Dollhouse and Furniture Advertising

1880s-1980s

Dian Zillner

Photography by Suzanne Silverthorn

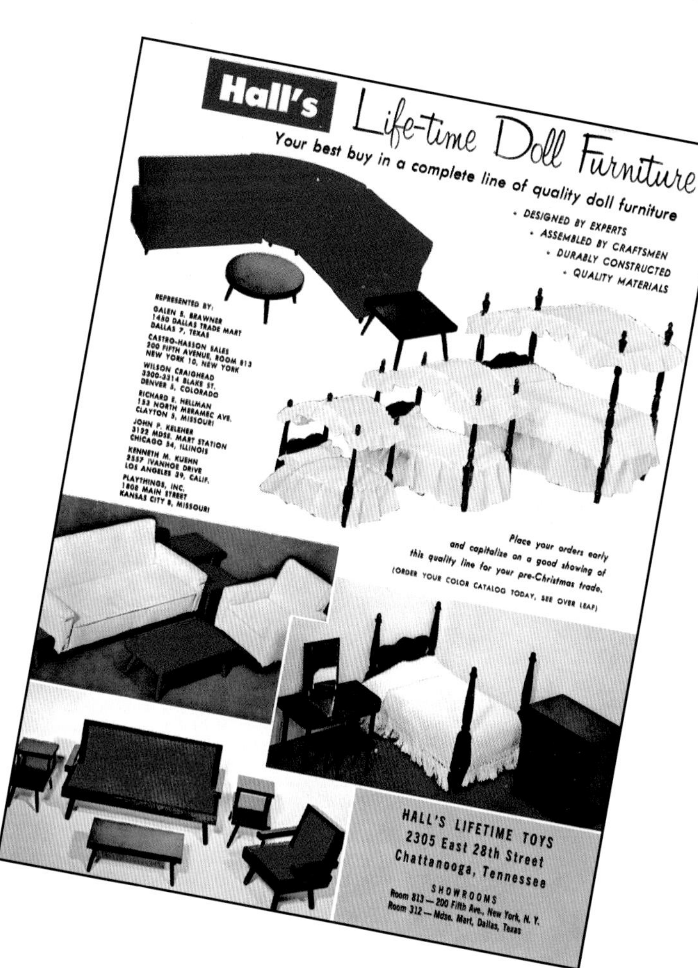

4880 Lower Valley Road, Atglen, PA 19310 USA

Dedication

Dedicated to Marilyn Pittman and Marcie Tubbs, fellow collectors and friends who have supplied photographs and materials to help make all the dollhouse books possible.

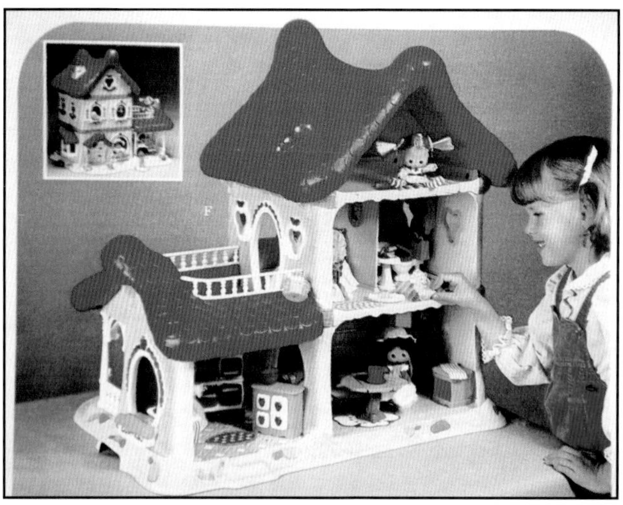

Notice: All of the items in this book are from private collections. Grateful acknowledgment is made to the original producers of the materials photographed. The copyright has been identified for each item whenever possible. If any omission or incorrect information is found, please notify the author or publisher and it will be amended in any future edition of the book.

Library of Congress Control Number: 2004108539

Designed by Ellen J. (Sue) Taltoan
Type set in Futura Hv BT/Souvenir Lt BT

ISBN: 0-7643-2112-9
Printed in China

Published by Schiffer Publishing Ltd.
4880 Lower Valley Road
Atglen, PA 19310
Phone: (610) 593-1777; Fax: (610) 593-2002
E-mail: Info@schifferbooks.com

In Europe, Schiffer books are distributed by
Bushwood Books
6 Marksbury Ave.
Kew Gardens
Surrey TW9 4JF England
Phone: 44 (0) 20 8392-8585; Fax: 44 (0) 20 8392-9876
E-mail: info@bushwoodbooks.co.uk
Free postage in the U.K., Europe; air mail at cost.

Contents

Introduction 4

Early Dollhouse and Furniture Advertising 5

1920s Advertisements 12

1930s Advertisements 26

1940s Advertisements 59

1950s Advertisements 85

1960s Advertisements 102

1970s Advertisements 118

1980s Advertisements 127

Dollhouse and Furniture Magazine and Newspaper Plans 133

Bibliography 142

Index 143

Introduction

Unlike the earlier dollhouse books by the author, this book pictures only advertisements for dollhouses and their furnishings instead of the actual toys themselves. It is hoped that the material in this book will allow collectors to identify products they own and to correctly date these items by referring to the dates of the advertisements pictured in this book. Note that if a company's products were produced during several decades, their ads are pictured in their most prolific decade.

An added chapter at the end of the book, "Dollhouse and Furniture Magazine and Newspaper Plans," is included to help in the identification and dating of handmade houses and furnishings. It is usually very hard to determine if these houses have been made from commercial patterns or were constructed using only the builder's imagination. Perhaps some collectors will recognize a house they own in this section of the book.

Help from fellow collectors has been given in the production of this book. As in all the previous books, Marcie Tubbs, Marilyn Pittman, and Roy Specht were especially generous in sharing materials and photographs for this publication.

Judy Mosholder and Carol Stevenson also sent numerous advertisements from their collections to be photographed for the book. Others who shared advertisements include Linda Boltrek, Gail Carey, Patty Cooper, Zelma Fink, Kathy Garner, Rita Goranson, George Mundorf, Betty Nichols, Becky Norris, C.S. Olson, Shirley C. Parks, Leslie and Joanne Payne, Ruth Petros, Marian Schmuhl, Evangeline Steinmeier, and especially Bob Tubbs, who took many photographs for the book. A special thanks also goes to Marge Meisinger for sharing her vast catalog collection so many vintage advertisements could be pictured.

December, 1929

630 CHILD LIFE

Just Like Mother's

. . . a little girl-size kitchen cabinet that isn't a make-believe . . . a *real* cabinet 40 inches high, sturdily built by the makers of the famous Kitchen Maid Equipment.

It has shelves, behind cunning latched doors, to hold cups, saucers, plates and goodies . . . a glistening porcelain table top . . . and a fascinating roll front that runs smoothly up and down.

Below, there is a space for pans and bowls and the whatnots of a well appointed kitchen. And, "just like mother," the little housekeeper will learn as she uses this cabinet that there is "a place for everything."

When you give your little girl this kitchen cabinet, you give her years of playday happiness . . . playdays that are habit forming and will remain in her memory always. Why not surprise her this Christmas with a cabinet "just like mother's"? Your choice of colors . . . ivory with green trim, green with ivory trim, or white.

PLAYROOM EQUIPMENT CO., 1812 Tribune Tower, Chicago, Ill.

Size, 30½ inches high, 31 inches deep, 26 inches wide

NEW!

With the same idea which prompted the manufacture of the Playroom Kitchen Cabinet . . . "Play-things That Build Character" . . . this new Doll House was developed. An amazingly realistic all-wood home for your little girl's doll family, built to last for years. Has brick-like outside walls in red and patterned green shingles . . . finished inside walls, a cozy fireplace and a tiny kitchen cabinet. Mounted on legs so the child need not sit on the floor while playing.

MAIL THIS

SEND NO MONEY
Simply fill in and send this order slip, or write a letter. The cabinet or doll house will be sent you by express. You pay on delivery, plus a slight shipping charge. Your money refunded if you are not completely satisfied.

PLAYROOM EQUIPMENT CO., 1812 Tribune Tower, Chicago, Ill.
☐ Enclosed is $........ for which send item checked. ☐ Send item checked C. O. D.
☐ Kitchen Cabinet ($12.00). ☐ Green with Ivory Trim. ☐ Ivory with Green Trim. ☐ Plain White.
☐ Doll House ($17.00). (If color is not specified, white will be shipped.)
Name........
Address........

Early Dollhouse and Furniture Advertising

Most of the dollhouses from the late 1800s to early 1900s were made of lithographed paper over wood (Bliss, Whitney Reed). The architectural details were printed on the paper on these houses. Cardboard houses from this period were produced in the same manner, with the windows, siding, and other details printed on the cardboard (McLoughlin Bros.). By the mid teens, these decorations were being printed directly on the wood by such firms as Mason & Parker and Morton Converse.

Advertising for these antique dollhouses and furniture is hard to find. It wasn't until the early 1900s that American magazines, which included advertisements of these types of toys, became more plentiful. Even then, many of the pictured dollhouses were only available as premiums for selling subscriptions to the magazines carrying the ad.

For the collector or researcher lucky enough to have access to early issues of the trade magazine *Playthings*, several well-known dollhouse firms sometimes carried ads in that publication during the early 1900s. The R. Bliss Mfg. Co. of Pawtucket, Rhode Island, and Grimm & Leeds located in Camden, New Jersey both advertised in *Playthings* during this time. Toys and Novelties was also a trade magazine, which began publication circa 1910. Early dollhouse ads were also scarce in that magazine. The issue for September 1919 contained no dollhouse advertisements although there were dozens of ads for dolls.

More plentiful are company or mail order catalogs, which picture dollhouses and furniture from the late 1800s into the early 1900s. In her book, *Dolls' Houses in America*, Flora Gill Jacobs reprints several pages of a 1902-3 Whitney-Reed catalog as well as pages from a 1901 catalog from the R. Bliss Mfg. Co. Blair Whitton, acting as editor, reprinted the entire 1911 Bliss catalog in her 1979 book called *Bliss Toys and Dollhouses*. Another reprinted early catalog is that of the Carl P. Stirn New York Importing & Wholesaling firm. Their 1893 catalog was reprinted by Dover Publications in 1990. The catalog included an early German Gottschalk dollhouse as well as several sets of furniture. Other early catalogs are being reprinted by various individuals and can be purchased on the Internet; Mason & Parker as well as Converse catalogs are available in this manner. *The Great American Antique Toy Bazaar 1879-1945*, edited and arranged by Ronald S. Barlow, is another great reprint of toy catalogs. It includes Biedermeier furniture (1880s), toy kitchens, Adrian Cooke Fairy Furniture (1905), a full page of assorted furniture (1917), Kilgore furniture (1930), Tootsietoy (1931), Converse (1931), and iron and other metal kitchen stoves throughout the catalog.

Although the very early mail order catalogs from Montgomery Ward and Sears are hard to find, those from the late teens and early 1920s are sometimes available on the Internet.

Advertising that pictures dollhouses and furniture is very important to collectors in this field for several reasons. It may enable collectors to match houses or furniture to magazine or catalog ads, which can help identify unknown makers. The time period when a toy was produced can also be verified in this manner. Additionally, collectors can learn if a piece already in a collection is complete and, if not, find out what's missing from the item. Through the pictures showing hundreds of advertisements in this book, dollhouse collectors can also identify houses or furniture they would like to add to their own collections and become knowledgeable enough about the product to locate the item(s) and make a purchase.

It is well to remember that most of the dollhouses owned by little girls before World War I were homemade by a relative or friend and, of course, no advertisements are available to record these houses unless they were made using a commercial pattern. This would change in the 1920s, when several new firms in the dollhouse industry began leaving a great paper trail for collectors of today to document their new products.

Althof, Bergmann & Co.

Tin dining room furniture pictured in the New York City based Althof, Bergmann & Co. catalog for 1874. The furniture was made of painted tin in the Victorian style with the addition of stenciled designs on some pieces. It was approximately 1.25"-1.5" to one foot in scale. The dining room furniture included six straight chairs, round table, fireplace, high-backed buffet, and a lounge. Sets were also provided for a kitchen, bedroom, and parlor.

Cass, N. D.

48B5402—Price, 21c
Shipping weight, 1 lb.
Pretty Doll's Kitchen Set. Made of hardwood, oak finish. Chairs height, 6⅞ in.; table, 7x4⅝x4 in. Nicely made and varnished.

The N. D. Cass firm was founded by Nathan David Cass in 1896. The company produced dollhouse furniture and a dollhouse similar to those made by Converse, which was featured in the company catalog for 1928. This dining room table and four chairs was advertised in the Montgomery Ward catalog circa 1916. The furniture was made by the N.D. Cass Co. of Athol, Massachusetts. The copy reads "Made of hardwood, oak finish." The chairs are approximately 6.75" high and the table measures 7" x 4.5" x 4". The set sold for 21 cents.

Solid Oak Bedroom Set

Five Pieces, all nicely varnshed and finished in natural color. Set consists of large double bed, table and three chairs, all strongly made. Shipping weight, 1½ lbs.
No. 37E1119 Price.............. 19c

Five-Piece Solid Oak Dining-Room Set

A beautiful little set, exceptionally well made and nicely finished in natural color. Consists of sideboard with hinged door, which opens; table with oilcloth cover, and three dining room chairs. Shipping weight, 1½ pounds.
No. 37E1120 Price.............. 19c

Beautiful Four-Piece Set

Consists of oak table, 7x5½ inches; fancy oak rocker, 7 inches high; two fancy 7½-inch chairs. Shpg. wt., 1½ lbs.
No. 37E1122 Price.............. 19c

Six-Piece Oak Kitchen Set

A dandy little set of good quality at a price lower than is usually asked for very poorly made sets. Consists of kitchen cupboard with curtains; oilcloth covered table, kitchen table, two chairs and a stool. Shipping weight, 1½ pounds.
No. 37E1121 Price.............. 19c

Four-Piece Mission Porch Set

All very large pieces, solidly made in very neat and attractive pattern. Made of strong, solid oak, with a dark mission stain. Set consists of 8-inch settee, 10-inch folding table, 9½-inch rocker and 8½-inch chair. All of the pieces in this set are exceptionally large. Shpg. wt., 4½ pounds.
No. 37E1125 Price.............. 39c

REAL DOLL COUCH HAMMOCK

Folds up just like a real big hammock. Made of brightly gilded steel with wood bottom. Extra strong. Steel frame with hammock upholstered in duck, well stitched.
No. 37E1123 Size, 21x20x-13 inches. Shpg. wt., 4 lbs. Price......79c
No. 37E1124 Same as above. Size, 14½x13x10 in. Shpg. wt., 2½ lbs. Price..39c

Large Folding Hammock

Frame made of heavy coppered steel wire, with bronzed steel brace. Has a fine large double woven hammock. Length over all, 35 inches. This strong, well made hammock is a low priced toy sure to give full satisfaction. The quality is much better than is usually found in toys at the price. Shpg. wt., 1 lb.
No. 37E1126 Price.............. 21c

Large Double Lawn Swing

A well made wooden swing, made just like a real lawn swing. Has a large canopy of good quality strong brown duck. Seats, 4 inches wide. Both seats and top are painted. Length of swing, 20 inches; height, 15 inches. Shpg. wt., 2½ lbs.
No. 37E1127 Price.............. 19c

512 GUARANTEED KANT KRACK DOLLS, LOW PRICED PRESENTS THAT LAST

The CHARLES WILLIAM STORES
New York City

The Charles Williams Stores, located in New York City, advertised a four-piece Cass mission porch set circa 1915. The pieces are pictured on the lower left of this ad. The copy reads "Made of solid oak with a dark mission stain." The set included an 8" settee, 10" folding table, 9.5" rocker and an 8.5" chair. It sold for 39 cents. Both the oak kitchen table and chairs and the porch set are identical to sets advertised by the N. D. Cass Co. in *Playthings* magazine in 1910. See page 42 of *International Dollhouses & Accessories* for an example of a boxed set of Cass dining room furniture. Other furniture pictured in the Charles Williams catalog includes an oak bedroom set for 19 cents, a five-piece dining set for 19 cents, and a folding hammock made of steel and wood in a doll size of 21" x 20" x 13". The dining room set is pictured on page 77 of the *Furnished Dollhouses* book. The table was covered with oilcloth. The furniture is in a large 1" to one foot scale. The four-piece set of oak table (7" x 5.5"), two chairs, and a rocker (7" high) would be too large to use for most dollhouses. It sold for 19 cents. The six-piece kitchen set also sold for 19 cents. No measurements are given. Included were a kitchen table, cupboard (with curtains), two chairs, stool, and another table. A "large folding hammock," 35" long, was priced at 21 cents and a double lawn swing, 20" high, cost only 19 cents.

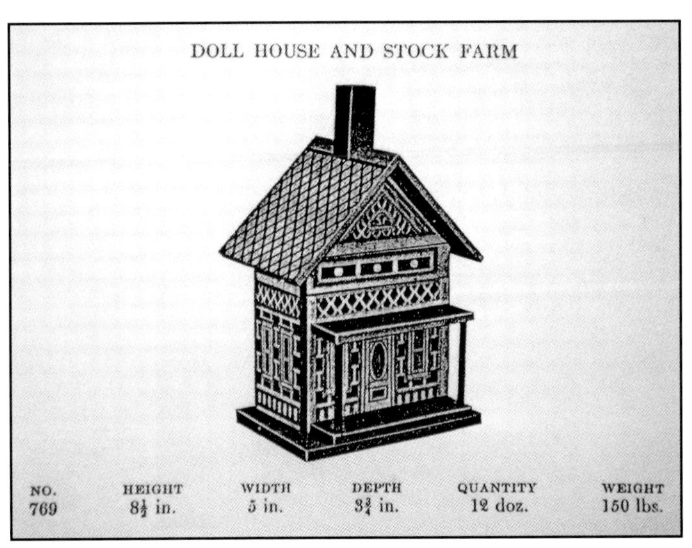

DOLL HOUSE AND STOCK FARM
NO. 769
HEIGHT 8½ in.
WIDTH 5 in.
DEPTH 3¾ in.
QUANTITY 12 doz.
WEIGHT 150 lbs.

Converse, Morton E.

This small wood one-room house was advertised in the Morton E. Converse catalog in 1919. The firm was located in Winchendon, Massachusetts and was founded by Morton E. Converse in 1884. The name was later changed to Morton E. Converse & Son. The Converse firm was sold in the early 1930s to the Mason Mfg. Co. of South Paris, Maine. The design was printed directly on the wood. The house opened from the front and measured 8.5" high x 5" wide x 3.75" deep. It was number 769. *Courtesy of Winchendon Historical Society, Home of Toy Museum of Converse and Mason & Parker Toys and Shirley Parks.*

Cooke, Adrian

Adrian Cooke pewter toy furniture sets were advertised in the 1905 Butler Brothers catalog. The furniture was produced by the Adrian Cooke Metallic Works in Chicago, Illinois. Included were a small parlor set in 1/2" to one foot scale, a wood table and four chairs (large 3/4" to one foot scale) and a larger, heavier set (1" to one foot scale, not pictured) which included a sofa, two chairs, and a rocker. See page 189 of *Antique & Collectible Dollhouses and Their Furnishings* for examples of this furniture. A pewter dollhouse size carriage was also shown in the ad. *Courtesy of Ronald S. Barlow from his book The Great American 1879-1945 Toy Bazaar.*

PEWTER TOY FURNITURE SETS.

F834—Parlor set, table, sofa, 2 chairs, 1 rocker, scroll design frames. 1 doz. in pkg........................ 36

F835—Sofa, rocker and chair, plush bottoms and fancy scroll frames. 1 doz. in pkg.. 75

F836—Dining room set—4 chairs with plush bottoms and 1 table. 1 doz. in pkg... 79

F837—Similar to F835, but larger and heavier, consists of 1 sofa, 2 chairs and 1 rocker. ½ doz. in pkg............. 1 85

PEWTER DOLL CARRIAGES.

F838—Openwork filigree body and parasol, upholstered, moving wheels, 3½x4. Each in box, 1 doz. in pkg...................... 80

F839—Similar to F838, larger and more fancy, 5¼x6. Each in box. 1 doz. in pkg.................... 75

The Cranford Doll House Co.

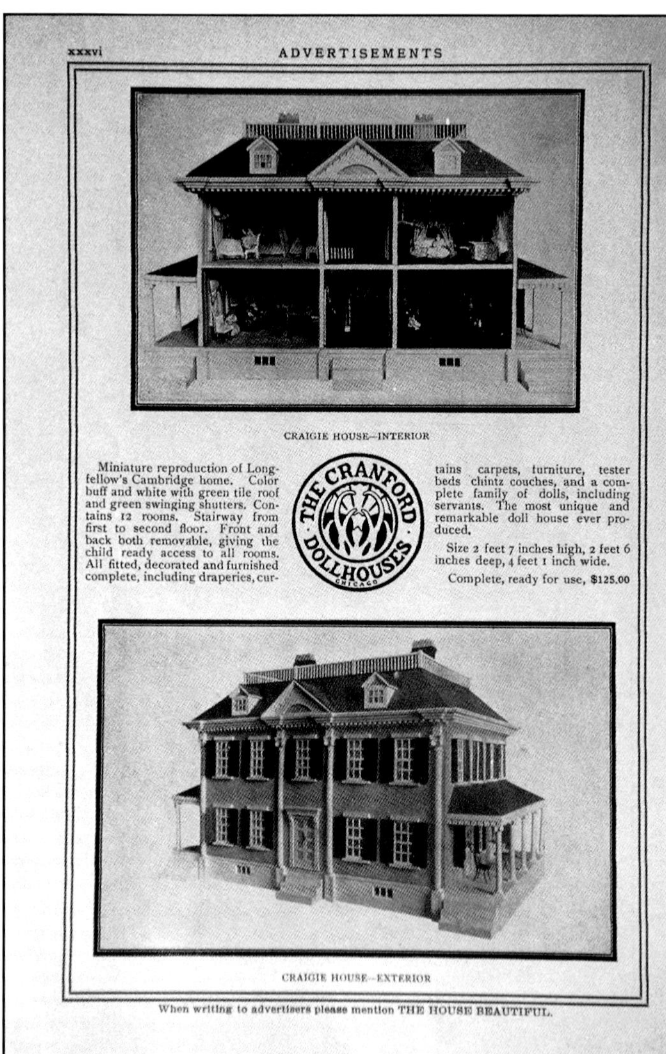

Advertisement for "The Cranford Doll House Co." from *The House Beautiful*, circa 1901. The Chicago based firm produced the houses of wood "with shingled roofs, latticed windows opening out or colonial windows with shutters, miniature stairways, and doors which opened and closed." The houses were "artistically painted and papered." Pictured is the "Craigie" House, a reproduction of Longfellow's Cambridge home. The house was buff and white with a green "tile" roof and green shutters. Both the front and back of the house were removable to allow access to its twelve rooms. A stairway was provided from the first to the second floor. The house came completely furnished including window coverings, carpets, tester beds, chintz couches, and a complete family of dolls including servants. It measured 31" high x 49" wide x 30" deep and sold for $125.

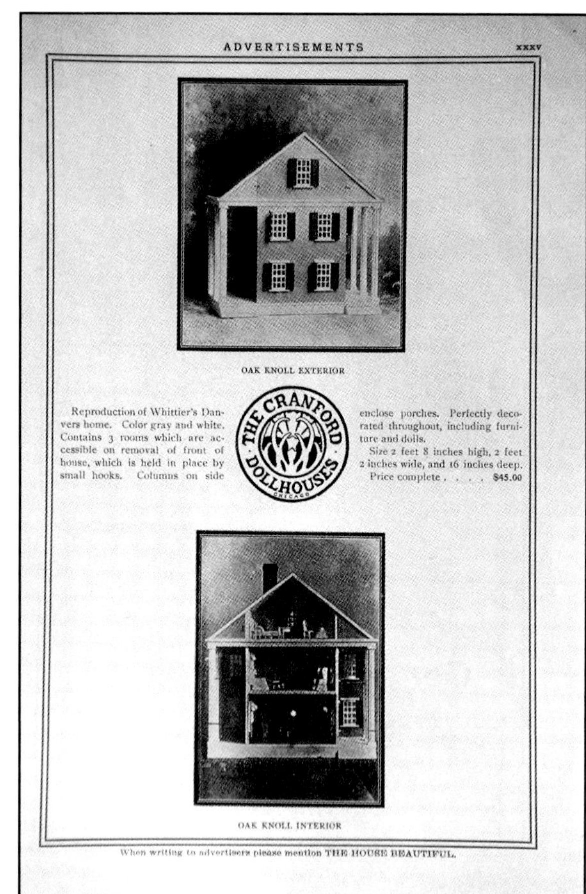

The Cranford firm also made cheaper models in their dollhouse line. Pictured here is Oak Knoll, the house representing Whittier's Danvers home. The house was painted gray and white and contained three rooms. The front of the house was removable to allow access to the inside. It came complete with furniture and dolls. It measured 32" high x 26" wide x 16" deep and was priced at $45.

The most inexpensive Cranford houses pictured in the advertisement were the "Red Cottage" and the "Elizabeth Cottage," each retailing for $35 complete with furniture and dolls. The Red Cottage contained three rooms with a removable front. A fenced in yard was supplied around its base. It measured 24" high x 31" wide x 17" deep. The Elizabeth Collage contained only two furnished rooms. Its front was also removable. It was 24" high x 30" wide x 24" deep.

Dorothy's Doll House (Keith, Max L.)

This open front dollhouse was advertised in *Scribner's Magazine* in November 1905. The copy read "This house is new and the first and only dollhouse on the market of good size and practical design." The house had glass windows and real wallpaper. It was 36" tall and weighed 27 pounds. A booklet could be ordered which gave prices on dollhouses and furniture. The house was offered by Max L. Keith of Minneapolis, Minnesota, who was publisher of *Keith's Magazine for Home Builders*.

Gottschalk, Moritz

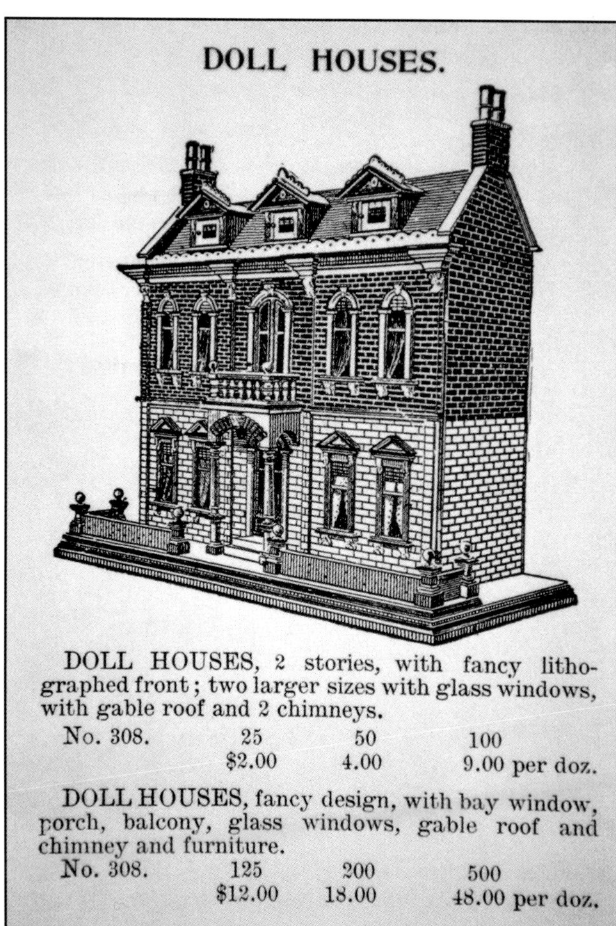

Dollhouse advertised in the Carl P. Stirn 1893 catalog. It was made by the German Moritz Gottschalk firm. In addition to the two-story paper lithographed over wood house pictured, other models were also available. A house with a bay window, porch, balcony, glass windows, gable roof, chimney, and furniture was available at a wholesale price of $48.00 per dozen. *Courtesy of Dover Publications, Inc. from their "Dover Pictorial Archive Series," Turn-of-The Century Dolls, Toys and Games. The Complete Illustrated Carl P. Stirn Catalog from 1893.*

John Smyth Catalog

This page of large scaled dollhouse furniture was advertised in the John Smyth 1917 catalog. It featured a set of Star Novelty Works dining room furniture in the top middle position priced at $1.25. This furniture is approximately 1.5" to one foot in scale. Other cheaper sets of wood furniture are also pictured, ranging in price from 9 cents to 48 cents. Japanese cane and reed furniture was also available for 29 cents and 45 cents a set. Interesting tin furniture is pictured in the center of the page. The set was enameled in blue and sold for only 29 cents for twelve pieces. The chairs were 3" high. *Courtesy of Ronald S. Barlow from the book The Great American 1879-1945 Antique Toy Bazaar published by Windmill Publishing Co.*

Letty Lane's Doll House (*Ladies Home Journal*)

Lettie Lane's Doll House

The Wonderful New Bungalow Home of a Most Delightful Little Lady

HAVE you ever seen a more charming doll house than this, or a more charming little doll than the one standing on the terrace? Of course you haven't. Months ago THE JOURNAL's architects and artists were asked to design the most beautiful doll house ever made, and even from the pictures of it here you can see how splendidly they have succeeded.

As for the dainty little girl who lives in this wonderful house, she comes to us from Germany; she is a jointed doll of bisque and practically indestructible. Pretty as she is, her dainty dress and braided straw hat add to her attractiveness. Moreover she just fits the house and harmonizes with every feature of it — its trellises of blooming roses and honeysuckle; its beds of Shasta daisies and forget-me-nots, and the sentinel bay tree on each side of the doorway beneath the lamp. And it is such a *big* house too. To be exact it is two inches wider than this whole page is long, and from front to back three inches deeper. And it is seventeen inches high.

The little mistress is very proud of her home; and she should be, don't you think?

Every Room is Ready for Doll Housekeeping

Its Little Mistress Bids You Welcome

TO TELL the truth another doll bungalow decorated and furnished in such perfect taste does not exist in all Dolltown. The living-room is finished and furnished in dark oak; the dining-room in tan and white and mahogany, while the blue bedroom's woodwork is ivory and its furniture mahogany too, like the charming dining-room. As for the kitchen, the walls, chairs and table appear cleanly painted, while the floor is in imitation of cork.

Moreover the furniture may be placed wherever the little girl who owns the house may choose to place it. For it is printed on heavy paper ready to be cut out, folded and pasted, while the house itself is printed on heavy coated cardboard, all cut out and clearly marked for bending, pasting and putting together. Indeed the setting up of the house and its furniture is one of the most interesting features of it, and yet very easy.

When done the house and furniture become as shown here, only of course much larger, both being in the same proportion to the charming little doll mistress that the actual house in which a real little girl lives, with its furniture, bears to her parents.

How to Obtain the House

ANY little girl may own house, doll and furniture if she will do this: Send to us THREE new yearly subscriptions for THE LADIES' HOME JOURNAL, accompanied by the regular subscription price ($4.50 for the three), requesting Lettie Lane's Doll House, whereupon the house, furniture and doll will be sent, all shipping expenses prepaid.

Remember four things: 1st, these must be 3 yearly subscriptions; 2d, they must all be sent at the same time, and must be accompanied by $4.50 remittance; 3d, they must all be NEW subscriptions (renewals of subscriptions already on the list, or transfers from one member of the family to another, will not count); 4th, the house must be asked for when the order is sent.

Perhaps Mother or Father will want to order some subscriptions as Christmas presents for friends this year. If so they can be ordered now and will count, but be sure that it is stated clearly that the subscriptions are not to be really started until Christmas. The house, however, will be sent at once. Above all, be very sure that the name and address to which the house is to be sent are written very clearly, and not confused with the names of the new subscribers. Address:

THE LADIES' HOME JOURNAL
INDEPENDENCE SQUARE
PHILADELPHIA, PENNSYLVANIA

Here is the Model Kitchen With its New Range

Imagine a Doll Dinner Party Being Given Here

Isn't This Dark Oak Living-Room Attractive?

Could a Doll Have a Prettier Bedroom Than This?

This is How the House Looks When Open and With All the Furniture in Place for a Doll Party

(Page 51)

Letty Lane's Doll House was offered by the *Ladies Home Journal* in this ad from their November 1912 issue. The cardboard house, German bisque doll, and cardboard furniture could be obtained by sending $4.50 for three new yearly subscriptions to the magazine. The house contained four rooms and measured 17" high x 17.5" wide x 18.5" deep. It apparently opened from both the front and the back. Furniture for a kitchen, dining room, bedroom, and living room was provided. It was printed on heavy paper and was to be cut-out and assembled by the owner. *Courtesy of Rita Goranson.*

Mason and Parker

MASON & PARKER MFG. CO.

DOLLS' BUNGALOWS

Painted in colors; handsomely printed both inside and and outside. Each bungalow packed in pasteboard box

NO.	HEIGHT	WIDTH	PACKED	WEIGHT
200	10 inches	9½ inches	6 dozen	120 lbs.
201	12½ inches	11 inches	3 dozen	120 lbs.
202	14¾ inches	13 inches	1 dozen	50 lbs.

DOLLS' BUNGALOWS

Made of wood, painted in colors; beautifully painted both inside and outside Each packed in carton.

NO.	HEIGHT	WIDTH	PACKED	WEIGHT
204	14 inches	15 inches	1 dozen	80 lbs.
205	16 inches	20 inches	½ dozen	60 lbs.
206	16 inches	20 inches	¼ dozen	40 lbs.

17

These two wood bungalows were pictured in the Mason & Parker catalog in 1914. The firm was located in Winchendon, Massachusetts and was founded by Orlando Mason and H.N. Parker circa 1899. The firm continued in business until 1956. The colors were printed directly on the wood to decorate both the insides and outsides of the houses. Both houses opened from the front. The house on the top came in three sizes, ranging from 10" to 14.5" high and 9.5" to 11" wide. The larger house pictured at the bottom of the page could be ordered in two different sizes ranging from 14" to 16" tall and 15" to 20" wide. Each house included only one room. See examples of these houses on pages 80 and 81 of the *Furnished Dollhouses* book.

Woman's World

40 WOMAN'S WORLD November, 1911

Our Wonderful Doll Outfit

Woman's World Big Christmas Doll Offer Given for Only Six New Subscribers

10 Different Doll Articles

1, Completely Dressed Life-Size Doll.
2, Doll's Baby Carriage or Go-Cart.
3, Doll's Chatelaine Watch.
4, Undressed Curly Haired Baby Doll.
5, Doll's Dining-Room Table.
6, Doll's Dining-Room Chair.
7, Doll's Dining-Room Chair.
8, Doll's Dining-Room Chair.
9, Doll's Dining-Room Chair.
10, Doll's Decorated Playhouse.

Our life-size doll is bigger than the ordinary baby—nearly two feet high. She is beautifully and stylishly dressed from head to toe, including large picture hat, trimmed with plume, lace, etc., fancy sateen dress with yoke, complete underwear, stockings, slippers with buckles, etc. Bisque body, jointed arms and legs, long curly waxen hair; opens and closes her eyes. Dolly's buggy or go-cart is substantially made and amply large enough for Dolly to sit in, as shown in the above picture. It is guaranteed to run smoothly. Dolly's little chatelaine watch looks just like a real watch, and she is very proud of it. Our little baby doll is very sweet and lovely, with long hair. The five piece furniture set is the cutest doll set you ever saw—regular dining-room table already set up and four upright dining-room chairs. Just imagine the good times the little girl can have dressing dolly, making clothes for baby doll, and taking both out riding in the go-cart, serving dinner and tea, etc., etc. Our Doll's House is made of cardboard, beautifully decorated in colors. It is small, but nevertheless any little girl will take great pleasure in keeping it with her Doll things and arranging it on the floor or table with her Dolls, furniture set, etc. These premiums are imported for us from Germany and Japan. We guarantee them to give satisfaction.

Premium Offer We will ship all ten of these grand Doll premiums—the large Dressed Doll, the Go-Cart, the Doll's Chatelaine Watch, the Baby Doll, the Five-Piece Dining Room Set and the Decorated Doll House—to anyone who will send us just **six 3-year subscriptions** to the Woman's World at 50 cents each or twelve 1-year subscriptions at 25 cents each. Premiums shipped, express prepaid, the same day subscriptions are received. The price of Woman's World will shortly be increased to 50c per year, and anyone can easily secure six 3-year 50c or twelve 1 year 25c subscriptions now for such a good magazine on these low terms and obtain all of these Doll presents for their trouble. Extra sample copies of the Woman's World sent on request. Present subscribers, whose names are sent, will have their subscriptions extended from the time they would originally expire. Use the coupon in sending in the subscriptions.

WOMAN'S WORLD, Premium Dept.
107 SO. CLINTON ST., CHICAGO

Woman's World,
Premium Dept.
107 So. Clinton Street
CHICAGO

Gentlemen: Enclosed find $3.00 subscription money to pay for the enclosed subscriptions (enter six 3-year 50 cent subscriptions or twelve 1-year 25 cent subscriptions). Send me express prepaid, at once, the big Dressed Doll, the Go-Cart, the Doll's Watch, the 5-Piece Furniture Set, the Baby Doll and the Doll's House. Enter the subscriptions to begin at once.

Name________________

Address________________

We distributed thirty thousand Doll outfits last year, and the following are a few of thousands of grateful letters we received:

"I received my doll and buggy, etc., on the 7th and was highly pleased and want to thank you for same. I am well *paid* for my work and can recommend this company to any little girl who wants to earn a nice doll outfit."—Thelma Leath, Wickliffe, Ky., April 8, 1911.

"I received the premiums and am perfectly delighted with them. *Their beauty far exceeds my expectations.*"—Hettie K. Fredrick, Corydon, Ky., April 19, 1911.

"I received my doll and doll go-cart and everything all O. K. and cannot express my joy over it. *They are beyond my expectations.* They are grand. I hope to serve you again soon."—Miss Lucile Rhine, care of Wm. Rhine, R. R. No. 7, Hartford City, Ind., April 19, 1911.

"I received my doll the 15th and am very much pleased with the things you sent. The go-cart is just fine, also the doll. I really think they are *better than I expected* them to be. Thank you very much for them all."—Helen Ritchie, Hillsboro, Va., April 17, 1911

"I received my doll and doll go-cart. I was very *well pleased* with them, so I thank you very much. They got here all right."—Daisy R. Porter, Bowling Green, Kentucky, April 16, 1911.

"We received the doll, go-cart, the set and other things O. K. *They are fine*, better than we expected."—Mrs. W. D. Lockwood, Highland, Mich., April 14, 1911.

"I have received my premiums and am very well satisfied with them. Thank you very much for the premiums, also for your kindness. I will always speak kindly of you. I know *you are a reliable firm.*"—Miss Freddie Brown, R. No. 2, Box 55, Michie, Tenn., April 12, 1911.

"I received the doll, go-cart and set today in good condition. Am well pleased. My little girl was *more than delighted.* Thank you for your premiums."—Mrs. John W. McGee, Laurel, Del., R. D. No. 2, Box 13, April 20, 1911.

"Received my premium last Friday, the 6th, and am very well pleased with it. *I never expected such nice premiums.* Thanking you ever so much for it all, I beg to remain yours respectfully."—Miss Effie Korslin, R. R. No. 2, Box 64, Grand Rapids, Wis., April 10, 1911.

"I received the premiums and found them O. K. I wish you could have seen *how delighted* my little daughter was with her doll and go-cart. Thanking you for the premiums I remain"—G. F. Hochstetler, Sand Patch, Pa., April 24, 1911.

"I received my premiums last night. They were *all O. K.* and much better than I expected. I thank you very much for them."—Ruby Thomas, Minneota, Minn., April 12, 1911.

This full page ad in *Woman's World* magazine for November 1911 promoted the premiums that could be earned by selling subscriptions to the magazine. The package included a life-sized doll, go-cart, doll's watch, undressed baby doll, dining room table and four chairs, and cardboard dollhouse. No sizes were given on the furniture but it is assumed to be large dollhouse size. The dollhouse is described as "small." All of the premiums could be earned with twelve new one-year subscriptions to the magazine for 25 cents each.

The Youth's Companion

The *Youth's Companion* advertised a toy parlor set and paper dolls, apparently as a premium, circa 1886-1889. The German Biedermeier furniture set included a settee, arm chair, three straight chairs, marble top table, and dresser, plus three paper dolls and clothing. The furniture was advertised as imitation ebony. *Courtesy of Ronald S. Barlow from the book The Great America 1879-1945 Antique Toy Bazaar.*

This premium offer from *Woman's World* is from October 1912. A set of large-scale dollhouse dining room furniture could be earned for three yearly subscriptions to the magazine at 35 cents each. The set was made of oak and was nicely varnished. It included a table, four chairs, and a cupboard 7" tall. The table measured 4" x 5.5". The furniture is similar to that being made by the Star Novelty Works during this period. *Courtesy of Becky Norris.*

1920s Advertisements

Dollhouse and dollhouse furniture advertisements were much more plentiful beginning in the 1920s. There are several reasons for this change. Children's magazines such as *Child Life* were becoming more popular and toy advertisers began directing their ads to the places where the child (and the parents) would be more likely to take notice. Another reason for the increase in advertising in the 1920s was the entry of two important firms into the dollhouse and furniture market during the decade. Their names were Dowst Brothers (later Dowst Manufacturing Co.), who marketed the Tootsietoy metal furniture, and the Arcade Manufacturing Co., who produced the 1-1/2" to one foot scaled iron furniture.

Both companies advertised heavily in the *Child Life* magazines of the decade and their products were also carried by many catalogs (both wholesale and mail order) during the 1920s. Ads can be found featuring at least five different Tootsietoy cardboard dollhouses and both lines of their small scale metal furniture. All of the Arcade furniture and the large house and individual rooms can be found in advertisements of the period. Even *Ladies Home Journal* carried one of these ads in 1927.

Iron Kilgore furniture, as well as other metal furniture, was also advertised during this decade. Kitchen pieces were especially popular.

The Tynietoy furniture, from the Toy Furniture Shop in Providence, Rhode Island, was also a frequent advertiser in the *Child Life* magazines. They also issued their own catalogs, as did Arcade and Kilgore. Some of these advertising products were more like booklets, as were those promoting Tootsietoy furniture.

More unusual advertisements from the 1920s include those from the Elastic Tip Co. for the metal Jenny Wren house, complete with furniture, and an advertisement from the Frier Steel Co. promoting a line of metal Cozytown houses. After studying all of these advertisements from the 1920s, it is surprising to note how many of the products from this period were made of metal. Neither the houses nor the furniture looked realistic (except for the kitchen pieces). Of course, the German firms, including Gottschalk, continued to produce houses and furniture of wood as did the English Lines firm.

Cardboard houses continued to be popular in the United States, both as houses to be used with the Tootsietoy furniture or to be furnished with various lines of cardboard pieces. Both the Wayne Paper Goods Co. and the Durrel Co. (Trixytoy) supplied these types of houses during the decade.

The 1930s would provide a change in both the cost and the supply of dollhouse-related products and the advertisements would tell the story.

Arcade Manufacturing Co.

January, 1929 PLAYTHINGS 431

Arcade Doll House

One of the most interesting features in the cast iron toy line this year is the Arcade Doll House completely furnished with Arcade Cast Iron furniture. The house as shown above is equipped with 3 bed rooms, two bathrooms, a living room, dining room, breakfast nook, kitchen, and laundry. It will be lighted throughout with 110 watt bulbs.

It is particularly interesting to note that not only the sets may be sold individually, but each separate piece may be sold as such.

In building this attractive little house, the Arcade Manufacturing Co., has made an effort to supply a set that will aid materially in selling for the dealer more individual items as well as more sets.

Toy Mack Stake Truck

The new Toy Arcade Mack Stake Truck dollar retailer was made by the Arcade Mfg. Co. because of the popular demand for a toy of this price styled after the larger Toy Arcade Stake Truck that has been so popular. It is complete in every detail and the box is of ample size to hold blocks and other toy luggage. It measures 8¾" long, 3" wide, and 3¾" high. As usual with Arcade Toys, it is modeled accurately after the real Mack Stake Truck.

Toy Ford Weaver Wrecker

The Arcade Toy Wrecker in the large size has been unusually popular this last year. It is an item that when shown on

Two New Big-Bang Celebrators

The Conestoga Corporation, manufacturers of Big-Bang Celebrators, is developing two new items—a 2-wheel Field Artillery piece to retail at $1.50, and a Bombing Plane with a real bang, to retail at $4.00. It is expected that these new items will be on display during the Toy Fair at the Permanent New York Show Rooms of the Conestoga Corporation, Room 461, Fifth Avenue Building. Further details will be published in this department in our next issue. In the meantime, interested buyers are invited to write to The Conestoga Corporation, Main Office and Factory, Bethlehem, Pa. The Conestoga Corporation also has in production a new long-spinning Ro-to-Top, attractively decorated, to retail at 10 cents.

Arcade dollhouse and furniture pictured in the trade magazine *Playthings* in January 1929. These products were produced by the Arcade Manufacturing Company, founded in 1885, located in Freeport, Illinois. The copy reads "One of the most interesting features in the cast iron toy line this year is the Arcade Doll House completely furnished with Arcade Cast Iron furniture." The house included three bedrooms, two bathrooms, a living room, dining room, breakfast nook, kitchen, and laundry. The furniture could be purchased by the piece or by the set. In 1946, the Arcade Manufacturing Co. was purchased by the Rockwell Manufacturing Co. in Buffalo, New York.

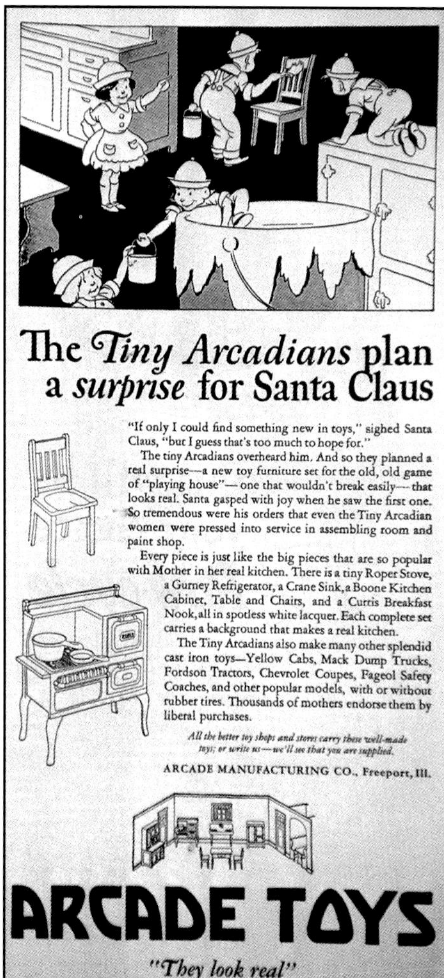

This Arcade ad from *Child Life* in December 1926 advertises the "new" toy iron furniture. Pictured is a kitchen stove, chair, and the entire kitchen set, which included a Roper stove, Gurney refrigerator, Crane sink, Boone kitchen cabinet, table, chairs, and a Curtis breakfast nook.

The Arcade bathroom set was pictured in this advertisement from the *Ladies Home Journal* of December 1927. It included Crane bathroom fixtures and a cardboard room setting. *Courtesy of Carol Stevenson.*

Modern Priscilla carried an Arcade ad in their November 1928 issue that pictured three pieces of the Arcade Thor laundry set. Besides the washer, double tub, and ironer, the other pieces in the set included a laundry tray, heater, and boiler. The cardboard room that came with the complete set measured 10.25" high x 14" wide x 11" deep. *Stevenson Collection.*

The Arcade Simmons bedroom was pictured in a *Child Life* advertisement in November 1928. The cast iron bedroom furniture included a double bed, dresser with working drawers, rocker, desk, and chair. The furniture was approximately 1.5" to one foot in scale. The cardboard room is also shown.

692
CHILD LIFE
SIMMONS
Every day
means real sport with
ARCADE CAST IRON TOYS
made by The Tiny Arcadians

Arcade Cast Iron Toys
"They Look Real"

Gas and Electric Kitchen Sets
Crane Bathroom Set
Simmons Bedroom Set
Thor Laundry Set
Yellow Cab and Coach
A. C. F. Coach
Fageol Safety Coach
McCormick-Deering Tractor, Plow, Truck, Wagon and Thresher
Buick and Chevrolet
Mack Trucks, Buses, Fire Trucks
Model A Ford Cars, Trucks, Fordson Tractor
Ford-Weaver Wrecking Truck

All large size Automotive Toys can be furnished with rubber tires at a small additional cost

Talk about fun! In the sand-box or the play-room Arcade Cast Iron Toys are the greatest kind of sport. They're exact small reproductions of grown-up things. They're sensible, wholesome toys; stimulate imagination, keep little hands and minds busy for joyous hours. And they're hard to break.

THE ARCADE MFG. COMPANY
1213 Shawnee Street Freeport, Illinois

See these famous toys at any good store or toy-shop. Look for this label. If you can't find Arcade Iron Toys, write us

Wonderful Story—Free!

A fascinating jingle about two children who visit the Tiny Arcadians—makers of Arcade Toys. Thousands of children have read and re-read it. Just send your name and address—we will send your copy.

Toy Cable Piano

This novel and very unusual cast iron model of a real Cable piano is another new item presented by the Arcade Manufacturing Co. of Freeport, Ill. It is accurate as to detail and very appropriate for the small doll house living room. This little piano is especially adaptable to the Arcade Toy Livingroom Set that has just been introduced this year.

The new Arcade Cable piano was pictured in *Playthings* for January 1929. It was part of the living room furniture that had just been introduced in 1929. Other pieces included a secretary, sofa, easy chair, ladder back chair, a reading table, and an end table. See pages 186 and 187 of *Antique & Collectible Dollhouses* for a photograph of the real furniture.

"ARCADE" METAL
BREAKFAST NOOK SET
1F3408 — 3x4¾ x3 table, 2 benches 4½x4¾x1¾, cast iron, white enameled, correctly modeled after large sizes.
1/12 doz. sets in pkg.
Doz sets $8.00

The Arcade iron breakfast nook set was advertised in the Butler Brothers catalog in 1929. It included a table and two benches.

In addition to dollhouses, Arcade also produced several toy buildings including fire stations, garages, and several models of gas stations. This wood example was advertised in the Marshall Field catalog in 1935. The Chicago based firm sold the toy for $1.00. It had two gas pumps and a door that opened on the side. It measured 9" high x 8" wide x 12" deep. *Courtesy of Marge Meisinger.*

The Carrom Company

The Carrom Company of Ludington, Michigan advertised a "Portable and Take-Down Doll House" circa 1920s. The house was made of plywood and finished in natural finish with trim done in mahogany. The house came in three sizes: two rooms, four rooms, and eight rooms. The prices ranged from $16.00 to $50.00. No measurements were given. The firm also advertised folding "bridge" tables and chairs for adults.

Elastic Tip Company

134 PLAYTHINGS January, 1924

FURNITURE
16 PIECES
Living Room—table and three chairs.
Dining Room—table, buffet and two chairs.
Kitchen — stove, chair, sink, table.
Bed Room—bureau, bed, table, chair.

"A Toyland Treasure—"

Jenny Wren
Doll House *and* Furniture

Happiness for the little miss. A lovely mansion for her dolly. Four fine rooms luxuriously furnished. All ready for housekeeping.

Substantially built of steel—both house and furniture. Beautifully painted in nine durable colors. And so light in weight that a tiny tot can easily carry the entire outfit.

Compactly boxed for shipment. Furniture complete or by rooms if desired. For further information write to your jobber or the manufacturer.

MANUFACTURED BY
THE ELASTIC TIP COMPANY
370 Atlantic Avenue, Boston, Mass., U. S. A.

The Elastic Tip Company, located in Boston, Massachusetts, advertised a metal dollhouse and furniture in *Playthings* magazine for January 1924. The "Jenny Wren" open front dollhouse was built of steel and included four rooms, The furniture was also made of steel and sixteen pieces were included to furnish the house. These consisted of a table and three chairs for the living room, a stove, chair, sink, and table to be used in the kitchen, and a dresser, bed, table and chair to furnish the bedroom. The Elastic Tip Co. was founded circa 1890s and was mostly known for its variety of dart games.

Florence V. Cannon Co., Inc.

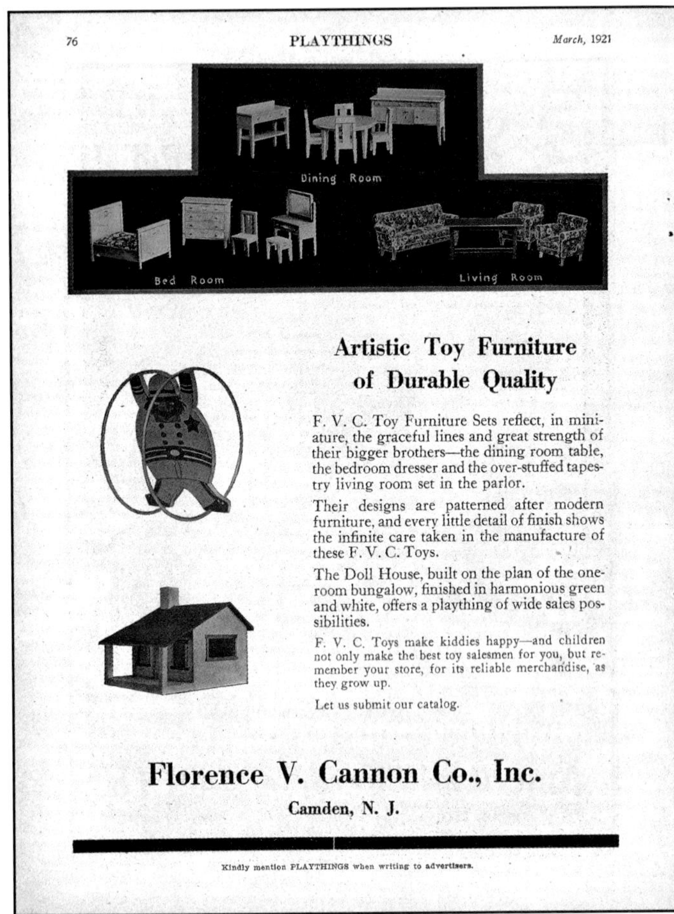

Left:
Large scale wood dollhouse furniture was advertised by the Florence V. Cannon Co. in 1921. This advertisement appeared in the March 1921 issue of *Playthings* magazine. Featured were pieces for a dining room (round table, four chairs, serving table, and buffet), bedroom (bed, chest-of-drawers, chair, vanity, and bench), and living room (sofa, two chairs, and a library type table). Tiny painted flowers were used for decoration on many of the pieces. The furniture is approximately 1.25" to one foot in scale. The dining room and several bedroom pieces are pictured in the *International Dollhouses* book on pages 29 and 81. A one-room wood bungalow dollhouse was also shown in the Cannon Co. ad. It was finished in green and white.

RED MINIATURE TOYS.

All metal bright red model toys; very popular for favors, Christmas tree ornaments or for doll play houses.

D4749. D4747. D4748.

D4749—Parlor Chair. Fancy scroll backs; imitation cane seat; four legs; 1 doz. Per doz. .... .44

D4747—A Porch Rocker; a very pretty doll house toy; 1 doz. Per doz. .... .44

D4748—Jitney Motor Bus; 2½ ins.; 1 doz. Per doz. .... .44

D4750. D4751. D4752.

D4750—Four Wheeled Doll Buggy; bright red; 2¼ ins. long; 1½ in. high; 1 doz. Per doz. .... .55

D4751—Novelty Airplane; revolving propeller; 2½ ins.; 1 doz. Doz... .55

D4752—Swinging Cradles. 1 doz. Per doz. .... .55

D4753. D4754.

D4753—New Red Taxi. Four turning wheels; spare; 2½ ins.; 1 doz. Per doz.................... .66

D4754 — Toy carpet sweeper with turning brush; adjustable pan; long metal handle; a wonder at the price. Per doz. .... .66

D4760. D4761.

D4760—Baby Grand Piano. Copper gilt; very fancy embossed rim; black and white key board; 1 doz. Per doz. .... .59

D4761—Folding Go-Cart with adjustable wheels and handle; copper gilt finish. 1 doz. Per doz....... .59

French Penny Toys

Most of the pictured metal toys have been found marked "France." These tiny toys were made as favors, or for use in tiny dollhouses, This ad in the G. Sommers & Co. (based in St. Paul, Minnesota) catalog from 1929 described the toys as being painted red to use in Christmas decorations instead of the more traditional gold. Included were a rocker, chair, buggy, cradle, carpet sweeper, piano, folding go-cart, three automobiles, and an airplane. The wholesale prices ranged from 44 cents to 66 cents per dozen. *Courtesy of Marge Meisinger*.

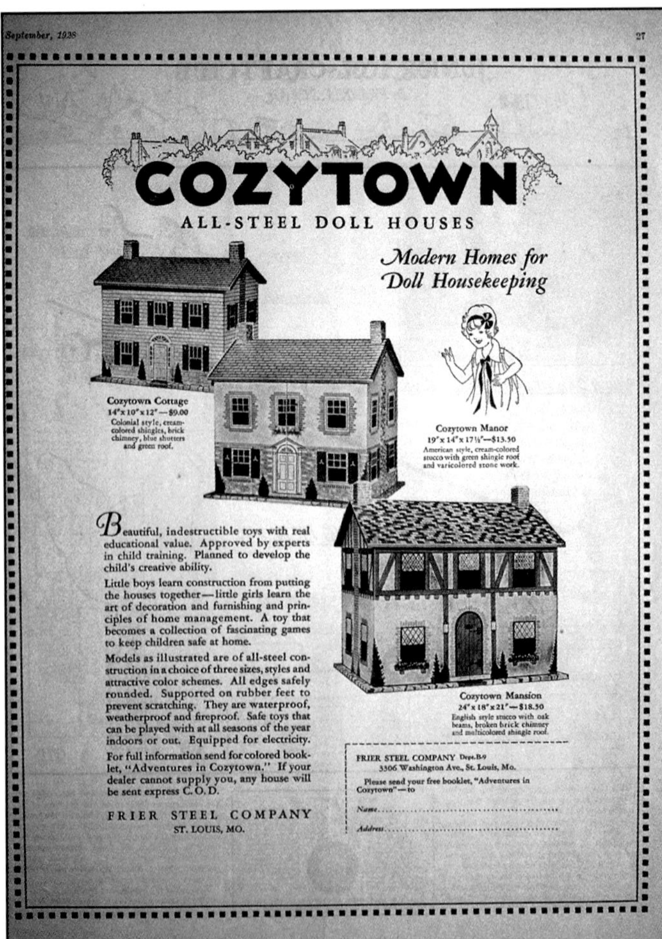

Frier Steel Co.

This Cozytown dollhouse ad is from September 1928. The houses were produced by the Frier Steel Co., located in St. Louis, Missouri. Three different houses were made. They included the smallest model called Cozytown Cottage, the medium sized house called Cozytown Manor, and the largest model named Cozytown Mansion. The smallest house measured 12" high x 14" wide x 19" deep. The Cozytown Manor was 18" high x 20.5" wide x 16.5" deep. The largest Mansion was 21" high x 24" wide x 18" deep.

Hubley Manufacturing Co.

Advertisement for toy kitchen stoves which appeared in the 1929 Butler Brothers catalog. The Chicago based firm offered several different designs of metal stoves, including those modeled from stoves that used coal, gas, wood, or electricity. The iron stoves labeled "Eagle" were produced by the Hubley Manufacturing Co., which was founded by John Hubley around 1894. The firm was located in Lancaster, Pennsylvania. The gas stoves ranged in size from 5" to 8" wide. The largest "Eagle" stove pictured was the coal model which measured 13.5" wide. *Courtesy of Marge Meisinger.*

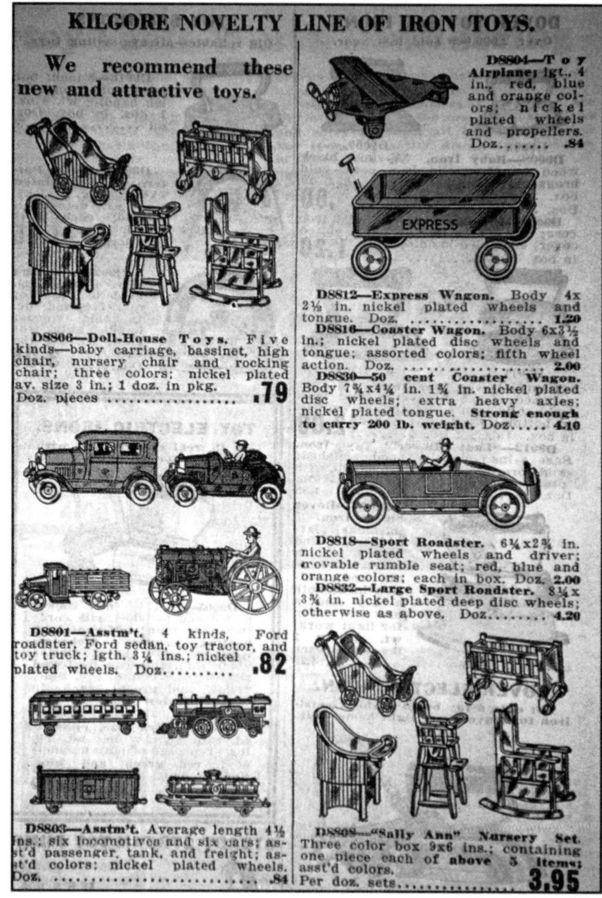

Katz Company

A set of "heavy gauge metal" kitchen furniture, produced by the New York based Katz Company, was also pictured in the 1929 Butler Brothers catalog. The set included a stove, refrigerator, sink, and cabinet. The cabinet was the tallest piece and measured 7.25" high x 4.5" wide. The stove was 5.75" high x 5.25" wide. See page 100 of *American Dollhouses and Furniture From the 20th Century* for a photograph of this kitchen set. *Marge Meisinger Collection.*

Kilgore Manufacturing Co.

Kilgore toy ad which appeared in the St. Paul based G. Sommers & Co. catalog in 1929. The iron toy dollhouse furniture was offered wholesale to retailers either packaged with a dozen assorted pieces or in a complete boxed Sally Ann Nursery Set of five pieces. The set included a crib, rocker, high chair, potty chair, and stroller. The Kilgore Manufacturing Co., located in Westerville, Ohio, produced iron dollhouse furniture in scales ranging in size from 1/2" to one foot to 1" to one foot. Other Kilgore toys are also pictured in the ad. *Meisinger Collection.*

Playthings for March 1930 also carried an ad for Kilgore dollhouse furniture. Pictured are the bathroom, bedroom, dining room, and kitchen sets. Each set was packed in a colorful carton that could be used as a room. When placed together, the four cartons made a four-room house. Each set retailed for 50 cents in 1930. These pieces are 1/2" to one foot in scale. The bathroom included a tub, sink, toilet, stool, and wastebasket. Bedroom pieces featured a bed, vanity and bench, wardrobe, and chair. Furniture for the dining room included a table, two chairs, china cabinet, and buffet. In the kitchen room box were an icebox, sink, stove, and table. *Courtesy of Marcie Tubbs.*

Mazda Lamps

This National Mazda Lamps ad appeared in *Literary Digest* magazine for September 22, 1928. It featured the firm's new light bulb boxes, which could also be used for dollhouses. The copy read "a light house for you – a doll's house for the little housekeeper." Three different styles are pictured: English, Spanish, and Colonial. The houses measured 8.5" high x 8.25" wide x 5.5" deep, not including the yards that were on some of the boxes. *Courtesy of Marcie Tubbs. Photograph by Bob Tubbs.*

Nit-Sal Company

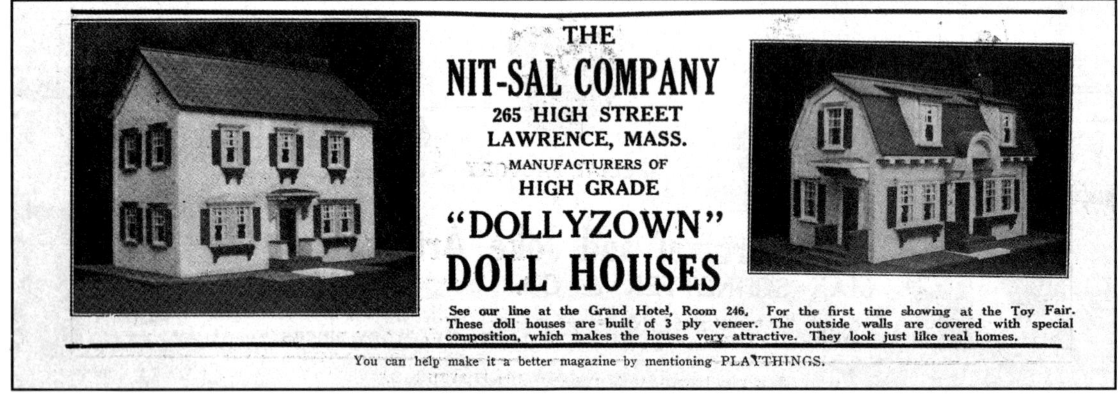

This Nit-Sal Company ad appeared in *Playthings* magazine for January 1928. This little known company produced "Dollyzown" dollhouses in Lawrence, Massachusetts. The houses were made of three-ply veneer. Two houses are pictured in the ad. The house on the right appears to be the house shown on page 74 of *International Dollhouses* as a product of the Converse firm. The house in the ad has fewer overhang decorations, no round holes in the shutters, and siding finish on the outside walls instead of stucco but otherwise the houses appear to be identical. Perhaps Converse purchased the firm or their leftover houses at a later date.

Playroom Equipment Co.

Advertisement from the Playroom Equipment Co., located in Chicago, Illinois, which appeared in the *Child Life* magazine of December 1929. Pictured were a children's version of a kitchen cabinet, and a bungalow dollhouse. The wood dollhouse had brick-like outside walls and patterned green shingles. The inside was completed with finished walls, a fireplace, and kitchen cabinet. The house was mounted on legs so it would be easy to reach. It sold for $17.00. The house measured 30.5" high x 26" wide x 31" deep. *Courtesy of Marilyn Pittman.*

Santa Claus Supply House

This ad appeared in the December 1923 issue of *Woman's World*. The bungalow dollhouse pictured "could be yours free" if the boy or girl sent in a postcard. The fine print stated that the postcard, in fact, would enable the child to obtain information on how to receive the house "free." It may have included new subscriptions for named magazines or the selling of other products. The house was made of "heavy fiberboard" and included four rooms. French windows opened on the wide sun porch. It measured 14.25" high x 21" wide x 20.5" deep. Furniture also came with the house. Listed are tables, chairs, beds, phonographs, stoves, and kitchen cabinets. The address was the Santa Claus Supply House in Chicago.

Schmidt Lithograph Co.

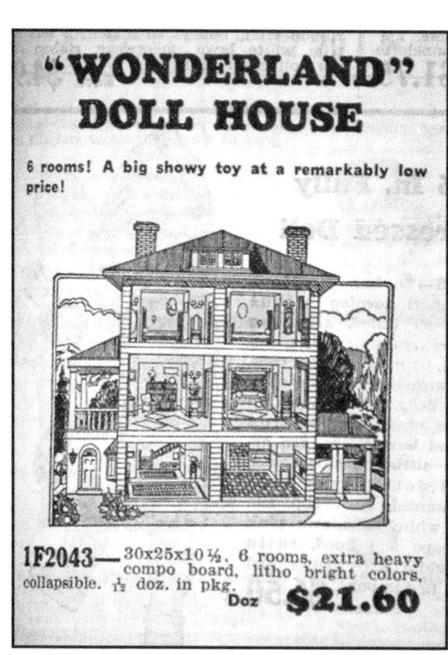

Right:
This compo board "Wonderland Doll House" was advertised in the Butler Brothers catalog in 1929. It was made by the Schmidt Lithograph Co. of San Francisco. The house contained six rooms, was collapsible, and measured 30" x 25" x 10.5". See page 200 of *Antique & Collectible Dollhouses* for a picture of the actual dollhouse. *Courtesy of Marge Meisinger.*

Sam'l Gabriel Sons & Co.

Left:
A set of thin cardboard furniture was advertised in the Chicago Mail Order Co. catalog for 1925-26. This same furniture was offered by *Needlework* magazine as a premium in 1921. It was also sold by Sam'l Gabriel Sons & Co. in a boxed set. The set included furnishings for a living room, dining room, bedroom, and kitchen. It sold for only 29 cents in this catalog. See page 132 of *International Dollhouses* for a photograph of the furniture.

Tootsietoy

Advertisement for metal Tootsietoy furniture from *Child Life* in December 1926. The furniture was produced by the Dowst Mfg. Co. in Chicago, Illinois from the early 1920s through the 1930s. The company was founded by brothers Charles and Samuel Dowst in 1878 but didn't begin making metal premiums (like Cracker Jack prizes) until around 1900. The later furniture pieces were approximately 1/2" to one foot in scale. Pictured is the earliest design of furniture. Included were sets to be used in a living room, bedroom, dining room, bathroom, and kitchen. A cardboard dollhouse to be used with the furniture is also shown. The house and furniture set was priced at $9.00. The house alone was $3.00 and individual sets of furniture sold for $1.00. The house was produced by the Wayne Paper Goods Co. It was made to look like red brick and measured 19" high x 21" wide x 15" deep.

Above right:
A differently styled six-room, two-story house was included in this Tootsietoy *Child Life* ad circa December 1927. These houses were usually marked with the Tootsietoy name but they may have been made by another firm for the Tootsietoy company. This house was decorated with dormers and the front opened in two sections. It measured 17.5" high x 17" wide x 11.5" deep. The prices remained the same, with the house selling for $3.00 unfurnished and $9.00 complete with furniture. Single sets still sold for $1.00 each. The metal furniture continued to be made with the early designs. *Courtesy of Marcie Tubbs. Photograph by Bob Tubbs.*

The G. Sommers & Co. wholesale catalog from 1929 offered the cardboard house and a variety of furniture sets. In addition to the boxes, which contain seven or eight pieces of Tootsietoy furniture, some of the sets include only four furniture items. *Courtesy of Marge Meisinger.*

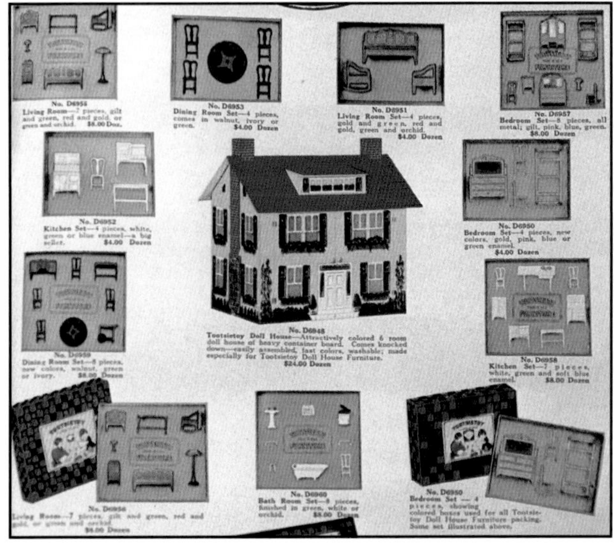

42F40—This new "tootsie toy" doll house is a six-room Spanish villa, painted in washable colors with a gay red roof. The living room has a fireplace and real stairs lead to the bedrooms. Of durable bookboard, 26 inches long, 16 inches high, $5. For furnishing this house to scale, we suggest the metal furniture sets described below. House with 7 sets which furnish it throughout, $11.65. Garden pieces listed at left.

Marshall Fields advertised the new "Tootsietoy" six-room Spanish Villa in their Christmas catalog in 1930. The house was described as having a fireplace and real stairs that led to the upstairs bedrooms. It was made of book board and sold for $5.00. The store also carried the metal furniture. The house, along with seven sets of furniture, could be purchased for $11.65. *Courtesy of Carol Stevenson.*

TOOTSIETOY DOLL MANSION

Sold by Mail Only at Ward's

$4.77

Beautiful Spanish Villa designed by a real architect. Colorfully lithographed inside to show rugs, curtains, pictures. Sturdily made of heavy book board. Exterior finished in **washable oil colors** to look like stucco; decorated with shrubs, vines, balconies. Stairway leads to upstairs rooms. Three wide doors on hinges make all rooms easily accessible to the little owner. Built in accurate proportion to the Tootsietoy furniture shown below. Size: 26 inches long by 17 inches wide by 17½ inches high. Packed in attractive carton with full directions for easy assembly. We Pay Postage.

448 G 979—Doll House Only $4.77

Tootsietoy Mansion—Furnished

Buy the TOOTSIETOY MANSION complete with the five rooms of Famous Tootsietoy Furniture below.

448 G 980—We Pay Postage............ $9.25

TOOTSIETOY Doll House Furniture

95¢ Bathroom

Nine metal pieces enameled orchid and white. 3½-in. tub, tile effect outside; toilet with raising seat; lavatory; medicine chest with mirror, opens; stool; clothes hamper; 2 towel racks; bathroom scale.

48 G 804 .... 95¢

95¢ Kitchen

Seven metal pieces; green lacquer and white finish. Kitchen Cabinet 2⅛ in. high, refrigerator, stove, 2 chairs, table, sink. All pieces in proportion. Doors and drawers of cabinet, refrigerator and stove really open.

48 G 803 .... 95¢

95¢ Bedroom

Pink and blue enameled metal bedroom set. 7 pieces: 2⅛-in. dresser with mirror, 3 drawers pull out; twin beds with spreads 3⅜ in. long, arm chair, rocker, night table and lamp. All in proportion.

48 G 800—Postpaid ... 95¢

PARLOR

DINING ROOM

Seven metal pieces; walnut lacquer finish. Extension table 3⅜ in. long, 3 straight chairs, 1 arm chair, corner cabinet door opens; buffet drawers open. All well made. 95¢

48 G 802—Postpaid .... 95¢

Parlor Set

95¢ Seven metal pieces. Grand piano is Chinese red and gold, 3 in. wide; top lifts, music rest; radio cabinet has gold panel, doors open; lamp, piano bench, arm chair, end table, foot stool.

48 G 801—Postpaid .... 95¢

DOLL SET

The Whole Family

Papa, Mama, Grandmother, Grandfather, Brother, Sister, Baby. Bisque; painted clothing. Father 2¼ inches tall. Postpaid. 42¢

48 G 2504—7 dolls .... 42¢

284 Montgomery Ward & Co CBA » » Swift Same-Day S

The Montgomery Ward Toys Spring and Summer catalog for 1931 also featured the new cardboard Tootsietoy Doll Mansion and the recently re-designed furniture pieces. The metal furniture was still produced in a 1/2" to one foot scale. The Mansion was priced at $4.77 and the furniture sets were 95 cents each. The house measured 17.5" high x 26" wide x 17" deep. It sold for $9.25 fully furnished. Furniture was produced for a parlor, dining room, kitchen, bedroom, and bathroom. The furniture was much more modern in design and reflected the styles of the time. *Courtesy of Marge Meisinger.*

Below:
Tootsietoy ad in color from *Child Life* in December 1931. It pictures two additional rooms of furniture called the "Boudoir," which included a chaise lounge and a vanity. The grand piano was included in the seven-piece music room set, shown at the bottom of the ad. The prices in this ad are slightly higher, with the Mansion selling for $5.00 unfurnished and $10 furnished. Individual sets were priced at $1.00 each.

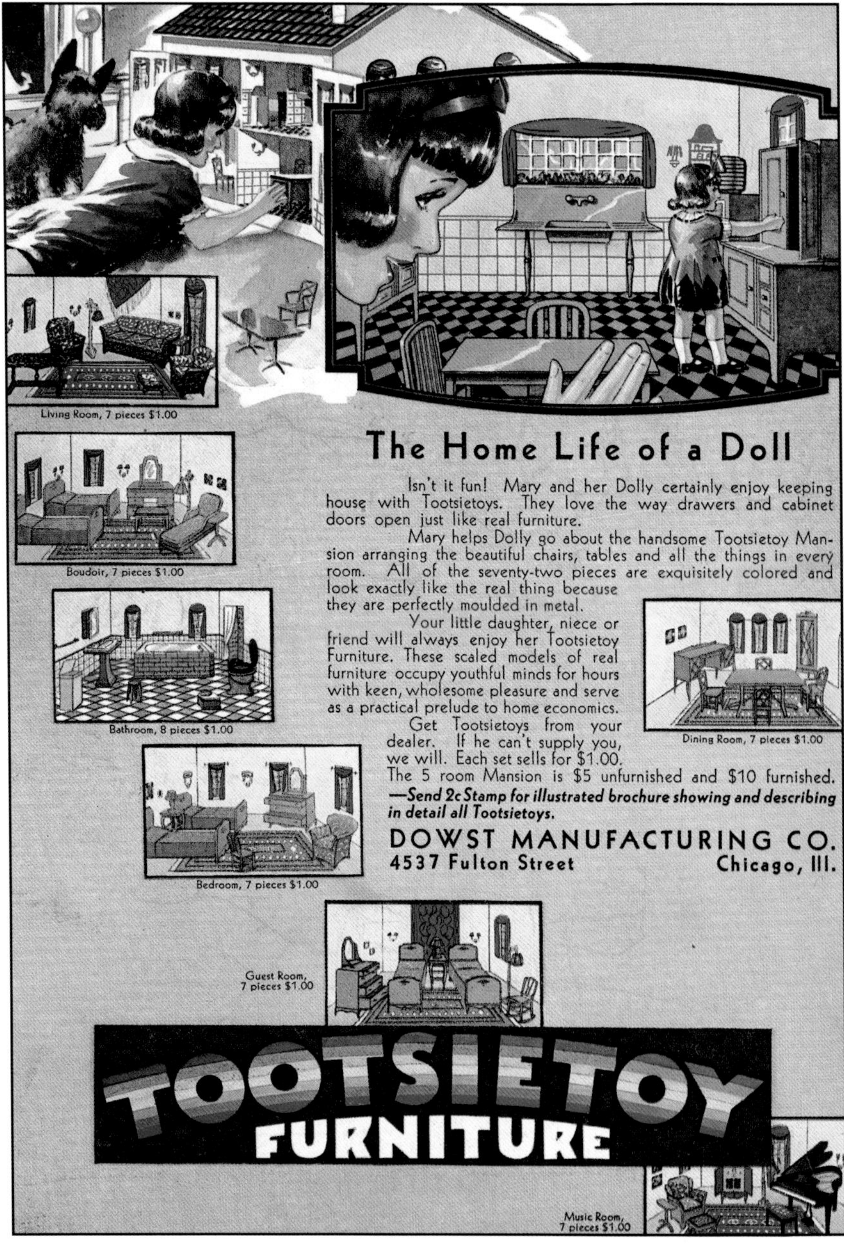

This "Add-A-Room" dollhouse was used to market Tootsietoy dollhouse furniture in the 1930s. Each large box of furniture also included a cardboard room for a dollhouse. The consumer could complete the house by purchasing all rooms of the furniture – there were five rooms in all. *Courtesy of Linda Boltrek.*

EDW. K. TRYON COMPANY, PHILADELPHIA

TOOTSIETOY FURNITURE

Practically Unbreakable – Lustrous Colors

No. 1—Living Room Set. Pink and blue assorted. 2 dozen in carton, 50 lbs. Each **$1.00**

No. 2—Bed Room Set. Pink and blue assorted. 2 dozen in carton, 48 lbs. Each **$1.00**

No. 3—Dining Room Set. Light walnut. 2 dozen in carton, 44 lbs. Each **$1.00**

No. 4—Kitchen Set. Green and white. 2 dozen in carton, 45 lbs. Each **$1.00**

No. 5—Bath Room Set. Orchid and white. 3 dozen in carton, 40 lbs. Each **50c**

No. 1505—8-Piece Living Room Set. Includes radio. Gold color. 3 dozen in carton, 42 lbs. Each **50c**

No. 1506—Bed Room Set. 8 pieces. Dresser not shown. Pink. 3 dozen in carton, 42 lbs. Each **50c**

No. 1507—Dining Room Set. 8 pieces. Includes 4 chairs. Light walnut. 3 dozen in carton, 42 lbs. Each **50c**

No. 1508—Kitchen. 8 pieces. Includes sink, step stool, table, range, refrigerator, cabinet and 2 chairs. 3 dozen in carton, 42 lbs. Each **50c**

No. 1—Living Room

No. 2—Bed Room

No. 3—Dining Room

No. 4—Kitchen

No. 1505—Living Room

No. 5—Bath Room

No. 1507—Dining Room

No. 1508—Kitchen

No. 1506—Bed Room

Toy Gro Educational Toys

Woman's World magazine for April 1921 carried an ad for a little known toy maker called Toy Gro Educational Toys. Their cardboard dollhouse furniture or truck (also made of cardboard) could be obtained through the purchase of magazine subscriptions. Offer #1 was for the dollhouse furniture. The set could be ordered by sending in two yearly subscriptions to the magazine. The set included an arm chair, rocking chair, table lamp, phonograph, library table, footstool, toy phonograph record, upholstery for chairs, set of metal fasteners, and instructions for assembling the furniture. The phonograph was 3.75" high.

Left:
As sales of the small metal furniture were slipping (probably due to competition from the new wood furniture, particularly from Strombecker) the firm began adding small accessories to its boxes of furniture. The Edward K. Tryon Co., based in Philadelphia, issued a catalog in 1939 which pictured some of these sets. The large boxed sets included extra pieces (piano, corner cabinets, chaise lounge, vanity, as well as many accessories) and still sold for $1.00 each. The earlier seven-piece sets were priced at 50 cents a box under the "Daisy" label. *Boltrek Collection.*

74 PLAYTHINGS *March,* 1921

These Toys Are Designed So Beautifully That They Sell Themselves

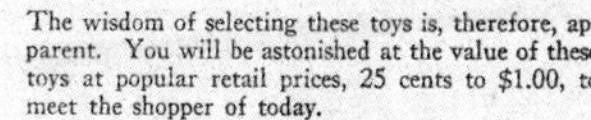

THE
Toymakers TOYS

The wisdom of selecting these toys is, therefore, apparent. You will be astonished at the value of these toys at popular retail prices, 25 cents to $1.00, to meet the shopper of today.

Our "Mary Jane" doll house fairly sparkles in its wonderful color scheme. Beautifully lithographed set-up red brick house with green window blinds and sunny flower garden. The front of the house is removable to enable the tots to place furniture and play with their dollies. The interior is lithographed in cream buff with ivory wainscot and rich chintz window drapes. A handsome rug adorns the floor.

This house is not a flimsy proposition, but is made of extra heavy fiberboard with a through ceiling piece which insures great rigidity and strength. When set up the size is 10 x 14 x 14 inches high. Packed in strong box with lithographed label.

The "Mary Jane" set-up doll cradles are graceful toys, lithographed in light cream buff color and daintily decorated with interesting little children play pictures.

They have a perfect balance responding to the slightest touch and the rocker has been made so that they cannot tip.

The "Broadway Limited" is an absolute reproduction of a standard railroad train in colors, reproduced by special permission from the railroad companies. This toy shows every detail of the standard equipment. The boys will appreciate this because it "looks real," and is highly instructive to the youngsters. Packed singly and in trains of four cars.

These toys are designed right and prices are right for your profit.

THE TOYMAKERS, INC.
223 to 233 No. California Ave.
CHICAGO, ILL., U. S. A.

New York Representatives
BAKER & BENNETT CO., 873 Broadway
DAVIS & VOETSCH, 43-54 East 19th St.
THE OWENS-KREISER CO., 31 EAST 17TH ST.

Kindly mention PLAYTHINGS when writing to advertisers.

The Toymakers, Inc.

An ad for the "Mary Jane" dollhouse appeared in *Playthings* magazine for March 1921. The cardboard house was made by The Toymakers, Inc. of Chicago, Illinois. The front of the house was removable to allow for play. The house measured 14" high x 14" wide x 10" deep. It eventually was marketed with several pieces of lightweight cardboard furniture. The actual house is pictured in the *International Dollhouses* book on page 136.

Trixytoy

PORTABLE DOLL HOUSES.

Practical, durable doll houses; made of wallboard. **New decorations.** Shipped flat but can be assembled in a "jiffy."

D8146—Lgt. 14½ ins.; 10 ins. high; imitation stucco walls; transparent windows; 4 color finish; a 50c retailer. Doz. **4.00**

D8148—Large 4-room doll house. Size 19x15x12 ins.; with 4 spacious rooms 9x10 ins.; beautifully finished with transparent windows; sets up without bolts or fastenings. Dozen **8.25**

The Trixytoy line of dollhouses and dollhouse furniture was made by the Durrel Company in Boston, Massachusetts. The one pictured here was advertised in the St. Paul based G. Sommers & Co. catalog in 1929. The house shown was 10" high x 14.5" wide. A larger four-room house was also offered by the company. It measured 15" high x 19" wide x 12" deep. For a photograph of the actual house, see page 110 of *Furnished Dollhouses. Courtesy of Marge Meisinger.*

Tynietoy

The Tynietoy houses and furniture were made and sold by The Toy Furniture Shop in Providence, Rhode Island. The firm was begun by Marion I. Perkins and Amey Vernon and they opened the Toy Furniture Shop around 1920. Their products were on the market for several decades from the 1920s until the 1940s. Pictured is one of the six models of houses produced by Tynietoy and shown in the catalog. It is called the New England Town House. It included six rooms, two halls, and an attic. It measured 2 feet, 5.5" tall x 4 feet, 2" wide x 1 foot, 4" deep. The pictured house includes a garden. Unfurnished and without the garden, the house was priced at $63.00 in the Tynietoy catalog. One of these houses is pictured in *Furnished Dollhouses* on page 112. *Courtesy of Leslie and Joanne Payne.*

Wayne Paper Goods Co.

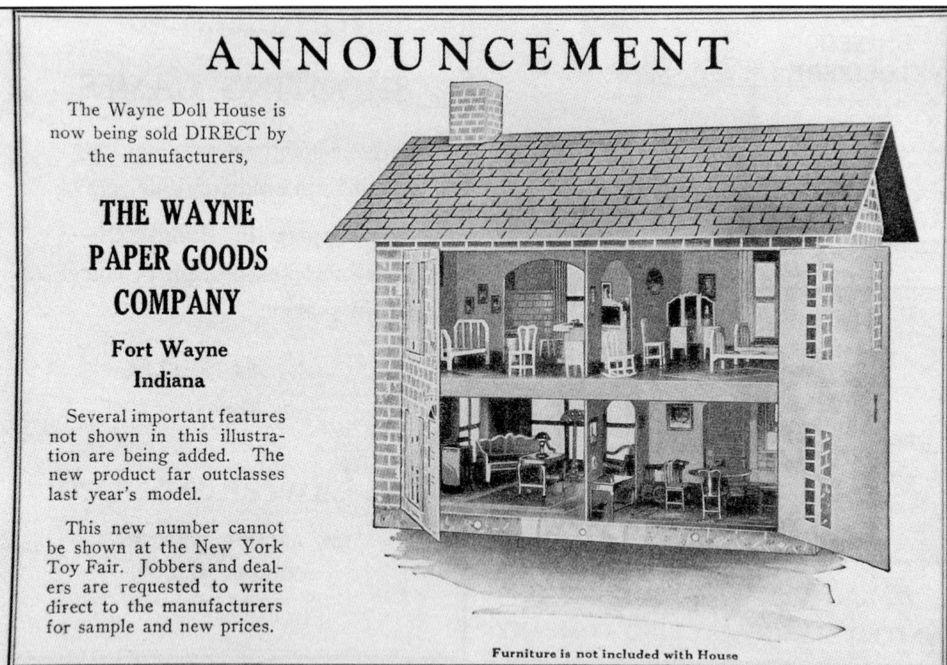

The Wayne Paper Goods Co. of Fort Wayne, Indiana produced different designs of cardboard dollhouses. The pictured house of "red brick" was sold for many years furnished with Tootsietoy metal furniture. This ad from the January 1927 issue of *Playthings* states that "The Wayne Doll House is now being sold DIRECT by the manufacturers." Perhaps the firm was trying to distance themselves from Tootsietoy, but the pictured house was furnished with Tootsie furniture. The house came in either four or six room models.

TYNIETOY DOLL HOUSE FURNITURE

SPECIAL CHRISTMAS OFFER from our catalogue of miniature Reproductions of Antiques

This completely furnished old time Kitchen 28 pieces . . $7.75

1 Kitchen Dresser, 1 Chair, 1 Set tub, 1 Rug, 1 Pitcher, 3 Bowls, 2 Foods, 1 Broom, 1 Kettle, 1 Table, 1 Sink, 1 Stove, 1 Clock, 1 Coffee Pot, 1 Ice Chest, 3 Plates, 1 Vacuum Cleaner, 1 Carpet Sweeper, 1 Frying Pan
Laundry Set, Basket, Board, Flatiron

Also individual pieces or rooms furnished in what ever period desired. Early American, Colonial, Victorian and Spanish.

Five types of TYNIETOY DOLL HOUSES varying in style from the South County Farm House to the Colonial Mansion.

A delightful and novel gift is our boxed "Assemble Your Own" TYNIETOY DOLL HOUSE. Materials cut and fitted, including stairs, fireplace, window casings, hinges, screws, door knobs, everything! with full directions. . . $15.00

WRITE FOR FREE CATALOGUE

TOY FURNITURE SHOP

The original designers of Miniature Antiques
29 Market Square, Providence, Rhode Island
(Ask The Toy Shop of your town for TYNIETOYS)

Left:
The Tynietoy furniture and houses were also sold through fine department stores and ads in magazines. This one appeared in *Child Life* magazine for December 1931. The kitchen pieces were pictured. The entire set, priced at $7.75, included a cabinet, table, chair, sink, stove, ice box, and accessories. The stove, ice box and many of the accessories were not made by Tynietoy but were carried by the firm to accompany their wood dollhouse pieces. This ad stated that an "Assemble Your Own" Tynietoy Doll House was available. The boxed package included the materials already cut and fitted along with directions for assembly. It sold for $15.00.

Miscellaneous

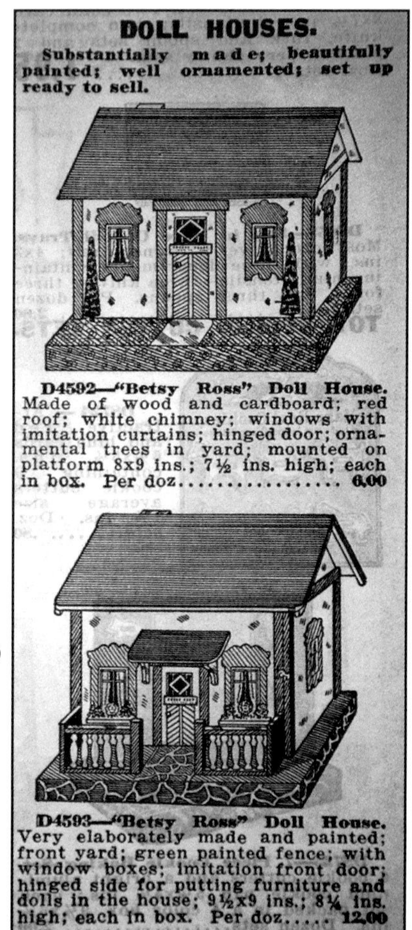

DOLL HOUSES.
Substantially made; beautifully painted; well ornamented; set up ready to sell.
D4592—"Betsy Ross" Doll House. Made of wood and cardboard; red roof; white chimney; windows with imitation curtains; hinged door; ornamental trees in yard; mounted on platform 8x9 ins.; 7½ ins. high; each in box. Per doz................ 6.00
D4593—"Betsy Ross" Doll House. Very elaborately made and painted; front yard; green painted fence; with window boxes; imitation front door; hinged side for putting furniture and dolls in the house; 9½x9 ins.; 8¼ ins. high; each in box. Per doz..... 12.00

The G. Sommers & Co. catalog for 1929 offered two inexpensive German dollhouses for sale. The houses were made of wood and cardboard. The house at the top was mounted on a platform measuring 8" x 9" and it was 7.5" high. The house on the bottom included a fence. It opened at the side and was 8.25" high x 9.5" wide x 9" deep. *Courtesy of Marge Meisinger.*

Dolls' Furniture Sets
763/6. Dining Room, chintz paper covered walls and imitation linoleum, fitted with seven pieces mahogany finish upholstered furniture; size set up 11x9¼x6¾ inches; ½ doz. sets in pkg. .... Doz. Sets $8.00

The Nerlich & Co. Holiday Season catalog from 1924 offered three different sets of German boxed dollhouse furniture. This dining room (which could also be used as a living room) included chintz paper covered walls and imitation linoleum. The seven pieces of furniture that completed the set included a settee, four chairs, small table, and a cabinet. When set up, the room measured 6.75" high x 9.25" wide x 11" deep.

763/3. Assorted Four Kinds, two living rooms, bedroom and parlor, oak finish furniture in one living room and bedroom, mahogany finish upholstered furniture in other rooms, in cardboard box 16x11x2¼ inches. .... Per Set $2.50
763/4. Assorted Two Kinds, parlor and living room as above; in cardboard box 16x11x2¼ inches. .... Per Set $2.50

The third boxed set of furniture pictured could be purchased to furnish a living or dining room. The finish came in oak. Bedroom and parlor furniture was also available. Some pieces were finished in mahogany with upholstery.

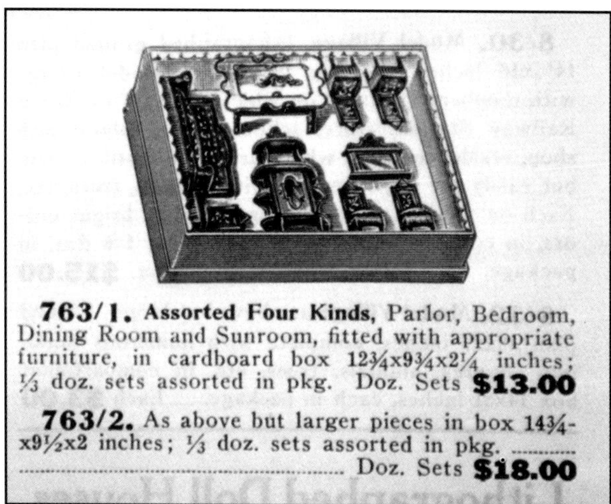

763/1. Assorted Four Kinds, Parlor, Bedroom, Dining Room and Sunroom, fitted with appropriate furniture, in cardboard box 12¾x9¾x2¼ inches; ⅓ doz. sets assorted in pkg. Doz. Sets $13.00
763/2. As above but larger pieces in box 14¾x9½x2 inches; ⅓ doz. sets assorted in pkg. .... Doz. Sets $18.00

A more expensive parlor set pictured in the Nerlich catalog included a sofa, five chairs, table, cabinet with shelves, and a mirror. These boxed sets were also available for the bedroom, dining room, and a sunroom. The boxes measured 2.25" high x 12.75" wide x 9.25" deep.

1F3106 — "General Electric," 7⅛ in. high, white enameled, cast iron frame, steel shelves and back, blue trim, nickeled removable ice cube pan, "G.E." label on door. 1/12 doz. in box.
Doz $8.00

This "General Electric" white enameled "electric" refrigerator was advertised in the Butler Brothers catalog in 1929. It was made with a cast iron frame, steel shelves, and back. The refrigerator included an opening door and removable ice cube pan. It was 7.25" tall. *Courtesy of Marge Meisinger.*

1930s Advertisements

During the 1930s, many additional companies joined the ranks as manufacturers of dollhouse and/or furniture products. Two of the most prominent were the A. Schoenhut Company and the Strombeck-Becker Manufacturing Co. (Strombecker). Although Schoenhut began producing dollhouses in 1917, they didn't add furniture to their line until 1928, and while Strombecker continued making their dollhouse furniture until the 1960s, the A. Schoenhut Co. filed for bankruptcy in 1934. Both companies produced similar wood dollhouse furniture in 3/4" to one foot and 1" to one foot scales. Advertisements from both firms dating from the 1930s are still available to collectors. Included are company ads or booklets as well as mail order catalog advertisements. A reprint of many of the A. Schoenhut company catalog pages picturing both houses and furniture was issued by Margaret Whitton some years ago. The catalogs that were used date from 1917 until 1934.

Other important firms from the era include Warren Paper Products (Built-Rite), who manufactured a line of cardboard houses and two lines of furniture. This company was a frequent advertiser in *Children's Activities* magazines and these ads are easily found by today's collectors. Their products were also carried in the Montgomery Ward mail order catalogs. The Rich Toy Co. also began their production of dollhouse in the 1930s. They were pictured in several different wholesale and mail order catalogs of the era as well as in many issues of *Children's Activities* magazine.

In addition to the major companies, Converse, Wisconsin Toy, J.L. Wright (Lincoln), Menasha Woodenware, Toy Tinkers, and the English Lines-Triang firm all manufactured wood dollhouse furniture during the era. The change had taken place – now wood furniture prevailed over the 1920s metal pieces. Meccano Ltd. in England still produced small metal dollhouse furniture but that firm provided only a very small amount of the furniture that was then being sold. Some of these firms, including Converse, Wisconsin Toy, Lines-Triang, and Meccano Ltd., also manufactured houses

Other new firms also arrived on the scene to enter the dollhouse market. Included were the Macris Co., Kiddie Brush and Toy Co., Vista Toy Co., Louis Marx, and the Playskool Institute. The advertisements from some of these companies are the only means collectors have to identify the firm's products if they are not marked.

In addition to Built-Rite's cardboard houses, the Sutherland Paper Co. also produced this type of house in the 1930s.

All of the products mentioned here, as well as many more, are featured in this chapter's advertisements gathered from magazines, company booklets, and wholesale and mail order catalogs. The decade of the 1930s remains one of the best for the variety of dollhouses and related products that were offered to the public. World War II in the 1940s subsequently brought many changes to the toy industry.

Brinkman

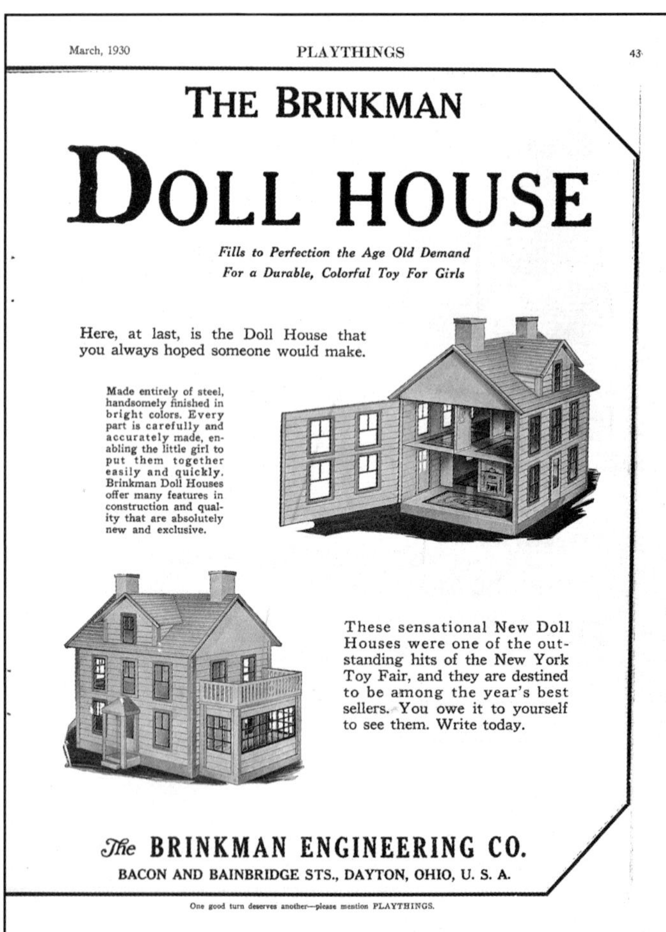

This ad for the new Brinkman steel dollhouse appeared in the March 1930 *Playthings* magazine. The house was produced by the Brinkman Engineering Co., located in Dayton, Ohio. The ad stated that the houses were a hit at the New York Toy Fair. They contained six rooms on two floors as well as a detachable porch and sun parlor. Each of these additions could be moved around to change the design of the houses. The only access to the house was the side opening. The houses were to retail for $5.00 each and measured 18" high x 21" wide x 17.5" deep. The actual house is pictured in *Furnished Dollhouses* on page 157. The Brinkman firm also produced toy bowling alleys, pool tables, and telephones.

Built-Rite-Warren Paper Products

This Built-Rite flyer was included with a boxed Built-Rite house, circa mid 1930s. It pictures the first set of cardboard furniture, four houses, a garage, and several toys for boys. The Built-Rite houses were made by Warren Paper Products of Lafayette, Indiana, beginning in the mid 1930s. The older houses were labeled "Play-Time Doll House." *Courtesy of Carol Stevenson.*

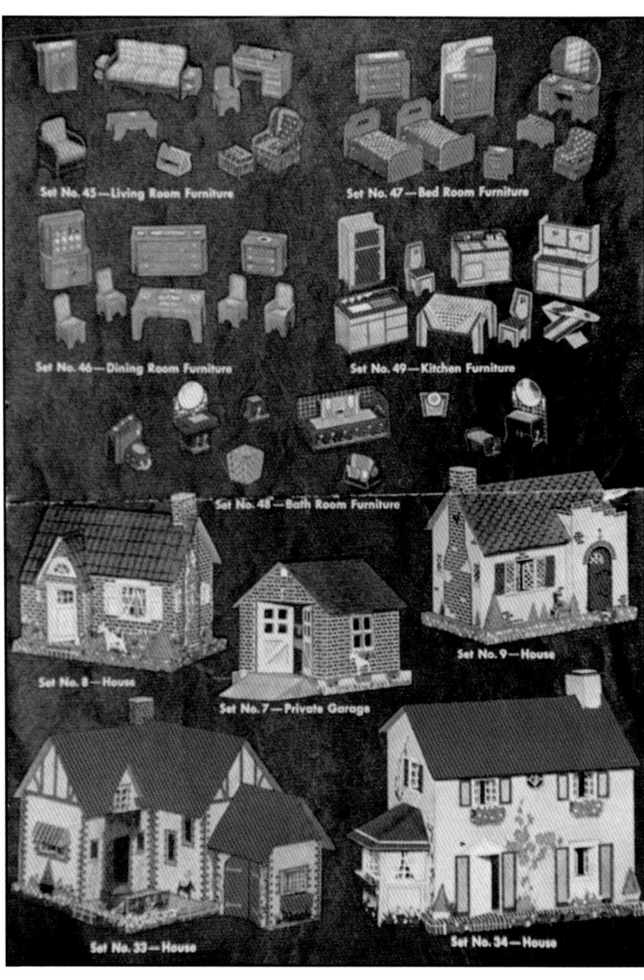

A later flyer, circa 1936, pictures five rooms of the "newer" line of cardboard furniture as well as four cardboard dollhouses and a garage. The smallest house on the upper right contained only one room. It measured 9.5" high (to top of chimney) x 10" wide x 6.5" deep. The largest house was the two-story house on the bottom right. *Courtesy of Linda Boltrek.*

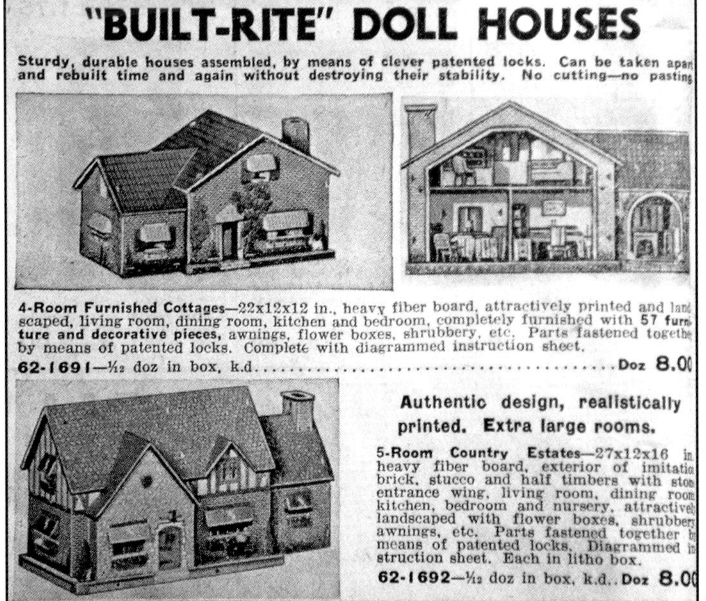

"BUILT-RITE" DOLL HOUSES

Sturdy, durable houses assembled, by means of clever patented locks. Can be taken apar and rebuilt time and again without destroying their stability. No cutting—no pasting

4-Room Furnished Cottages—22x12x12 in., heavy fiber board, attractively printed and land scaped, living room, dining room, kitchen and bedroom, completely furnished with **57 furn ture and decorative pieces**, awnings, flower boxes, shrubbery, etc. Parts fastened togethe by means of patented locks. Complete with diagrammed instruction sheet.

62-1691—1/12 doz in box, k.d. .... Doz **8.0**

Authentic design, realistically printed. Extra large rooms.

5-Room Country Estates—27x12x16 in heavy fiber board, exterior of imitati brick, stucco and half timbers with sto entrance wing, living room, dining roo kitchen, bedroom and nursery, attractive landscaped with flower boxes, shrubber awnings, etc. Parts fastened together b means of patented locks. Diagrammed i struction sheet. Each in litho box.

62-1692—1/12 doz in box, k.d.. Doz **8.0**

Two additional Built-Rite houses were advertised in the 1936 Fall and Winter Butler Brothers catalog. These larger houses included four and five rooms. Both cardboard models were sold by the company for many years. The four-room cottage came furnished with fifty-seven pieces of Built-Rite cardboard furniture. It measured 12" high x 22" wide by 12" deep.

The four-room cottage and the five-room Country Estate dollhouse were advertised in *Child Life* magazine for December 1938. The smaller house came with fifty-seven pieces of furniture and decorative pieces and sold for $1.00. The larger house included 88 furniture and decorative pieces and was priced at $2.00. Both houses included awnings and the "new" line of Built-Rite cardboard furniture. Also advertised was the Built-Rite Miniature Village, which included a railroad station, firehouse, drugstore, church, school, six houses, and a big business block. The set was priced at $1.00. *Courtesy of Carol Stevenson*.

The Warren firm continued to advertise the four-room cottage house in the December 1939 issue of *Child Life*. It was still priced at only $1.00, complete with cardboard furniture. *Courtesy of Patty Cooper*.

The Montgomery Ward Christmas catalog for 1940 featured the Country Estates house furnished with Strombecker wood furniture. Montgomery Ward's Christmas catalogs continued to offer this house for the next several years. With the advent of World War II and the shortages it entailed, cardboard dollhouses proved easier to produce. The ad copy stated that for the first time, wallpaper, pictures, blinds, rugs, and carpets were printed on the interior. The house plus five rooms of wood Strombecker 3/4" to one foot furniture was priced at $1.98.

A full page of Built-Rite cardboard toys was advertised in *Children's Activities* magazine for December 1942. The "Country Estates" dollhouse was called a "Dream House." It was priced at $2.00 complete with eighty-eight pieces of cardboard furniture and accessories. The Village set was also featured at a price of $1.00. In addition, a cardboard Railroad Station and a Castle Fort were also available. The "Train Scenery" set included three sections that totaled 60" long. One section included a mountain tunnel. Also available was the Railroad Accessory set, consisting of a station, signal tower, bridge, signs, billboards, and twenty miniature freight packages. Each boxed set sold for $1.00. The Castle Fort set was called "U.S. Army Unit and Fort." It included ninety-four pieces and featured troops, mechanized equipment, sand bag barricades, and a fort. A cardboard pistol which shot rubber bands was also part of the package. It was priced at $1.00.

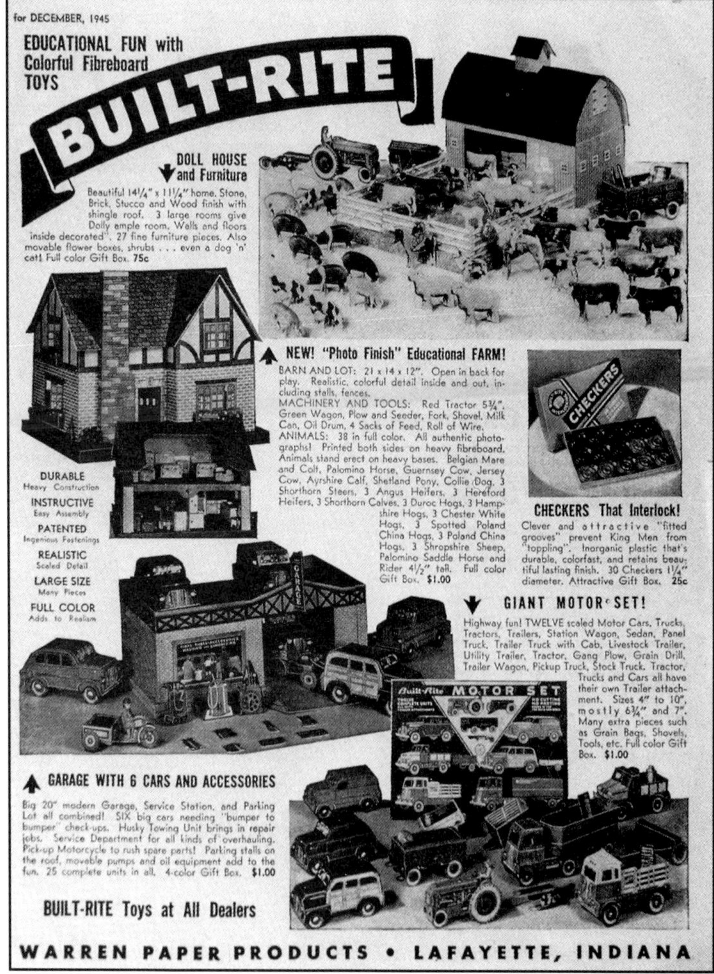

The full page Built-Rite ad in *Children's Activities* for December 1945 no longer offered the military fort. With the end of World War II, these toys were probably not as popular as previously. The boxed toys included a "New Photo Finish Educational Farm," a three-room dollhouse and furniture, a garage, and a "Giant Motor Set." The cardboard farm included a barn and lot measuring 21" x 14" x 12", red tractor, green wagon, plow and seeder, fork, shovel, milk can, oil drum, four sacks of feed, roll of wire, and 38 animals (which were authentic photographs). A palomino saddle horse and 4.5" tall rider were also part of the set. The total cost was only $1.00. The three-room dollhouse sold for only 75 cents and measured 14.25" x 11.25". The inside walls were decorated, unlike earlier models of this house. The set featured 27 Built-Rite cardboard pieces of furniture. The two-story house included two rooms downstairs and one room upstairs. The 20" Modern Garage, Service Station and Parking Lot was also priced at $1.00. The set included six cardboard cars, a motorcycle, movable pumps, and oil equipment. The "Giant Motor Set" included twelve cardboard cars, trucks, tractors, and trailers measuring from 4" to 10" long. This package also sold for $1.00.

Built-Rite
To Make Her Happy
Modern 5 Rooms -- all Yours
Modern suburban design . . . beautiful with full color detail thruout. Heavy, strong fibreboard construction . . . 3 large downstairs rooms, 2 more upstairs. Plenty of room for exciting doll and furniture play. Size 20 x13x11 in. Comes knocked down, in full color Gift Box, for easy assembly. Only $1.25
$1.25

Command these 25 Rugged Fighters!

Place your men! Be ready! Defend . . then counter-attack! Get these 25 Officers and Soldiers . . . handsome miniatures, every one . . . 3¼" tall, full color detail. This fine U.S. Army outfit also includes Fort 13½x 9½ x 10½" with ramp to Tower. 4 movable Sand Bag emplacements. All sturdy fiberboard construction. 2 Army Trenches 11" long. Each soldier has rank insignia. Set in attractive Gift Box. Only
$1.25
Boyhood Thrills! Run this Modern Farm!
Girls and boys love this big Stock Farm. Efficient, true-to-life. Exclusive: all animals from REAL PHOTOS of famous breeds. Jersey cows . . Poland China Hogs, etc. Fascinating, educational. Overall size 21x14x12" open in back for play, lots of fence, tools, tractors, equipment. It's Life on the Farm. Handsome Gift Carton. Only
$1.75

A different Built-Rite dollhouse was advertised in *Children's Activities* magazine for November 1949. It included three rooms downstairs and two rooms in the upper story. It measured 13" high x 20" wide by 11" deep. The house was priced at $1.25 and did not include furniture. A smaller version of the 1942 fort was advertised for $1.25. The fort measured 13.5" x 9.5" x 10.5". It came with 25 officers and soldiers, four sandbag emplacements, and two army trenches. The 1945 cardboard barn was still for sale but the price had escalated to $1.75 for the set.

Converse, Morton E.

(See also Chapter 1, Early Advertisements)

Dollhouse and furniture made by the Morton E. Converse firm located in Winchendon, Massachusetts. This advertisement appeared in the Montgomery Ward Spring and Summer catalog in 1931. The house was 10" high x 13.75" wide x 11.75" deep, and priced at $2.69. The catalog stated that the house had wallpapered walls. Converse dollhouse furniture was also shown, priced at 89 cents for each room. Other Converse advertisements of the time state that four different "stucco" houses were available. *Courtesy of Marge Meisinger.*

The complete set of wood Converse furniture was offered for sale in the Sears catalog for 1930. Realy Truly furniture included sets to furnish a parlor, dining room, bedroom, and kitchen. Each set was priced at 89 cents in the Sears advertisement. The furniture is similar to the Schoenhut furniture.

Craftsman's Model Co.

DOLL HOUSES THAT WILL THRILL. THE HEART OF ANY CHILD

Any child will be proud to own this Mansion style Doll House. It has six well arranged rooms with a winding stairway. The front of this Doll House is removable, exposing all rooms. Doll House stands approximately 24" high, is 36" long and 16" wide. The plan for this Doll House is complete in every detail, every part clearly dimensioned.

Cat. No. A1—Plans and instructions $0.75

KNOCK DOWN DOLL HOUSE

Kit comes to you with every part neatly cut to perfect fit from select 3/8" plywood, all brads and nails furnished. Plan and instructions also included.

Cat. No. KA1—Shipping Wt. 35 lbs. $14.75

COMPLETELY ASSEMBLED DOLL HOUSES

Doll House comes to you completely assembled, ready to paint.

Cat. No. CA1—Shipping Wt. 40 lbs. $19.75

Model A1 Doll House completely assembled and painted, ready for use.

Cat. No. CPA1—Shipping Wt. 40 lbs. $24.50

COLONIAL MODEL

Here we have a typical Colonial type Doll House of six rooms. It is 18" high, 24" long and 12" wide, and the entire back is open, making all rooms easily accessible. Very easy to make from our fully detailed plans.

Cat. No. A2—Plans and instructions $0.50

KNOCK DOWN KIT

All parts cut to perfect fit from select plywood, ready to assemble. Plans and instructions included.

Cat. No. KA2—Shipping Wt. 12 lbs. $5.95

COMPLETED DOLL HOUSES

Model A2 Doll House completely assembled, ready to paint.

Cat. No. CA2—Shipping Wt. 14 lbs. $7.95

Model A2 Doll House completely assembled and painted, ready for use.

Cat. No. CPA2—Shipping Wt. 14 lbs. $10.95

SPANISH MODEL

A one-story Spanish Type Doll House having three rooms. House stands 15" high, is 22" long and 14" wide. Entire back open for easy access.

Cat. No. A3—Plans and instructions $0.50

KNOCK DOWN KIT

Consists of all parts neatly cut to perfect fit from select plywood. Plans and instructions included.

Cat. No. KA3—Shipping Wt. 10 lbs. $4.75

COMPLETED DOLL HOUSES

Model A3 Doll House completely assembled, ready to paint.

Cat. No. CA3—Shipping Wt. 12 lbs. $6.85

Model A3 Doll House completely assembled and painted, ready for use.

Cat. No. CPA3—Shipping Wt. 12 lbs. $9.00

24

The Craftsman's Model Co. of Delafield, Wisconsin issued a catalog circa late 1930s that offered three different styles of dollhouses. The buyer could purchase a pattern and produce the house himself; buy the kit, which could then be built according to instructions; purchase the house ready to paint; or buy the completed house ready for use. The houses included a mansion with six rooms and a winding stairway. The front of this house was removable for play. It measured 24" high x 36" wide x 16" deep and sold completely furnished for $24.50. The Colonial model also included six rooms with an open back. It measured 18" high x 24" wide x 12" deep and sold for $10.95 complete. The Spanish model contained only three rooms and also included an open back. It was 15" high x 22" wide x 14" deep; it sold for $9.00. All of the houses were made of plywood.

Dinky Toys

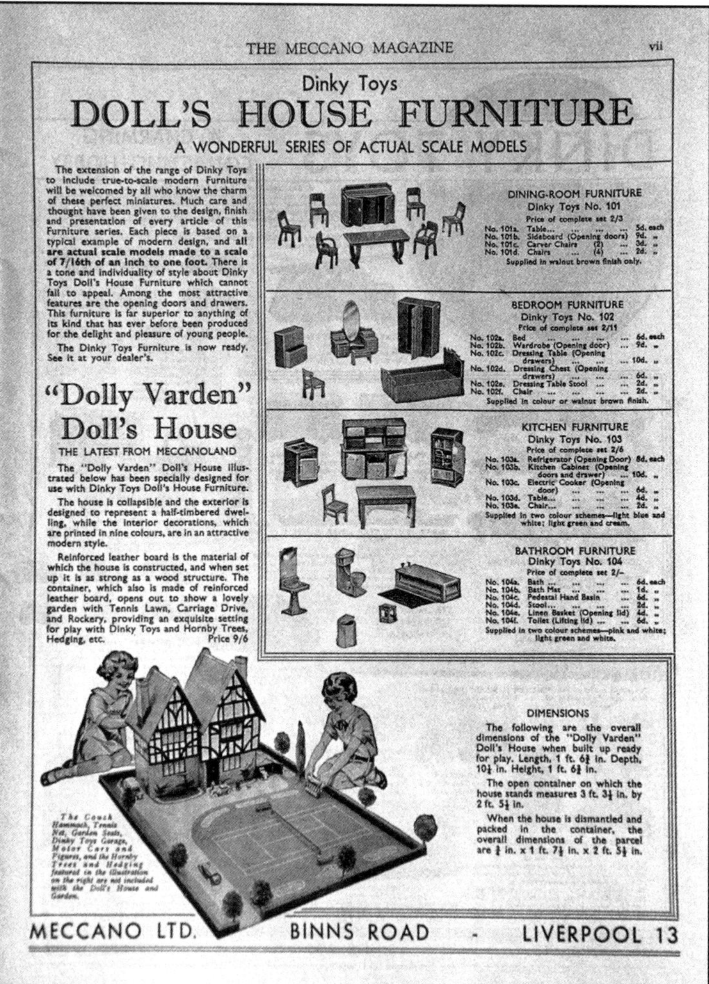

THE MECCANO MAGAZINE vii

Dinky Toys

DOLL'S HOUSE FURNITURE

A WONDERFUL SERIES OF ACTUAL SCALE MODELS

The extension of the range of Dinky Toys to include true-to-scale modern Furniture will be welcomed by all who know the charm of these perfect miniatures. Much care and thought have been given to the design, finish and presentation of every article of this Furniture series. Each piece is based on a typical example of modern design, and all **are actual scale models made to a scale of 7/16th of an inch to one foot.** There is a tone and individuality of style about Dinky Toys Doll's House Furniture which cannot fail to appeal. Among the most attractive features are the opening doors and drawers. This furniture is far superior to anything of its kind that has ever before been produced for the delight and pleasure of young people.

The Dinky Toys Furniture is now ready. See it at your dealer's.

"Dolly Varden" Doll's House

THE LATEST FROM MECCANOLAND

The "Dolly Varden" Doll's House illustrated below has been specially designed for use with Dinky Toys Doll's House Furniture.

The house is collapsible and the exterior is designed to represent a half-timbered dwelling, while the interior decorations, which are printed in nine colours, are in an attractive modern style.

Reinforced leather board is the material of which the house is constructed, and when set up it is as strong as a wood structure. The container, which also is made of reinforced leather board, opens out to show a lovely garden with Tennis Lawn, Carriage Drive, and Rockery, providing an exquisite setting for play with Dinky Toys and Hornby Trees, Hedging, etc. Price 9/6

DINING-ROOM FURNITURE
Dinky Toys No. 101
Price of complete set 2/3

No. 101a. Table... ... ... 5d. each
No. 101b. Sideboard (Opening doors) 9d. "
No. 101c. Carver Chairs (2) ... 3d. "
No. 101d. Chairs ... (4) ... 2d. "

Supplied in walnut brown finish only.

BEDROOM FURNITURE
Dinky Toys No. 102
Price of complete set 2/11

No. 102a. Bed ... ... 6d. each
No. 102b. Wardrobe (Opening door) ... 9d. "
No. 102c. Dressing Table (Opening drawers) ... ... 10d. "
No. 102d. Dressing Chest (Opening drawers) ... ... 6d. "
No. 102e. Dressing Table Stool ... ... 2d. "
No. 102f. Chair ... ... 2d. "

Supplied in colour or walnut brown finish.

KITCHEN FURNITURE
Dinky Toys No. 103
Price of complete set 2/6

No. 103a. Refrigerator (Opening Door) 8d. each
No. 103b. Kitchen Cabinet (Opening doors and drawer) ... 10d. "
No. 103c. Electric Cooker (Opening door) ... ... 6d. "
No. 103d. Table... ... ... 4d. "
No. 103e. Chair... ... ... 2d. "

Supplied in two colour schemes—light blue and white; light green and cream.

BATHROOM FURNITURE
Dinky Toys No. 104
Price of complete set 2/-

No. 104a. Bath ... ... 6d. each
No. 104b. Bath Mat ... ... 1d. "
No. 104c. Pedestal Hand Basin ... 6d. "
No. 104d. Stool... ... ... 2d. "
No. 104e. Linen Basket (Opening lid) 4d. "
No. 104f. Toilet (Lifting lid) ... ... 6d. "

Supplied in two colour schemes—pink and white; light green and white.

The Couch Hammock, Tennis Net, Garden Seats, Dinky Toys Garage, Motor Cars and Figures, and the Hornby Trees and Hedging featured in the illustration on the right are not included with the Doll's House and Garden.

DIMENSIONS

The following are the overall dimensions of the "Dolly Varden" Doll's House when built up ready for play. Length, 1 ft. 6¾ in. Depth, 10¼ in. Height, 1 ft. 6¾ in.

The open container on which the house stands measures 3 ft. 3½ in. by 2 ft. 5½ in.

When the house is dismantled and packed in the container, the overall dimensions of the parcel are ¾ in. x 1 ft. 7½ in. x 2 ft. 5½ in.

MECCANO LTD. BINNS ROAD - LIVERPOOL 13

Advertisement for Dinky Toys "Doll's House Furniture" which appeared in the October 1936 edition of *Meccano Magazine.* The cast metal furniture was produced by Meccano Ltd., located in Liverpool, England, during the 1930s. The furniture was approximately 1/2" to one foot in scale. There were four rooms of the small furniture, which included pieces for a dining room, bedroom, kitchen, and bathroom. There was no living room furniture, evidently because the cardboard Dolly Varden house the firm sold to use with the furniture contained only four rooms. The house measured 18.75" high x 18.75" wide x 10.25" deep. The container for the house could be used as a base and lawn, complete with a tennis court. These houses are very hard to find and, therefore, are expensive for a collector to purchase.

Meccano Magazine from December 1935 pictured a full page ad for the "Dinky Builder." This toy (No. 2 set) could be used to construct seven groups of miniature furniture. Pictured are the bedroom and office groups.

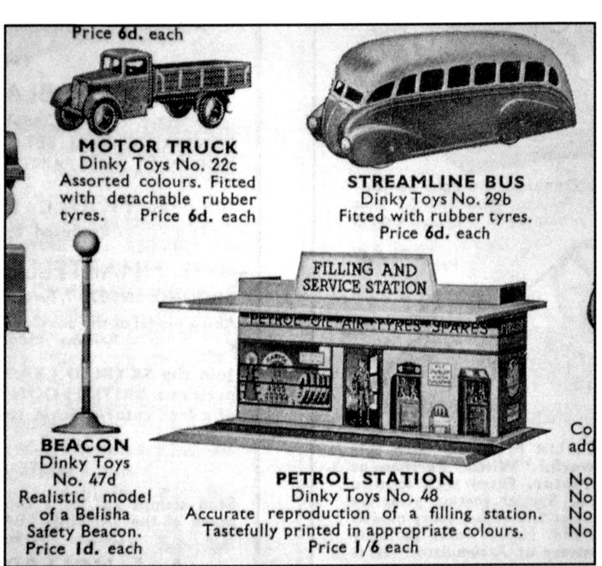

In addition to dollhouses, the English firm also produced Dinky Toys "Petrol Stations." Pictured is one advertised in *Meccano Magazine* for October 1936.

Lincoln (J.L. Wright)

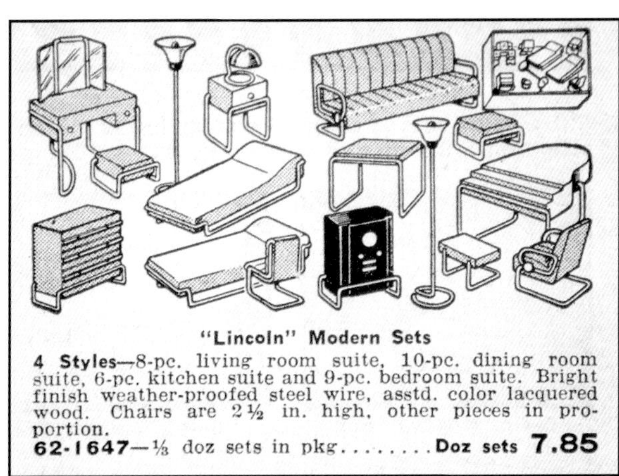

"Lincoln" Modern Sets
4 Styles—8-pc. living room suite, 10-pc. dining room suite, 6-pc. kitchen suite and 9-pc. bedroom suite. Bright finish weather-proofed steel wire, asstd. color lacquered wood. Chairs are 2½ in. high, other pieces in proportion.
62-1647—⅙ doz sets in pkg........Doz sets 7.85

"Lincoln" furniture made by J.L. Wright, Inc. of Chicago, as pictured in the 1936 Butler Brothers catalog. Furniture was made for a kitchen, dining room, bedroom, and living room according to the advertisement. The pieces were "modern" in style and were made of wood and steel wire. The furniture is approximately 3/4" to one foot in size. The J. L. Wright firm was famous for its production of Lincoln Logs, designed by John Lloyd Wright in 1916. See page 160 of *International Dollhouses* for pictures of the furniture. The company merged with Playskool in 1943.

The Embossing Company

The Montgomery Ward and Co. Toys Spring and Summer catalog for 1931 featured an advertisement for wood furniture made by the Embossing Company of Albany, New York. Although the company was founded in 1870, most of the firm's collectible toys and games were made from the 1920s through the early 1940s. The sets pictured in the catalog included a bedroom (69 cents) and dining room set (48 cents). In addition, a set was also produced for a living room. The 3/4" to one foot furniture came in pieces and was to be assembled by "fitting lugs into slots provided." In some sets, heavy cardboard rooms came with the furniture. The tops and bottoms of the boxes as well as an extra three-sided wall piece were to be used to make the rooms. The boxes were labeled "Tiny Town Furniture" or "Toys that Teach." See page 108 of *American Dollhouses and Furniture* for photographs of the actual furniture. The Embossing Co. was purchased by the Halsam Co. in 1957. *Courtesy of Marge Meisinger.*

Macris Company

Dollhouse advertised in the Marshall Field and Co. (Chicago) Christmas catalog in 1929. Even though no trade name is given, it appears to be an early Macris example. Although no shutters are included in the outside decoration, the two chimneys, removable front and back panels, and metal window frames are like those used on a similar Macris house. The front door pillars, yellow painted exterior, and green roof also follow the Macris pattern. The house measured 22.75" high and sold for $25. See page 152 of *Furnished Dollhouses* for photographs of a similar house.

EVERY child wants a Dolly Ann House—the gift that brings the most delightful thrill, the most constant pleasure and lasting interest. There is big play value and educational benefit in one of these beautiful electric lighted Dolly Ann Houses. Here is the gift supreme, the one thing that every child will enjoy and cherish.

The Dolly Ann House comes to you completely and permanently set up—ready to use. Lift it out of its strong shipping carton and it's ready for play in every detail. No assembling necessary.

The construction is rigid, strong and enduring. The Dolly Ann House is sturdily built. Its beautiful, bright colors are fadeless and indestructible. It is sanitary—it can be washed repeatedly. Leading dealers in many cities sell Dolly Ann Houses. Or—

We will send you a Dolly Ann House direct from the factory at the regular price of $12.00. Good condition on arrival absolutely guaranteed. All carrying charges fully prepaid. To assure early arrival *order one now.*

Showing the interior of the Dolly Ann House—

Full electric lighted—including vestibule. Complete with lamps, cord and plug. Attaches to any light socket.

Lacquered in bright attractive colors inside and out with durable waterproof lacquer. Can be washed inside and out repeatedly without damage.

Size 17¾ x 18½ x 14¼. Made of heavy, high grade composition board with wooden frame.

Four rooms. Steel window frames with heavy clear panes of non-shatter glass-like material.

No removable parts. Two strongly hinged back sections give access to every room.

Absolutely safe.

MACRIS COMPANY—TOLEDO, OHIO

Advertisement for a Dolly Ann dollhouse made by the Macris Company of Toledo, Ohio. It appeared in *Child Life* magazine for December 1930. The house sold for $12.00. It was made of composition board with a wood frame. The house had steel window frames with clear non-shatter glass-like material used for the windows. The four-room house measured 17.75" high x 18.5" wide x 14.25" deep. The firm also produced several other sizes and designs of dollhouses during the 1930s.

Marshall Fields

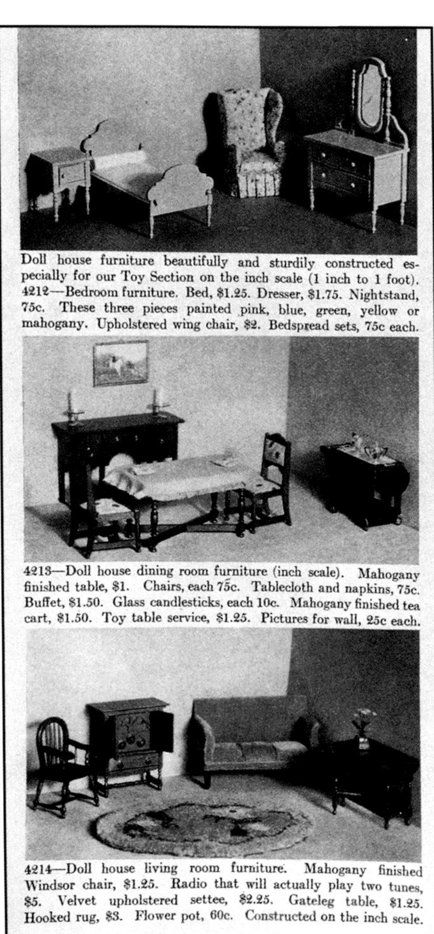

Doll house furniture beautifully and sturdily constructed especially for our Toy Section on the inch scale (1 inch to 1 foot). 4212—Bedroom furniture. Bed, $1.25. Dresser, $1.75. Nightstand, 75c. These three pieces painted pink, blue, green, yellow or mahogany. Upholstered wing chair, $2. Bedspread sets, 75c each.

4213—Doll house dining room furniture (inch scale). Mahogany finished table, $1. Chairs, each 75c. Tablecloth and napkins, 75c. Buffet, $1.50. Glass candlesticks, each 10c. Mahogany finished tea cart, $1.50. Toy table service, $1.25. Pictures for wall, 25c each.

4214—Doll house living room furniture. Mahogany finished Windsor chair, $1.25. Radio that will actually play two tunes, $5. Velvet upholstered settee, $2.25. Gateleg table, $1.25. Hooked rug, $3. Flower pot, 60c. Constructed on the inch scale.

Wood dollhouse furniture in the 1" to one foot scale was pictured in the Marshall Fields & Co. catalog for 1929. The ad copy stated that the furniture was "constructed especially for our toy section." The bedroom furniture included a bed ($1.25), dresser ($1.75), nightstand (75 cents), and upholstered wing chair ($2.00). The dining room included a mahogany finished table ($1.00), chairs (75 cents each), buffet ($1.50), tea cart ($1.50), picture for wall (25 cents), tablecloth and napkins (75 cents), glass candlesticks (10 cents each), and toy table service ($1.25). The living room featured a mahogany finished Windsor chair ($1.25), radio that would play two tunes ($5.00), velvet upholstered settee ($2.25), gate leg table ($1.25), hooked rug ($3.00), and flower pot (60 cents).

Interior Decorating on a Small Scale

SUCH a bustle on Christmas morning! The doll house telephone must be installed, the grand piano has to be in the best light, baby's crib must have southern exposure! All the enchantingly tiny furniture listed below is sturdily built and scaled about one inch to one foot.

42F31—LIVING ROOM. (Furniture in mahogany finish.)
High back chair, velours or chintz upholstery . . . $1.25
Davenport in velours or chintz, loose cushions . . . 2.25
Fireplace and mantel $1.50 — Fire tongs and poker .50
Book cases, apiece . 1.25 — Painted books, each . .15
Brass candlestick . . . .25 — Mantelpiece clock . .25
Bird cage with stand .95 — Pictures from 10c to .35
Coffee tables. .75 and .95 — Real pewter tea set . 1.25
Bookends . . .25 and .35 — Potted plants, each . .25
Table lamp and shade 1.00 — Floor lamp and shade 1.50
Large hooked rug . 3.75 — Small hooked rug . 1.50
Gateleg table . . . 1.25 — Colonial spinet desk 1.50
Piano with music box 5.00 — Radio with music box 5.00
Ladderbacked chair .95 — Windsor rocking chair 1.50
Dial telephone . . . .60 — Corner cupboard . . 1.25

42F32—DINING ROOM. (Furniture in mahogany finish.)
Tea set of wood, gaily painted pink, white or yellow .$0.75
Table flatware, service for 6, knife, fork, spoon 36
Oblong dining table .$1.25 — Chintz seat chair. 75 to 1.25
Serving table . . . . 1.25 — All-enclosed buffet . 1.50
Set of table linen . . .75 — Floral centerpiece . . .60
Double toaster . . . .75 — Percolator set . . . 1.25
Glass goblets, each . .10 — Limoges plates, each. .50

42F33—BEDROOM. (Furniture in mahogany finish or in charming soft shades of blue, green, yellow or pink.)
A comfortable chaise longue covered in chintz . . .$1.75
Single size bed . . .$1.25 — Dresser with mirror . 1.75
Low dressing table . 1.50 — Chair or rocker 75
Bedside night table . .75 — Lamp with silk shade 2.00
Set: 2 bedspreads and 2 dresser scarfs . . 1.25 — Painted powder box. .15
Tiny perfume bottle . .20

42F34—BATHROOM pieces, in green, white or orchid.
Medicine chests available in white only $1.00
Modern bathtub . .$1.50 — Waterproof bath mat .25
Lavatory on base . . .95 — Toilet seat and cover .75

42F35—NURSERY furniture in pastel pink or baby blue.
Roomy wardrobe to keep baby's clothes neat . . . $1.75
Cunning crib . . . . $1.75 — Baby's high chair . 1.50
Dressing table . . . .50 — Low nursery chair . 1.00

42F36—GARDEN furniture painted in gay red or green.
Wicker lamp with a tiny bulb that will light . . .$2.00
Wicker armchair . .$1.00 — Outdoor tea cart . . 1.75
Canvas beach chair . .50 — Canvas camp chair . 25
Iced tea set for 4 . . .50 — Lawn or terrace table. .75

42F37—KITCHEN pieces, yellow or green. Stove, 50c. Cabinet, $1.50. Sink, $1.50. Table, 75c and Chair, 75c.

Several of the large department stores, including Marshall Fields, had dollhouses or dollhouse furniture made just for their stores. This Marshall Fields advertisement from Christmas 1930 lists furniture and accessories that may have been produced in this manner. It is likely that the furniture came from Germany. Furniture and accessories included items for a living room, dining room, bedroom, bathroom, nursery, garden, and kitchen. The scale of the furniture pictured was 1" to one foot. *Courtesy of Carol Stevenson.*

GOOD HOUSEKEEPING HINTS

4230—Dining room furniture for the doll house, very well designed and made. Mahogany finish.

Chairs with red leather seats.......*each*	$ .60
Server	.95
Table	1.00
Buffet	1.00
Clock	.15
Tea cart	1.25

4231—Living room furniture in maple finish.

Green chintz wing chair	$1.00		
Fire-place with marble top	1.50		
Marble top coffee table	.75		
Windsor rocker	$1.00	Floor lamp	1.50
Spinet desk	1.25	Tilt top table	1.00
French rug	1.00	Red chintz divan	1.50
Desk chair	.75	Magazine rack	.45

These toys from the 4th floor and the Evanston, Oak Park and Lake Forest Stores.

4233—The perfect doll cab is equipped with hand brake, baby carriage style gear and pusher, drop back and sliding hood adjustments. Round fiber reed in sand and brown, or green and willow. 19" x 11", with sturdy 10" wheels. $7.50.

4234—The perfect doll house furniture for a bedroom. In pink or green.

Bed	$ .95	Chest	$1.25
Dressing table	1.50	Night table	.50
Bench	.50	Lamp	.85
		Hooked rug	1.00

Additional furniture was pictured in a 1932 Marshall Fields Christmas advertisement. Like the furniture in 1930, each piece was priced separately. The red chintz divan was $1.50, tea cart $1.25, dressing table with mirror $1.50, and the floor lamp $1.50. Pictured are pieces for a dining room, living room, and bedroom. Although the furniture was a little cheaper than that pictured in 1930, it was still too expensive for most little girls. The bedroom set would total over $6 while a set of Realy Truly furniture was priced at only 89 cents. *Stevenson Collection.*

Louis Marx and Co.

(Early, from 1930s; see also 1950s chapter)

Cardboard Newlywed dollhouse made by Louis Marx and Co. in the 1920s and early 1930s, as pictured in the National Bellas Hess catalog for 1930. The house included four furnished rooms. Each of the rooms was made of lithographed sheet steel. The walls were decorated to represent the different rooms. The tiny furniture was also lithographed metal. The rooms consisted of three sides and a floor and measured 3" high x 5.5" wide x 2.5" deep. The pictured house included a kitchen, bedroom, dining room and parlor. A bathroom and a library were also available. The house measured 8.5" high x 10.25" wide x 2.75" deep and sold complete for 44 cents. The front opened with two large doors. The metal rooms were housed in the cardboard house container. The Marx firm was begun by Louis Marx shortly after World War I. *Courtesy of Marge Meisinger.*

Copy of the No. 190 Newlyweds kitchen box. The furniture included a cabinet, sink, stove, table, and two chairs. The box is marked "Louis Marx New York U.S.A." *Courtesy of Patty Cooper.*

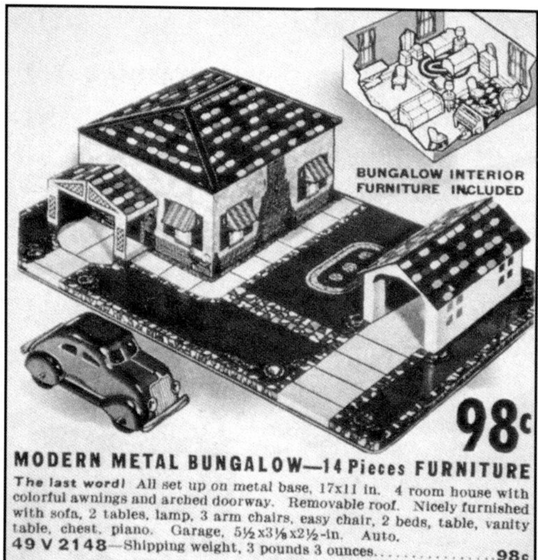

The 1938 Sears Christmas catalog featured another early Marx dollhouse. The small metal house and garage came on a metal base measuring 17" x 11". The four-room house came with awnings and "Midget" Tootsietoy metal furniture. Included were a sofa, two tables, lamp, three arm chairs, easy chair, two beds, vanity table, table, chest, and piano. A car was also included in the package. The roof was removable for play. The price for the "Modern Metal Bungalow" was listed as 98 cents. See page 26 of the *Toy Buildings* book for a photograph of the actual house. *Courtesy of Marge Meisinger.*

The same 1938 Sears Christmas catalog also offered a cardboard "carton" dollhouse that included a double deck tea wagon holding a tea set, as well as a kitchen set consisting of a Marx metal refrigerator (4.5" x 3.75"), stove, sink, and cabinet. The other metal kitchen furnishings measured approximately 4" x 4.25" each. The set was priced at 79 cents. *Meisinger Collection.*

Besides dollhouses, Marx also produced many buildings for boys during this period. Included were a fire station, police station, grocery store, bank, drug store, and other buildings similar to the Newlywed rooms, plus railroad stations, bus stations, airports, garages, and service stations. Pictured is an ad from the Montgomery Ward 1940 catalog for a Marx electrically lighted service station. The firm made several different designs of these stations throughout the 1930s. This one includes a "fast food" addition. A 6" steel roadster came with the set. The steel station and platform measured 13.5" x 10" and sold for $1.00.

Menasha Woodenware Corp.

Menasha Woodenware Corp. advertised their Tyke Toys in *Playthings* in August 1934. Besides dollhouse furniture, the company also made baby bassinets, a table and chairs, nursery chairs, and shoo flys. The firm, located in Menasha, Wisconsin, produced two different scales of wood dollhouse furniture during a few years in the 1930s. One line was in a small 1" to one foot scale while the other line was approximately 1.5" to one foot in scale. See pages 135 and 136 of *Antique & Collectible Dollhouses* for photographs of the furniture.

Miniaform

Miniaform furniture was produced by the Hugh Specialty Co. of Chicago beginning in 1939. This ad appeared in the Chicago Mail Order Company Fall and Winter catalog for 1939-1940. Included were pieces suitable to furnish a dining room, living room, kitchen, and bedroom. The set of four rooms sold for $1.69 while each set was priced individually for only 45 cents. The actual furniture is pictured on page 84 of *International Dollhouses*. The house pictured with the furniture was made by The Kiddie Brush & Toy Co. (Susy Goose) in Jonesville, Michigan. *Courtesy of Marge Meisinger.*

Playskool Institute

December, 1930 CHILD LIFE 665

Playthings With A Purpose

Give them more than "just toys" this Christmas

PLAYSKOOL PRODUCTS

are designed and built to promote *"Learning While Playing"*.

For Christmas, and all the year, Playskool Institute offers a complete line of educational playthings to meet the play requirements of children of pre-school, kindergarten and primary age.

From the simple sets of large-sized pegs and blocks, for tiny tots, up to Playskool, The Home Kindergarten, and the marvelous Build-At-Will Doll House for the "older" youngsters—each Playskool Product provides valuable benefits in mental stimulation, coordination of mind and muscle, and general sense training.

The Playskool idea and ideal of "Learning While Playing", as expressed in Playskool Products, is approved by recognized authorities on child training and pre-schooling.

The Build-At-Will Doll House and Playskool, The Home Kindergarten, are two Playskool Products which provide many happy play hours for children of kindergarten and primary age.

See Them At Leading Stores

DEPARTMENT stores and other alert retailers are well aware of the tendency toward educational playthings, and are featuring the products of Playskool Institute in their holiday displays.

They will be glad to show you the complete Playskool line, and to suggest the proper items for the good little boys and girls you want to remember this Christmas.

We, too, will be glad to help you with your shopping by sending you the colorful new folder describing Playskool Products, together with an interesting booklet entitled "Pre-school Training in The Home". Just send the attached coupon and enclose Ten Cents to cover mailing cost of booklet.

Playskool Junior — of lighter construction and contains fewer play materials than Playskool. Has bench instead of chair.

Playskool Sandie .. This modern sand table combines the benefits of sand play with the Playskool idea.

Hammer-Nail .. Makes the child's desire to pound, a constructive pastime. A popular number.

Cart-Block Peggy — a colorful collection of large sized pegs and blocks, and a fascinating pull-toy, too.

Playskool Peggy Box .. Pegs, blocks and peg-board in sturdy wood container.

Playskool Parquetry Blocks — stimulate a sense of color and design. In various assortments and sizes.

PLAYSKOOL INSTITUTE
594 COMMERCE ST. MILWAUKEE, WIS.

PLAYSKOOL INSTITUTE C.L.-12-30
594 Commerce Street, Milwaukee, Wis.

Please send me the booklet and folder mentioned above. I enclose Ten Cents to cover mailing cost.

Name..........
Address..........
City.......... State..........

Playskool Institute advertisement from *Child Life* magazine in December 1930. The ad features "The Build at Will" dollhouse but no further information about the house is given. It appears to be a large house that perhaps could be taken apart and re-assembled easily. The company was located in Milwaukee, Wisconsin and produced wooden toys suitable for use in a classroom. These products were also marketed to individuals. The firm acquired the popular Lincoln Logs when J.L. Wright merged with Playskool in 1943.

Rich Toys

The Rich Toy Co., was founded by Maurice Rich Sr. and Edward M. Rich in 1921 in Sterling, Illinois. In 1935, the company moved to Clinton, Iowa. That same year, this Rich house was advertised in the Chicago Marshall Field & Co. catalog. The house was white with maroon trim. The furniture pictured with the house was the new wood Strombecker 1" to one foot design. The five-room house was 24" tall (including chimney) x 27.5" wide x 15"deep. It sold for $6.50 while the furniture was priced at $1.50 per box. *Courtesy of Marge Meisinger.*

ENGLISH TYPE DOLL HOUSES

5 Rooms—24x12x22 in., heavy composition, yellow with brown and buff trim, metal hinges and door knob, 3 imitation leaded pane isinglass windows with painted shutters, 2 with flower boxes. Open back.
62R-1694—1 in carton, k.d., 14 lbs. **Each 2.15**

"English Type Doll House," thought to have been made by the Rich Toy Co. It was advertised in the Minneapolis based Butler Brothers Fall and Winter 1936 catalog. The five-room house was made of heavy composition with three imitation leaded pane isinglass windows with painted shutters. The house was yellow with brown and buff trim. It measured 24" high x 22" wide x 12" deep.

English Type Doll House

This is a beautiful six-room, electrically lighted doll house, a quality product by Rich. It is 31" x 16½" x 20". Bisque with brown trim and brown blinds. Chimney realistically made of wood, with painted stone effect and iron chimney supports. Celluloid windows. The material of the house is a pressed hardwood, stronger than wood and will not warp. Open at back, and also back half of roof is removable. Shipped knocked down, with hardware and directions for easy assembling. **Price, complete with electric lights, prepaid, $7.80.**

Right:
A Tudor designed Rich house was advertised in *Children's Activities* magazine in December 1937. This house, called an "English Type House," included six rooms and was electrically lighted. It was bisque in color with brown trim and brown shutters, and measured 20" high x 31" wide x 16.5" deep. The chimney was made of wood finished with a stone effect. The windows were described as being made of celluloid. The open-backed house was made so that the back half of the roof was removable. It sold for $7.80.

Three Rich houses with totally different designs were advertised in the 1939 Edw. K. Tryon Co. catalog. Included were a two-story dollhouse numbered 382, which included five rooms. The ad copy described the house as being cream color with brown trim. The house included two swinging windows. It measured 17.5" high x 25" wide x 11" deep. The "Avon" two-story example included only three rooms. It was white with a red roof. It measured 18.5" high x 22.5" wide x 9.75" deep. The third house, called "Cottage," looks more like an Art Deco example. Although it is a two-story house, it contained only three rooms and was the cheapest house pictured. It was light yellow with green shutters and shrubs. It measured 12" high x 18" wide x 8" deep. *Courtesy of Linda Boltrek.*

DOLL HOUSES — FORT — MUSICAL CRADLES

No. 382—Doll House. 25 x 11 x 17½ inches. 5-room. Cream color, brown trim. Inside finished bisque, light brown floors. 2 swinging windows. Weighs about 10 lbs. Each **$3.25**

No. 281—Avon. 22½ x 18½ x 9¾ inches. 2-story American cottage. White with black stenciled clapboard effect, red roof. Inside bisque walls, light brown floors. Swinging windows. Weight, 8½ lbs. Each **$2.00**

No. 380—Cottage. 18 x 12 x 8 inches. 2-story. 3-room. Light yellow, green shutters and shrubs, celluloid windows. Weight, 62 lbs. to dozen. Each **$1.00**

Left:
Rich toys were featured in an ad from *Children's Activities* magazine in December 1939. The two houses pictured included a "Colonial Mansion" and a "6 room Suburban" Tudor designed house. The Mansion contained six rooms and a stairway and measured 24.5" high x 34" wide x 21" deep. The outside was decorated with four pillars, green shutters, metal windows, and red brick chimneys. It also included electric lights and was priced at $14.00. The Suburban house included a garage at its side. The house measured 21" high x 33.5" wide x 15.5" deep and sold for $6.95. *Courtesy of Carol Stevenson.*

Right:
Two different designs of Rich dollhouses were featured in the 1940 Christmas catalog from Massey's Drug Store in Shirley, Indiana. A different cottage was pictured, which sold for $2.25. It included four rooms and measured 18.5" high x 22.5" wide x 3.75" deep. The larger house on the left was designed after a "Southern Mansion" with its four front pillars. The two-story house contained four rooms and sold for $3.25. *Meisinger Collection.*

The Montgomery Ward Christmas catalog of 1940 also included two Rich houses for sale. The cottage shown was exactly like the one offered by Massey's Drug store but priced more cheaply at $1.79. The more expensive Rich house cost $3.69. It featured four rooms, windows that opened, a doorbell that rang, a metal balcony, a lantern on the front porch, and built-in dummy cabinets and sink. The kitchen and bathroom were designed with "tile-effect" floors and the living room and bedroom were carpeted with felt-like fabric. The house was white with a green roof and red shutters. It measured 19.5" high x 27" wide x 14" deep. Both houses were made of Gypsum board. *Courtesy of Marge Meisinger.*

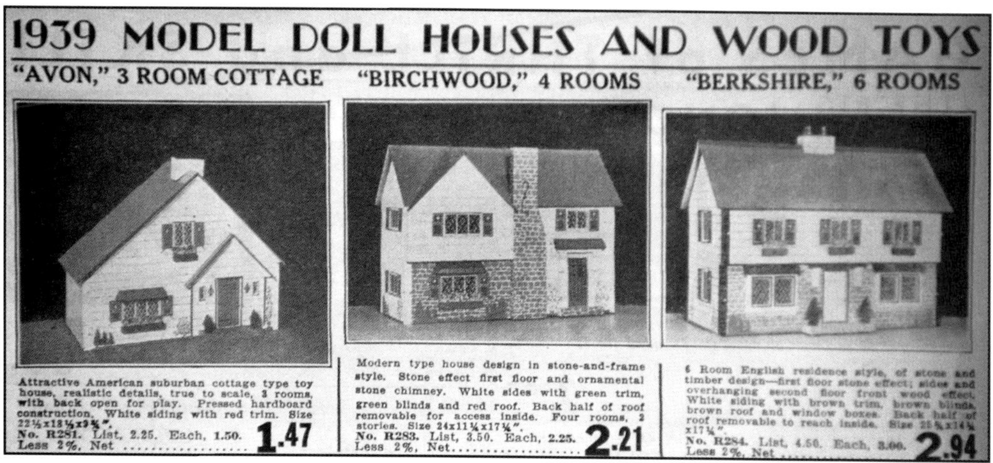

The All-American Products Corp. of Chicago wholesale catalog for 1939 also featured three dollhouses made by Rich. Included were the "Avon" three-room cottage, plus a four room "Birchwood" house and a six room "Berkshire" example. The outside of the "Birchwood" two-story house included a first floor and chimney with a stone design. The house also featured an overhanging second floor. The house's siding was white with brown trim and a brown roof (the back half was removable). It measured 17.5" high x 25.75" wide x 14.5" deep. *Courtesy of Marge Meisinger.*

GEOGRA-KIT This unique kit contains everything necessary for children to make their own maps in a simple but effective way. They can make four large maps, each 13½" x 18". The maps are of the United States; Canada and Alaska; Mexico and Central America; and South America. The basic part of each map is a sheet of heavy black cardboard on which is printed the outlines of states, provinces and countries. Then there are sheets of colored gummed paper. On each sheet are printed outlines and geographical features of the various states, provinces and countries. Children cut out the colored paper and stick it on the proper places on the black outline maps. The finished products are beautiful six color maps. There are also over 150 stickers of small pictures which can be stuck on the maps, showing the principal industries and resources of the various sections. A folder gives key maps showing the location of industries and resources as well as other interesting geographical information. **Price, postpaid, $1.35.**

COLONIAL DOLL HOUSE WITH RUGS We think this house by Rich is one of the finest and most beautiful doll houses to be found. It is of typical colonial style, painted white with red blinds. Green roof with black stenciled shingles. Colonial porch with white wooden pillars. Outside walls decorated with green shrubbery and red flowers. Metal frame windows of heavy cellophane, red chimneys. Large size, 34" x 24" x 22" with 6 large rooms and stairway. Porch lamp. The rugs are of rayon flock sprayed on the floor. Made of U. S. Gypsum hardboard. **Price, express prepaid, $15.00.**

The *Children's Activities* magazine for December 1942 also offered a Rich house for sale. It was yet another example of a Colonial house. The pillars on this model were round instead of square. The house was white with red blinds and a green roof with black stenciled shingles. Also included were windows made of heavy cellophane framed in metal, a stairway, and a porch lamp. The two-story, six room house measured 24" high x 34" wide x 22" deep. The postpaid cost was $15.00.

A house produced by Rich Industries was featured in "The Toy Yearbook 1946-47" from the Grover C. Hughes Hardware & Appliance store in Waynesburg, Pennsylvania. The six-room house was made of Gypsum and was 27" wide. The floors were painted and stenciled. It was priced at $6.50. *Courtesy of Judy Mosholder.*

HOUSE TO LET. Desirable tenants wanted for well-built English country home; six rooms freshly decorated, carpets on floor. Move into your dream house today. Only $10. Completely furnished and with family of five, $21.50. What young mother wouldn't snap up such a buy for her dolls who have no roof over their heads! Prepaid from J. J. Anthony, 1517 W. North Ave., Milwaukee, Wisc.

A Rich Tudor house was offered for sale in a *House Beautiful* advertisement from the October 1948 issue. This two-story, six-room house sold for $10.00. It could be purchased completely furnished along with a family of five for $21.50. No clue is given to what type of furniture or dolls were to be included. No house measurements were listed. The ad came from the J. J. Anthony firm in Milwaukee, Wisconsin.

No. 1044 SIX ROOM DOLL HOUSE

Your little "pigtailed mother" needs this lovely home for her dolls! There are few things a little girl wants more than a doll house. This one is really super. It is two stories high, has six rooms and is decorated in gay colors of red, bisque and green. Green roof—red chimneys. Floors are painted to represent rugs and linoleum. Of hinged construction—it is shipped flat—no tools are needed for quick and easy assembly. Size 27" long—17½" high—13½" deep. **$6.50.**

Mayfair Gifts located in Forest Hills, New York offered a Rich dollhouse for sale in their Fall 1948/Spring 1949 catalog. It was a two story, six-room example with a green roof, red chimneys, and stenciled outside decorations. The unusual chimney placement was used on several different designs of Rich houses of the era. This house measured 17.5" high x 27" wide x 13.5" deep and was priced at $6.50.

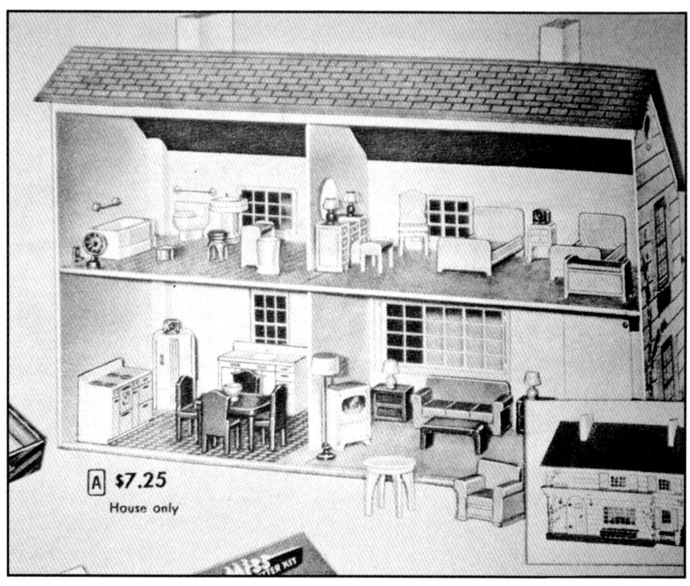

As the metal dollhouses produced by various firms in the 1950s became more popular, fewer Rich dollhouses were advertised in the mainstream catalogs. This example from the Sears 1955 Christmas catalog is an exception. The two story, four-room house still features the familiar Rich designer floors and a plain white interior. The outside of the white house is decorated with the usual stencil designs with a red roof and white plastic windows. The house measured 17.5" high x 27" wide x 10.5" deep and sold for $7.25 unfurnished. The ad pictured the house furnished with 3/4" to one foot Strombecker wood furniture from the period. The furniture included separate boxed sets of ten pieces each for a living room, bedroom, bathroom, and kitchen. Each boxed set was $1.85. The total cost was nearly $15.00 for a furnished dollhouse. The same catalog pictured two Marx metal dollhouses complete with plastic furniture priced at $3.19 and $5.29 for a larger six room example. For most parents, the cost difference was the deciding factor in their choice to purchase a metal Marx house instead of a Rich hardboard model.

6-ROOM ENGLISH DOLL HOUSE . . . made of U.S. Gypsum Hardboard. Two stories; plastic stairway. Finished in bisque with red, brown and green stenciled designs. Red blinds, green roof, stone chimneys and plastic windows. Interior painted and stenciled to represent linoleum in kitchen, bath. Flocked floors in other rooms like carpets.
89-2125 C1050 Size: 35x23¼x14" $14.95
6-ROOM EARLY AMERICAN DOLL HOUSE. A junior homemaker's delight! Made of U.S. Gypsum Duron and finished in white with red blinds and chimneys; green roof. Two stories. Exterior stenciled in red, green and black designs simulating trees, ivy, etc. Painted floors stenciled to look like rugs, linoleum.
89-2133 C665 Size: 29¼x21¼x14" $9.50

The John Plain catalog for 1956 features ads for two Rich houses. The Tudor house included six rooms in two stories and featured a plastic stairway. The familiar flocked floors and stenciled linoleum in the kitchen and bathroom were still being used in both houses. The outside decorations on both models included red shutters, green roofs, and plastic windows. The Tudor measured 23.5" high x 35" wide x 14" deep and sold for $14.95. The six-room "Early American" house was 21.25" high x 29.25" wide x 14" deep and sold for $9.50.

Colonial-styled just like real houses—open in back for play
B

This Colonial styled dollhouse was advertised in the 1958 General Merchandise Co. catalog. It could have been made by Rich Industries because of its similarity to the Rich model featured in the Bing Allen & Co. example from 1960 (see next picture). The house was made of wood and Tekwood with plastic window frames and wood grained flooring according to the copy. The two-story house included six rooms. The outside was finished with a simulated brick design and white shutters. The house measured 22" high x 28" wide x 14" deep and was priced at $9.98 retail.

Bing Allen & Co. catalog dollhouse ad dating from 1960. This six-room Colonial house is a late Rich design featuring an outside decoration of red "brick" and four columns. It also includes the simulated tile and rug designs of earlier years. It was made of U.S. Gypsum board and measures 20.5" high x 28" wide x 15.5" deep.

6-ROOM COLONIAL DOLL HOUSE. Extra big, extra strong—will house a large doll family for many happy years. True Williamsburg styling from its red "brick" front to its graceful white columns. Decorated interior with simulated tile and rug designs. Heavy, warp-resistant U.S. Gypsum board. Scaled for 1" furniture. 28x15½x20½".
89-2497 C865 Colonial Doll House $12.95

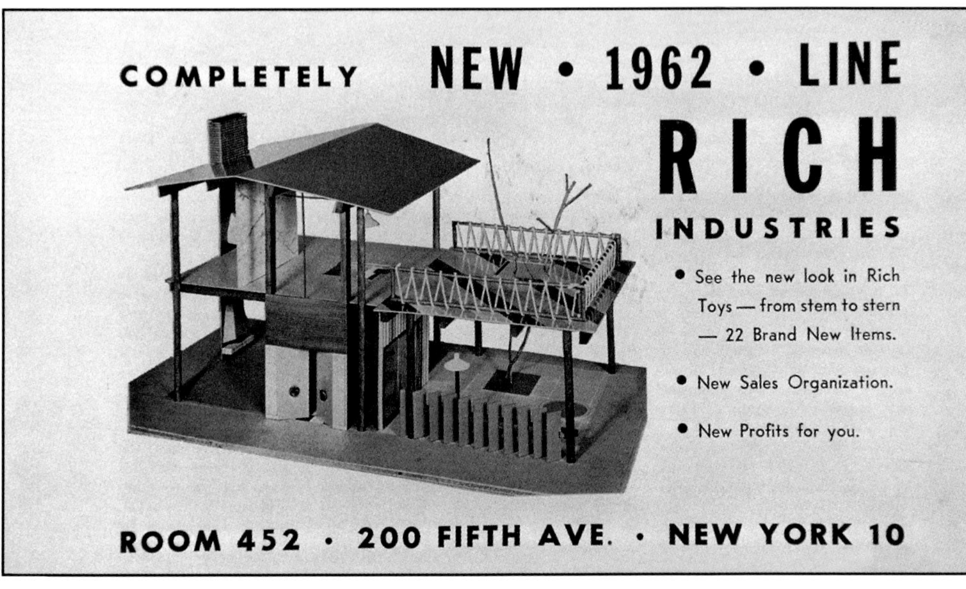

This ad for Rich Industries appeared in *Playthings* magazine for March 1962. The copy reads "See the new look in Rich Toys – from stem to stern – 22 Brand New Items. New Sales Organization." The dollhouse pictured was very different than anything Rich Toy Co. had done before. After a move to Tupelo, Mississippi in the 1950s, the firm fell on hard times and it is thought that 1962 was the last year of business for the once successful company.

Left:
The Sears Christmas catalog for 1962 carried the new Rich "House of the Future" priced at $17.99. The house was made of wood, masonite, and pressed wood and measured 36" x 20". There were no outside walls and the inside partitions were movable. The house included a patio and pool.

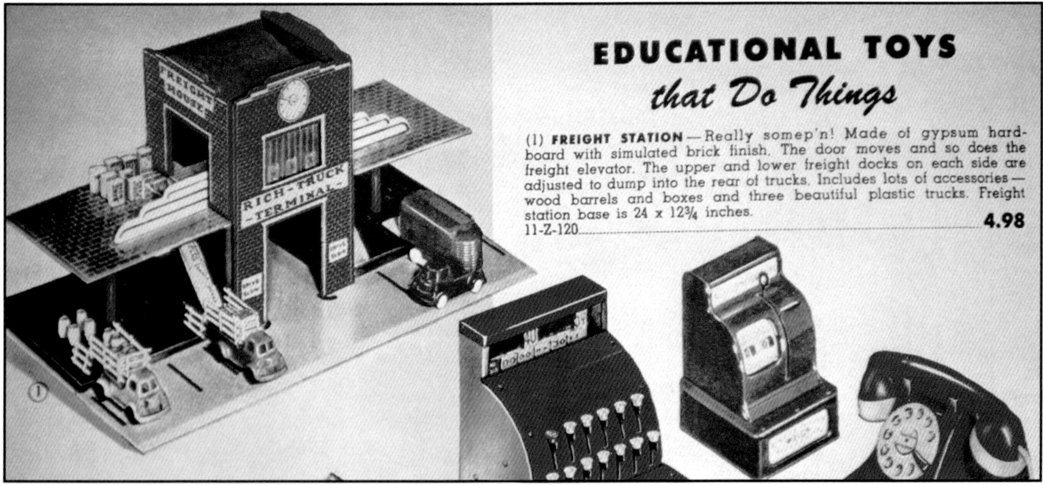

Besides dollhouses, Rich Industries also produced many toy buildings during their many years in business. Included were gas stations, barns, garages, airports, and freight stations. Pictured is an ad for a Rich truck terminal from the 1948 Firestone Fall and Winter catalog sent from the Sibley's Firestone Dealer Store in Little Falls, Minnesota. It was made of Gypsum hardboard and measured 24" wide x 12.75" deep. Accessories included three plastic trucks, wood barrels, and boxes. A moving freight elevator was also part of the terminal. It sold for $4.98. *Courtesy of Roy Specht.*

A. Schoenhut Company

The Schoenhut firm was located in Philadelphia, Pennsylvania. Beginning in 1917, the firm began the manufacture of dollhouses. This Schoenhut ad is from the November 1926 *Ladies Home Journal*. It pictures a bungalow made of wood and fibreboard. The walls were embossed to represent stone and the roof was finished in a tile design. The inside of the house was covered with lithographed paper to represent wallpaper, doors, and other interior decorations. It measured 19.5" x 26.5" x 18.5" and contained three rooms. *Courtesy of Marilyn Pittman.*

Schoenhut's Doll Houses and
Bungalows are made in a wide
range of styles and prices.

Schoenhut offered a new line of dollhouses in 1927. This *Child Life* ad from December 1927 pictured two of the houses. The new houses no longer included a stone look but instead were painted a pale yellow, maybe to tie in to the stucco look then popular on real houses. The two-story house included five rooms and measured 15.75" x 18.75" x 20.25". The smaller, one-story bungalow included two rooms and an attic and measured 18.25" x 13.5" x 18.25". *Pittman Collection.*

Advertisement for "Schoenhut's Doll Houses Entire New Line for 1927." The houses could be purchased with or without the garden, trees, shrubbery, and garage pictured. They were made of wood and fibreboard and included embossed roofs to represent tile. The inside of the houses were covered with tinted wallpaper. The two-story pictured house included eight rooms. It measured 23.5" x 24" x 23.25".

In addition to the eight-room house shown at the bottom of this Schoenhut 1927 advertisement, two smaller two-story houses are pictured at the top of the ad. On the left is a two-story house which contains four rooms and measures 12" x 17.75" x 17". On the right is a two-story house which includes five rooms. Its dimensions are 15.75" x 18.75" x 20.25".

The one-story Schoenhut Bungalows were pictured in the third page of the 1927 advertisement. They ranged in size from one-room to four-room structures. The large house in the middle contained four rooms and an attic. It measured 16.75" high x 24.5" wide x 26" deep.

This full page Schoenhut ad appeared in *Child Life* magazine in December 1929. It pictured two of the company's pianos, the popular circus, and one of their dollhouses. *Courtesy of Marilyn Pittman.*

Schoenhut's Latest New Large Size Doll House Wood Furniture—Many New Features—Larger Pieces—Finer Designs—Prices Greatly Reduced.
7 Pc. Orchid Enameled Bedroom Set 69c
Twin beds, 5¼x2⅞ in. 4 in. width dresser with two removable drawers. Two chairs, night table and floor lamp in proportion.
49K7152—Shpg. wt., 1 lb. 4 oz. 69c
7 Pc. Bright Red and Green Enameled Parlor Set 69c
Piano, 4¼x4½ in. and bench, enameled green. 6⅜x3¼ in. settee enameled red. Arm chair, ottoman, end table and floor lamp in proportion.
49K7150—Shpg. wt., 1 lb. 8 oz. 69c
7 Pc. White Enameled Kitchen Set 69c
Table, 5x2¾x2⅝ in.; 4½ in. Ice Box with hinged door. Gas range, sink, stool and two chairs in proportion. Shpg. wt., 1 lb. 8 oz.
49K7153......69c
7 Pc. Light Green Enameled Dining Set 69c
Table, 5⅞x3¼ in.; buffet has hinged doors. Server with removable drawer and four chairs in proportion. Shpg. wt., 1 lb. 4 oz.
49K7151......69c
7 Pc. Orchid Bathroom Set 69c
Bath-tub, 5¼x2½ in. Shower, toilet, wash-basin, make-up table, bench, chest in proportion. Shpg. wt., 1 lb. 4 oz.
49K7154......69c

The Schoenhut firm produced five different lines of dollhouse furniture from 1928 until 1934. Three of these lines were scaled 3/4" to one foot and the other two lines were in a small 1" to one foot scale (1928) and a larger 1" to one foot scale (1932). Pictured is an ad for the larger line of 1" to one foot scale furniture as advertised in the 1932 Sears catalog. Schoenhut made furniture for a living room, dining room, bedroom, kitchen, and bathroom in all of its lines of dollhouse furniture. These sets were sold by Sears for only 69 cents each. *Courtesy of Patty Cooper.*

A close-up of the dollhouse pictured in the 1929 *Child Life* advertisement. This was from the new line of houses. The house was furnished with the small 1" to one foot wood furniture that had been added to Schoenhut's toy line in 1928. The two-story house included a removable front which allowed access to its four rooms and two halls. A stairway connected the two floors. Furniture was made for a bathroom, bedroom, living room, dining room, and kitchen. The house measured 31" x 22" x 16.5". *Pittman Collection.*

SOLD EVERYWHERE
MADE IN U. S. A. SINCE 1872—AMERICAN INGENUITY AND INVENTION
Toys that Teach and inspire the Children as well as amuse
SCHOENHUT TOY PIANOS
Schoenhut pianos, ukeleles and other musical toys are most interesting and instructive. The Schoenhut Toy Piano has great educational value. It teaches familiarity with the standard piano keyboard, for even the smallest model has keys spaced correctly and is tuned accurately. There are forty different models including both Baby Grand and Upright Pianos, ranging from five keys to three full octaves with half tones. Priced from 50c to $35.00 each. Be sure that the name SCHOENHUT appears on the front of the piano you buy; any other name appearing designates that it is not a Schoenhut.
SCHOENHUT'S TOY PIANOS have been the standard for 57 years. Accept no substitute. Schoenhut Toy Pianos can be had in three different finishes: Mahogany, Two-tone Ivory and Jade Green. Very beautiful.
SCHOENHUT'S DOLL HOUSES
When you buy a Doll House, be sure it is a Schoenhut Make. It will give the best satisfaction and the most pleasure to the child.
Shoenhut's Doll Houses and Bungalows. Strong and Stylishly Built, American Style Houses. Made in a wide range of styles and prices.
Schoenhut's Doll House Furniture, made out of clean hardwood, just the right size. Better than the average in quality. Made in five different sets for the various rooms.
SCHOENHUT'S Humpty Dumpty Circus Toys
The Greatest Show on Earth
A TOY TO AMUSE THE WHOLE FAMILY
GET YOUR DEALER TO SHOW YOU THIS NEW BIG TENT WITH SIDE SHOW EFFECTS
Probably the most beloved of all Schoenhut toys is the Humpty Dumpty Circus. This consists of all the familiar figures of the saw-dust ring, from the clown to the elephant, so marvellously jointed that they can be made to do all sorts of tricks. As a never failing source of delight, there is probably nothing else like it. Sets cost from $1.00 to $35.00 depending on the number of figures.
LOOK FOR THE NAME "SCHOENHUT" APPEARING ON EVERY TOY OR LABEL

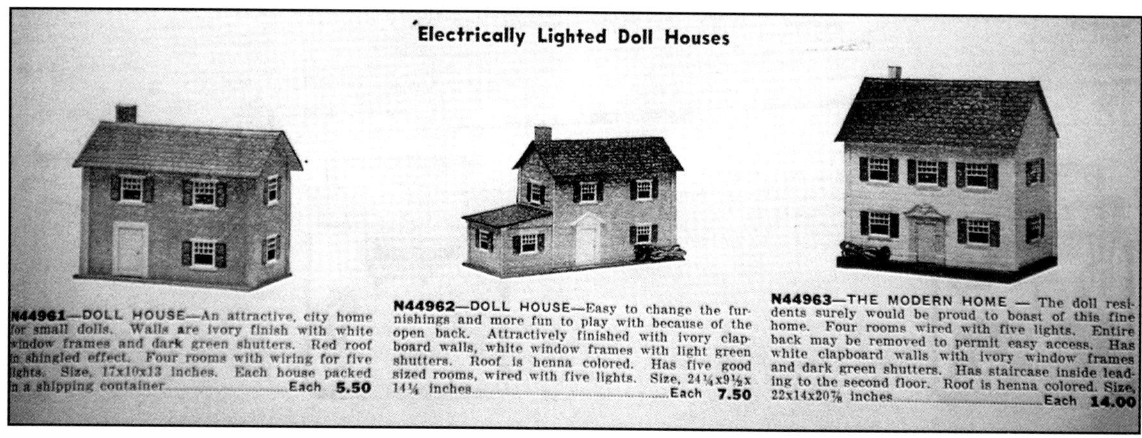

Three Schoenhut dollhouses were advertised in the Chicago based McClurg's Fall and Winter catalog in 1934. This was the last year of business for the A. Schoenhut firm. The house on the left contained four rooms and an open back. It could be purchased with or without electric lights. It came with a red roof and green shutters. It measured 13" high x 17" wide x 10" deep. The middle house was a very unusual design for the Schoenhut firm. It contained four rooms in the two-story part of the house and an extra room on the first floor. This house provided enough room to use a complete set of Schoenhut furniture (five rooms). The back was removable. It was finished with ivory clapboard walls and light green shutters. The house was electrified with five lights. It measured 14.25" high x 24.25" wide x 9.5" deep. The house on the right was the largest and the most expensive. It contained four electrified rooms, a stairway, and a removable back. The outside was finished with white clapboard walls and dark green shutters. It measured 20.75" high x 22" wide x 14" deep. *Courtesy of Marge Meisinger.*

The Sears Fall and Winter catalog for 1933 advertised a set of 3/4" to one foot scale Schoenhut wood furniture. The price was only 47 cents for each room set. *Courtesy of Marge Meisinger.*

Strombecker

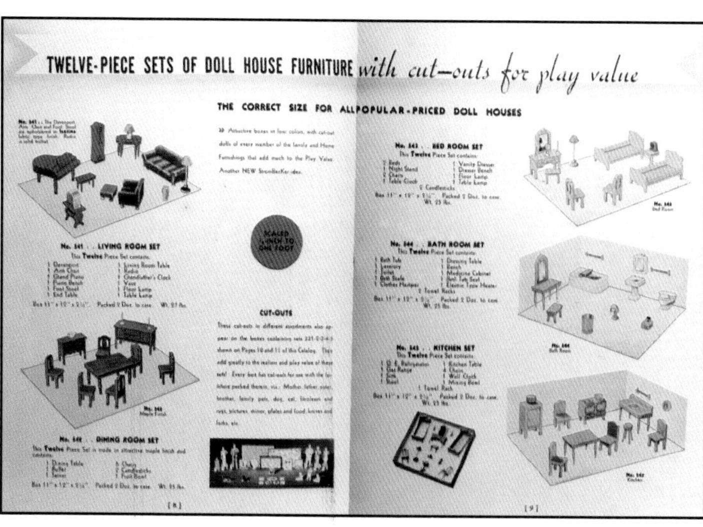

The Strombeck-Becker Manufacturing Co. of Moline, Illinois, was founded by J.F. Strombeck and R.D. Becker in 1911 and the firm began the production of wood handles. The company added wood dollhouse furniture to their line in 1931. The first furniture was 1" to one foot in scale. In 1934, the firm added 3/4" to one foot scaled furniture that could be sold more cheaply than the larger furniture. The Strombecker 1936 catalog pictured the early set of 3/4" scale furniture as well as the larger 1" to one foot pieces. The same 3/4" furniture designed in different colors was also shown in the 1934 catalog. Furniture was made for a living room, dining room, bedroom, bathroom, and kitchen. Each 1936 set consisted of twelve pieces including accessories. *Courtesy of C.S. Olson.*

In 1938, Strombecker offered a whole new design of the 3/4" to one foot scaled dollhouse furniture. The company called it the "Modern" design. Shown are the catalog pages from that year picturing the new line of furniture. *Courtesy of C.S. Olson.*

By the early 1940s, Strombecker had again made changes in the 3/4" line of dollhouse furniture. They were still featuring this design in an advertisement from the *Toy Yearbook for 1946-47*. The booklet was from the Grover C. Hughes Hardware and Appliance firm in Waynesburg, Pennsylvania. There were still five rooms of furniture but the pieces had been given a new look to match the changing times. The boxed sets sold for $1.39 for each room. *Courtesy of Judy Mosholder.*

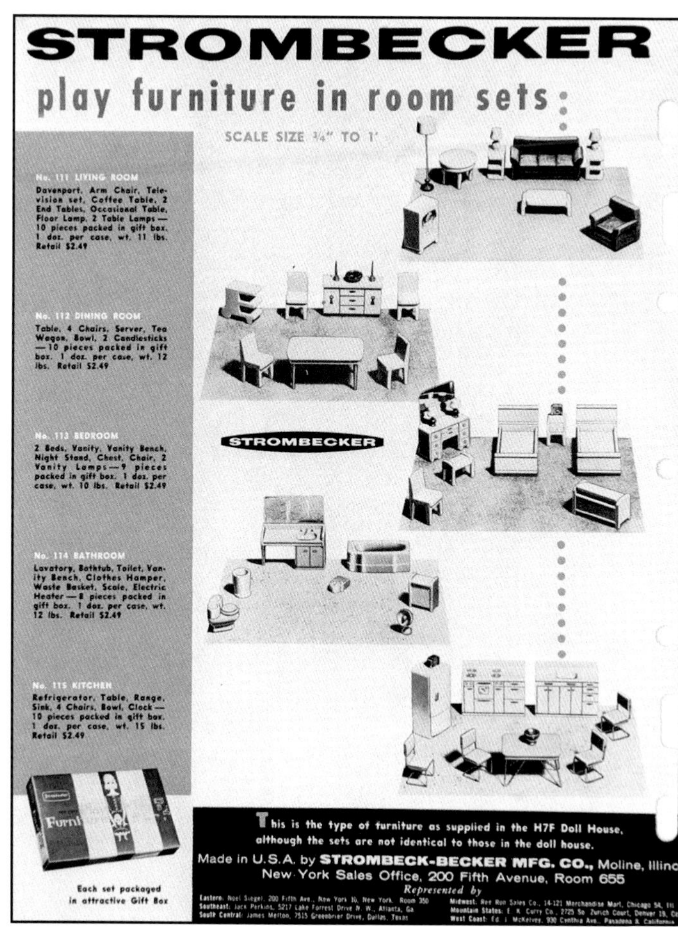

The 3/4" to one foot designs had changed again in the company's advertising from 1950 (see *American Dollhouses and Furniture*, page 50). The 3/4" furniture continued to evolve over the 1950s. A television was added as well as new kitchen furniture. By the late 1950s, a new, more modern design of furniture was being offered. The pictured five rooms of the modern design sold for $2.49 for each boxed set. *Courtesy of George Mundorf.*

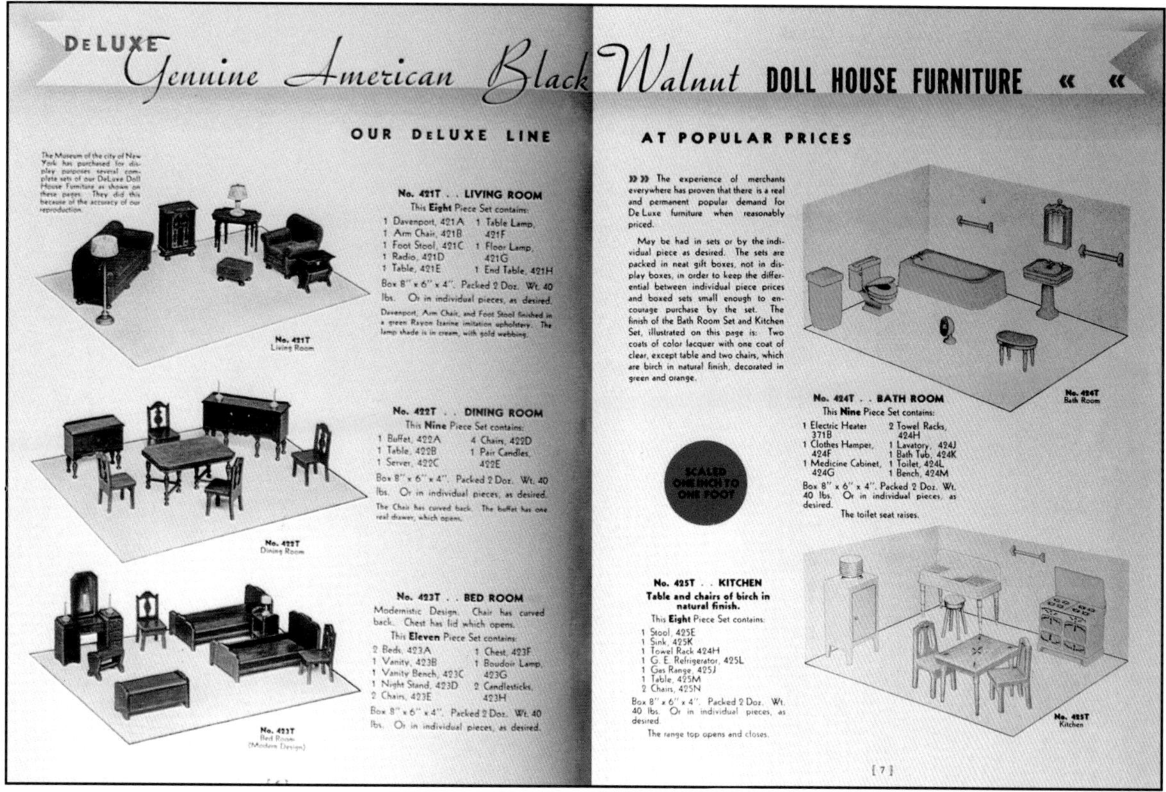

Several designs of the 1" to one foot scale Strombecker wood furniture were also produced. Five rooms of the larger scaled furniture were made in each design. The earliest line is pictured in *Furnished Dollhouses* on page 136. The 1936 company catalog offered a new line in the 1" scale. Some of the pieces were made of walnut while the new living room couch and chair were finished with flocking. Instead of being on legs, the kitchen stove was a floor model. A radio that no longer included legs was also part of the new design. *Courtesy of C.S. Olson.*

Strombecker advertised heavily in *Children's Activities* magazines during several decades. This ad appeared in the November 1937 issue. It pictures several pieces from the new line of 1" to one foot "Custom-Built Doll House furniture." The pieces ranged in price from 40 cents for a coffee table to $5.00 for the piano, which contained a music box. Free cardboard play rooms came with a purchase of $1.00 or more. *Courtesy of Carol Stevenson.*

DOLL HOUSE FURNITURE
GENUINE HAND-RUBBED - AUTHENTIC - ONE INCH TO ONE FOOT
INDIVIDUAL LIVING ROOM PIECES
INDIVIDUAL DINING ROOM PIECES
INDIVIDUAL BEDROOM PIECES

Strombecker offered a two-page spread in its 1938 catalog to promote the new, more expensive 1" to one foot walnut furniture. *Courtesy of C.S. Olson.*

In an ad from *Children's Activities* magazine in December 1939, yet another line of 1" to one foot scaled furniture is pictured. It had been introduced in 1938. Included were a bathroom, dining room, bedroom, living room, kitchen, and nursery. Each boxed room of furniture sold for $2.00. Pieces from the "Custom " line and the 3/4" to one foot "Modern" line were also pictured. *Courtesy of Carol Stevenson.*

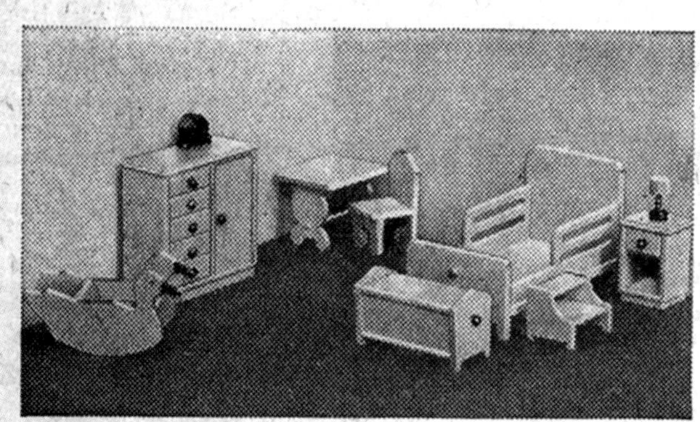

DE LUXE DOLL HOUSE FURNITURE StromBecker Toys have created a beautiful new series of six rooms of doll house furniture, authentically designed, and built accurately to a scale of one inch to one foot. **Nursery (illustrated).** A 10 piece set of wood, beautifully enameled in cream and colors. Youth bed, step-up for bed, chifforobe, toy chest, shoofly, writing table, chair, lamp, clock, night stand. **Living Room** (illustrated). An 8 piece set. Sofa, lounge chair, and ottoman are finished in Dubonnet Izarine simulated upholstery; "Philco" radio, occasional table and coffee table in solid American Walnut; table lamp, and floor lamp. Additional sets include: **Dining Room set.** 10 piece set in genuine American Walnut. **Bedroom set.** 9 piece set in cream enamel. **Bathroom set.** 8 piece set in blue enamel. **Kitchen set.** 9 piece set in cream and orange enamel. **Price of each room set, $2.50, prepaid.** Specify set or sets by name when ordering.

This Strombecker ad from *Children's Activities* magazine for December 1942 pictured the 1" to one foot nursery and living room sets that had been introduced in 1938. The boxed set of furniture for each room was priced at $2.50.

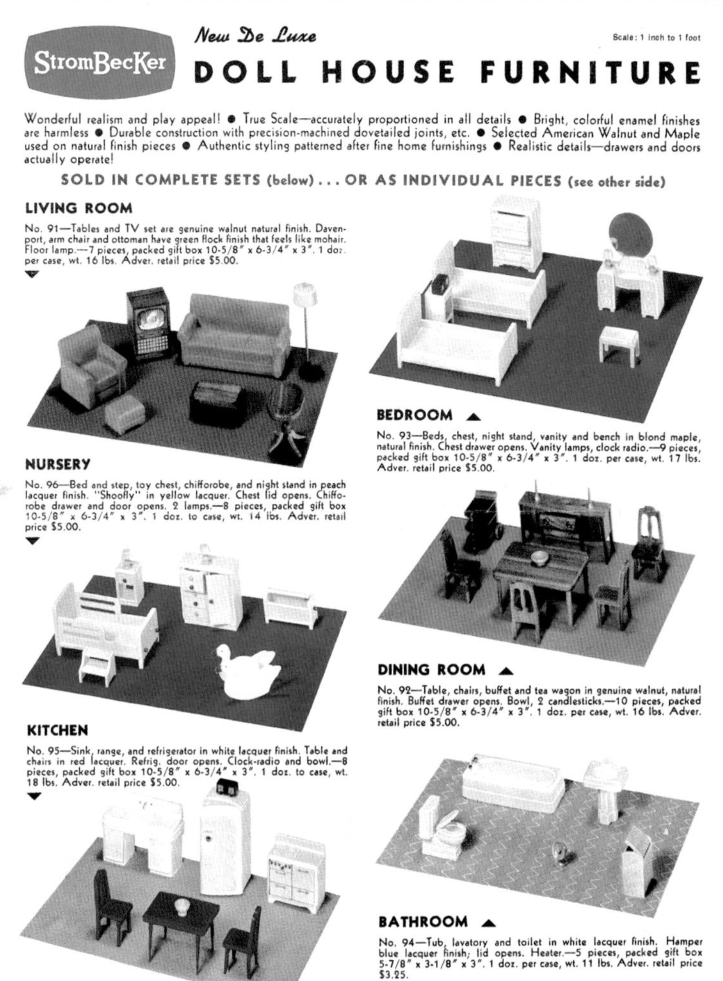

StromBecKer

New De Luxe

Scale: 1 inch to 1 foot

DOLL HOUSE FURNITURE

Wonderful realism and play appeal! ● True Scale—accurately proportioned in all details ● Bright, colorful enamel finishes are harmless ● Durable construction with precision-machined dovetailed joints, etc. ● Selected American Walnut and Maple used on natural finish pieces ● Authentic styling patterned after fine home furnishings ● Realistic details—drawers and doors actually operate!

SOLD IN COMPLETE SETS (below) . . . OR AS INDIVIDUAL PIECES (see other side)

LIVING ROOM

No. 91—Tables and TV set are genuine walnut natural finish. Davenport, arm chair and ottoman have green flock finish that feels like mohair. Floor lamp.—7 pieces, packed gift box 10-5/8" x 6-3/4" x 3". 1 doz. per case, wt. 16 lbs. Adver. retail price $5.00.

BEDROOM

No. 93—Beds, chest, night stand, vanity and bench in blond maple, natural finish. Chest drawer opens. Vanity lamps, clock radio.—9 pieces, packed gift box 10-5/8" x 6-3/4" x 3". 1 doz. per case, wt. 17 lbs. Adver. retail price $5.00.

NURSERY

No. 96—Bed and step, toy chest, chifforobe, and night stand in peach lacquer finish. "Shoofly" in yellow lacquer. Chest lid opens. Chifforobe drawer and door opens. 2 lamps.—8 pieces, packed gift box 10-5/8" x 6-3/4" x 3". 1 doz. to case, wt. 14 lbs. Adver. retail price $5.00.

DINING ROOM

No. 92—Table, chairs, buffet and tea wagon in genuine walnut, natural finish. Buffet drawer opens. Bowl, 2 candlesticks.—10 pieces, packed gift box 10-5/8" x 6-3/4" x 3". 1 doz. per case, wt. 16 lbs. Adver. retail price $5.00.

KITCHEN

No. 95—Sink, range, and refrigerator in white lacquer finish. Table and chairs in red lacquer. Refrig. door opens. Clock-radio and bowl.—8 pieces, packed gift box 10-5/8" x 6-3/4" x 3". 1 doz. to case, wt. 18 lbs. Adver. retail price $5.00.

BATHROOM

No. 94—Tub, lavatory and toilet in white lacquer finish. Hamper blue lacquer finish; lid opens. Heater.—5 pieces, packed gift box 5-7/8" x 3-1/8" x 3". 1 doz. per case, wt. 11 lbs. Adver. retail price $3.25.

Strombecker continued producing both scales of dollhouse furniture through the 1950s. This advertisement from the period pictures the six rooms of 1" to one foot scaled furniture with some changes in the living room pieces including the addition of a television and an updated refrigerator for the kitchen. The back of this company ad gave prices for "Do-it yourself" assembly sets for $2.50 each as well as prices for each piece of furniture. The boxed sets were to retail for $5.00 each, except for the bathroom set which was $3.25.

Although Strombecker marketed several cardboard houses to be used with this furniture, it is likely that they were made by other companies. The first house of this type was pictured in the 1934 Strombecker catalog as well as the *Good Housekeeping* magazine for December 1933. The house contained five rooms and was sold complete with thirty pieces of 3/4" to one foot scaled furniture. It measured 16.25" high x 19.5" wide x 14.5" deep. The price listed in the *Good Housekeeping* magazine was $3.25.

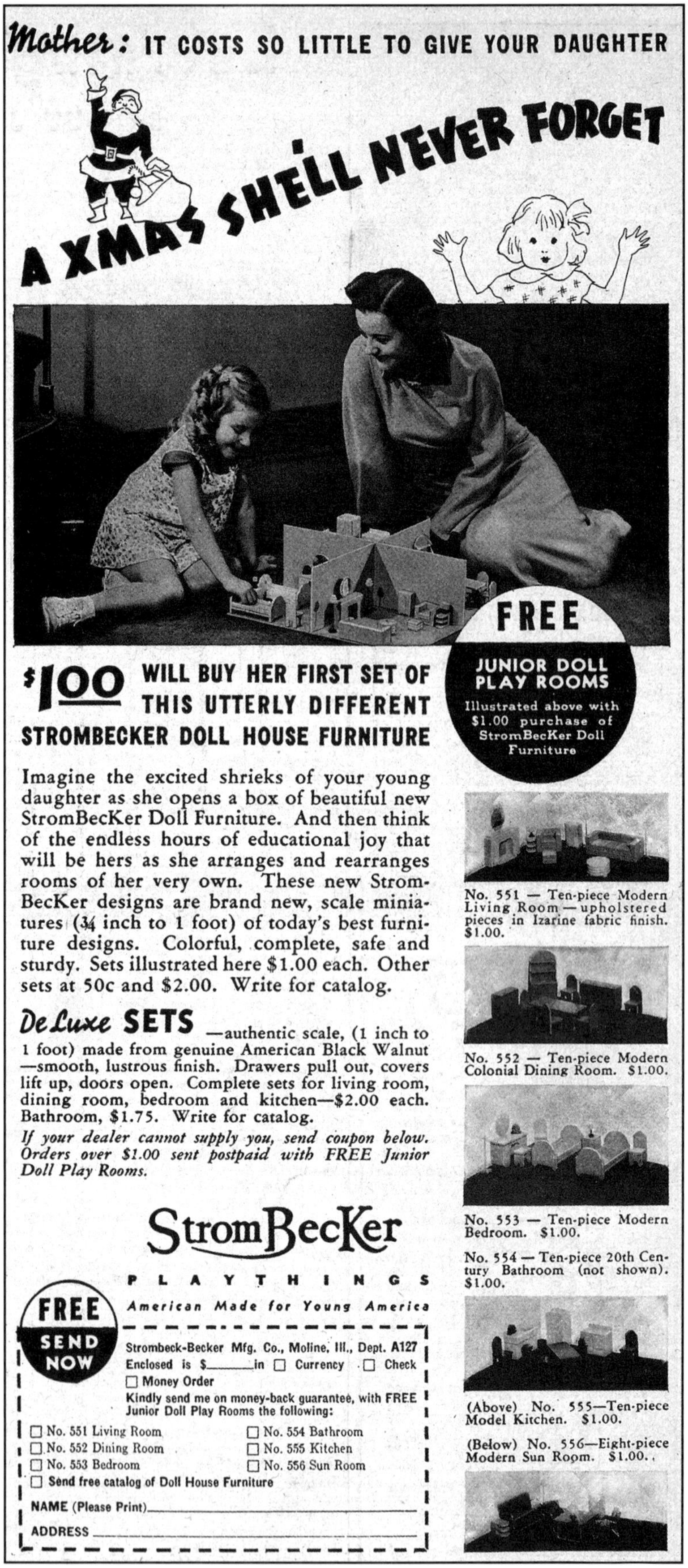

Mother: IT COSTS SO LITTLE TO GIVE YOUR DAUGHTER
A XMAS SHE'LL NEVER FORGET
FREE
JUNIOR DOLL PLAY ROOMS
Illustrated above with $1.00 purchase of StromBecKer Doll Furniture
$1.00 WILL BUY HER FIRST SET OF THIS UTTERLY DIFFERENT STROMBECKER DOLL HOUSE FURNITURE
Imagine the excited shrieks of your young daughter as she opens a box of beautiful new StromBecKer Doll Furniture. And then think of the endless hours of educational joy that will be hers as she arranges and rearranges rooms of her very own. These new StromBecKer designs are brand new, scale miniatures (¾ inch to 1 foot) of today's best furniture designs. Colorful, complete, safe and sturdy. Sets illustrated here $1.00 each. Other sets at 50c and $2.00. Write for catalog.
DeLuxe SETS —authentic scale, (1 inch to 1 foot) made from genuine American Black Walnut —smooth, lustrous finish. Drawers pull out, covers lift up, doors open. Complete sets for living room, dining room, bedroom and kitchen—$2.00 each. Bathroom, $1.75. Write for catalog.
If your dealer cannot supply you, send coupon below. Orders over $1.00 sent postpaid with FREE Junior Doll Play Rooms.
StromBecKer
PLAYTHINGS
American Made for Young America
No. 551 — Ten-piece Modern Living Room — upholstered pieces in Izarine fabric finish. $1.00.
No. 552 — Ten-piece Modern Colonial Dining Room. $1.00.
No. 553 — Ten-piece Modern Bedroom. $1.00.
No. 554 — Ten-piece 20th Century Bathroom (not shown). $1.00.
(Above) No. 555—Ten-piece Model Kitchen. $1.00.
(Below) No. 556—Eight-piece Modern Sun Room. $1.00.
FREE
SEND NOW
Strombeck-Becker Mfg. Co., Moline, Ill., Dept. A127
Enclosed is $____ in ☐ Currency ☐ Check ☐ Money Order
Kindly send me on money-back guarantee, with FREE Junior Doll Play Rooms the following:
☐ No. 551 Living Room ☐ No. 554 Bathroom
☐ No. 552 Dining Room ☐ No. 555 Kitchen
☐ No. 553 Bedroom ☐ No. 556 Sun Room
☐ Send free catalog of Doll House Furniture
NAME (Please Print)
ADDRESS

In a *Children's Activities* magazine for December 1937, the Strombecker "Play Rooms" are again offered free with purchase of a set of the 3/4" to one foot scaled "Modern" furniture priced at $1.00 for each of the five sets. The cardboard "rooms" apparently opened out into a four-room "house." *Courtesy of Carol Stevenson.*

66 StromBecKer GIFTS FOR BOYS AND GIRLS
6-ROOM "PLAY-HOUSE"
$6.00
4-ROOM "PLAY-HOUSE"
$4.00
DOLL HOUSE FURNITURE SETS
50c
$1.00
Special DeLuxe DOLL HOUSE FURNITURE
Scale:—one inch to one foot
$2.00
No. 446 NURSERY
$2.00
No. 441 LIVING ROOM
$2.00
No. 443 BEDROOM
$2.00
Custom Built DOLL HOUSE FURNITURE
Scale—one inch to one foot
LIVING ROOM PIECES
DINING ROOM PIECES
BEDROOM PIECES

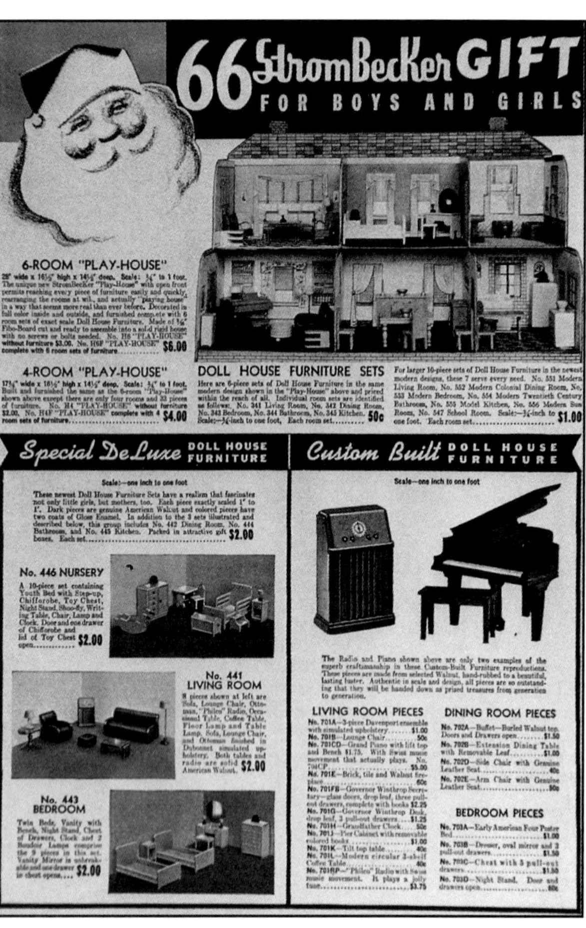

A different cardboard house was advertised in *Children's Activities* magazine for December 1938. It was one of three similar models pictured in the Strombecker catalog for 1938. The pictured example is the largest of the three houses. It contained six rooms, came completely furnished and was priced at $6.00 in the magazine. A smaller furnished four-room house cost only $4.00. The 3/4" to one foot scaled furniture was a combination of the "Modern" line and the regular pieces. The 1" to one foot scaled furniture was available for $2.00 for each room. The "Custom Built" furniture was also listed. *Courtesy of Carol Stevenson.*

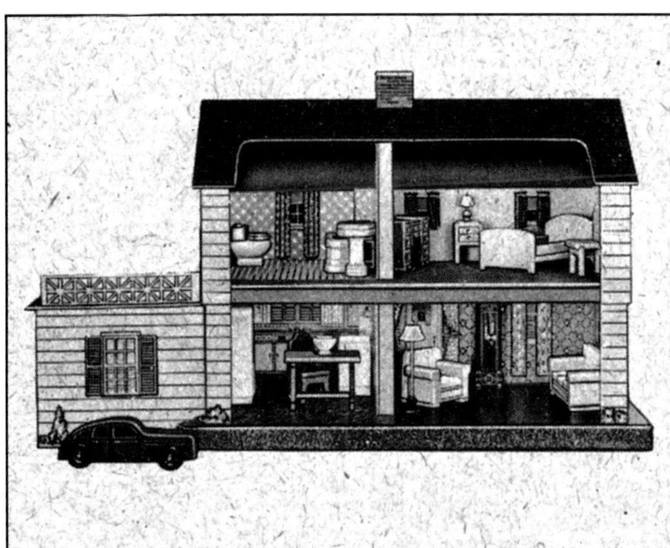

STROMBECKER 4-ROOM DOLL HOUSE
Strombeck Becker have produced a new "Dream Home" doll house which we predict will prove to be extremely popular. It is a very attractive low priced 4-Room fiber-board house with attached garage. The illustration shows the open back of the house with the 4 rooms fully equipped with 18 pieces of painted wooden StromBecker furniture. Floors and walls are printed in pleasing decorations. House and furniture are built to true scale of ¾" to 1'. The front and sides of the house are tastefully decorated in colors to represent brick, white clapboards, and green roof. There is a toy automobile with the set and a cardboard baby carriage and Scottie dog. An exclusive idea is the "lift-off" feature, whereby the second story may be lifted off to provide easier access to the first floor. Over all dimensions are 23" long, 11" wide, and 13" high. House comes knocked down but is easily put together. **Price, postpaid, $2.50.**

A cardboard house, probably made by Built-Rite, was pictured in *Children's Activities* magazine for November 1945. It came with eighteen pieces of the 3/4" to one foot scaled Strombecker furniture. The house contained four rooms and a garage (complete with wood automobile) and sold for $2.50 postpaid. The house measured 13" high x 23" wide by 11" deep.

This unusual house was also sold under the Strombecker name circa late 1950s. It contained five rooms and a deck. The roof could be lifted to allow additional access to the rooms. Instead of cardboard, the house was made of masonite and wood. The house could be purchased furnished with forty-three pieces of 3/4" to one foot furniture (later style) for $19.95. Unfurnished, the house sold for $14.95. It measured 14.5" high x 24.25" wide x 12.75. deep. *Courtesy of George Mundorf.*

During the late 1950s, because of the popularity of the 8" Vogue Ginny and Ginnette dolls, Strombecker began the production of larger furniture suitable for these dolls. The line included bunk beds, single beds, canopy beds, tables and chairs, rocking chairs, a sofa bed, arm chair, corner lamp table, coffee table, baby crib, high chair, chest, wardrobe and an umbrella table and chairs. The doors and drawers in the furniture were functional. Some of the pieces were painted white, decorated with flowers, and sold as Betsy McCall pieces to accompany the famous McCall Inc. 8" doll. Pictured is a flyer from Strombecker with prices for some of the products. The bunk beds were listed at $2.50, single bed $1.50, table and chairs $2.79, rocker $1.79, and single chair 59 cents. The furniture was made of birch wood.

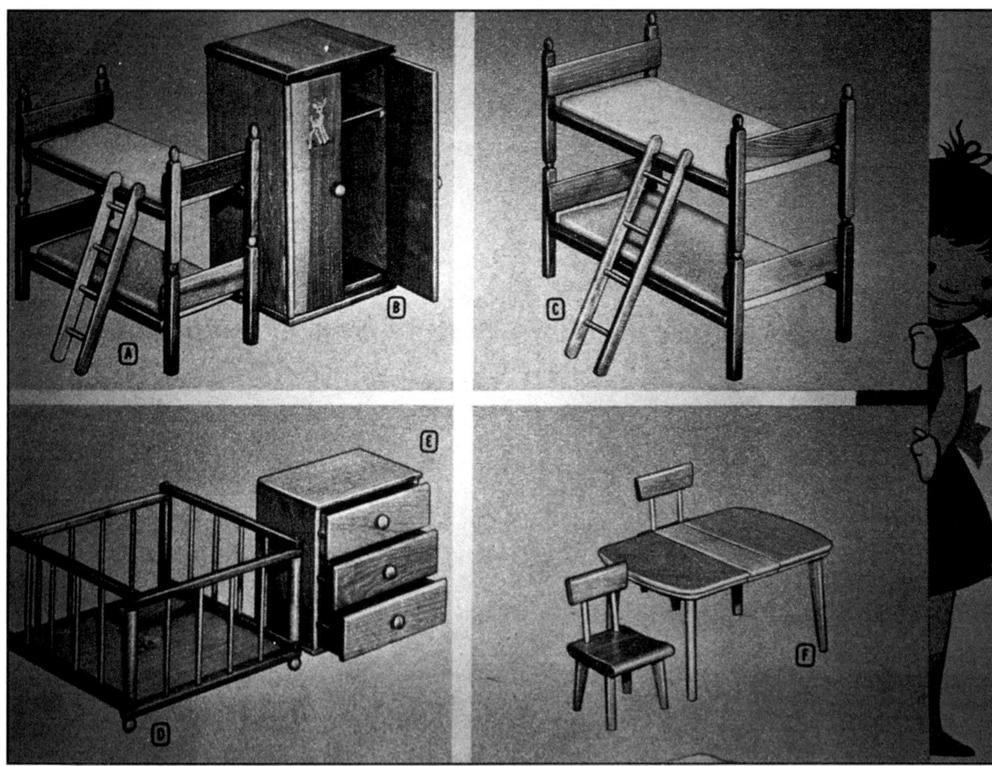

The May Company of Los Angeles featured the late Strombecker furniture in their 1957 Toy Time catalog. Included were the bunk beds for $2.98, wardrobe $3.50, playpen $2.59, chest $3.29, and table and chair set $2.98. Toy dollhouse and larger doll furniture was no longer produced by Strombecker by the early 1960s. The company name was changed to the Strombeck Manufacturing Co. and the firm continued to produce custom wood-working products, mainly handles, for many years. *Courtesy of Marge Meisinger.*

Sutherland Paper Co.

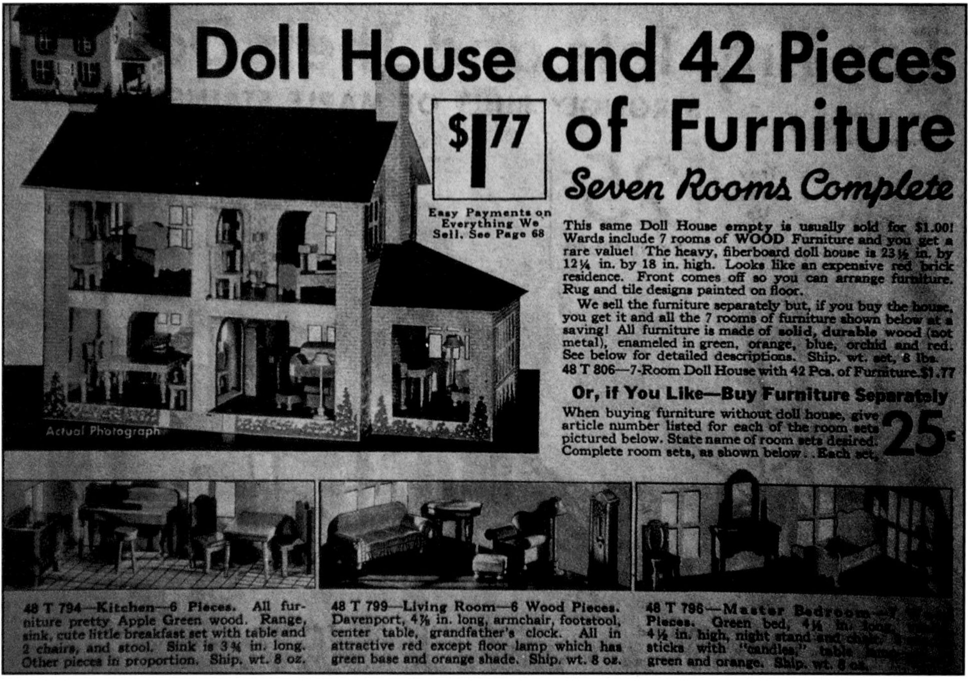

The Sutherland cardboard dollhouse, complete with forty-two pieces of Strombecker wood furniture, was also advertised in the Montgomery Ward catalog in 1934 priced at $1.77. The individual sets of furniture could be purchased for 25 cents a set.

4221

4220

Wolff-Cooley

4220—A toy carpet sweeper is our first thought for a housekeeper aged anywhere under twelve. She will love to use it and incidentally (mothers please note) it really gets the nursery carpet clean. It is 9" x 5½" and has a 26" handle. $1.

4221—A sturdy cardboard doll house comes folded ready to put up and looks exactly like the nicest red brick house with window boxes painted on the outside and a sun porch, and six light, airy rooms inside. 12" x 16" and 18" high. $1.

Left:
This cardboard dollhouse was advertised by Marshall Fields for Christmas 1932. It was made by the Sutherland Paper Co. in Kalamazoo, Michigan. The inside of the house contained a sun porch and six rooms. It measured 18" high x 23" wide x 12" deep and sold for $1.00. *Courtesy of Carol Stevenson.*

Toy Tinkers, Inc.

A complete living room set of furniture, walnut finish, is illustrated. There are 13 pieces from two to four inches in size. Assortment is nested in fibre mailing package.

In 1930, Toy Tinkers, Inc. of Evanston, Illinois (famous for Tinkertoys beginning in 1914) produced a set of dollhouse living room furniture. As pictured, the set included thirteen pieces which were finished in walnut with colorful accents. They ranged in size from 2" to 4". Apparently no other furniture was ever made by the firm. The furniture is very hard to find since it was made for such a short time. See page 180 of *Antique & Collectible Dollhouses*.

Tri-ang-Lines Brothers

The December 1935 *Meccano Magazine* carried this advertisement from the English Lines Brothers firm. It pictured many pieces of Tri-ang's two lines of wood dollhouse furniture then available. The furniture was advertised as being scale model reproductions of both Queen Anne and Jacobean styles. The pieces were 1" to one foot in scale and featured opening doors and drawers. Furniture was provided for living rooms, bedrooms, and dining rooms. An interesting "Queen Anne Period Scale Model" construction set was also advertised. The pieces were cut-out and were to be finished by the consumer. Stain, lacquer, upholstery, and instructions were provided to assemble the furniture.

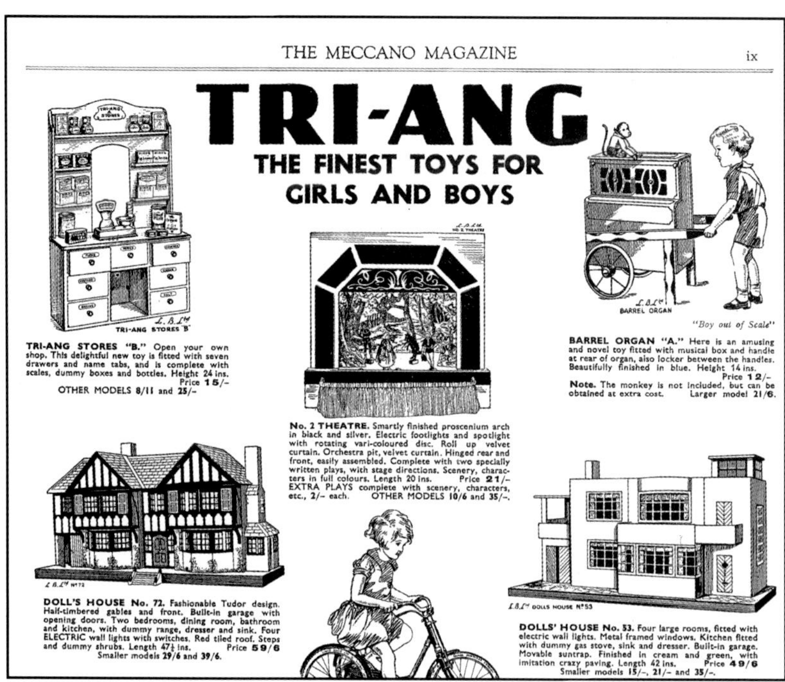

Left:
English Lines Bros. Ltd. – Tri-ang advertisement in *Meccano Magazine* for December 1935. Two dollhouses as well as other toys were featured. Included was the house collectors call the Stockbroker Tudor #72 (see page 109 of *Furnished Dollhouses* for a photograph of the house) and a "Modern Doll's House No. 53." It came in four different sizes in this ad. *Courtesy of Leslie and Joanne Payne.*

Vista Toy Company

Left:
Vista dollhouse, marketed by the Vista Toy Company, as pictured in *Playthings* magazine for April 1934. The four-room house was made of plywood and came in five styles. The houses included electric lights and scenes visible through the windows. The houses were open for play.

Playthings magazine also carried an ad for the Vista houses in their June 1934 issue. A different style of house was pictured. It included four rooms and scenes visible through the windows. The Cassopolis, Michigan firm's houses retailed from $10.00 and up, according to the ad. A style #7 house came with six rooms, a colonial front, ceiling lights, lighted fire place, and with or without a hidden five tube Fada Radio installed in the house.

Wisconsin Toy Co.

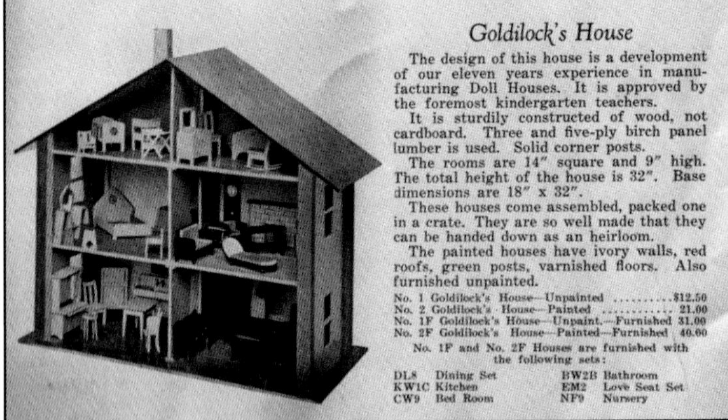

Goldilock's House

The design of this house is a development of our eleven years experience in manufacturing Doll Houses. It is approved by the foremost kindergarten teachers.

It is sturdily constructed of wood, not cardboard. Three and five-ply birch panel lumber is used. Solid corner posts.

The rooms are 14" square and 9" high. The total height of the house is 32". Base dimensions are 18" x 32".

These houses come assembled, packed one in a crate. They are so well made that they can be handed down as an heirloom.

The painted houses have ivory walls, red roofs, green posts, varnished floors. Also furnished unpainted.

No. 1 Goldilock's House—Unpainted $12.50
No. 2 Goldilock's House—Painted 21.00
No. 1F Goldilock's House—Unpaint.—Furnished 31.00
No. 2F Goldilock's House—Painted—Furnished 40.00

No. 1F and No. 2F Houses are furnished with the following sets:

DL8	Dining Set	BW2B	Bathroom
KW1C	Kitchen	EM2	Love Seat Set
CW9	Bed Room	NF9	Nursery

The Wisconsin Toy Co. was located in Milwaukee, Wisconsin during the 1920s and 1930s. The firm produced both wood dollhouses and dollhouse furniture during this period. This wood dollhouse appeared in one of their catalogs circa mid 1930s. It was an open front model which included six rooms on three floors. The larger rooms were 14" square x 9" high. The house measured 32" tall x 32" wide x 18" deep. It sold for $21.00 painted and unfurnished and $40 furnished. *From the collection of Leslie and Joanne Payne.*

Kitchen Sets

All modern pieces. Finishe[d] in green or white. Drawers pu[ll] out.

Set K. W. 1 C

Sewed into a gift box $3.75

K 1—Table
K 2—Chair
K 3—Sink
K 4—Ice box
K 5—Cabinet
K 6—Stool

Set K. W. 1A

Sewed into a gift box $2.00

K 1—Table
K 2—Chairs (2) 25c each
K 3—Sink
K 4—Ice box

Goldilock's
KITCHEN SET

Pictured is one of the kitchens from the mid 1930s Wisconsin Toy catalog. The furniture was usually sold under the "Goldilock's" trademark. This kitchen set came in green or white. A set including the table, chair, sink, ice box, cabinet, and stool sold for $3.75. *Payne Collection.*

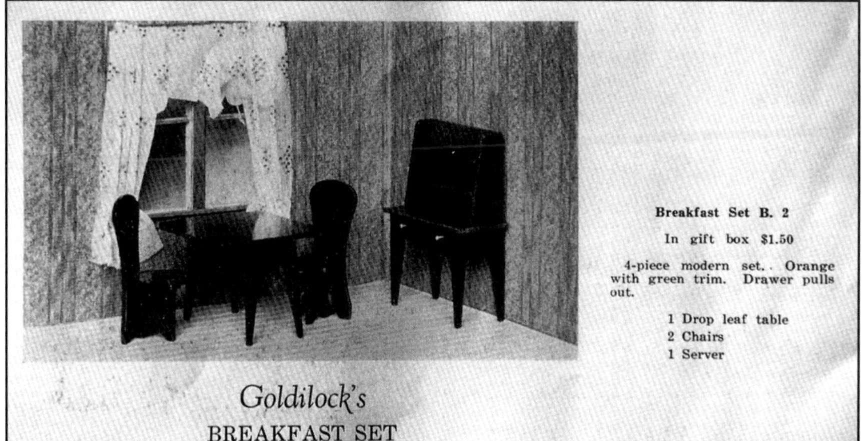

A breakfast set pictured in the same catalog included a drop leaf table, two chairs, and a server. It sold for $1.50. The modern set was orange with green trim. Most of the furniture was marked in a triangle "Wis/ToyCo." *Payne Collection.*

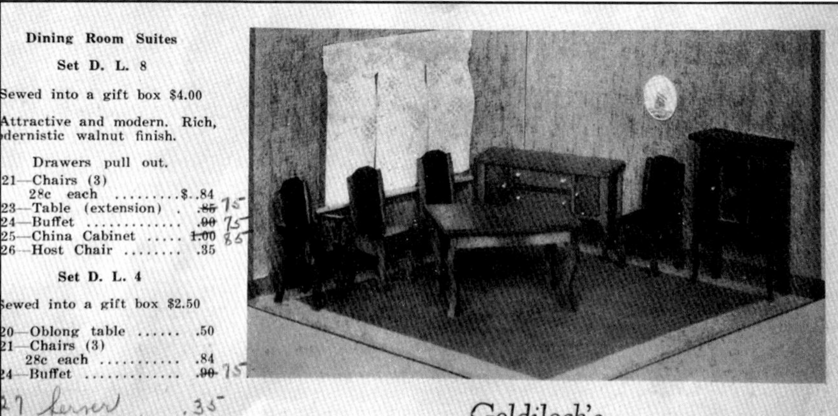

Dining Room Suites
Set D. L. 8
Sewed into a gift box $4.00
Attractive and modern. Rich, modernistic walnut finish.
Drawers pull out.
21—Chairs (3) 28c each ....$..84
23—Table (extension) . ~~.85~~ 75
24—Buffet .... ~~.90~~ 75
25—China Cabinet ..... ~~1.00~~ 85
26—Host Chair .... .35
Set D. L. 4
Sewed into a gift box $2.50
20—Oblong table ...... .50
21—Chairs (3) 28c each .... .84
24—Buffet .... ~~.90~~ 75
27 Server .35
28 Corner Cabinet .60
Goldilock's
DINING ROOM

Goldilock's dining room furniture was finished in walnut. The set was priced at $4.00 and included three straight chairs, one host chair, an extension table, buffet, and a china cabinet. *Payne Collection.*

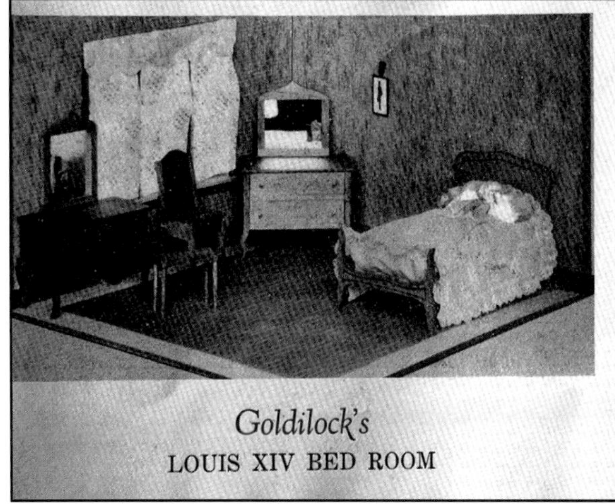

Louis XIV Bed Room

This furniture is a direct copy of authentic Louis XIV style. Finished in early American maple.

L 1—Dresser .... $ ~~.75~~
L 2—Chair .... .28
L 3—Dressing table ..... ~~.90~~
L 4—Bed (without bedding) . ~~.65~~

Goldilock's
LOUIS XIV BED ROOM

One of the many Wisconsin Toy bedroom sets was called the "Louis XIV Bedroom." It was finished in early American maple. Included were a dresser, chair, dressing table, and bed. The firm's furniture ranged in size from a regular 1" to one foot scale to 1.5" to one foot scale. *Payne Collection.*

Bed Room Suites

The designs in these sets are modern. Can be had in the following colors—pink or green. High grade mirrors. Drawers pull out.

Set C. W. 9

Sewed into a gift box $2.75

C 19—Vanity and bench..$1.00
C 11—Chair .... .28
C 13—Chiffonier .... .50
C 16—Large Bed .... .60

Set C. W. 33

Sewed into a gift box $2.00

C 16—Bed .... .60
C 12—Rocker .... ~~.45~~
C 11—Chair .... .28
C 10—Dresser 65

Extra items that can be had.

C 17—Small bed .... .50
C 20—Folding Screen ..... .50

Goldilock's
BED ROOM

Another "Bed Room Suite" pictured in the catalog came in pink or green with flower decorations. Pieces that could be purchased singly or in a set included a bed, vanity and bench, chair, chiffonier, rocker, and dresser. A smaller bed and folding screen were also available. All of the drawers and doors were functional on the Wisconsin Toy furniture. *Payne Collection.*

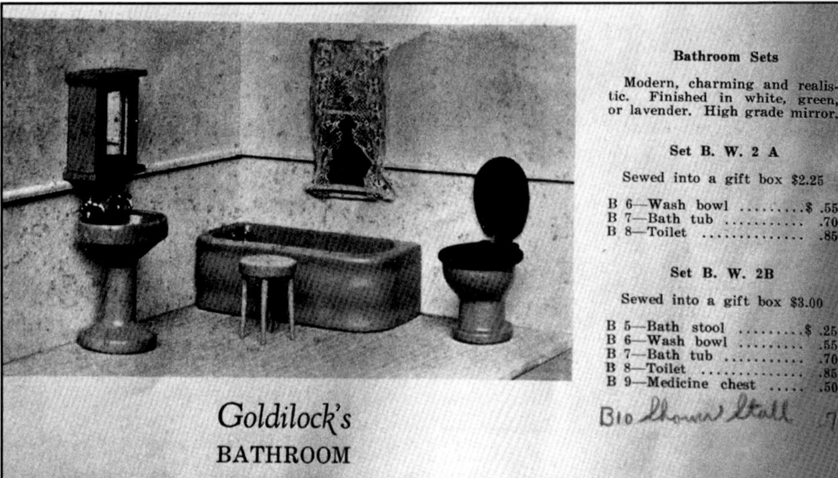

Bathroom Sets
Modern, charming and realistic. Finished in white, green, or lavender. High grade mirror.
Set B. W. 2 A
Sewed into a gift box $2.25
B 6—Wash bowl ....$ .55
B 7—Bath tub .... .70
B 8—Toilet .... .85
Set B. W. 2B
Sewed into a gift box $3.00
B 5—Bath stool ....$ .25
B 6—Wash bowl .... .55
B 7—Bath tub .... .70
B 8—Toilet .... .85
B 9—Medicine chest ..... .50
B10 Shower Stall .75
Goldilock's
BATHROOM

Several of the bathroom pieces were made of a breakable plaster-like material. Included were a tub, washbowl, toilet, stool, and medicine chest. The complete set sold for $3.00. *Payne Collection.*

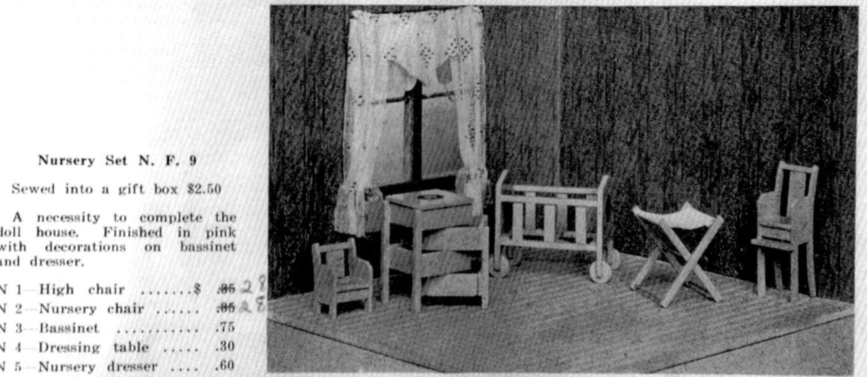

The Goldilocks nursery is one of the favorites for today's collector. Although the set sold for only $2.50, it included a high chair, potty chair, crib, dressing table, and nursery dresser. *Payne Collection.*

Occasional Set O. M. 5
Sewed into a gift box $3.50
This set is made up of
casional pieces that will en-
ch the atmosphere of any doll
use.
inished in Mahogany or Maple.
2—Gate Leg Table....$ .70
3—Console Table ..... .50
4—Console Mirror .... .25
5—Secretaire 1.50
34—Pull Up Chair ..... .60 50
Extra items are:
1—Tilt Top Table .... .50
6—High Boy 1.50
Goldilock's
OCCASIONAL SET

The music room included pieces that could also be used in a living room. It sold for $3.35 and featured a baby grand piano, floor lamp, fireplace, pull up chair, and a clock. *Payne Collection.*

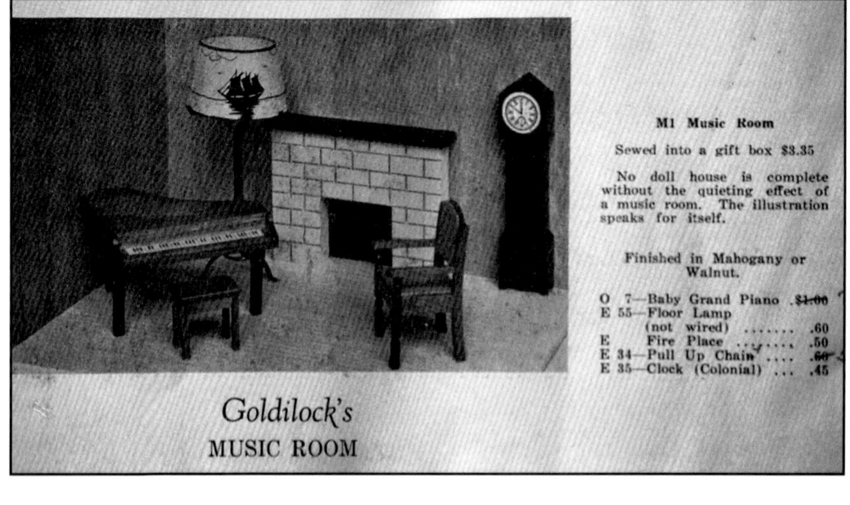

M1 Music Room
Sewed into a gift box $3.35
No doll house is complete without the quieting effect of a music room. The illustration speaks for itself.
Finished in Mahogany or Walnut.
O 7—Baby Grand Piano .$1.00
E 55—Floor Lamp (not wired) .... .60
E Fire Place .... .50
E 34—Pull Up Chair .... .60
E 35—Clock (Colonial) ... .45
Goldilock's
MUSIC ROOM

The pieces listed under "Occasional set" could be used in a variety of rooms in a dollhouse. Included were a gate leg table, console table, console mirror, secretary, pull up chair, tilt top table, and high boy. The total set sold for $3.50. *Payne Collection.*

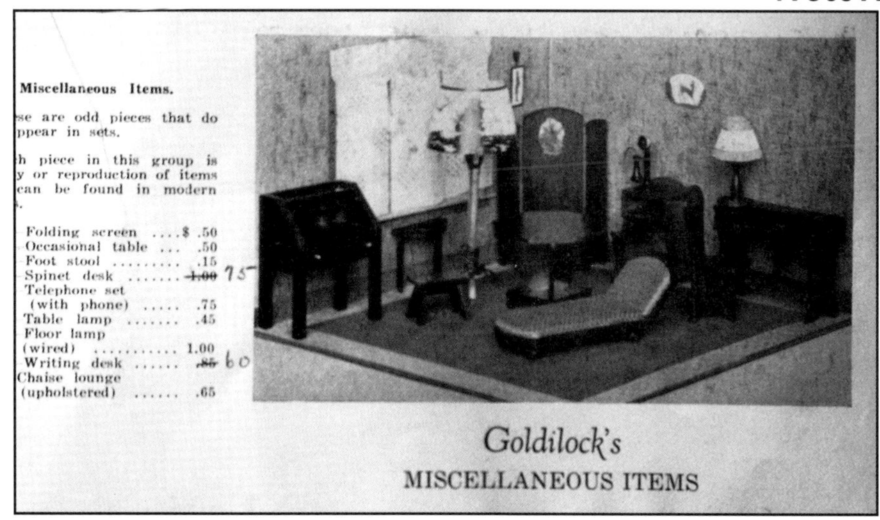

A page of miscellaneous items was also included in the Wisconsin Toy catalog. Pictured were a folding screen, occasional table, foot stool, spinet desk, telephone set, table lamp, floor lamp, writing desk and chaise lounge. Other catalog pictures can be seen in *Antique & Collectible Dollhouses,* page 143. *Payne Collection.*

Miscellaneous

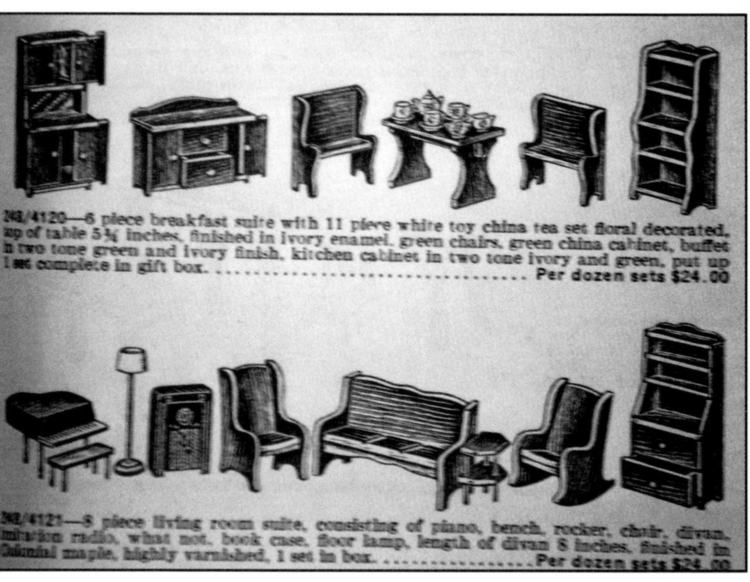

This unidentified dollhouse furniture was pictured in the Blackwell Wielandy Co. catalog in 1936. The St. Louis based firm sold a number of imported toys so the sets may not have been produced in the United States. The six-piece "Breakfast Suite" was painted in ivory and green . The top of the table measured 5.75". The eight-piece living room furniture was finished in Colonial Maple.

Wolverine Toy Co.

Wolverine bathroom advertised in the 1940 catalog for Massey's Drug Store, located in Shirley, Indiana. The metal room includes a bathtub, sink, toilet, hamper, and doll. Water could be stored in a small reservoir in the back of the room so the taps on the tub and sink would function. The lid on the metal hamper was also functional. The fixtures were made of Tenite. The room measured 17.25" wide and sold for $1.98. See 1980s Chapter for more Wolverine products. *Courtesy of Marge Meisinger.*

The Butler Brothers catalog for 1936 pictured a three-piece bathroom set, made of china, in assorted colors. A four-piece kitchen set was also available. It included a cabinet, gas range, electric refrigerator, and kitchen sink. The sets were probably imported from Japan.

The Montgomery Ward Christmas catalog for 1933 offered a selection of dollhouse dolls for sale. Included were a set of eight bisque dolls ranging from 2.5" to nearly 3" in size. Their hats, hair, features, shoes, and stockings were painted. Included in the set were Grandma, Grandpa, Mother, Father, Maid, big Brother, and two little Twin Sisters. The whole set sold for only 59 cents. Larger bisque dolls were also pictured in the Montgomery Ward 1933 Christmas catalog. The boy and girl measured 6.25" tall and the baby with a pacifier was 5" tall. These may have been painted over bisque dolls as the set of three sold for only 29 cents. *Courtesy of Marge Meisinger.*

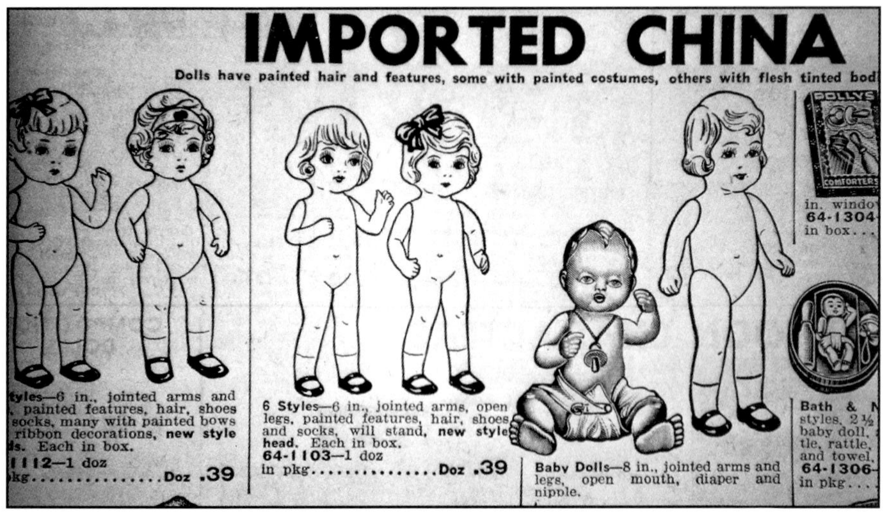

The Butler Brothers catalog of 1936 also offered small dolls ranging from 6" to 8" tall. These dolls appear to be the cheaply made white bisque dolls "Made in Japan."

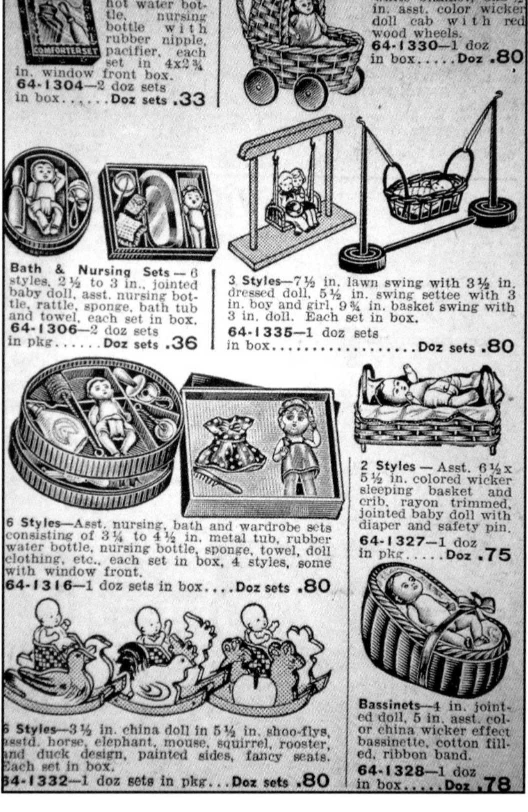

The same Butler Brothers catalog of 1936 also offered several different sets of small dolls, some of which included accessories. Most of the dolls measured 2.5" to 3" tall. It is likely that all of these sets were "Made in Japan."

1940s Advertisements

Although dollhouses and their furnishings had become more prolific and less expensive in the decade of the 1930s, the scarcity of materials during the war years of the 1940s limited the production of many toys to a large extent.

In looking over the mail order catalogs from 1940-1945, few dollhouses were available for purchase except for those made of cardboard. Built-Rite houses were still being marketed as were cardboard houses made by the O.B. Andrews Co. of Chattanooga, Tennessee. A material called Tekwood (wood center with heavy craft paper covering) was used by the DeLuxe Game Corp. in their new line of dollhouses circa 1945.

Wood furniture made by Strombecker was still available but the more inexpensive Nancy Forbes furniture was carried more often in the mail order catalogs. Even the cheaper Donna Lee furniture and houses made by the Woodburn Manufacturing Co. were featured in the Aldens catalogs during these years. The houses were made of heavy construction board. The more expensive Lynnfield type furniture and the Tynietoy pieces were still being produced, as were some models of Rich and Keystone houses. Perhaps, as in doll production during the period, the firms were selling stock already on hand as new materials became harder to buy. The war years proved profitable for the Dolly Dear firm, which was located in Union City, Tennessee. The company received extra exposure when their accessories were featured in the Montgomery Ward Christmas catalog in 1943. There were so many orders, the firm had to move to larger quarters.

After World War II ended in 1945, major changes occurred in the dollhouse and furniture industry. New designs of plastic furniture appeared on the market and this material dominated the inexpensive lines of dollhouse furniture during the rest of the decade. The best selling furniture was made by the Renwal Manf. Co. of Mineola, Long Island, New York. The Ideal Toy Co. and the Plastic Art Toy Corp. also marketed successful lines of plastic dollhouse furniture.

Although both the Rich and Keystone firms continued to produce their houses made of wood and masonite, the most popular dollhouses manufactured after the war were made of metal. One of the first companies to enter this field was T. Cohn Inc., located in Brooklyn, New York. Their first lithographed steel house was featured in the Montgomery Ward Christmas catalog in 1948 priced at $4.75 unfurnished. A set of plastic Renwal furniture could be purchased for $5.98 to furnish the house. The National Can Corp. marketed their own metal Playsteel dollhouses the same year. The Louis Marx firm soon took advantage of the popularity of the new metal houses and plastic furniture and that company began making newly designed houses and furniture beginning in 1949.

The dollhouse industry survived the upheaval of the war years and the drastic changes made to the designs of furniture and houses in the later 1940s to emerge stronger than ever. These years brought new companies into the field and ended the reign of others in the industry. The advertisements in this chapter reflect those changes. (T. Cohn and Marx are both featured in the 1950s chapter because that is when their products were the most popular).

Andrews, O.B.

This seven-room wood pulpboard furnished house was advertised in the Sears Christmas catalog for 1938. The cost of the house was 69 cents, complete with cardboard furniture. The house came with a six-piece living room, five-piece dining room, three-piece kitchen, two six-piece bedrooms, three-piece front porch set, and lamps, pictures etc. The house measured 16.5" high x 31.25" wide x 12" deep. This same house and a "Country Estate" house were advertised in the Sears 1940 Christmas catalog. The "Country Estate" came furnished with forty-five pieces of metal Tootsietoy furniture to be used in the living room, dining room, kitchen, two bedrooms, and a bathroom. It sold for $1.98 complete. It is thought that both houses were made by the O.B. Andrews Co., located in Chattanooga, Tennessee. The company also produced several other cardboard houses during this period, as well as cardboard furniture. See page 204 of *Antique & Collectible Dollhouses* for examples of another Andrews' house and its furniture. *Courtesy of Marge Meisinger.*

Banner Plastics Corp.

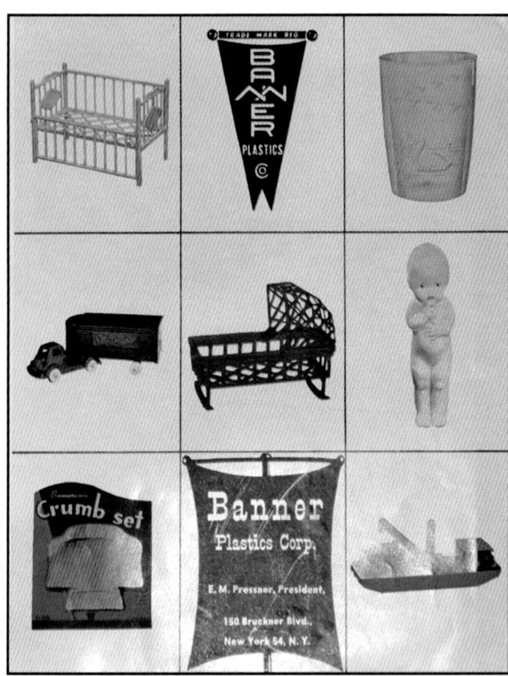

Banner Plastics Corp. products were featured in an ad in *Playthings* in 1947. The New York firm produced a number of dollhouse related items, including the crib, cradle, and doll pictured here. They also marketed a set of five small metal rooms furnished with plastic furniture. *From the collection of Marcie Tubbs. Photograph by Bob Tubbs.*

De Luxe Game Corp.

READY FOR IMMEDIATE DELIVERY

"De Luxe"

DOLL HOUSES
ACTION AND
SKILL GAMES

PAINT SETS
CLAY SETS
CHALK & SLATE SETS
SEWING SETS
RING TOSS GAMES
DUCK PIN SETS
TARGET GAMES
ROLLING GAMES
BANGO BENCHES
HAMMER & NAIL TABLES
BOWLING ALLEYS
SHOO FLYS
DRAWING SETS
ACTION GAMES

DeLUXE
GAME CORPORATION
Room 363
200 Fifth Ave. New York 10

JUNE, 1946—PLAYTHINGS 39

This ad for De Luxe Game Corp. appeared in *Playthings* magazine for June 1946. The firm, located in Richmond Hill, Long Island, marketed a wide variety of dollhouses during the mid to late 1940s. The houses were made of Tekwood and some included both inside and outside decorated walls. Two of their two-story houses are shown in this company advertisement. See page 160 of *Furnished Dollhouses* for more examples of De Luxe houses. *Courtesy of Marcie Tubbs.*

Budget-priced 5-room Doll House on turn table
This charming house too, has a turn table. The little owner can sit in one position, turn house easily, and play from front or open back. Big picture window and 2 upstairs windows covered with specially molded plastic material. Two windows and two doors open. Airy patio with fabric awning is especially attractive. Made of sturdy tekwood (wood-center fiberboard), decorated insid and outside. Overall size 11¾x20½x31½ in. long. Simple to set up; instructions included.
$4.69
79 N 02115—Unfurnished Doll House. Shipped unassembled. Shpg. wt. 5 lbs. $4.69

Tekwood house advertised in the Sears Christmas catalog from 1948. It may have also been a De Luxe Game Corp. product. The five-room house included a turntable and a patio with awning. The windows for the two-story house were made of a "specially molded plastic material" and the inside as well as the outside were decorated. The house sold for $4.69. *Courtesy of Betty Nichols.*

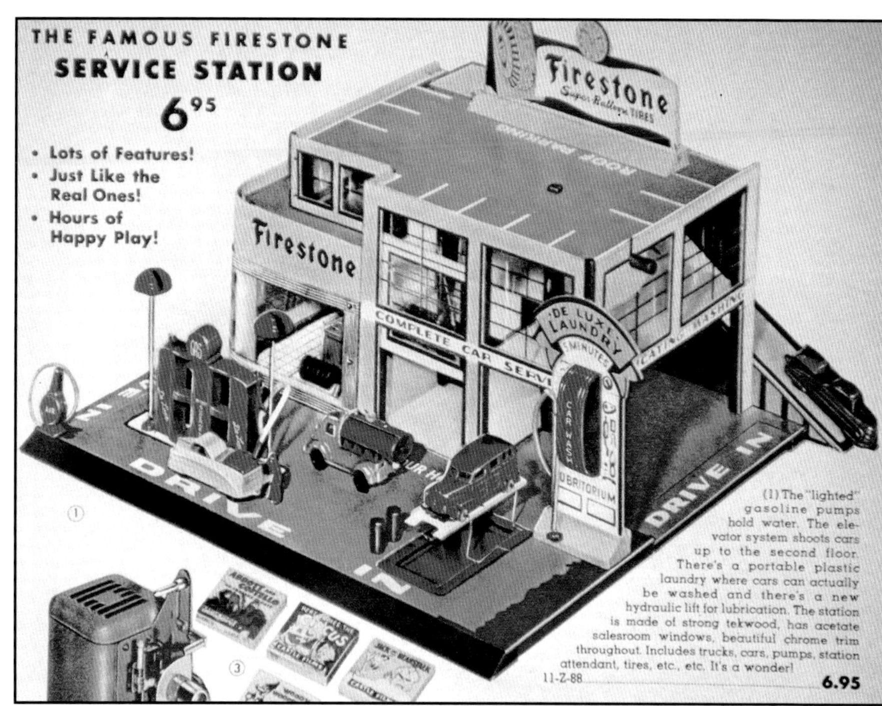

The De Luxe Game Corp. produced many different styles of toy buildings, including a variety of service stations, a fire station, and perhaps barns and stores. One of the firm's stations was this Firestone model. It was advertised in the 1948 Firestone Fall & Winter catalog issued by Sibley's Firestone Dealer Store in Little Falls, Minnesota. The station was made of Tekwood with acetate windows and included trucks, cars, station attendant, and other accessories. The gasoline pumps held water and the station also included an elevator and a car wash. The station sold for $6.95. See page 163 of the *Toy Buildings* book for photographs of other De Luxe service stations. *Courtesy of Roy Specht.*

Dennison's

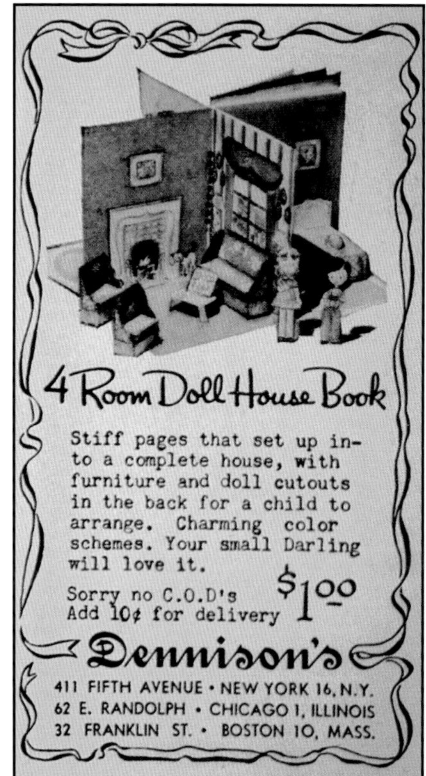

This "4 Room Doll House Book" was advertised in the October 1948 *House Beautiful* magazine. The house was marketed for $1.00 by Dennison's of New York City. Furniture and doll cutouts were included in the back of the book to be used with the house. The pictured book was called Doll House and was created by Marion Moss with pictures by Lisl Weil. It was a "Rainbow Playbook" published by the World Publishing Co. in 1946.

Dolly Dear Accessories

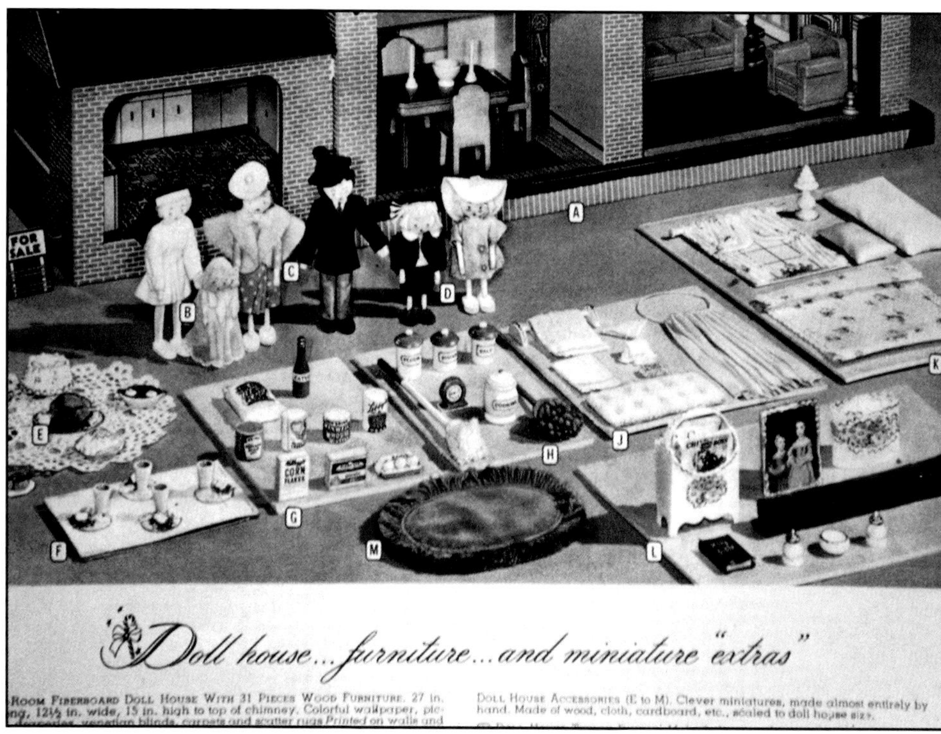

Business boomed for the small Dolly Dear firm in Union City, Tennessee when Montgomery Ward included the 1" to one foot scaled accessories in their Christmas catalog in 1943. The accessories came in sets. Included were a turkey dinner (89 cents), living room accessories (picture, Bible, mantel decorations, waste basket, magazine rack, and rug, $1.35), and a scatter rug (57 cents). The business was begun in 1928 by Rossie Kirkland under the R.T. Kirkland name, but later became known as Dolly Dear Accessories.

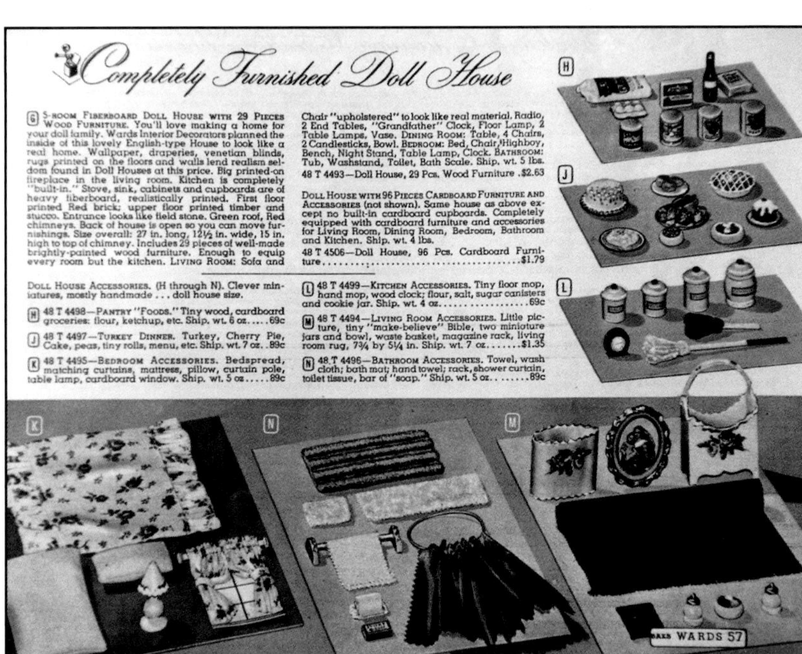

Left:
Similar Dolly Dear items were also offered in the Montgomery Ward Christmas catalog for 1945. The bathroom accessories included a towel, washcloth, bathmat, hand towel, towel rack, shower curtain, toilet tissue and a bar of soap. The set sold for 89 cents.

Donna Lee (Woodburn Manufacturing Co.)

The Donna Lee line of furniture as well as one of the dollhouses was advertised in *Playthings* magazine for January 1946. The Woodburn Manufacturing Co. of Chicago produced the furniture. Dave Rapaport headed the company and the furniture and dollhouse line was named for his daughter Donna Lee. The ad included sets of wood furniture for a living room, dining room, kitchen, bedroom, and bathroom. A dollhouse was also pictured but no prices were listed.

A Dolly Dear catalog page circa 1958 pictures the same style magazine rack as that pictured in the Montgomery Ward catalog in 1943. The price was 59 cents in 1958. Other items shown are the Victorian lamp (59 cents), table lamp (59 cents), floor lamp (89 cents), clock (49 cents), vase of flowers (49 cents), bookcase ($1.29), and bookends (59 cents). At the time of this catalog, Alberta Kitchell Allen (Mrs. Kirkland's niece) had purchased the business and moved it to Rives, Tennessee. The company continued in business until 1966. *Courtesy of Zelma Fink.*

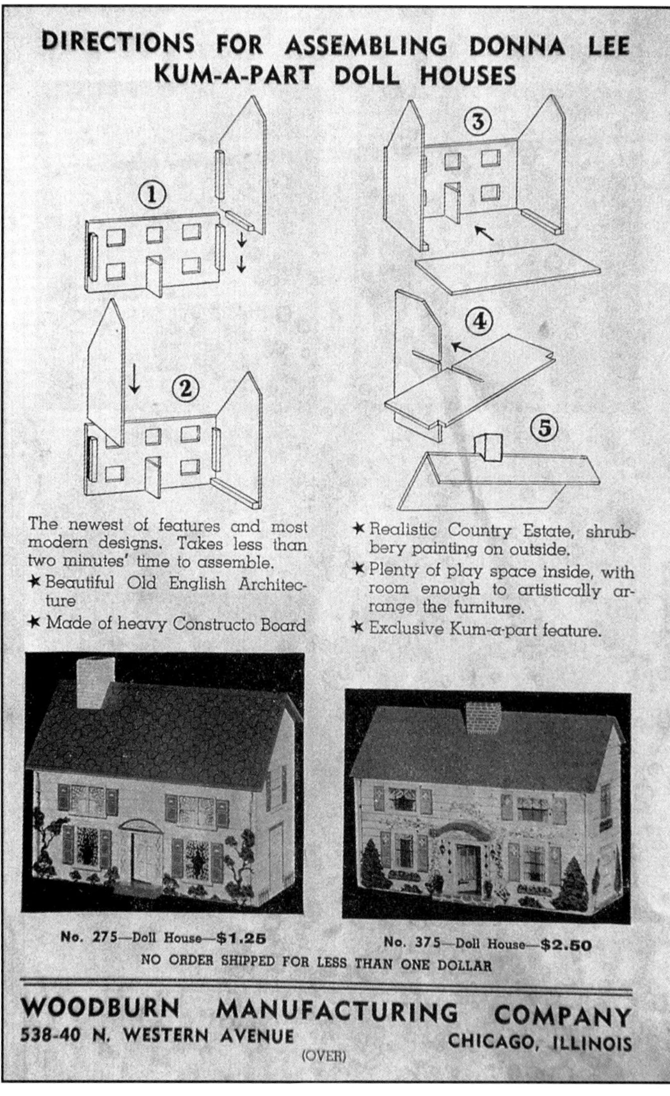

Left:
Flyer from the Chicago based Woodburn Manufacturing Co., picturing two of the company houses. Both houses were two-story. The larger four-room house on the right sold for $2.50 and measured 15" high x 21" wide x 7.25" deep. The houses were made of constructo board. The cheaper house on the left was priced at only $1.25.

Electric Game Co. Inc.

This advertisement appeared in *Child Life* magazine in 1942. The room measured 8" high x 16" wide x 14" deep. It came with an electric floor lamp, table lamp, and fireplace, as well as an assortment of living room furniture. Batteries for the "electricity" were also included. The package sold for $2.50. The set was made by the Electric Game Co. in Holyoke, Massachusetts. *From the collection of Marcie Tubbs. Photograph by Bob Tubbs.*

ECA Toys

This ECA Toys advertisement is from 1944. Boxes of composition dollhouse furniture for the living room and kitchen are pictured. The furniture was sold in plain white and the buyer was to finish the furniture by using watercolors that were included to apply decorations. See page 164 of *Antique & Collectible Dollhouses* for a photograph showing a boxed set of this furniture.

Faber, David H.

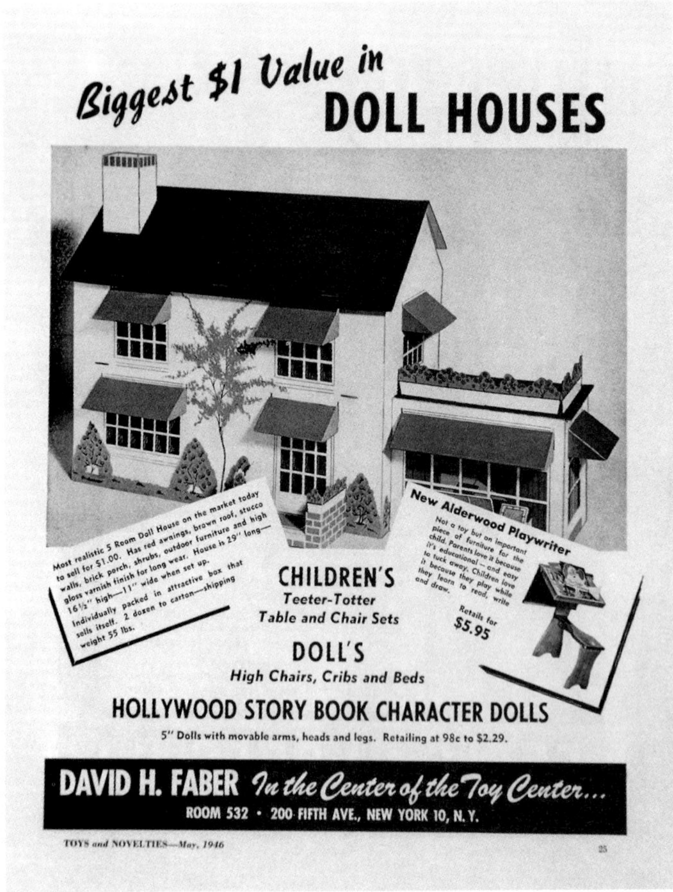

"The Nels Doll House" was advertised in *Toys and Novelties* in May 1946 (see page 112 of *American Dollhouses and Furniture* for a photograph of the actual house). The ad described several toys that were being marketed from the listed David H. Faber firm in New York City. The five-room cardboard house retailed for $1.00 and measured 16.5" high x 29" wide x 11.5" deep.

Ideal Novelty & Toy Co.

No.	Retail	No.	Retail	No.	Retail	No.	Retail	No.	Retail
dz. KR-25	.25	dz. BWC-25	.25	dz. PFL-10	.10	dz. DCH-10	.10	dz. GA-25	.25
dz. KS-25	.25	dz. BT-25	.25	dz. PTL-5	.05	dz. DBR-20	.20	dz. GB-20	.20
dz. KC-5	.05	dz. BH-10	.10	dz. PLC-20	.20	dz. DBU-25	.25	dz. GBB-10	.10
dz. KT-10	.10	dz. BMC-25	.25	dz. PH-10	.10	dz. SM-40	.40	dz. GC-20	.20
dz. KF-20	.20	dz. BB-10	.10	dz. PRT-75	.75	dz. SBE-25	.25	dz. GDH-30	.30
dz. KST-50	.50	dz. PSY-25	.25	dz. PRD-10	.10	dz. SVD-30	.30	dz. GD-5	.05
dz. KRA-50	.50	dz. PIA-40	.40	dz. PTT-15	.15	dz. SBC-15	.15	dz. GSP-35	.35
dz. LW-35	.35	dz. PSO-25	.25	dz. PCT-10	.10	dz. SHB-20	.20	dz. GPT-30	.30
dz. LM-35	.35	dz. PWC-20	.20	dz. RTR-15	.15	dz. SNT-10	.10		
dz. KRF-40	.40	dz. PFP-40	.40	dz. DCA-10	.10	dz. GTU-40	.40		
dz. KC-5	.05	dz. PPF-10	.10	dz. DTA-20	.20	dz. GT-40	.40		

The Ideal Novelty & Toy Co. was begun by Morris Michtom in Brooklyn, New York in 1903. The firm started with the production of Teddy bears, and manufactured thousands of different toys and dolls throughout the years. Their 3/4" to one foot plastic Ideal furniture was advertised in the February 1948 *Toys & Novelties* magazine. The furniture had initially come on the market in 1947. This 1948 advertisement pictured five rooms of furniture, a deluxe kitchen, and pieces for a garden area. In this ad, the furniture was priced by the piece instead of by the set. Prices ranged from 25 cents to 40 cents each.

This full page Ideal ad appeared in *Toys & Novelties* in July 1948. It pictured the 3/4" to one foot scale Ideal plastic furniture packaged in house shaped room boxes for $1.19 each. The box contained a "full color interior room that could be lifted out of the house." Rooms available included: kitchen, nursery, living room, music room, bathroom, and bedroom. The rooms included five or six items.

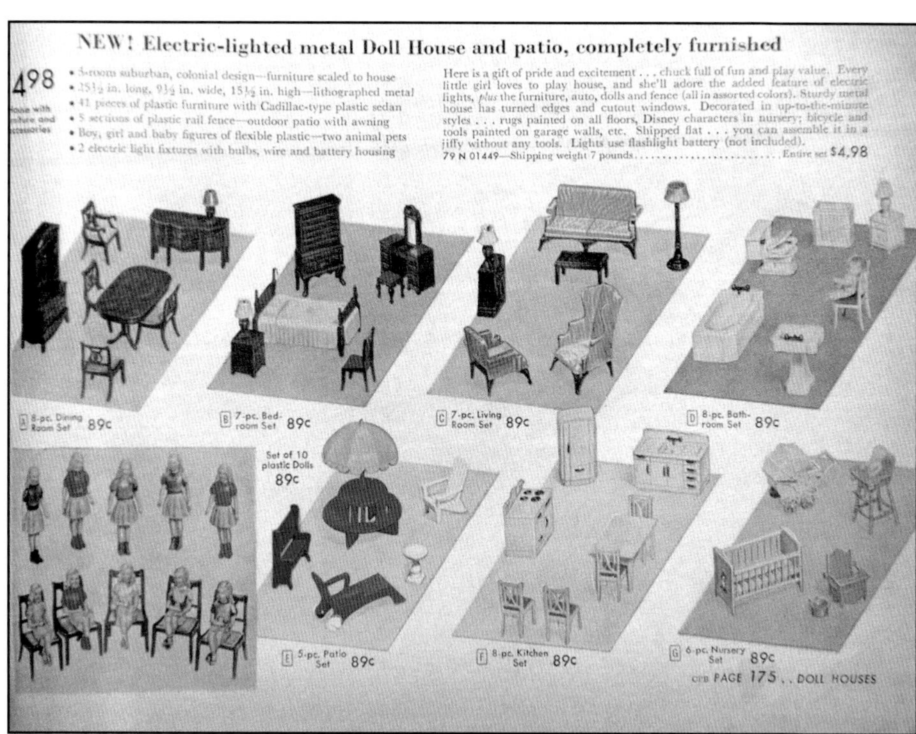

Plastic furniture made by Ideal was featured in the Sears Christmas catalog for 1949. Included were sets to be used to furnish a dining room, bedroom, living room, bathroom, kitchen, patio, and a new nursery set. The boxed sets were priced at 89 cents each.

The Sears Christmas catalog for 1966 advertised a vinyl "suitcase" two-story house furnished with twenty pieces of the Petite Princess furniture. The house folded into an 18" x 21" x 8" case. The house and furniture sold for $9.99. The Marx dolls were sold separately. *Courtesy of Marilyn Pittman.*

Ideal brought out a new line of 3/4" to one foot plastic furniture in 1964 called Petite Princess. Several pages of the 1964 Sears Christmas catalog were devoted to pictures of this new, rather expensive furniture. The prices ranged from 77 cents for a coffee table set to $2.47 for a piano and bench. The Princess Patti kitchen and bathroom pieces were added in 1965. A special set of dolls was available to be used with the furniture. The four-piece family was priced at $2.44.

Luxurious Styling!

Fantasy Doll House with Patio by Ideal 4.99

MAJESTIC, FULL COLOR doll house, 2 Complete floors of furnishings scaled for all popular small size dolls. Features—fireplace, leaf table, piano, bed, dresser, staircase with chandelier. Molded and vinyl house closes up into portable carrying case. 349 Y 5980—14x16¾x7-in. Mailable. Wt. 2 lb. 15 oz.........4.99

The Aldens Christmas catalog from 1967 pictured a "Fantasy House" with patio by Ideal. The two-story vinyl house closed up into a portable carrying case. The copy stated that the furniture was suitable for all popular small sized dolls. The furnishings included a fireplace, table, piano, dresser, and bed. It sold for $4.99 and measured 16.75" tall x 14" wide x 7" deep. *Courtesy of Marilyn Pittman.*

An "Ideal Deluxe 3 Story Doll House Case" was advertised in the True Value *Santa's Preview Booklet* in 1968. The house was furnished with plastic furniture, which included a sink, range, piano, bedroom and dining sets. When the front was opened, a yard and patio were revealed. The house measured 14.5" x 17" x 12.5". It sold for $7.77. The Ideal firm was sold to the Columbia Broadcasting System in 1983.

Keystone Mfg. Co.

The Keystone Mfg. Co., of Boston, Massachusetts, was founded in the early 1920s by Chester Rimmer and Arthur Jackson. The firm produced dollhouses from the late 1930s until the early 1960s. This Keystone dollhouse was advertised in Filene's Christmas catalog for 1938. The house was made of masonite and wood and included an opening door. The exterior featured metal casement windows and awnings. The house contained four rooms with plain brown walls and floors. It measured 16" high x 24" wide x 10" deep and sold for $1.95. See page 165 of *International Dollhouses* for a picture of the actual house. Strombecker wood 3/4" to one foot furniture was advertised for use in furnishing the house. The set includes nine pieces for the living room, an eight-piece bedroom set, six pieces for the bathroom and seven pieces for the kitchen. The total furniture cost was $1.95.

KEYSTONE
COMPLETELY FURNISHED
Four Rooms Of Miniature Furniture
Doll house furniture was never so beautiful! Sturdily made of metal, ttractively finished in colors. The living room furniture is shown below at the ıft, with davenport, rocker, tables, lamps, radio. Bedroom furniture inludes twin beds, dresser, vanity, rocker, table and lamp. The kitchen furniure is shown below at the right, with refrigerator, range, table, chairs, ink and footstool. The dining room furniture is shown at the right above. An immense value.
126390 Four Rooms of Furniture............$2.95

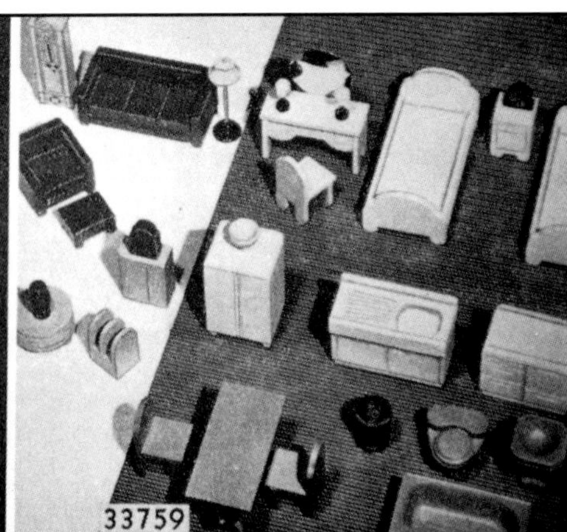

Left:
The John Plain wholesale catalog for 1938 included this Keystone dollhouse. The house was made of wood and masonite and contained four rooms. The outside included metal opening casement windows along with a stonelike chimney. The inside was painted. The house was 16" high x 25" wide x 10" deep. *Courtesy of Marge Meisinger.*

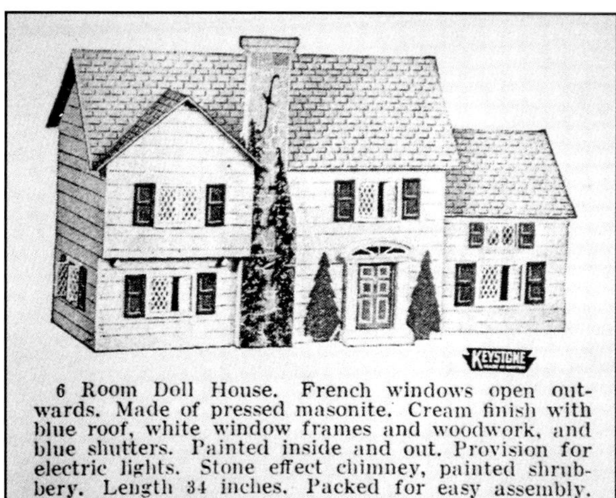

KEYSTONE
6 Room Doll House. French windows open outwards. Made of pressed masonite. Cream finish with blue roof, white window frames and woodwork, and blue shutters. Painted inside and out. Provision for electric lights. Stone effect chimney, painted shrubbery. Length 34 inches. Packed for easy assembly.
No. 42N100. Each......................$6.50

A different model of a Keystone house was pictured in the N. Shure Co. catalog for 1938. This larger six-room house was made of pressed masonite and had a provision for electric lights. Its design also included a tall "stone" chimney, metal casement windows, and painted shrubbery. The inside was painted. The house was 34" wide. *Meisinger Collection.*

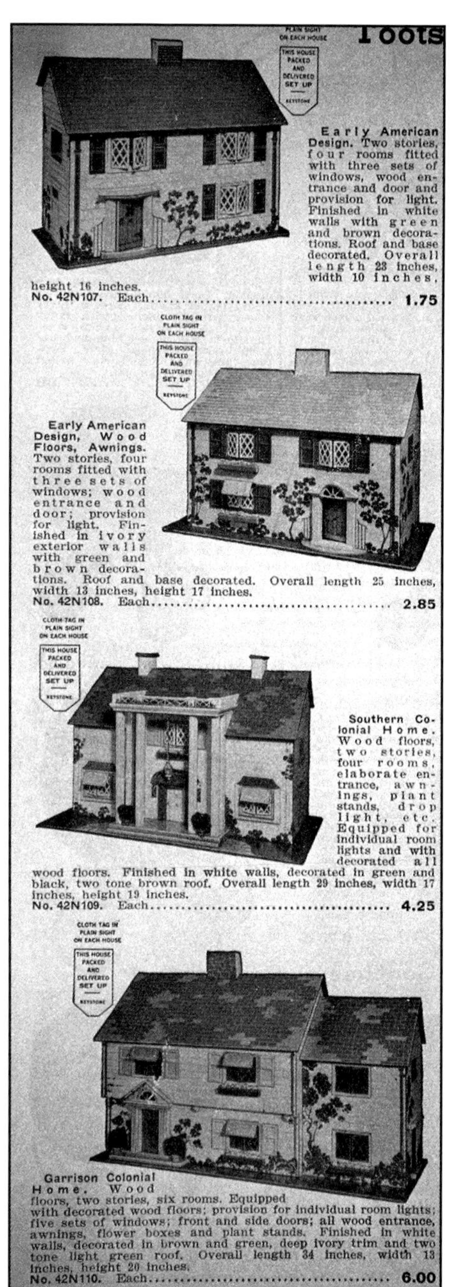

PLAIN SIGHT
ON EACH HOUSE
THIS HOUSE PACKED AND DELIVERED SET UP
KEYSTONE
Early American Design. Two stories, four rooms fitted with three sets of windows, wood entrance and door and provision for light. Finished in white walls with green and brown decorations. Roof and base decorated. Overall length 23 inches, width 10 inches, height 16 inches.
No. 42N107. Each.................................... 1.75
CLOTH TAG IN PLAIN SIGHT ON EACH HOUSE
THIS HOUSE PACKED AND DELIVERED SET UP
KEYSTONE
Early American Design, Wood Floors, Awnings. Two stories, four rooms fitted with three sets of windows; wood entrance and door; provision for light. Finished in ivory exterior walls with green and brown decorations. Roof and base decorated. Overall length 25 inches, width 13 inches, height 17 inches.
No. 42N108. Each.................................... 2.85
CLOTH TAG IN PLAIN SIGHT ON EACH HOUSE
THIS HOUSE PACKED AND DELIVERED SET UP
KEYSTONE
Southern Colonial Home. Wood floors, two stories, four rooms, elaborate entrance, awnings, plant stands, drop light, etc. Equipped for individual room lights and with decorated all wood floors. Finished in white walls, decorated in green and black, two tone brown roof. Overall length 29 inches, width 17 inches, height 19 inches.
No. 42N109. Each.................................... 4.25
CLOTH TAG IN PLAIN SIGHT ON EACH HOUSE
THIS HOUSE PACKED AND DELIVERED SET UP
KEYSTONE
Garrison Colonial Home. Wood floors, two stories, six rooms. Equipped with decorated wood floors; provision for individual room lights; five sets of windows; front and side doors; all wood entrance, awnings, flower boxes and plant stands. Finished in white walls, decorated in brown and green, deep ivory trim and two tone light green roof. Overall length 34 inches, width 13 inches, height 20 inches.
No. 42N110. Each.................................... 6.00

The N. Shure Co. catalog of 1941 offered four different models of Keystone houses. All were two story models and featured metal casement windows. Three of the houses included four rooms, while the house pictured at the bottom included six rooms. All except the one at the top included awnings. The house at the top measured 16" high x 23" wide x 10" deep. The second house was 17" high x 25" wide x 13" deep. The third house was 19" high x 29" wide x 17" deep. The six-room house at the bottom was 20" tall x 34" wide x 12" deep. A lighting unit for the dollhouses was also available. *Meisinger Collection.*

KEYSTONE ALL-SET DOLL HOUSES
• SHIPPED SET UP
• READY TO USE XMAS MORNING
• NO LOOSE PARTS — NO LOST PARTS
• DELIVER AND SHIP IN ORIGINAL CARTON
Available with
WOOD FLOORS
(See Model Numbers)
No. 1241
Six room Georgian Colonial House. Gray roof in shingle pattern. White walls decorated in brown and green. Blue shutters. All wood entrance and door and swinging windows. All wood floors. Second floor slotted for two single lights. Packed completely set up. Length 28", width 13", height 17". Weight 18 lbs. each.

This Keystone house was advertised in the Keystone catalog for 1942. The two-story house included six rooms, metal casement windows, blue shutters, and two chimneys. The house measured 17" high x 28" wide x 13" deep.

G. Fox & Co. of Hartford, Conn., advertised this Keystone house in their December 1942 catalog. The two-story house included four rooms and metal casement windows. It measured 17" high x 24" wide x 13" deep. Strombecker 3/4" to one foot wood furniture could be purchased to furnish the house. *Meisinger Collection.*

New! 6-room Doll House on built-in turn table
Turns easily without lifting . . . comes already assembled
Big improvement in doll house construction! Built-in wooden turn table enables the little housekeeper to turn house and play from front or open back—without changing her position.
$969
Roomy house is remarkably strong: built of very durable Masonite presdwood with wood corner posts and partition supports. Impressive wooden doorway and steps, enameled white. Door and metal casement windows open and close. Two floors connected by circular wooden staircase. Living room, dining room and kitchen downstairs; 2 bedrooms and bath upstairs. Colorfully decorated interior and exterior. Overall size 12⅛x22⅛x24½ in. long. See opposite page for furniture and dolls.
79 NM 2178—Unfurnished House. Shpg. wt. 29 lbs. Freight or Express $9.69

A Keystone house with a built-in turntable was featured in the Sears Christmas catalog for 1948. The two-story house included six rooms connected by a circular wooden staircase. Metal casement windows were included in the house, which was made of masonite presdwood. Both the interior and the exterior were "colorfully" decorated. The house measured 22.25" high x 24.5" wide x 12.25" deep. It sold for $9.69. *Courtesy of Betty Nichols.*

New Doll House on turn-table
• 6 rooms and garage—42x12¾x19 in. high overall • Plastic windows in front
• Two wings pivot . . . nest into house reducing length for storage to 23 inches.
• Built of sturdy Masonite Presdwood and tekwood (wood-center fiberboard)
$969
Has built-in turntable . . . the little owner can turn the house around and play from front or open back without changing her position. Roof slides off, making it possible to play from top of house as well as front and back. Two floors connected by staircase. Living room, dining room and kitchen downstairs; 2 bedrooms and bath upstairs. Closet, 2 outdoor terraces, porch, garage with sliding door. Transparent plastic windows on front of house. Beautifully decorated inside and out . . . bathroom has built-in "shower" . . . living room has bookcase with movable "books."
79 N 01437—Unfurnished house. Shipped completely assembled. Shipping weight 21 pounds. $9.69
174 . . SEARS, ROEBUCK AND CO. c

A Keystone dollhouse on a turntable was also featured in the Sears 1949 Christmas catalog. The house was made of masonite presdwood and teakwood (wood-center fiber board). It included six rooms and a garage and could be turned from the front to the open back. The roof was removable for easier access to the inside. Extra features included a closet, shower, two terraces and a porch. Both the inside and outside of the house were decorated. The two wings pivot to nest into the main house for storage. The house measured 19" high x 42" wide x 12.75" deep and sold for $9.69.

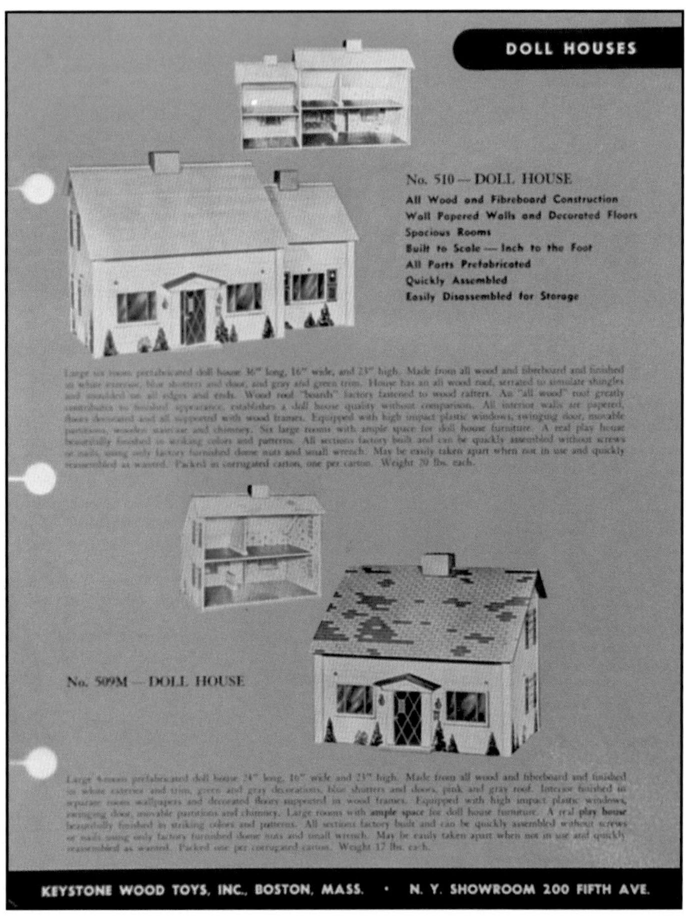

DOLL HOUSES
No. 510 — DOLL HOUSE
All Wood and Fibreboard Construction
Wall Papered Walls and Decorated Floors
Spacious Rooms
Built to Scale — Inch to the Foot
All Parts Prefabricated
Quickly Assembled
Easily Disassembled for Storage
No. 509M — DOLL HOUSE
KEYSTONE WOOD TOYS, INC., BOSTON, MASS. • N. Y. SHOWROOM 200 FIFTH AVE.

Right:
Keystone houses pictured in the company catalog for 1955. The houses were made with wood and fibreboard construction. They featured decorated walls and floors. The larger, open-backed house contained five rooms. It was 23" high x 36" wide x 16" deep. The smaller house in the catalog contained four rooms and measured 23" high x 24" wide x 16" deep. *Courtesy of Linda Boltrek.*

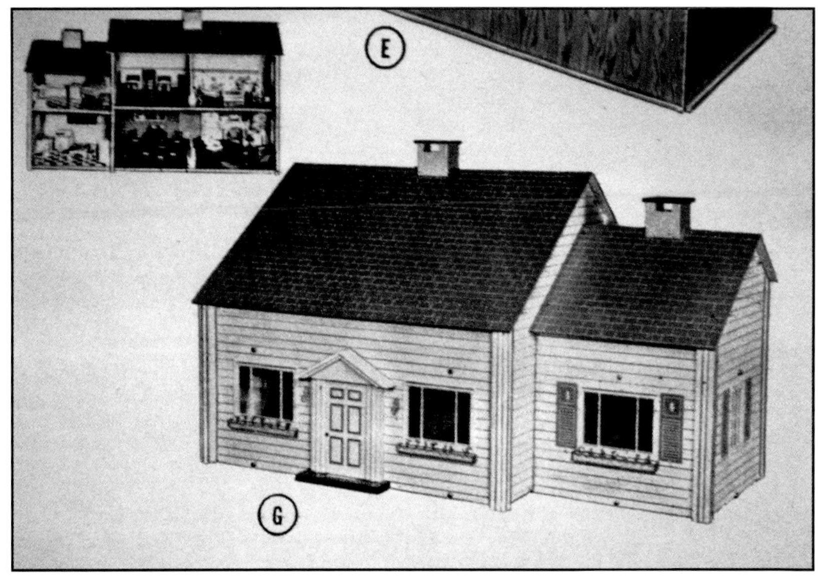

The FAO Schwarz Christmas catalog for 1959 featured a house that looked very much like the Keystone house advertised in the Keystone catalog for 1955. The houses are exactly the same size, both contain six rooms, include movable partitions, and are to be assembled using dome nuts. The Schwarz version was priced at $28.95 unfurnished. The house could also be purchased for $35.00 furnished with plastic furniture or for $42.50 with mostly Strombecker furniture except for the nursery pieces which were made of plastic.

In addition to houses, the Keystone Company also produced a number of toy buildings. Included were villages, barns, fire stations, a lumber yard, warehouse, railroad station, bus station, parking garages, forts, and many different designs of service stations. Pictured is one of the Keystone fire stations. It included an alarm, opening doors, two fire engines, a car, and a hose that could be used to spray water on the "burning warehouse." The toy sold for $4.95 in this ad from the Billy and Ruth catalog for 1949. *From the collection of Marcie Tubbs. Photograph by Bob Tubbs.*

Left:
Besides houses and toy buildings, the Keystone Mfg. Co. issued a line of small doll furniture to accommodate the 8"-11" dolls popular in the 1950s. The firm's 1955 toy catalog offered an 8" baby doll packaged with a wood wardrobe, crib, playpen, baby tender, and bathinet. The furniture could also be purchased by the piece. *Courtesy of Linda Boltrek.*

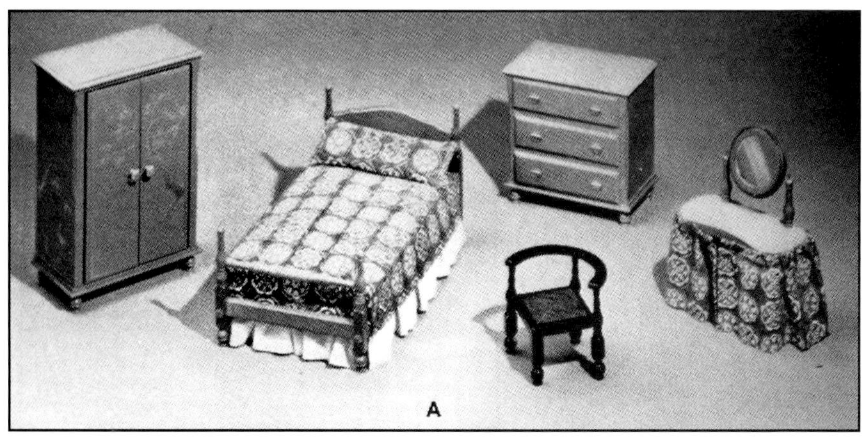

The Keystone firm also produced furniture for the 11" styled dolls like Vogue's Jill and Jeff. Several examples of this furniture were advertised in the 1956 catalog issued by Pomeroy's in Reading, Pennsylvania. The pieces from the bedroom set included a bed ($3.98), wardrobe ($2.98), dresser ($2.79), vanity with mirror ($2.00), and chair ($1.50). The complete set was priced at $12.95. *Courtesy of Marge Meisinger.*

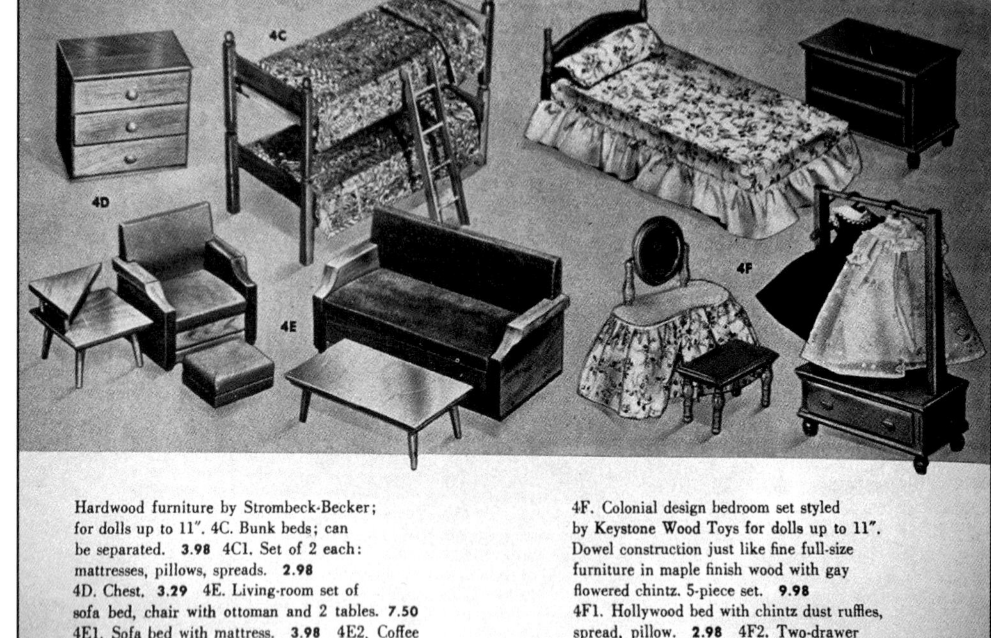

4C
4D
4E
4F
Hardwood furniture by Strombeck-Becker; for dolls up to 11". 4C. Bunk beds; can be separated. **3.98** 4C1. Set of 2 each: mattresses, pillows, spreads. **2.98** 4D. Chest. **3.29** 4E. Living-room set of sofa bed, chair with ottoman and 2 tables. **7.50** 4E1. Sofa bed with mattress. **3.98** 4E2. Coffee table. **69c** 4E3. Two-tier corner table. **69c** 4E4. Arm chair and ottoman. **2.29**
4F. Colonial design bedroom set styled by Keystone Wood Toys for dolls up to 11". Dowel construction just like fine full-size furniture in maple finish wood with gay flowered chintz. 5-piece set. **9.98** 4F1. Hollywood bed with chintz dust ruffles, spread, pillow. **2.98** 4F2. Two-drawer dresser. **2.59** 4F3. Clothes rack with drawer. **2.59** 4F4. Vanity with bench. **2.59**

Kilpatricks in Omaha, Nebraska also advertised Keystone furniture, in addition to pieces made by Strombecker, in its 1957 catalog. The Keystone five-piece bedroom set was priced at $9.98. A bench had been added to the vanity, a two drawer chest replaced the earlier one with three drawers, and a clothes rack with a drawer ($2.59) had replaced the earlier wardrobe. Strombecker pieces for the 8"-11" dolls included a living room set of five pieces priced at $7.50, bunk beds for $2.98, and a three-drawer chest for $3.29. *Meisinger Collection.*

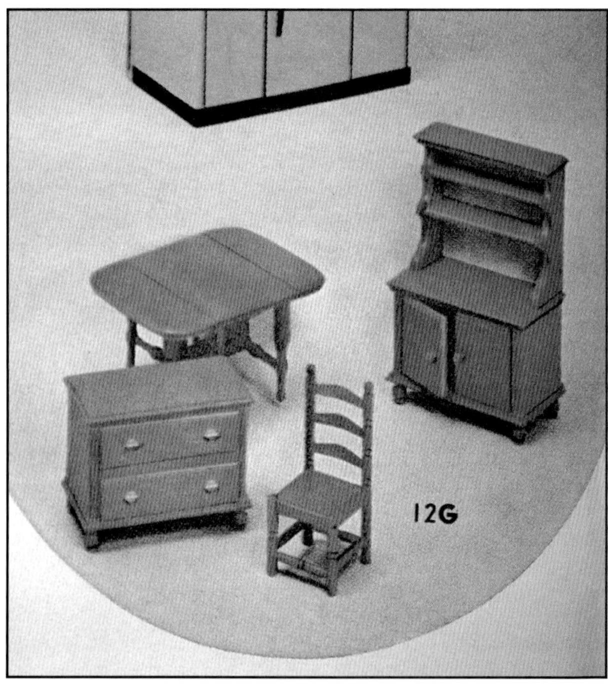

Keystone also produced furniture for a dining room to be used with the popular 8"-11" dolls of the period. Mihlbaugh's from Sharon, Pennsylvania pictured this set in their 1957-58 catalog. The maple finished pieces included a drop leaf table ($2.79), ladder back chair ($1.59), Hutch cupboard ($2.98), and a buffet ($2.59). Halls produced dollhouses large enough to accommodate this large furniture. The Child Life Dolly Home was also made in this scale.

Melco Toys

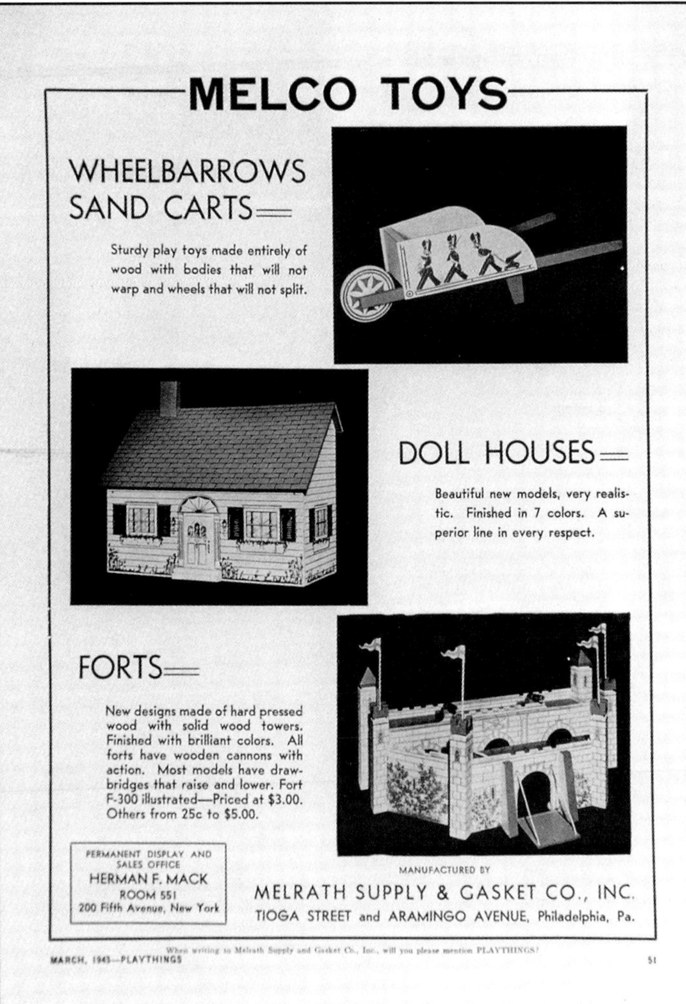

This Melco Toys ad appeared in *Playthings* magazine in March 1943. The pictured toys included a wheelbarrow, a dollhouse, and a fort. The dollhouses were made of hard pressed wood. No information is given about the house pictured but the copy reads "Beautiful new models, very realistic" so several different designs must have been available. The ad came from Melrath Supply and Gasket Co., Inc. in Philadelphia. See another design of a Melco house at the top of page 163 in *Antique & Collectible Dollhouses*.

Meritoy

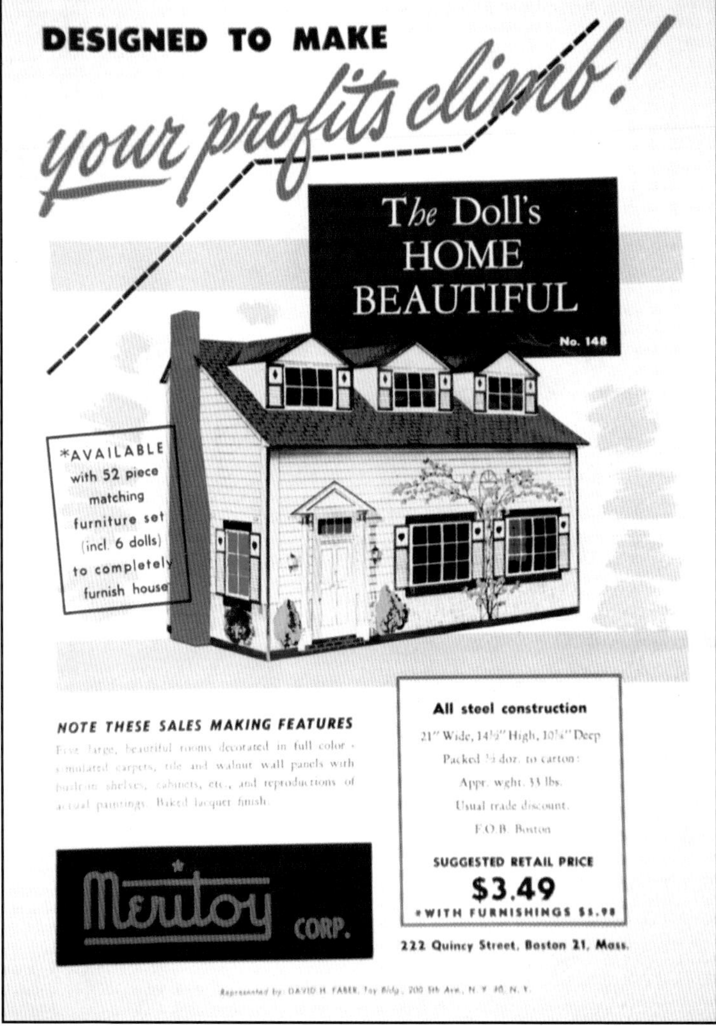

Meritoy Corp. advertisement for their metal dollhouse, circa 1949. The Boston based firm marketed only this one dollhouse. In the ad, the steel house sold for $3.49 unfurnished and for $5.98 complete with fifty-two pieces of furniture and six dolls. It is not known what brand of furniture came with the house. The six-room, two-story house measured 14.5" high x 21" wide x 10.25" deep.

Nancy Forbes (American Toy & Furniture Co., earlier called Rapaport Bros.)

New "FOLD-AWAY" *Type*

- ★ Beautiful Cape Cod Designs
- ★ Large and Roomy
- ★ Heavy, Strong Construction
- ★ Exclusive FOLD-AWAY Feature
- ★ Real Paint Finish
- ★ Exclusive PLAY Features

★

THE LATEST in doll houses. A beautifully shaped series of authentic houses in the popular Cape Cod style of architecture. Roomy interior and many play features. Realistic exterior in color finished in durable paint. BUT — the best feature of all is that **each house can be taken apart and put away flat within a few moments time!** Hidden integral parts are used in the simple but ingenious interlocking construction.

★

AMERICAN TOY and FURNITURE CO.

725 S. LaSalle St., Chicago, Illinois
200 Fifth Avenue, New York City

★

Also Manufacturers of Electric Woodburning Sets, Tapping Sets, Woodcarving Sets, Metal Tooling, Foil Writing, Glass Painting, Casting Sets, Sand Painting Sets, Combination Sets.

INSTRUCTIONS FOR ASSEMBLING

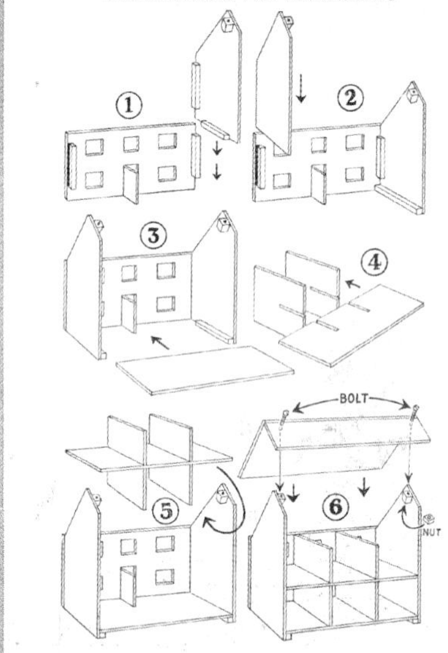

Nancy Forbes DOLL HOUSES!

← 6 ROOM HOUSE, ELECTRIC LIGHTING

No. 503 . . . . $3.00

Size 24x19x10. Front door opens, large circular veranda with steps and upstairs porch, supported by columns. Miniature awnings, flower boxes and transparent windows covered with movable shutters. Six large rooms open to rear. Green, White, Yellow and Red Paint finish in full detail. Corrugated box 24x10x5½. 4 in shipping carton. Weight 35 lbs. Electric lighting for extra play value.

← 2 ROOM HOUSE

No. 501 . . . . $1.00

Size 18x12½x8. Complete with front door that opens, transparent windows, and two rooms opening in rear. Each house finished in durable Ivory, Green and Red paint for shingles, shrubbery, "Lap-board" walls, etc. Corrugated box 18x9x3½. 12 in shipping carton. Weight 50 lbs.

↑ 4 ROOM HOUSE

No. 502 . . . . $2.00

Size 20x18x11. A two story Cape Cod house. Front door opens. Four transparent windows, four room open in rear convenient for play. White, Green and Red paint finish for shingles, shubbery, shutters, etc. Attractive Window Boxes. Front porch with steps. Corrugated box 20x11x5. 6 in shpg. carton. Wt., 40 lbs.

Nancy Forbes GENUINE WALNUT *Doll Furniture*

No. 270—Genuine Walnut Living Room $2.00
11 piece cozy outfit consists of Large Fireplace with beveled glass mirror, Davenport, Armchair and Footstool, Modernistic Radio, Pair of Right and Left End Tables, Conventional and Coffee Tables with mirror top and Two Lamps.

No. 271—Genuine Walnut Dining Room $2.00
Consists of 10 useful pieces. Buffet with mirror, Serving Table, beautiful China Cabinet with beveled mirror, Dining Room Table, 4 Chairs and Two Lamps.

No. 272—Genuine Walnut Bedroom . . . $2.00
9 pieces, neatly arranged, will make a comfortable room. Full size Bed, Dresser and Vanity with beveled glass mirrors, Vanity Seat, Night Table, Chest of Drawers, hinged cover Cedar Chest and two Dresser Lamps.

No. 381—Genuine Walnut Upholstered Dining Room $3.00
Consists of 10 realistic pieces. Beautiful China Cabinet with beveled mirror, Serving Table, Dining Room Table, Four shaped and upholstered Dining Room Chairs, full size Buffet with mirror and Two Table Lamps.

No. 380—Genuine Walnut Upholstered Living Room $3.00
12 pieces include Modernistic Upright Piano, upholstered Piano Bench, upholstered Armchair and Ottoman, upholstered Davenport, Radio, Pair of Right and Left End Tables, Coffee Table with mirror top, Conventional Table and Two Lamps.

No. 382—Genuine Walnut Upholstered Bedroom $3.00
Nine pieces, full size Bed with beautiful padded Bedspread and Bolster, upholstered Bedroom Chair, Dresser and Vanity with beveled Glass mirrors, upholstered Vanity Seat, High-boy Chest, hinged Cedar Chest and two Dresser Lamps.

Each set in beautifully lithographed box 12¼"x16¼". 12 sets in shipping container. Wt. 24 lbs.

Flyer for three styles of Nancy Forbes dollhouses offered by the Chicago based American Toy & Furniture Co. during the 1940s. The houses included two rooms, four rooms, or six rooms. The smallest two-room house, pictured on page 95 of the *International Dollhouses* book, measured 12" high x 16" wide x 8" deep and sold for $1.00. The house had transparent windows and an open back. The four-room, two-story house measured 18" high x 20" wide x 11" deep. It, too, included transparent windows and an open back and was priced at $2.00. The largest house, which contained six rooms, measured 19" high x 24" wide x 10" deep. It included an upstairs porch supported by columns, awnings, and movable shutters. It was also an open-backed house. Electric lighting was available for this house, which was priced at $3.00. All of the houses were "New Fold-Away Type Houses" according to the advertising copy.

Nancy Forbes GENUINE WALNUT *Doll Furniture*

No. 270—Genuine Walnut Living Room $2.00
11 piece cozy outfit consists of Large Fireplace with beveled glass mirror, Davenport, Armchair and Footstool, Modernistic Radio, Pair of Right and Left End Tables, Conventional and Coffee Tables with mirror top and Two Lamps.

No. 271—Genuine Walnut Dining Room $2.00
Consists of 10 useful pieces. Buffet with mirror, Serving Table, beautiful China Cabinet with beveled mirror, Dining Room Table, 4 Chairs and Two Lamps.

No. 272—Genuine Walnut Bedroom . . . $2.00
9 pieces, neatly arranged, will make a comfortable room. Full size Bed, Dresser and Vanity with beveled glass mirrors, Vanity Seat, Night Table, Chest of Drawers, hinged cover Cedar Chest and two Dresser Lamps.

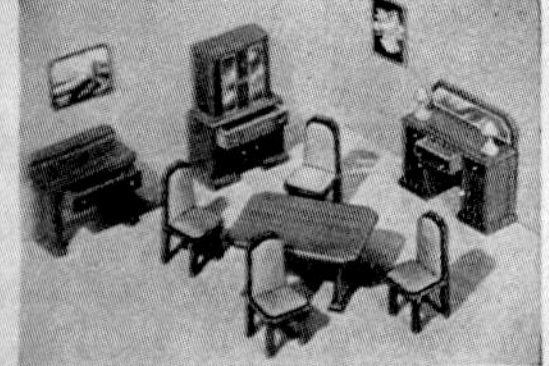

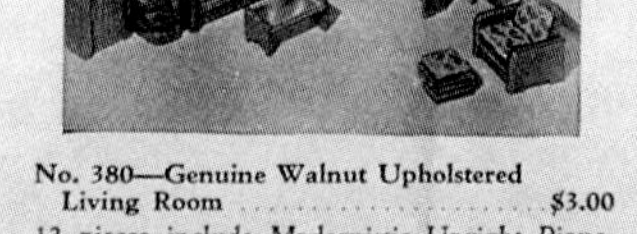

No. 381—Genuine Walnut Upholstered Dining Room $3.00
Consists of 10 realistic pieces. Beautiful China Cabinet with beveled mirror, Serving Table, Dining Room Table, Four shaped and upholstered Dining Room Chairs, full size Buffet with mirror and Two Table Lamps.

No. 380—Genuine Walnut Upholstered Living Room $3.00
12 pieces include Modernistic Upright Piano, upholstered Piano Bench, upholstered Armchair and Ottoman, upholstered Davenport, Radio, Pair of Right and Left End Tables, Coffee Table with mirror top, Conventional Table and Two Lamps .

No. 382—Genuine Walnut Upholstered Bedroom $3.00
Nine pieces, full size Bed with beautiful padded Bedspread and Bolster, upholstered Bedroom Chair, Dresser and Vanity with beveled Glass mirrors, upholstered Vanity Seat, High-boy Chest, hinged Cedar Chest and two Dresser Lamps.

Each set in beautifully lithographed box 12¼"x16¼". 12 sets in shipping container. Wt. 24 lbs.

Nancy Forbes furniture was sold in two scales in the early 1940s. This flyer advertising the larger 1" to one foot scale included pieces for a walnut living room ($2.00), walnut dining room ($2.00), and walnut bedroom ($2.00), as well as sets of the three rooms with upholstery added. The more elaborate upholstered sets were priced at $3.00 for each set. A piano was also included in the more expensive set.

Left:
The 3/4" to one foot scaled Nancy Forbes furniture was issued in both walnut and maple finish. This flyer advertised the sets, which included only six pieces in each boxed set and sold for 50 cents each. Other boxed sets were sold that included nine pieces. The line also featured furniture for a child's room. These sets sold for $1.00.

Plasco (Plastic Art Toy Corp)

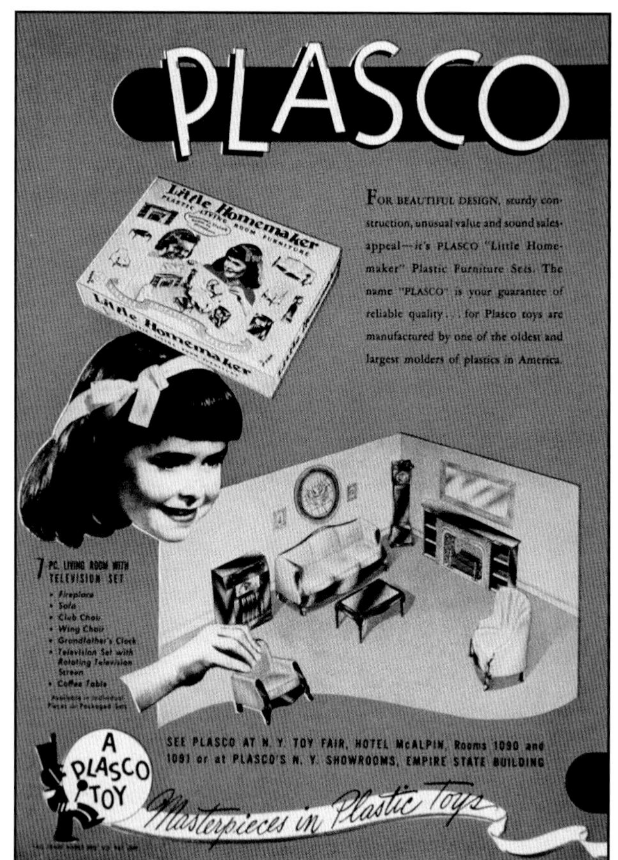

The Plastic Art Toy Corp. (Plasco), located in East Rutherford and East Patterson, New Jersey, was begun in the 1940s by Vaughan D. Buckley. The firm first manufactured plastic dollhouse furniture around 1944 during World War II. In the late 1940s, the furniture came in boxed sets with the insides of the boxes printed to represent the rooms themselves. On this Plasco brochure from that period, the boxed 3/4" to one foot scaled living room furniture is shown placed in its "room." The seven-piece set included a television with rotating pictures. *Courtesy of Roy Specht.*

The American Toy & Furniture Co. placed a full page ad in the November 1945 issue of *Children's Activities* magazine to advertise their new line of Nancy Forbes "Dream House" furniture. Five rooms of furniture could be purchased for $6.00 by mail, or the sets sold for $1.00 each at retail stores. No child's room was offered in the newer line of 3/4" to one foot furniture (really a little smaller in scale.)

All of these early Plasco boxes are marked "Little Homemaker" on the top and include a trademark on the box of a little drummer boy. Marked on the base drum is "A Plasco Toy." These sets of furniture also included a separate paper rug to make the "room" complete. The bathroom pictured here included only six pieces. *Specht Collection.*

The boxed Plasco dining room of the period included nine pieces of furniture, while the kitchen box contained eleven pieces of plastic furniture. *Specht Collection.*

The bedroom furniture consisted of seven pieces of furniture. The furniture was also sold individually. *Specht Collection.*

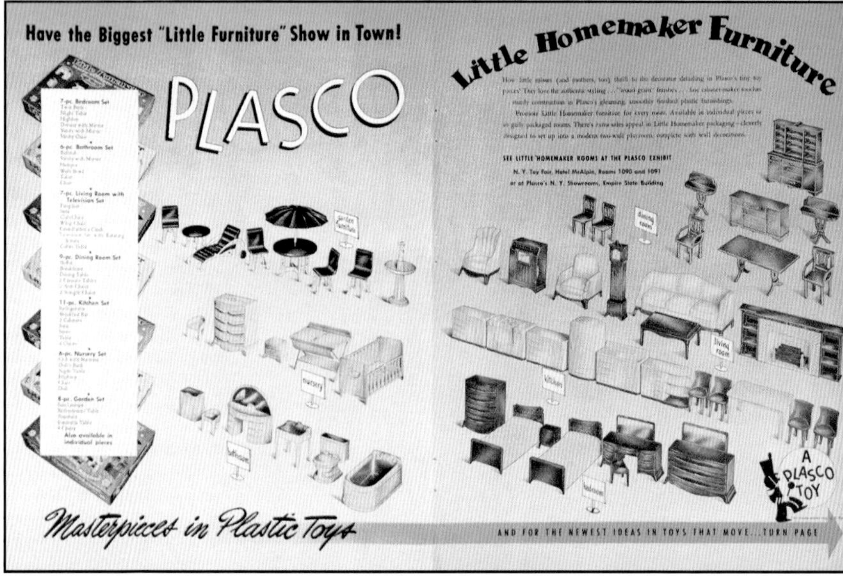

A Plasco brochure from a little later pictures all of the furniture individually. Besides the earlier sets, a garden set and a nursery set of furniture were also available. *Specht Collection.*

Left:
This Plasco brochure states that the "Plasco 'Little Homemaker' Furniture and 'Open House' Doll House were selected as the winners of the Toy Award in the Modern Plastics 1948 Competition sponsored by *Modern Plastics* magazine." The earlier "room" boxes were discontinued because the firm was marketing the new "Open House" dollhouse to use with the furniture. The ad copy reads "Built like the house of the future...Circular exterior. Easily the most popular doll house on the market." *Specht Collection.*

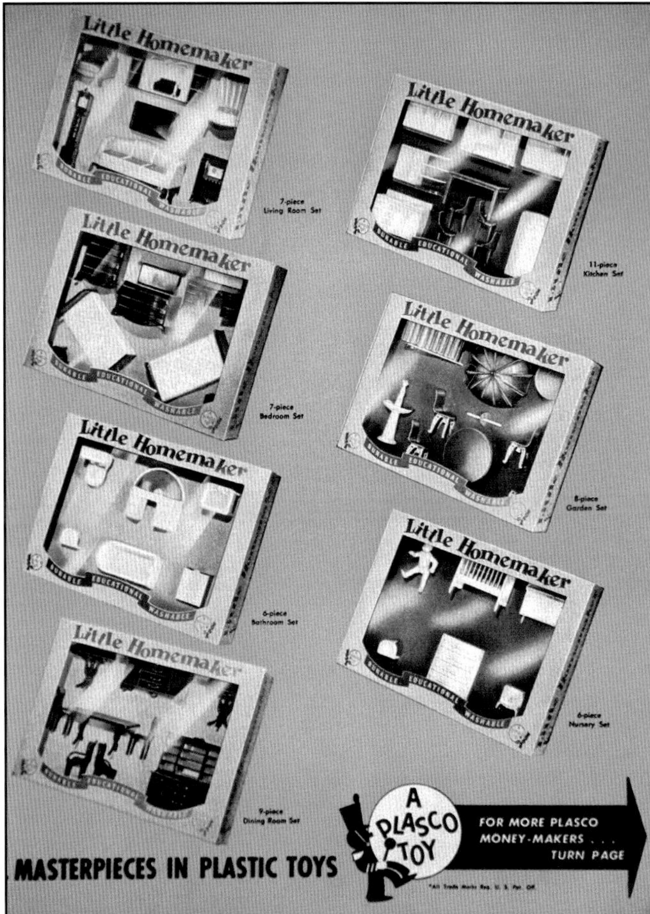

The new design of Plasco furniture boxes included a clear plastic front to reveal the furniture contained inside. In this circa 1948-49 brochure, seven different sets of furniture were offered for sale. *Specht Collection.*

The "Open House" dollhouse and five rooms of Plasco furniture were pictured in the Firestone catalog in 1948. It was issued by Sibley's Firestone Dealer Store in Little Falls, Minnesota. The six-room house was made of heavy pressed board with acetate panels. An upstairs terrace was also part of the design. The house measured 12.75" high x 23" in diameter and sold for $8.95. The ad copy indicated the house was sold furnished. Nine rooms of plastic furniture were also available from the Firestone catalog. They were priced at $1.00 each and included the dining room, living room, bedroom, music room, kitchen, lawn furniture, bathroom, day nursery, and night nursery. Neither the day or night nursery, the lawn furniture, or the kitchen are pictured. *Specht Collection.*

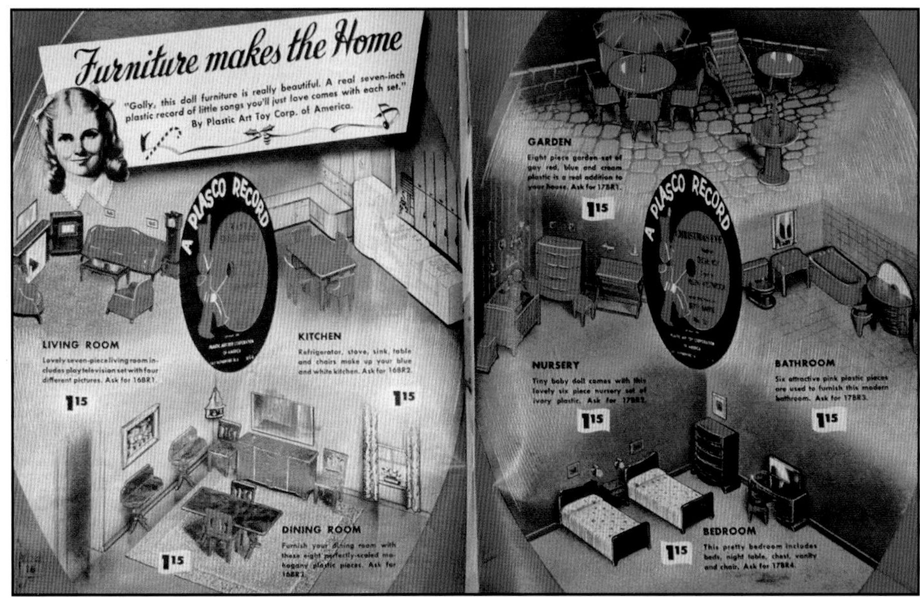

The Billy and Ruth catalog from 1949 featured a two-page spread of Plasco furniture that was packaged with a 7" plastic record which played children's tunes. Each set of furniture was priced at $1.15. Seven sets of furniture were pictured (no nursery or music room). *Courtesy of Marcie Tubbs. Photograph by Bob Tubbs.*

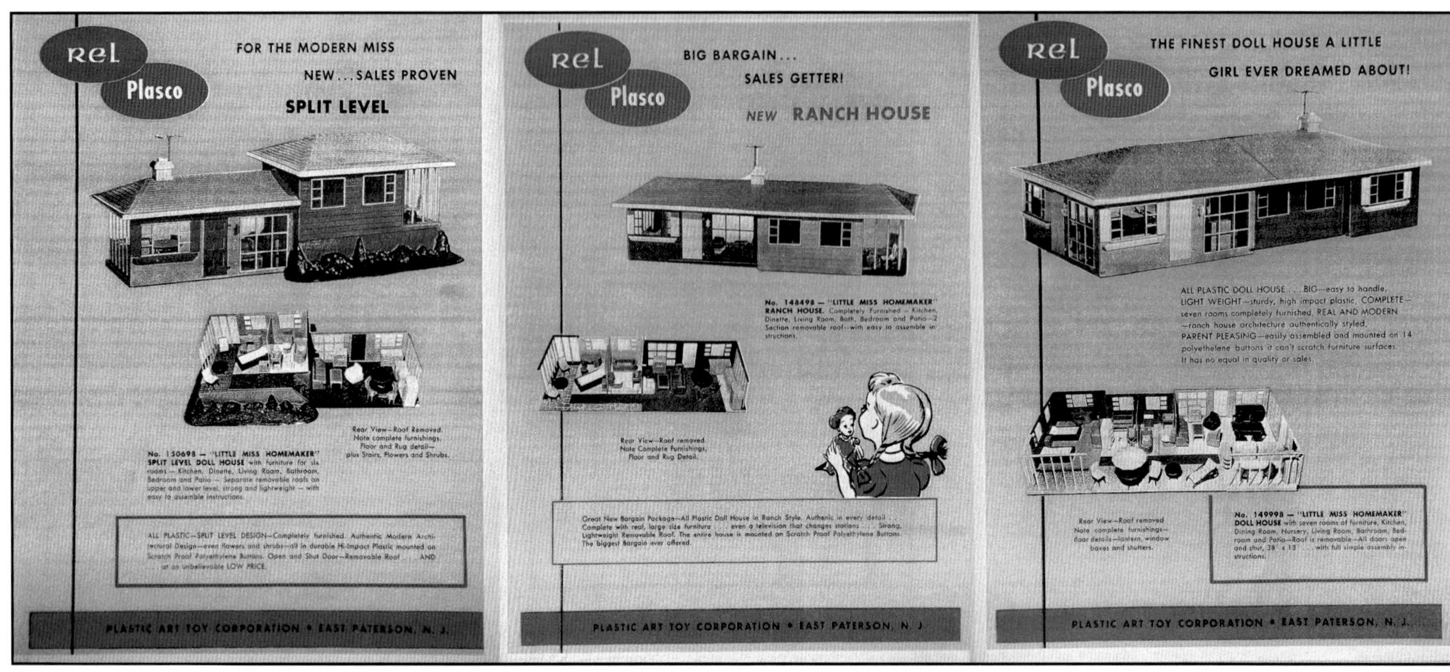

A Plasco brochure circa late 1950s advertised three different Plasco dollhouses. Included was this "Split Level" house which came furnished with furniture for six rooms. The furniture had been restyled using a cheaper version of the original pieces. Head and foot boards were removed from the beds, legs were eliminated from the living room sofa and chairs, and fewer pieces of furniture were produced. The same furnished house was advertised in the Sears Christmas catalog in 1957. It was priced at $6.21. The roofs were movable. The house was made of plastic mounted on scratch proof polyethylene buttons. *Courtesy of Roy Specht.*

A Ranch House was also part of the line. It included a television antenna on top of the roof. It, too, came furnished with the cheaper furnishings. It included furniture for a kitchen, dinette, living room, bath, bedroom, and patio. This roof was also removable. *Specht Collection.*

The third "All Plastic Doll House" pictured in the brochure came with seven rooms of furniture. Room for a nursery was provided for in this house. A television antenna was also to be placed on this roof, and the roof was removable for play. The house measured 38" wide x 18" deep. *Specht Collection.*

Brightly-painted plastic with landscaping, and flag-stoned terrace
D

This Plasco house was pictured in the General Merchandise Co. catalog in 1958. It is furnished with the more cheaply made plastic furniture. The house was produced with plastic construction and includes four furnished rooms and a terrace in back. The roof was removable and the house had permanently hinged walls. Furniture for a living room, bathroom, bedroom, and kitchen was included. The house measured 11.5" high x 34" wide x 14" deep and retailed for $7.98. See page 170 of *International Dollhouses* for a photograph of the actual house.

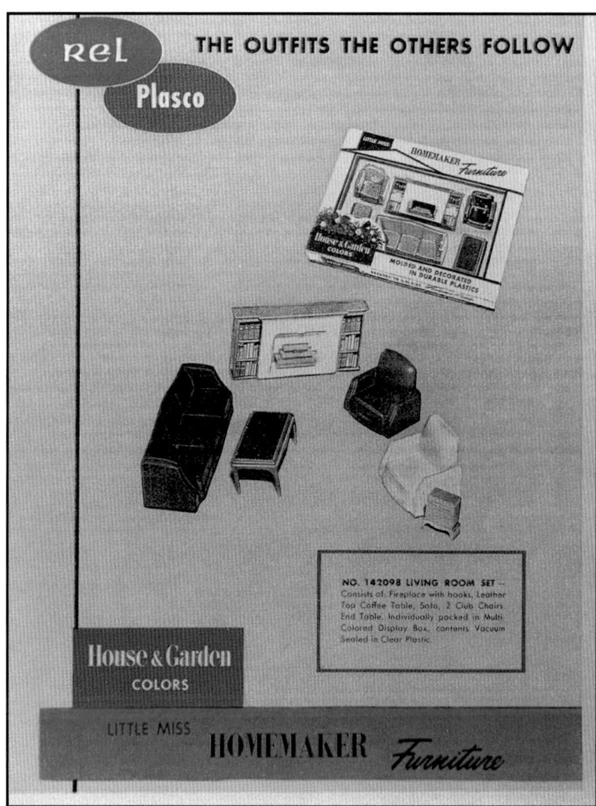

The furniture included in this later Plasco Brochure pictured the new living room furniture in "House and Garden Colors." The new box still carried the "Little Miss Homemaker" trademark. The bottoms had been removed from some pieces of furniture and the head and footboards were no longer included on the beds. This set includes only six pieces of furniture. Cards of this later furniture were sold labeled "Plastic Toy & Novelty Corp. Brooklyn, New York." Later versions also can be found with the package marked "REL Manufacturing Corp. East Patterson, New Jersey." *Specht Collection.*

Playsteel (National Can Corporation)

The Playsteel Colonial dollhouse was marketed by its maker, National Can Corp. of New York, beginning in 1948. This ad for the new house appeared in *Toys & Novelties* in February 1948. The all-metal house included five rooms decorated in nine colors. The box for the house could also be used as a yard. The house measured 19" high x 22" wide x 12" deep.

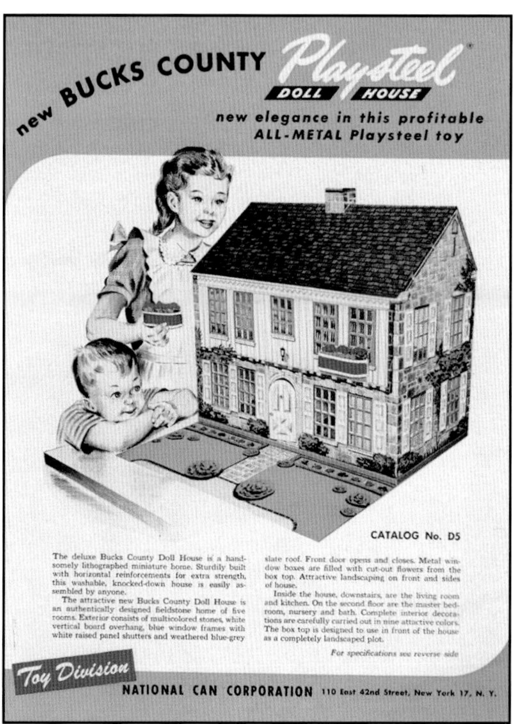

The July 1948 issue of *Toys & Novelties* pictured another similar Playsteel house using different outside decorations. It was called the Bucks County House. It was the same size as the Colonial house.

Both of the metal Playsteel houses included the same décor inside and were packaged in containers designed as landscaped plots. The houses were to be assembled by the consumer.

Renwal Manufacturing Co.

The Renwal plastic furniture was placed on the market in 1946. It was produced by the Renwal Manufacturing Co. located in Mineola, Long Island, New York. The firm was founded in 1939 by Irving Lawner (backward Renwal). This ad appeared in *Playthings* magazine in January 1946. It pictured the eight-piece kitchen and dining room sets. The furniture was boxed in sets under the "Jolly Twins" trade name.

BEAUTIFUL PLASTIC DOLL FURNITURE OUTFITS

PLASTIC KITCHEN SET

Cool white furniture in eight pieces. Each an excellent adaptation of actual modern kitchen equipment, including four white frame mahogany seat chairs, refrigerator, kitchen table, kitchen sink and midget stove that will delight every child. Eight pieces in set in attractive box with room setting. Box size 12½ x 9 x 3".

No. 17A1957—Doz. $11.20.
Less 2%, net........ $10.98

PLASTIC LIVING ROOM SET

Cozy, comfortable living room set of sturdy colorful plastic, consisting of floor lamp, dainty table lamp, cocktail table, end table, club chair, barrel chair, sofa, radio, grand piano and bench, and fireplace. Her dolly's home is not complete without this new colorful plastic furniture wonder. 13 pieces in set with attractive room setting. Box measures 14 x 10½ x 3".

No. 17A1954—Doz. $19.20. Less 2%, net........ $18.82

PLASTIC BATHROOM SET

Smooth, glistening, frost white set, perfectly molded. Including oblong bathtub, full shaped bath sink, toilet and hamper. So cleverly designed it is really a joy for dolly. Four pices in set with attractive room setting. Box size 10¼ x 7½ x 3".

No. 17A1956—Doz. $8.00.
Less 2% net........ $7.84

PLASTIC DINING ROOM SET

Handsomely finished plastic dining room set with a Duncan Phyfe table, breakfront, four mahogany frame, white-seat chairs, server and buffet beautifully finished and not lacking in one detail. Eight pieces in set in attractive box with room setting. Box size 12½ x 9 x 3".

No. 17A1953—Doz. $11.20. Less 2%, net........ $10.98

PLASTIC DINING ROOM SET

A complete dining room, 4 chairs, table, china closet and buffet, all perfectly scaled and authentically styled after the real thing. Attractively packaged in many-colored printed box, size 12" x 11¼" x 2¾".

No. 17A1908
Doz. $8.00.
Less 2%, net.... $7.84

PLASTIC BEDROOM SET

Perfectly detailed bedroom set consisting of twin beds, Vanity and Dresser with frame and mirror, Night Table, and High Boy. Drawers have tiny nobs and slide in and out. Vanity has matching Dressing Bench. Seven pieces in each set with attractive room setting. Box measures 12 x 9 x 3".

No. 17A1955—Doz. $13.50. Less 2%, net........ $13.23

Chicago Wholesale Co., 230 South Franklin St., Chicago 6, Illinois Page 151

The Chicago Wholesale Co. Fall and Winter catalog from 1946-47 carried a full page of pictures showing the new Renwal 3/4" to one foot furniture. Cardboard rooms accompanied the Jolly Twins boxed sets of furniture. In addition to the kitchen and dining rooms, the living room, bathroom, and bedroom were also shown. *Courtesy of Marge Meisinger.*

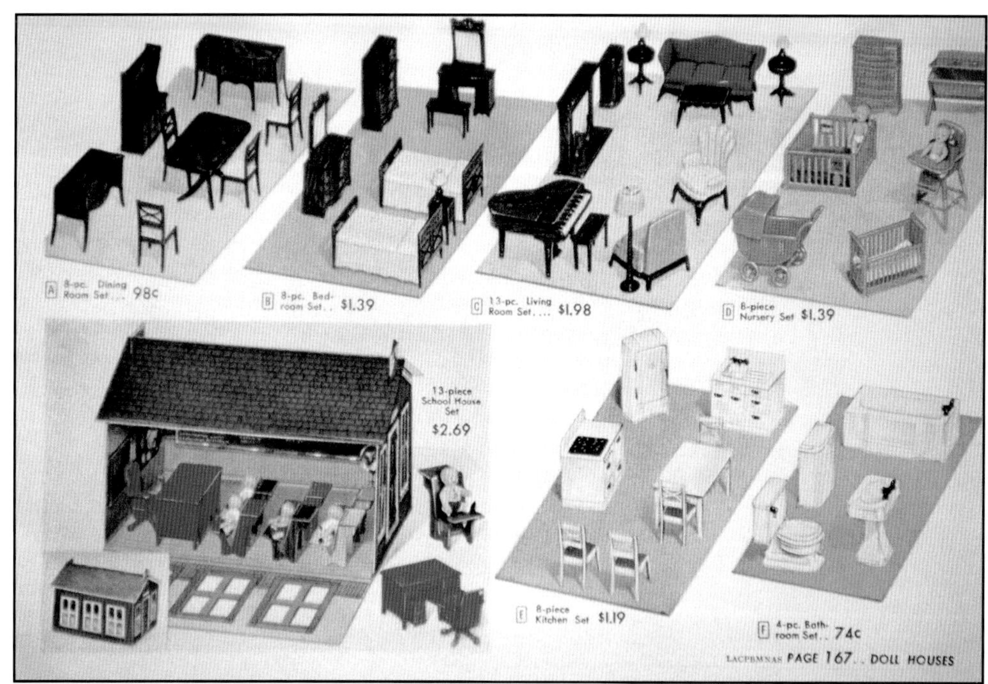

The Sears Christmas catalog from 1947 also offered the Renwal plastic furniture and included the new nursery furniture as well as the earlier rooms. The sets were priced from 74 cents for the bathroom to $1.98 for the living room. The nursery cost $1.39 for eight pieces (including two babies). The Renwal School is also pictured. It cost $2.69 for a teacher's desk and chair, six school desks, four pupils, and the cardboard school.

This 1948 Woolworth's ad pictured the Play Steel house priced at $4.59 and eight different sets of Renwal plastic furniture priced at $1.00 each. Individual pieces could be purchased, ranging in price from 5 cents to 39 cents each.

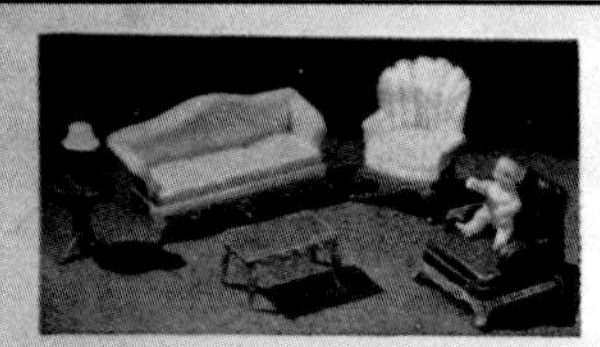

No. 1038
PLASTIC DOLL HOUSE LIVING ROOM FURNITURE

Beautifully made, exquisite little pieces that will thrill any little girl. Set consists of sofa, coffee table, end table, table lamp, club chair, easy chair and tiny doll. In acetate window gift box. **$1.25.**

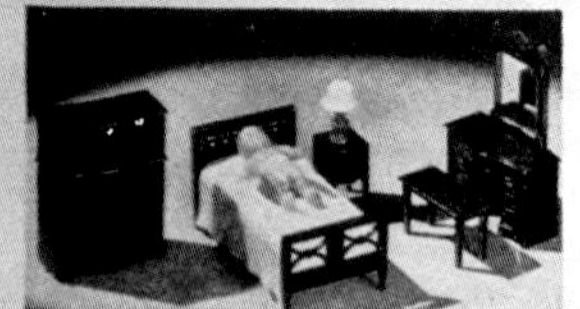

No. 1039
DOLL HOUSE BED ROOM FURNITURE

Made to scale of colorful, durable plastic, these lovely little pieces are perfect for your little housekeeper. Set includes bed, vanity, vanity bench, night table, table lamp and doll. In acetate window gift box. **$1.25.**

No. 1040 DOLL HOUSE KITCHEN

Another set that is standard equipment for any little girl who plays house! Made of plastic in contrasting varying colors. It is both decorative and durable. Set: refrigerator, cooking range, table, 4 chairs and doll. In window gift box. **$1.25.**

No. 1041 DOLL HOUSE BATHROOM

Complete to the last detail—all pieces made to scale. Set includes bath tub, sink, toilet, laundry hamper, weighing scale, stool, night table and doll. In window gift box. **$1.25.**

Mayfair Gifts, located in Forest Hills, New York City offered four sets of Renwal furniture for sale in their 1948-49 catalog. The sets sold for $1.25 each and included the living room, bedroom, kitchen, and bathroom. *Courtesy of Marge Meisinger.*

This Dow Plastics ad from the December 1949 *Parents* magazine included several pieces of Renwal furniture, including the sewing machine, child's rocking chair, stroller, garbage can, and dust pan. The Ferris wheel was made by Thomas Manufacturing Co. *Courtesy of Judy Mosholder.*

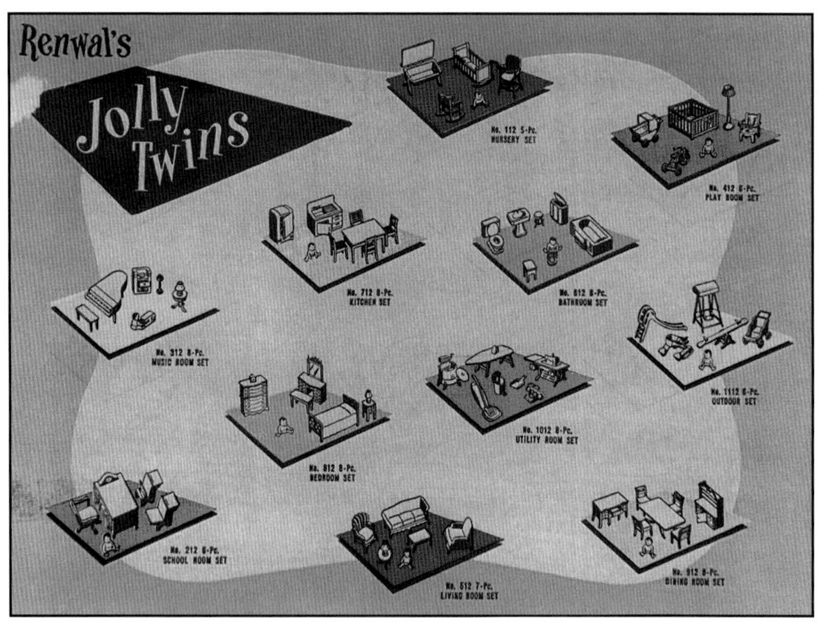

This later Jolly Twins box pictures all of the furniture sets made at that time. An outdoor set which included a slide, teeter totter, swing, kiddie car, baby and stroller is especially desirable for collectors. The utility room set offered a "working" sewing machine and washing machine as well as an iron, ironing board, vacuum cleaner, telephone, garbage can, and dustpan. *Courtesy of Judy Mosholder.*

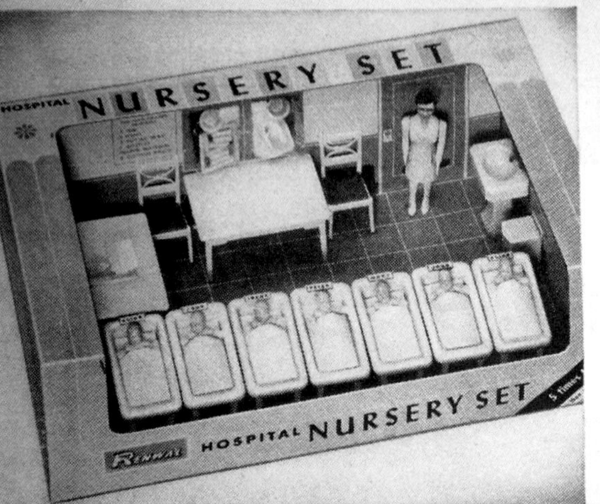

Fun! Educational!

HOSPITAL NURSERY SET

Children aren't usually allowed in hospitals, but now they can play with and nurse a whole nursery full of "new" babies. 7 hospital cribs, 7 baby dolls, blankets, tables, chairs, sink, night table, scale, bottles, pans, everything to make nursery "real" to little girls from 4 to 10. Plastic, 5 times tougher than ordinary toys. $2.98.

RENWAL MANUFACTURING CO., INC.
Toyland Park, Mineola, N. Y.

In addition to the basic sets of furniture, Renwal produced a variety of different packages combining their furniture with new products. This circa mid 1950s ad is for the "Hospital Nursery Set." It included seven hospital cribs and baby dolls along with blankets, tables, chairs, sink, night table, scale, bottles, and pans. A "nurse" was also included. The toy sold for $2.98 and was first introduced in 1954. A smaller version was marketed in 1956. *Courtesy of Carol Stevenson.*

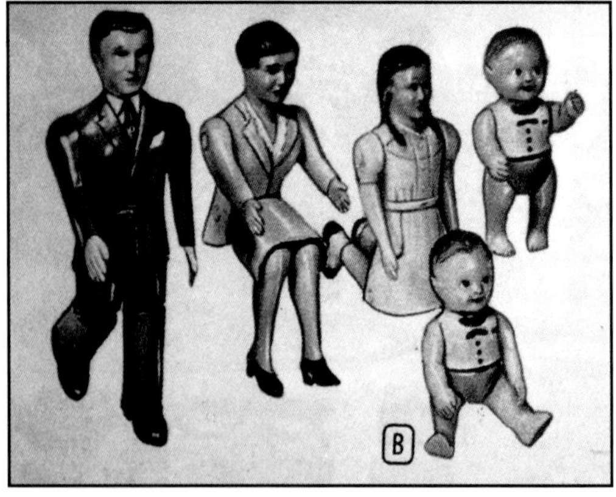

The popular jointed Renwal family of dolls was offered for sale in the Montgomery Ward Christmas catalog in 1952. The five-piece plastic family included the father, mother, daughter, and two babies (no son). The father was listed at 4.25" tall. The five-piece set sold for 95 cents.

Ready-to-decorate

DOLL HOUSE FURNITURE

A whole doll house full of furniture. 5 rooms, 29 pieces, to decorate to suit a little girl's own tastes. Transfer sheet with many designs included plus brush and harmless water-soluble paint which can be washed off for repainting. Furniture is new plastic, 5 times tougher than ordinary plastic toys. For ages 5 to 10. $4.98.

RENWAL MANUFACTURING CO., INC.
Toyland Park, Mineola, N. Y.

Renwal advertised their "Ready-to-decorate" boxed set of furniture in a special advertising section of *Life* magazine circa 1950s. Twenty-nine pieces of furniture were included in the set along with transfer sheets which featured designs and water colors to use to decorate the furniture. It sold for $4.98. *Stevenson Collection.*

The 1955-56 Toy Yearbook from Norberry's Toy Headquarters in West Seattle, Washington included a "Renwal Decorated Play Furniture Set." The furniture came in a dollhouse type box with decorated walls and floors for six rooms. The furniture included decal type decorations and workable parts (opening doors and drawers). There were forty-five pieces in the set, which sold for $8.95. Individual room sets were also available for $1.49 each. *Courtesy of Roy Specht.*

Campbell Kids PLAY FURNITURE

Complete 6-room set! Doors and drawers open, just like real furniture. Set contains sofa, club chair, barrel chair, 2 end tables, cocktail table, 4 table lamps, 2 floor lamps, dining table, china closet, server, 4 chairs, 2 beds, vanity, dresser, night table, highboy, stove, sink, refrigerator, table, 4 kitchen chairs, bathtub, bathroom sink, toilet, hamper, toydee chair, cradle, baby bath, carriage, night table, rocking chair, play pen, baby doll. Keeps tiny homemakers happily occupied for hours and hours. Educational, too! And you get all *45-pieces for only $9.00.*

RENWAL MANUFACTURING CO., INC.
Toyland Park, Mineola, New York

This "Campbell Kids Play Furniture" set was advertised in the special toy advertising section of *Life* magazine in 1955. It appears to be the same six room "house" advertised in the 1955-56 Toy Yearbook, with the addition of a Campbell Kids logo on the top of the box. The set sold for $9.00. Renwal plastic furniture continued to be made until the early 1960s. The company was sold in the early 1970s. *Courtesy of Marcie Tubbs. Photograph by Bob Tubbs.*

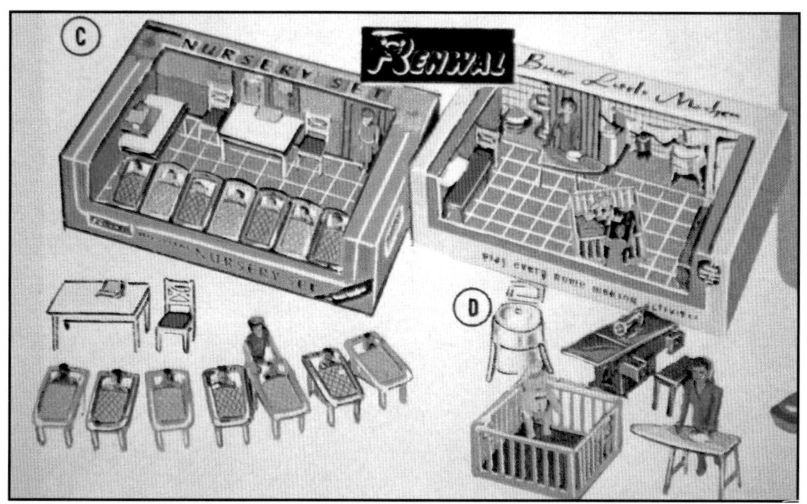

Left:
The 1955-56 Toy Yearbook also offered the Renwal hospital nursery set for $2.98 and the "Busy Little Mother Set," also priced at $2.98. The Little Mother boxed set included a washing machine, sewing machine, iron and ironing board, playpen, table, chairs, bench, table lamps, telephone, toilet, bathroom sink, garbage can, dust pan, vacuum sweeper, and hamper, plus mother, girl, and baby dolls. *Specht Collection.*

Miscellaneous

Life magazine featured an unusual article on dollhouses circa 1940. Among the houses shown was a Southern Colonial Mansion that was priced at $98 furnished. A full page photograph of a variety of furniture was also included in the article. Tynietoy pieces, as well as Lynnfield furniture, was pictured. The very modern house shown here was also featured. It sold for $25.00 unfurnished. Several pieces of 3/4" to one foot scaled Strombecker furniture can be seen on the open spaces of this house. Unidentified porch furniture decorates the front. *Courtesy of Carol Stevenson.*

5-Room Doll House With Furniture
She'll jump with joy when she gets this adorable 5-room doll house, completely furnished. Charming house in latest design, made of gypsum pressed wood—strong and practically unbreakable—easy to set up. Measures 24¾x16½x11½ inches high. House is enameled white with blue stripes and smart red shutters. Furniture in colors to harmonize includes: 4-piece bedroom set, 4-piece bathroom set, 4-piece kitchen set, 4-piece living room set, 5-piece dining room set. Shpg. wt. 13 lbs. 2 oz.
45F5J 8766..............................2.98
LOW!

This unidentified dollhouse was offered for sale in the Chicago based Spiegel catalog during the 1942 holiday season. The five-room house was made of Gypsum pressed wood and measured 11.5" high x 24.75" wide x 16.5" deep. The house came furnished with Tootsietoy metal furniture from an earlier period. It sold for $2.98. *Courtesy of Marge Meisinger.*

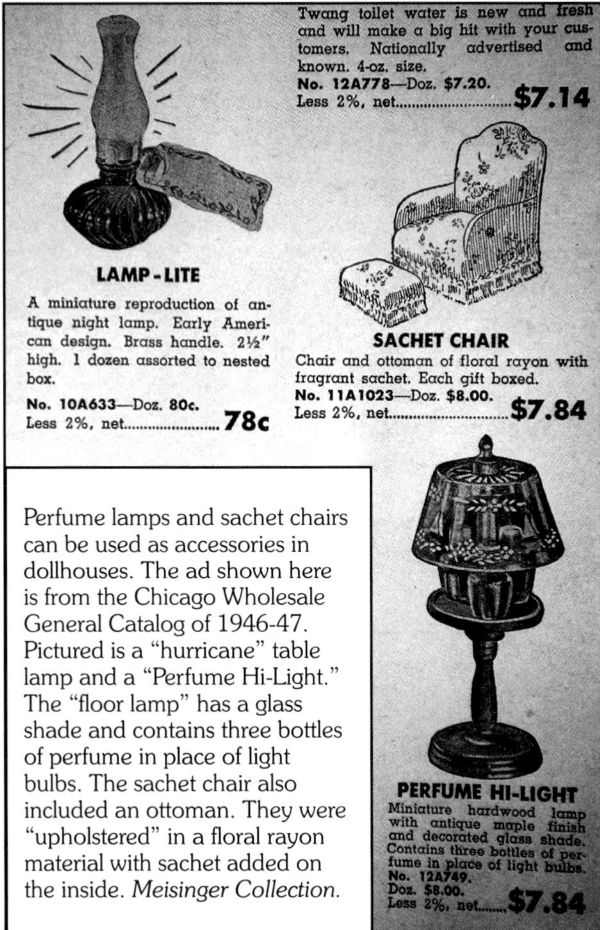

Perfume lamps and sachet chairs can be used as accessories in dollhouses. The ad shown here is from the Chicago Wholesale General Catalog of 1946-47. Pictured is a "hurricane" table lamp and a "Perfume Hi-Light." The "floor lamp" has a glass shade and contains three bottles of perfume in place of light bulbs. The sachet chair also included an ottoman. They were "upholstered" in a floral rayon material with sachet added on the inside. *Meisinger Collection.*

WALLS IN THIS
HOUSE WITH
D FURNITURE!
d Venetian
n the floor!
real home.
s). Houses
here at $3.
$198
$3 VALUE
urniture. Well made, bright-
ROOM: Sofa, arm chair, foot
randfather clock, vase, end
G ROOM: Table, 4 chairs, 2
HEN: Table, 2 chairs, range,
M: Chair, bed, vanity, night-
lesticks, clock. BATHROOM:
oilet, scale. Dolls not in-
ipped flat; easily assembled.
t. 5 lbs..............$1.98
es of Wood Furniture
. 12 oz............ 1.29
Doll House Family 29c
7 tiny Dolls to live in your doll house. Papa, Mama, Aunt, Maid and Servant, each 3⅛ inches tall. Boy and Girl 2⅝ inches tall. Bisque, with jointed arms and legs. Painted hair. Real clothes . . . not painted on. Made in Japan.
48 T 675—7 Dolls. Wt. 10 oz.....29c

This unidentified dollhouse family was pictured in the 1940 Montgomery Ward Christmas catalog. The dolls were "Made in Japan" and ranged in size from 2.5" to a little over 3" tall. Included were a Papa, Mama, Aunt, Maid, Servant, Boy, and Girl. The bisque dolls had jointed arms and legs and real clothes. The set sold for 29 cents. *Meisinger Collection.*

Doll House Dolls Added to Grandmother Stover's Family

GRANDMOTHER STOVER'S, INC., 1504 W. First Ave., Columbus 8, Ohio, is introducing a complete family of doll house dolls to be sold through toy and department stores.

These dolls, unique in appearance and method of manufacture, are made completely by hand. The bodies are made of cloth over a wire frame which permits them to bend into any desired position for doll house play. The features are embroidered and the hair is either real hair or yarn. They are completely attired from underthings to leather slippers.

The father, mother, mammy, nurse and maid are approximately 5" high; the children 2½", and the baby 1½".

This nationally advertised line of miniatures now comprises more than 100 items, covering practically every doll house accessory with the exception of furniture. All of the items are carded and heat-sealed in cellophane to protect them against handling, dust, or moisture. The line carries the *Parents' Magazine* Commendation Seal, and dealers report it has proved equally popular with young doll housekeepers and miniature collectors.

A new catalog illustrating all of the Grandmother Stover miniatures in actual size is available, and will be sent upon request.

TOYS *and* NOVELTIES—*March, 1947*

This set of dolls was advertised in *Toys & Novelties* magazine of March 1947. They were to be carried by the popular Grandmother Stover's firm as well as in toy and department stores. The bodies were made of cloth over a wire frame. The hair was fashioned from either yarn or real hair and their faces were embroidered. The dolls came completely dressed. The larger dolls were 5" tall while the children measured 2.5" and the baby 1.5." *From the collection of Marcie Tubbs. Photograph by Bob Tubbs.*

Another set of unidentified dollhouse dolls was offered in the Montgomery Ward 1943 Christmas catalog. The dolls were made of wood and cardboard and ranged in size from 2.25" (Baby) to 4" (Mother, Father, Nurse). The hand painted dolls came fully dressed with yarn hair and jointed arms and legs that allowed them to stand or sit. Each pair of dolls (Nurse and Baby, Father and Mother, or Brother and Sister) sold for $1.79.

Gerber Plastic Co., located in St. Louis, Missouri, advertised their new "Play Dolls" in *Toys & Novelties* in September 1948. The plastic dolls sold for as little as 20 cents each or as a boxed set of four for 98 cents. The dolls were to be used in dollhouses and came in sitting or standing positions. Without hand painted clothes and features, the dolls cost only 10 cents each. The standing dolls measured a little over 3.5" tall.

1950s Advertisements

With Eisenhower serving as president, the 1950s are remembered as good "status quo" years for most people in the United States. The same was true in the dollhouse industry. After the years of rationing and doing without during the war years of the 1940s, prosperity was back for the first time since before the Depression of the 1930s. World War II veterans were married with new families and it was time to spoil the children. Most little girls received at least one metal Marx dollhouse, furnished with inexpensive plastic furniture, during these years. So many different models were marketed, it would be hard to count them all. T. Cohn also continued to produce these types of houses furnished with their "Superior" line of plastic furniture. Although the nicer Plasco and Renwal pieces of furniture were still available, the houses that sold completely furnished must have been easier (and cheaper) for parents to purchase. These types of houses continued to dominate throughout the decade.

The only real innovations seemed to come in the dollhouse dolls line. The most interesting were the jointed plastic dolls called Twinky dolls by their creator Ethel R. Strong. In 1950, Grandmother Stover's catalog offered the dolls for sale and increased their exposure. The dolls were priced from $1.00 to $3.50 each. The Flagg Doll Company of Jamaica Plain, Massachusetts was advertising their "Flagg Flexible Play Dolls" in sizes that could be used in dollhouses during the decade of the 1950s. They were sold in a variety of family groups. They measured from 1.5" to 4.5" tall. German Caco dollhouse dolls were also available in the 1950s. These family groups could be purchased in 3/4" to one foot scale or 1" to one foot scale.

At the end of the 1950s, there was one new innovation that foretold changes in the industry for the 1960s. In order to address the new popularity of dolls 8" to 11" tall, houses and furniture appeared on the market to accommodate these larger dolls. Some of these houses were made of heavy cardboard (Fibre-Bilt) and others were made of wood (Hall's Lifetime Toys). Furniture also had to be manufactured in these larger sizes and Keystone, Strombecker, and Halls all tried to fill the void.

The advertisements in this chapter will reflect these changes as manufacturers tried to adjust their products to keep up with the times.

Caco Dolls

These German Caco dollhouse dolls labeled "Peasant Family" were advertised in the FAO Schwarz Christmas catalog in 1959. They ranged in size from 2.25" to 4" tall. The dolls had molded hair, metal feet and hands, and heads made of a composition type material. The set sold for $3.95.

A set of Caco dolls in a larger size was also featured in the 1959 Schwarz catalog. They ranged in size from 3.5" to 5" tall and were priced at $5.95 for a set of six dolls. Besides the usual family, a maid and baby were also included.

Right:
A newer style set of Caco dolls was advertised in the Mark Farmer catalog in 1968. Eight different dolls were pictured, including a father, mother, grandmother, grandfather, baby, and two little girls. The mother, grandmother, and one of the girls had "real" hair while the hair on the other dolls was molded. All of the dolls were 1" to one foot in scale and were priced from $1.50 to $3.00 each. They ranged in size from 2.5" (baby) to 5.5" (adults). *Courtesy of Roy Specht.*

Child Life Toys, Inc.

This "Dollyhome" dollhouse was produced by Child Life Toys, Inc. (located in Seattle, Washington) during the late 1950s. The advertisement comes from the General Merchandise Co. in 1958. The "Cedarwood Ranch-style" house was scaled for 8"-10" tall dolls. The house had four rooms, including a living room, bedroom, bathroom, and kitchen. It came with a built-in wardrobe closet, kitchen and bathroom fixtures, a television set, Swedish coffee table, dining room table and chairs, bed, bureau, chair and couch. It measured 12" high x 42.25" wide x 24.25" deep and sold for $17.95. The house also came in a smaller size of 26.5" wide x 16.5" deep.

Fibre-Bilt Toys

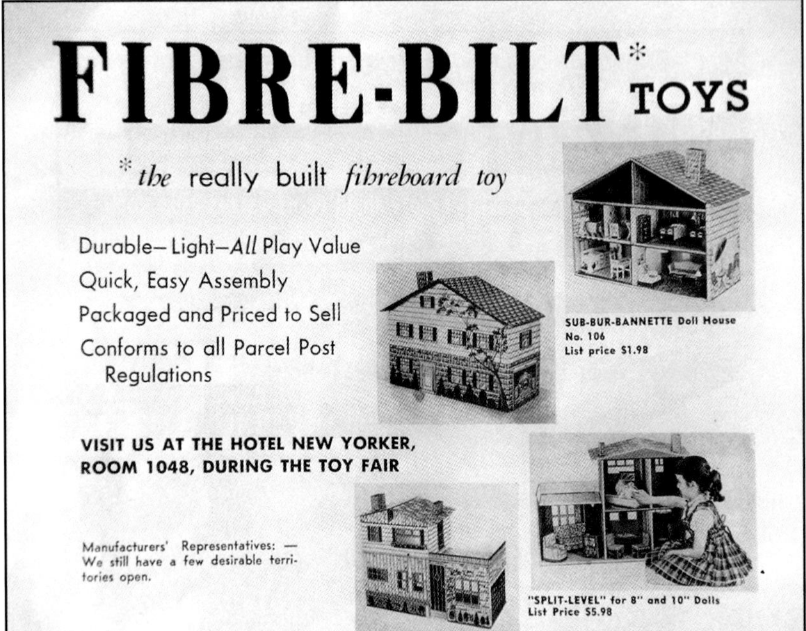

This ad for Fibre-Bilt Toys appeared in *Playthings* magazine in March 1958. Fibre-Bilt was a division of the Atlantic Container Corp. from Long Island City, New York. Two dollhouses were included in the full page ad. One was the SUB-BUR-BANNETTE dollhouse, which included five rooms plus two attic rooms and had a list price of $1.98. It was made of corrugated cardboard and was decorated on both the inside and outside of the house. It measured 16" high x 21.5" wide x 9" deep. (See actual house on page 211 of *Antique & Collectible Dollhouses*). The other Fibre-Bilt house featured in the ad was a "Split-level" model that could be used with 8" to 10" dolls. It contained five rooms and the list price was $5.98.

Flagg Dolls

Flagg Flexible Dolls from Jamaica Plain, Massachusetts advertised their dolls in this ad from *American Home* magazine in November 1952. The firm had been producing these flexible plastic dollhouse dolls since the late 1940s. The ad offered a four-piece family set for $3.75 with sizes ranging from 3.5" to 4.5" tall. The firm also offered a 7" Ballerina and her partner for $2.00 plus a 7" Rumba Dancer and partner for $2.50. The consumer could write for a catalog showing "70 Originals."

Flexible Plastic DOLLS by FLAGG
WILL BEND AND HOLD LIFE-LIKE POSITIONS!
DOLLHOUSE DOLLS—Educational—realistic—children love and learn with these almost human dolls. Hand painting and handmade costumes add to realism. Washable—durable. 4½" Father, Mother; 3½" Son, Daughter; 1¼" Baby—all in Dollhouse Box $4.95 ppd. 10 piece set illustrated—$10.95 ppd.
8" DANCING DOLLS—in Beautiful, Authentic, Foreign Costumes. Specify countries desired: Cuban, Scottish, Egyptian, Hawaiian, Swiss, Haitian, Spanish, Gypsy, Greek, Panamanian, Russian, Chinese, Balinese, Irish, Japanese, Dutch, French, Eskimo, Israeli, Can-Can, Ballerina and Drum Majorette $2.95 ea. ppd. Collector's set of 8 assorted dolls—$21.00 ppd.
Renee—8" CAMPUS QUEEN WARDROBE DOLL: Snap-on washable costumes. Wash and set hair—removable high-heeled shoes. RENEE—in bra, panties and shoes—$1.50. A—Basic tan coat, matching hat & bag. Hi-heels & nylons. Dressed—$3.00. Outfit only—$1.50. B—Softly tailored print PJ's, matching robe, lace trim. Dressed—$3.00. Outfit only—$1.50. C—Short tennis skirt—a whirl of pleats—sleeveless sailor blouse, panties. Jacket, tennis racket & case. Dressed—$3.00. Outfit only—$1.50. D—Exquisite Formal Gown of Taffeta & lace, fluffy petticoat, lace stole, clutch bag, hi-heels, nylons. Dressed—$3.50. Outfit only—$2.00. E—Sleek cotton tapered slacks, print over-blouse, hair tie, sunglasses. Dressed—$2.50. Outfit only—$1.00. F—Classic white felt blazer, pleated plaid skirt, tailored jersey, hi-heels and bag. Dressed—$3.50. Outfit only—$2.00. G—Sleek jersey top, 5 gored swirling gay felt skirt, organdy petticoat with lace trim, kerchief, hi-heels, nylons. Dressed—$3.00. Outfit only—$1.50.
SEND 10¢ FOR New Catalog OF OVER 100 DOLLS
FLAGG FLEXIBLE DOLLS
BOX 205-MC • JAMAICA PLAIN • MASS.
A
B
C
D
E
F
G
137

This Flagg Flexible Dolls ad dates from 1959-60 when it appeared in the *McCalls Needlework* book. It offered the ten-piece set of dollhouse dolls pictured at the top of the page for a price of $10.95. The larger dolls were listed as 8" tall and included a "Campus Queen Wardrobe Doll." She could be purchased dressed in a variety of outfits for $4.00 or wearing only underwear and shoes for $1.50. All of her many outfits could be purchased separately, priced from $1.00 to $3.50 each. The company catalog contained over one hundred dolls.

Flexible DOLLHOUSE DOLLS

Children love—and learn—with these almost human dolls. Soft plastic bodies can be bent into 1000 life-like positions—sitting, standing, dancing, etc. Hand painting and handmade, authentic costumes add to realistic appearance. Washable—durable. 4½" parents; 3½" children; 1¼" baby. Dollhouse box. $5.00 ppd. 10 pc. set (shown) $11.95 ppd. Large scale family dolls (Father 6")—$6.95 ppd. 10 pc. set—$15.95 ppd.

New! NATIONALITY DOLLS

42 AUTHENTIC COSTUMES

Exquisite, handpainted dolls; lovely vinyl hair; authentically detailed costumes. 7" flexible bodies retain any position. CHOICE: Austria, Korea, France, Turkey, Arabia, Mexico, Lebanon, Holland, Switzerland, Panama, Czechoslovakia, Italy, Port de France, China, Sweden, Haiti, Hawaii, Ireland, Germany, Orient, Norway, Calypso, Eskimo, Egypt, Russia, Scotland, Greece, Spain, Israel, India, Denmark, Philippine, Bali, Poland, Argentina.

ONLY $2.95 ea. ppd. Collector's set of 8 —$21.00

SEND 10¢ FOR NEW color catalog showing over 100 dolls.

FLAGG *Flexible Dolls*

BOX 205-10, JAMAICA PLAIN, MASS.

This Flagg ad appeared in the *McCalls Needlework* catalog for 1963-1964. A set of larger scale dollhouse dolls was offered in this ad, with a father 6" tall. A set of parents, two children, and perhaps a baby in this larger scale sold for $6.95. This size Flagg dollhouse family is hard to find. Nationality Dolls in the 7" size were available in forty-two different costumes for $2.95 each or a collector's set of eight for $21.00.

Members of the doll-house set bend into lifelike positions. Of flexible plastic, packed in doll-house box. Dad stands 6 in. tall; $5.98, ppd. Younkers, Des Moines, Ia.

Left:
The larger scaled set of Flagg dollhouse dolls was also advertised in the November 1961 issue of *Better Homes and Gardens*. The set (with a 6" father) could be purchased for $5.98 from Younkers in Des Moines, Iowa. The hair styles on these larger dolls are different than those used on the smaller dollhouse dolls.

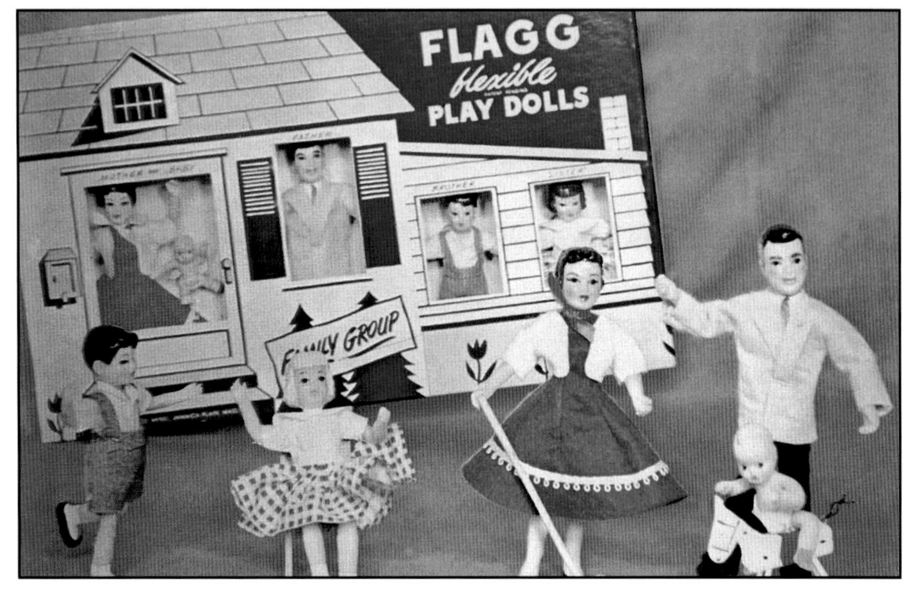

This Flagg Doll postcard, circa 1960s, pictures the larger 1" to one foot scaled dollhouse family of dolls (father 6" tall). The hair colors of the mother and daughter apparently varied from blonde to brown in the various sets. The family sold for $6.95. The smaller scale family (father 4.5") was priced at $4.95. *Courtesy of Judy Mosholder.*

Advertisement for the Flagg Nationality Dolls, circa 1960s. The dolls were listed as 8" tall and came in seventy different costumes. The Flagg firm was sold in 1973 and the new owners closed the business in 1985. *Mosholder Collection.*

Carl Forslund Inc.

Brochure from Carl Forslund, Inc. of Grand Rapids, Michigan advertising "Quaint American Miniatures" made by Hilleary House of Cleveland, Ohio. The furniture was made of cherry with working parts. The pieces were marked with a stamp reading "Copied exclusively for Carl Forslund by Hilleary House." There were fifteen pieces offered for sale, priced from $3.95 to $14.95 for each piece. *Courtesy of Leslie and Joanne Payne.*

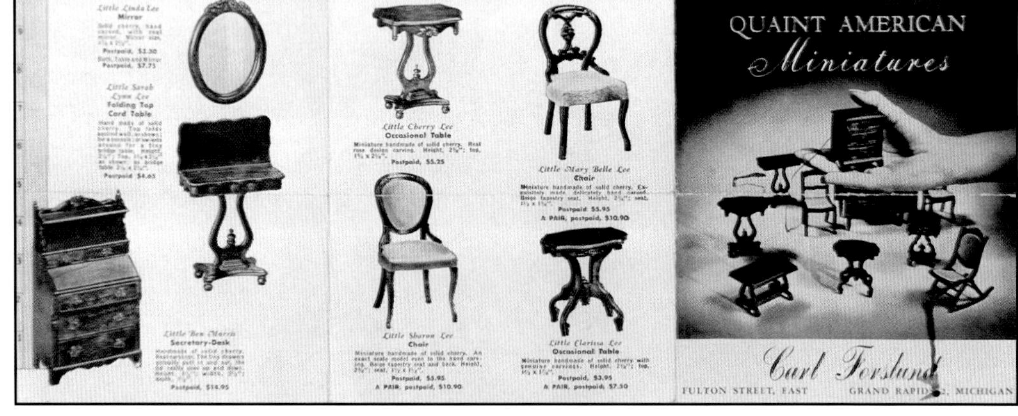

The second page of the circa 1950 brochure offered the whole collection for $77.65. A shadow box was sent free with a $15 purchase. The hand made furniture was 1" to one foot in scale. *Payne Collection.*

Grandmother Stover's Inc.

This Grandmother Stover's Inc., advertisement appeared in *Toys and Novelties* in March 1947. The dollhouse miniature firm was founded by John Stover in Columbus, Ohio. The copy in this ad reads "For the past 4 years, these nationally advertised Made-in-America miniatures have been the fastest selling line in leading toy and department stores." There were 125 different carded items in the line at that time. Pictured in the ads are telephones, groceries, dishes, clocks, pictures, a salad set, and much more. *Courtesy of Judy Mosholder.*

Left:
The Grandmother Stover firm issued several catalogs picturing their products. This one dates from 1950. *Courtesy of Marcie Tubbs. Photograph by Bob Tubbs.*

Twinky dolls marketed by Ethel R. Strong, of Lynnfield, Massachusetts, beginning in 1946 were featured in a two-page insert of the 1950s Grandmother Stover's catalog. The jointed plastic dolls are in 1" to 1 foot scale with the father measuring 6" tall. The special dolls that could be purchased from Grandmother Stover in the 1950s catalog included a nurse and maid for $2.50 each, a bridal couple for $3.50 each, and an aunt and uncle for $3.00 each. *Tubbs Collection.*

All of the Twinky dolls had painted features, molded hair and removable clothing. The family of dolls included a baby ($1.00), boy and girl ($1.50 each), and a mother and father ($2.25 each). *Tubbs Collection.*

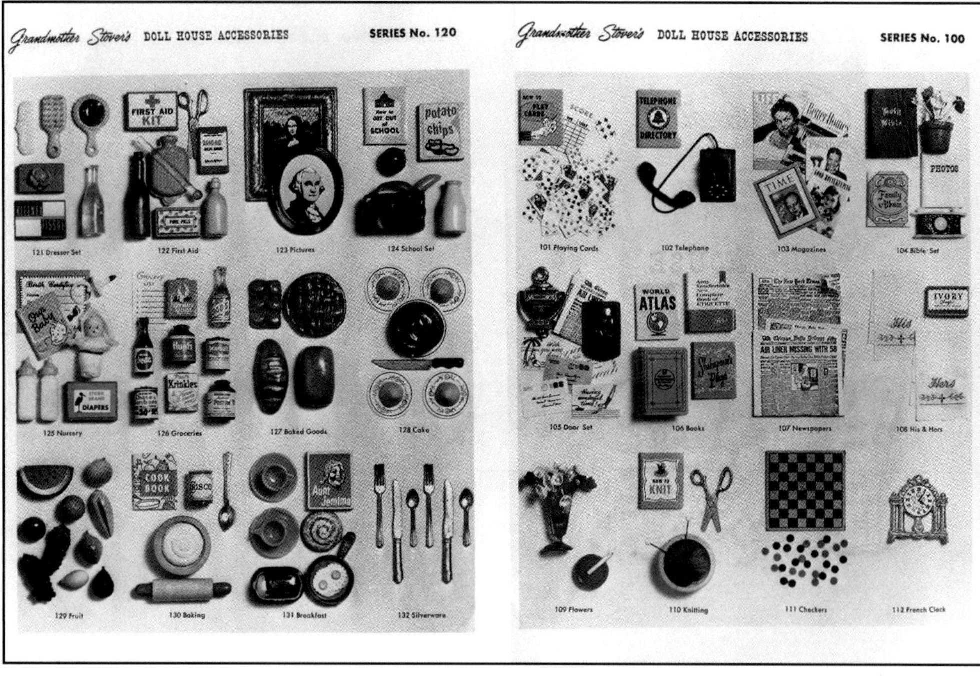

Two pages from a later (circa early 1970s) Grandmother Stover's catalog. Included were a telephone, magazine, books, newspaper, clocks, kitchen utensils, food products, games, sewing supplies, and much more.

Hill, P. J.

Ad for a Cindy Walker doll and her dollhouse from the November 1958 *American Home* magazine. The package was offered by P.J. Hill Co. from Newark, New Jersey. The 8.5" tall walker doll came with five clothing pieces. The "Modern Ranch" house was furnished with two chairs, table, television set, and a bed. The house was made of fibre board and the complete outfit sold for $2.98 plus shipping. The house was 24" wide x 16" deep.

Jayline Toys, Inc.

Left:
An advertisement from the Chicago Wholesale Co. catalog for Fall and Winter 1946-47 featured a variety of dollhouses. The houses pictured include several models by Rich Toys on the right, a cardboard Concord house at the upper left, a Nancy Forbes house at the lower left and a four-room house in the left center labeled "Jaylene." The house was made of Masonite and wood with cut-out windows. The house measured 16" high x 24" wide x 8" deep. An unusual five-room bungalow is pictured at the bottom right. It was also made of Masonite and wood. It measured 14" high x 24" x 21". Jayline Toys was located in Philadelphia, Pennsylvania. *Courtesy of Marge Meisinger.*

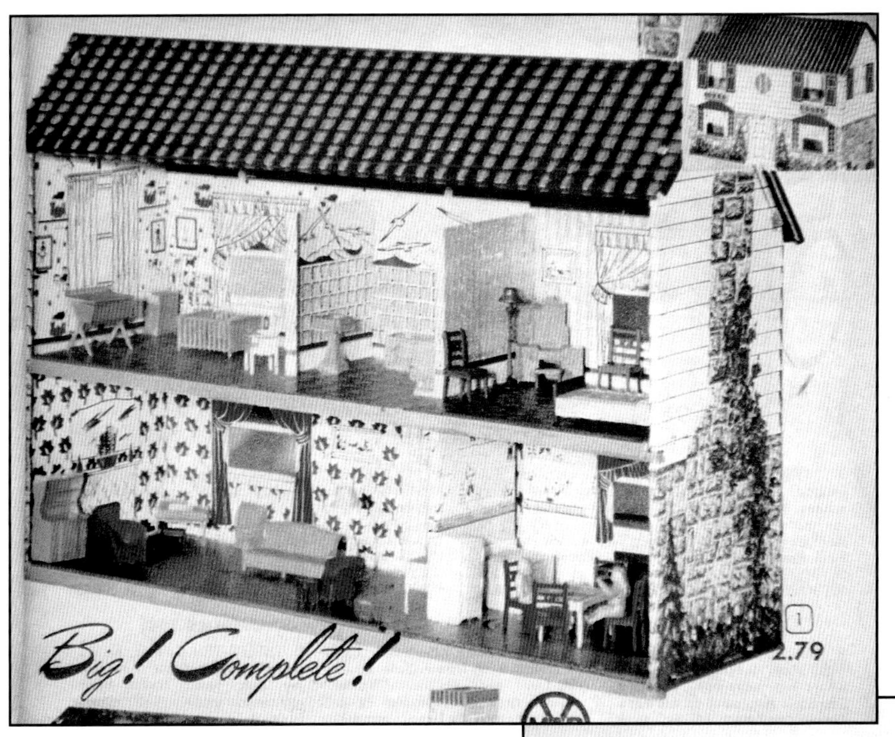

This metal dollhouse was advertised in the Aldens Christmas catalog in 1952. It was made by Jayline Toys, Inc. The same house with an attached garage had been advertised by Aldens in 1950. The house without the garage was furnished with thirty-four pieces of small scale plastic Allied furniture for the nursery, bathroom, bedroom, living room-dining room, and kitchen. It sold for $2.79 and measured 16.5" tall x 19.5" wide x 6.5" deep. *Courtesy of Marilyn Pittman.*

Kiddies Treasure Line

Advertisement for the Terry Lynn Doll House which appeared in *Playthings* magazine in March 1953. The house was manufactured by Kiddies Treasure Line in San Fernando, California. It was described as "California Modern" with cotton loop carpeting, acetate patio doors, and a removable Bermuda roof. The firm also provided six rooms of upholstered furniture to be used in the house. A boxed bedroom is pictured in the ad.

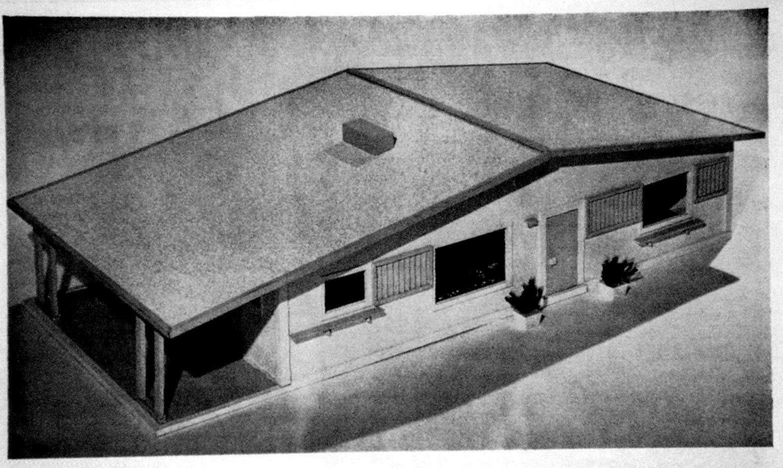

The Terry Lynn dollhouse with its roof in place, from *Playthings* magazine in May 1953. Victor and Teresa Evelyn Mortensen and Gordon and Olive Hayne were partners in the company. The pressed board house contained six rooms and measured 10" high x 41" wide x 21" deep. The retail price was $17.95.

The Kiddies Treasure six-piece living room set, one of five in the series of sets designed for furnishing the doll house.

Kiddies Treasure-Terry Lynn dollhouse furniture made for the living room, as pictured in *Playthings* for May 1953. Additional upholstery sets were made to furnish a bedroom, sectional den, dinette, and patio. A nursery set may have been added later. The furniture sets sold for $1.98 each.

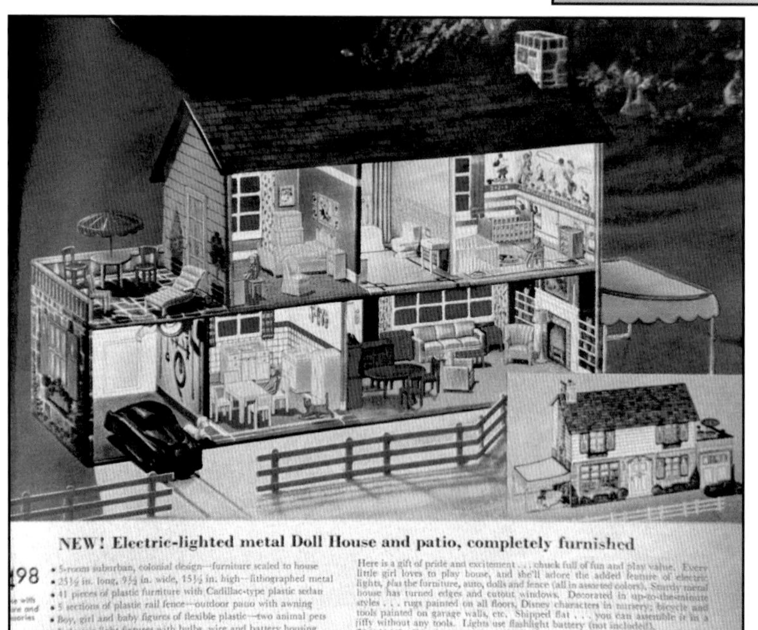

NEW! Electric-lighted metal Doll House and patio, completely furnished

Louis Marx & Co.

Louis Marx & Co., headquartered in New York City, began producing metal dollhouses and plastic furniture in the late 1940s. This early metal Marx "Disney" house was advertised in the Sears 1949 Christmas catalog. The house gets its name from the Disney characters used to decorate the walls of the nursery. The five-room house came with two "electric light" fixtures, forty-one pieces of hard plastic furniture, a plastic automobile, five sections of 1/2" to 1 foot plastic rail fence, an outdoor patio with awnings, boy, girl, and baby figures of flexible plastic, and two animal pets. The lithographed metal house featured a colonial design and measured 15.5" high x 25.5" wide x 9.5" deep. It sold for $4.98 complete. The house also included a garage to house its plastic automobile.

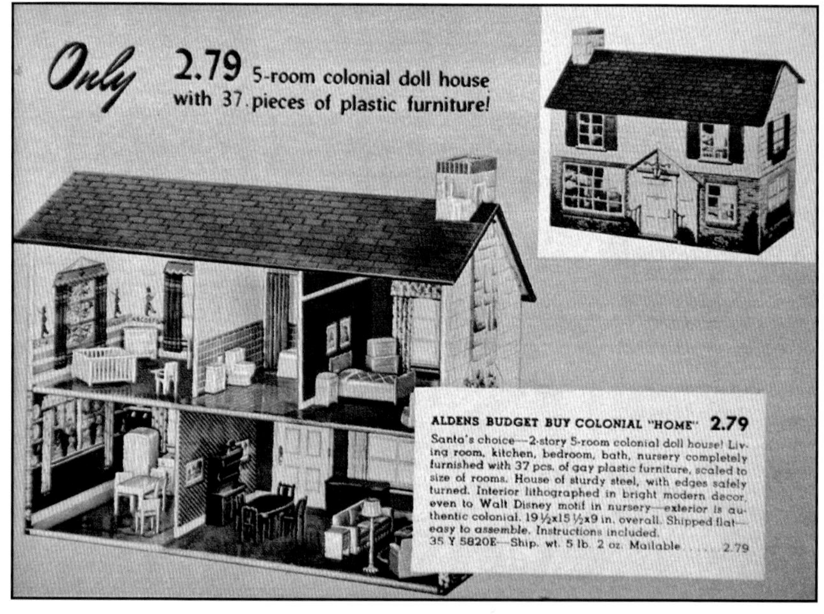

A smaller lithographed Marx metal house was pictured in the 1950 Aldens Christmas catalog. This five-room colonial house included no garage or patio. The decorations on the nursery of this house featured marching toy soldiers in the advertisement, but a Walt Disney motif was mentioned in the ad copy. The house measurements were 15.5" high x 19.5" wide x 9" deep. It sold for $2.79 including the plastic 1/2" to 1 foot Marx furniture.

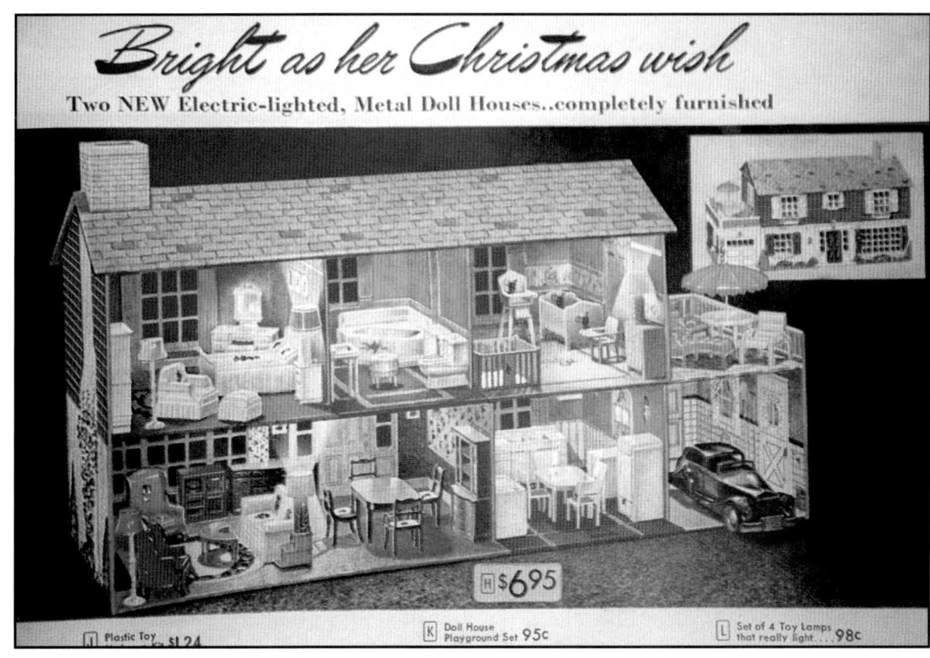

A larger Marx lithographed dollhouse was offered in the 1950 Sears Christmas catalog. This five-room colonial house featured a garage with an upstairs deck. The plastic Marx furniture included with this house was in a larger 3/4" to 1 foot scale. Decals that came with the house could be used to decorate the hard plastic furniture. The house came with forty-six pieces of furniture, three electric lamps (battery operated), and a plastic Rolls-Royce type automobile. Patio furniture was also included. The house measured 18.75" high x 33" wide x 12" deep. It sold for $6.95 complete.

A breezeway had been added to the featured Marx lithographed metal house in the 1952 Sears Christmas catalog. The house included the five basic rooms, plus a garage, breezeway and rumpus room. An upstairs deck over the garage was still part of the design. The house came with fifty-three pieces of plastic furniture in a 1/2" to 1 foot scale. The rumpus room furniture included a piano, juke box, and ping pong table. Plastic figures of a boy, girl, and baby came with the house, as did an automobile. The house measured 15.5" high x 38" wide x 9.5" deep. It sold for $5.29.

A "New! Modern L-shaped Ranch Home with Patio" was pictured in the Sears 1953 Christmas catalog. This Marx lithographed metal house included five rooms on one floor. Newly designed Marx plastic furniture was included with the house, which featured a kitchen, combination living-dining room, bedroom, bathroom, and nursery. A plastic Cadillac sedan and fourteen flexible plastic people came with the house. A weathervane and TV antenna were also included as house accessories. The open-backed house featured a large furnished patio at the rear. Furnishings for the house were as follows. Living room: 3-piece sectional sofa, corner table, occasional chair, TV console, table lamp, floor lamp, and coffee table. Dining room: dining table, two side chairs, two arm chairs, and buffet server. Kitchen: sink, refrigerator, stove, breakfast bar, and two stools. Bedroom: modern bed with headboard, lamps, dresser, vanity and bench. Bathroom: Hollywood tub, commode, hamper, vanity-type wash stand, and vanity bench. Child's room: crib, two-piece high chair, and hobby horse. Patio: chaise lounge, coffee table, chair, settee, table, and umbrella. The house measured 13.24" high x 32" wide x 16.25" deep and sold for $7.29 complete.

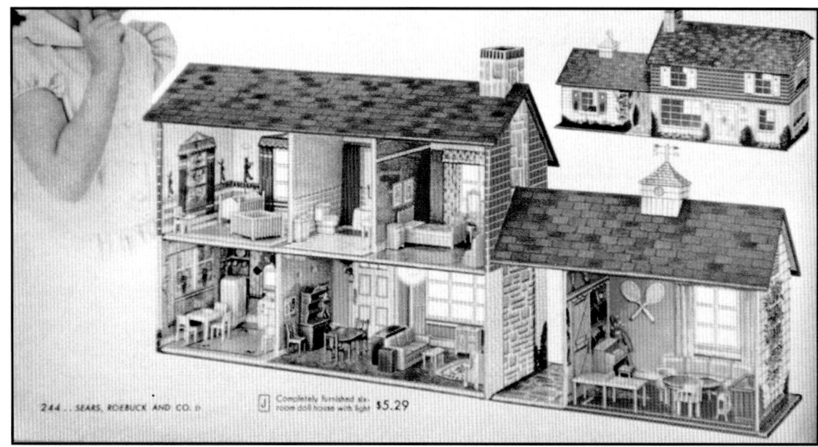

One of the Marx lithographed metal houses offered for sale in the Sears 1955 Christmas catalog was an example of the "breezeway" house. This model featured a red and white front décor and no garage. It did include a door bell and a weather vane. It came with forty-eight pieces of plastic furniture including pieces for the den (no longer called rumpus room). The 1/2" to 1 foot scale furniture was the same as that pictured with the earlier "breezeway" houses. The house measured 15.5" high x 31.5" wide x 9" deep and sold for $5.29.

A new Marx split level house was featured in the Sears Christmas catalog for 1958. The new three-level house came with a pool, patio, light (battery), and doorbell. The soft plastic furniture used to furnish the house was the same design as that used earlier for the L-shaped ranch house. The house included a plastic door that opened, plastic stairs and railings for the front entrance, and a two-way barbecue unit. Furniture was provided for a living room, dining room, kitchen, dinette, bathroom, bedroom, nursery, utility room, and back patio. Pool accessories included a diving board, ladder, and water toys. Plastic figures representing a family of six were also part of the package. The house measured 14" high x 29.5" wide x 16" deep and was priced at $8.99

The Marx colonial mansion is probably the most collectible dollhouse the company ever made. The first version was issued in 1961. Sears featured the luxury house in its 1962 Christmas catalog. The house included eight rooms, a ringing doorbell, vinyl framed walk lined by plastic shrubs, a plastic picket fence, and a swimming pool. Twenty-two plastic inhabitants came with the house. The furnished house included a bathroom, nursery, bedroom, "Florida" room, kitchen, laundry room, and living-dining room. Cloth draperies were provided for five windows, and three outside awnings also came as accessories. A plastic porch and shutters added to the outside décor. Fifty-two plastic pieces were included to furnish the house. Tableware, lawn pieces, and furniture were part of the package. The 3/4" to 1 foot plastic furniture was the earlier 1950 design made in soft plastic. The "Florida" room with jalousie windows was a new innovation for this house. The house measured 18" high x 44" wide x 14" deep. The pictured model sold for $15.88. All of the Marx steel lithographed houses came in pieces and were to be assembled by the buyer. This example probably took a good deal of Santa's time on Christmas Eve.

A furnished ranch house made by Marx was pictured in the 1962 Sears Christmas catalog. It included a bedroom, bathroom, combination living room-dining room, and kitchen-laundry room. A furnished patio was also part of the house's design. The 1/2" to 1 foot scaled plastic furniture was, for the most part, the early design from 1950. The house measured 10" high x 33" wide x 9" deep. It sold for $3.99.

This Marx furnished lithographed steel contemporary house was featured in the Montgomery Ward Christmas catalog in 1965. Unlike other Marx houses, this one included a removable roof in order for the child to access its six living areas. This house had an open floor plan with no walls separating the living room, dining area, and kitchen. The enclosed rooms included two bedrooms and a bathroom. It was furnished with later styled Marx plastic furniture. The house sold for $6.99 and measured 9" high x 32" wide x 16" deep. *Courtesy of Marilyn Pittman.*

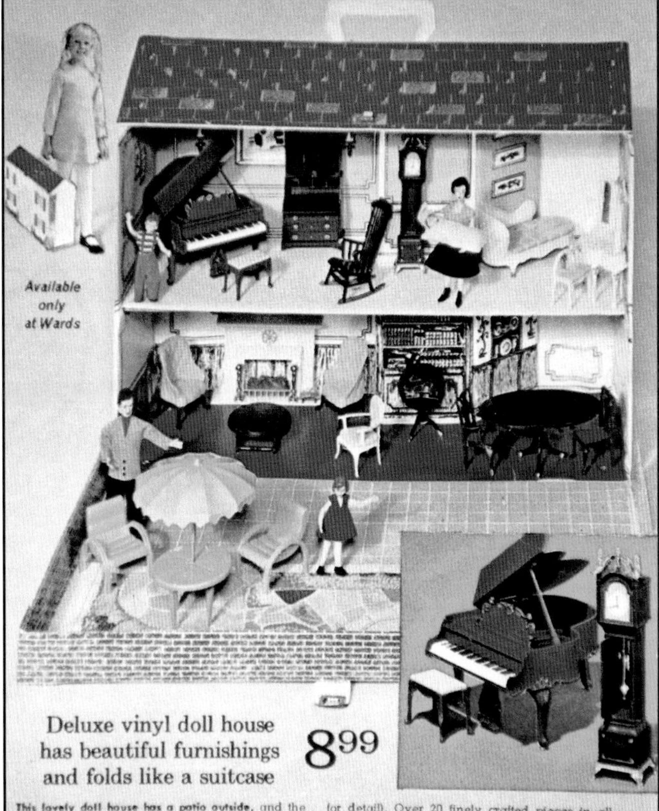

Left:
Several pieces of the Marx Little Hostess plastic furniture were included in this vinyl suitcase dollhouse in 1967. The more expensive 3/4" to one foot furniture had been introduced in 1964. The package was pictured in the Montgomery Wards Christmas catalog for 1967. This house included four rooms and a patio. Little Hostess furniture was used in a music room, bedroom (with no bed), living room, and dining room. The plastic patio set was not part of the Little Hostess designed furniture. The house was approximately 15.5" high x 20" wide x 7.25" deep in size and sold furnished for $8.99. The dolls were not included.

The same pieces of Little Hostess furniture were offered in the 1969 Montgomery Ward Christmas catalog for only $3.99.

MEMO: "METAL WORK AT MARX"
In our continuing interest in safety at play, Marx all steel doll houses (and Service Stations too) are engineered and manufactured to eliminate all sharp edges when assembled. Our colorful packaging carries age-use recommendations and cautionary consumer notices to assist in speedy, trouble free assembly.

Left:
This Marx catalog page, circa 1970, pictures two of their new suitcase houses then being made by several companies. Although other firms' examples were made of vinyl, these two Marx suitcase styled houses were produced of steel. Included on the left is the "Fantasy Doll House," which came with plastic people, an automobile, beds, dresser, table and chairs, and more. The house measured 10.5" high x 11.5" wide x 9.25" deep. This house was made for younger children, as was the similar Disney carryall house pictured on the top right. Mr. And Mrs. Mickey Mouse and Mr. And Mrs. Donald Duck lived in this house. The house contained plastic living room, dining room, and bedroom furniture. The other steel house pictured is the basic five room, two story Colonial house that had been marketed in one design or another for twenty years. It came complete with plastic 1/2" to 1 foot scaled soft plastic furniture. *Courtesy of Marcie Tubbs. Photograph by Bob Tubbs.*

This page from the same circa 1970 Marx catalog pictures a ranch style house plus three varieties of the Colonial dollhouse. *Tubbs Collection.*

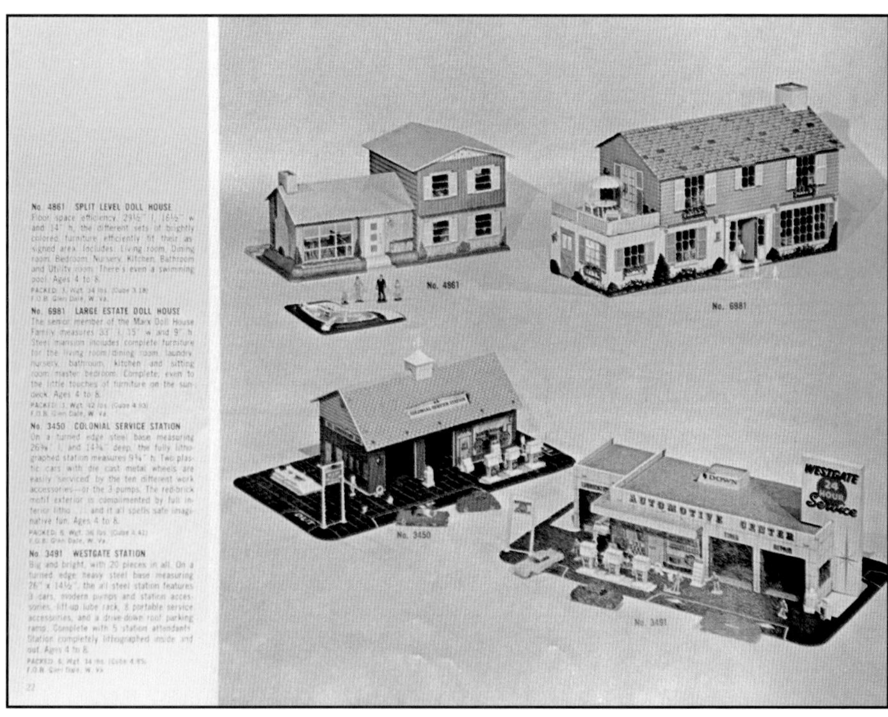

The third page of the catalog featured a slightly different version of the split level house, a blue and white "Estate Dollhouse," and two Marx service stations. The stations were called a "Colonial Service Station" on the left and a "Westgate Station" on the right. *Tubbs Collection.*

The Marx Colonnade dollhouse was advertised in the Sears Christmas catalog for 1973. This newer house came on the market in 1972. The house was made of lithographed steel with a molded plastic roof and other plastic parts. There were six columns across the front and windows that opened. A battery operated porch light was also included. The inside of the house included two bedrooms, bathroom, kitchen, and a combination living room and dining room. An attached patio was on the ground floor. The plastic furniture was made in the Colonial style according to the ad copy. The house measured 16.5" high x 26" wide x 14.25" deep and sold for $9.88.

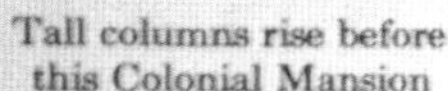

This earlier Marx Colonial Mansion was offered for sale in the Sears 1960 Christmas catalog. It included the basic design for the later Colonnade house. It featured a metal roof, no base, and different columns, but the basic design was the same. It sold for $3.44 and measured 15" high x 19" wide x 11" deep. *Courtesy of Marilyn Pittman.*

In addition to doll figures, Marx also marketed this family of dolls for many years. This ad is from the 1966 Montgomery Ward Christmas catalog. The dolls had flexible bodies and wore real clothing. The father was 4.5" tall. The set of five dolls was priced at $1.89.

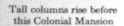

BELOW: For the doll house owner—a family, outdoor playground, housewares!

3. PLASTIC HOUSEWARES—Cute plastic housewares to make Dolly's house even more complete! 19-piece plastic set is scaled to fit doll house E35Y5821E at right. 1 vacuum cleaner; 1 golf bag; 1 snow shovel; 1 carpet sweeper; 1 hose reel; 1 broom; 1 dry mop; 1 scrubbing board, 1 dust pan; 3-pc. canister set; 1 bread box, 1 utility can, 5 venetian blinds. All pieces about 4-inches high. Aldens ideal gift!
35Y5902—1 set. Wt. 11 oz. 89c

4. 15-PC. PLAYGROUND SET—Doll's plastic playground set means hours of quiet fun for the child who likes miniature toys. Set is scaled to go with most doll houses. 4 vinyl plasitc people in sitting position are included—1 Boy, 1 Girl, 2 Babies. Figures measure about 1½-inch high. Set consists of 1 slide, sand box, wading pool, see-saw, sail boat, pail, shovel, 4 sections of picket fence 6¾-in. long. Cute as can be in doll house "yard".
35 Y 5904—1 Set. Wt. 11 oz. 94c

5. DOLL HOUSE FAMILY—Playing house is lots more fun with a real doll family. This set of 14 people is made of vinyl plastic and has been designed to fit furniture in any standard doll house. There is a Father, a Mother, 5 daughters, 3 sons, 3 babies, 1 cat all in various sitting and standing positions. Father is the tallest measuring 3¼-in. high—the others in life-like proportion. The perfect addition to any doll house.
35Y5903—Set of 14. Wt. 9 oz. 89c

Other dollhouse related sets were also offered by Marx over the years. Several different packages were featured in the Aldens Christmas catalog for 1952. Included were a "Plastic Housewares" set that sold for 89 cents and included cleaning tools, a canister set, bread box, and five Venetian blinds along with other items. The plastic "Playground Set" featured fifteen pieces relating to playground activities. A slide, sand box, and see-saw were included in the 94 cent package. Plastic dollhouse figures were in a separate set that sold for 89 cents. Fourteen stationary "people" of all ages were provided to be used with dollhouses. *Courtesy of Marilyn Pittman.*

$1.97

Set for outdoor fun .. pool holds water

Luxurious patio has built-in barbecue, shuffle-board court and is beautifully furnished with outdoor furniture. Pool is equipped with diving board, sail boat, life ring, etc. Set of playground equipment .. swings, slide, teeter-totter, sand box. 4 miniature people. Of colorful plastic, about 18x11x2 inches high.
49 N 1404—Shipping weight 1 lb. $1.97

Sears offered this later Marx "Outdoor Fun" set in 1960. It included a pool, deck, bar-b-que, outdoor furniture, and playground set. It sold for $1.97. *Pittman Collection.*

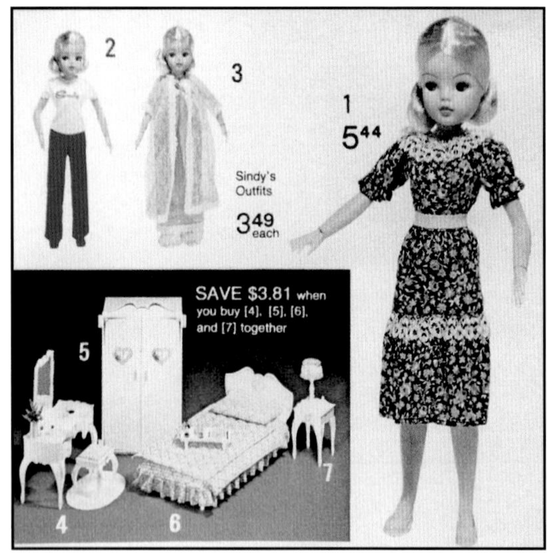

The J.C. Penney Christmas catalog for 1978 featured the 11" Sindy doll priced at $5.44. Her plastic bedroom furniture could be purchased by the piece for $5.95 each. The lamp worked with a battery.

THE THINGS THAT DREAMS ARE MADE OF.
She's only a little girl once. And like every little girl, she dreams of wonderful things like Sindy and her World.
Sindy's World is a loveable 11-inch doll, a spectacular three-level home and a collection of the most carefully detailed furnishings that ever lit up her imagination.
The star is Sindy. She's an innocent little charmer that can be posed in more ways than any other doll. The showplace is Sindy's new home with electric elevator, spiral staircase and beautiful graphics inside and out. It's the perfect play setting for Sindy's rooms of finely crafted furnishings.
And such furnishings! No detail has been overlooked to guarantee endless hours of enchanting play. Drawers and doors open with ease. The bedroom lamp lights. Sindy's Music Centre has a working AM radio. Her new shower and washing machine really work. In the kitchen, the refrigerator has miniature 'food'. The dining room is so complete there's even 'silver' candelabra.
And because each piece or setting is sold separately, you can select any part of Sindy's World now and add to it later.
Of course every Christmas is special for little girls. Sindy and her world may just make this one remembered forever.
Sindy
SINDY'S WORLD BY MARX.

Right:
In 1978, after the earlier Louis Marx firm had been purchased by the English toy company, Dunbee-Combex, a new larger scale line of plastic furniture and houses was issued by the company. This advertisement pictures the 11" Sindy vinyl doll, as well as her house. The ad was from Marx Toys Canada Limited. The house was on three levels and included furniture for a kitchen, bathroom, bedroom, dining room, and living room. (See pages 155 and 156 of *American Dollhouses and Furniture* for photographs of this doll and furniture.)

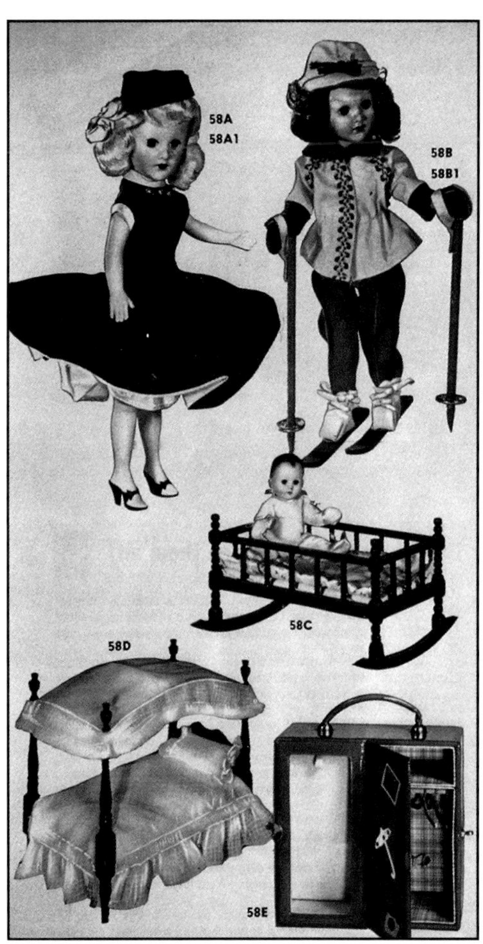

Richwood Toys, Inc.

Richwood Toys, Inc. was located in Annapolis, Maryland. The firm produced the 8" hard plastic Sandra Sue doll during the 1950s. Two of the Sandra Sue dolls and the Colonial Canopy bed were advertised in the Strawbridge and Clothier catalog from Philadelphia in 1956. The undressed Sandra Sue sold for $1.98 while outfits were priced at $2.50 each. The 8" baby doll called Tina Sue sold for $1.98 and the cradle was $4.98. The canopy bed was priced at $5.98. *Courtesy of Marge Meisinger.*

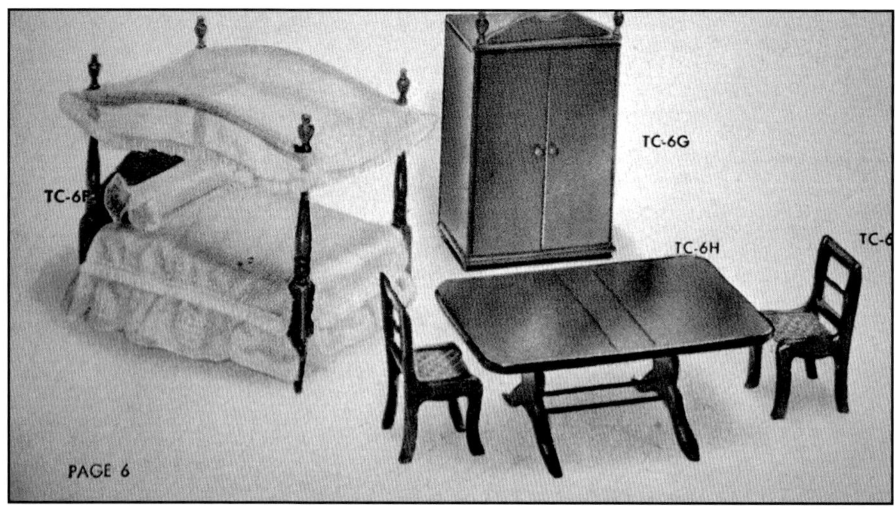

Additional pieces of Richwood Toys' furniture were featured in the 1954 Emporium (San Francisco) catalog. The bed was priced at $4.98, the wardrobe cost $3.98, and the "Duncan Phyfe" extension table and two chairs sold for $5.98. Extra matching chairs could be purchased for $1.50 each. All of the furniture was suitable for 8" dolls. A dresser was also available. *Meisinger Collection.*

T. Cohn, Inc.

Left:
T. Cohn, Inc., located in Brooklyn, New York, produced many collectible dollhouses over a period of many years. The company was responsible for what appears to be one of the first modern metal dollhouses. It was featured in the Montgomery Ward Christmas catalog in 1948. As shown here, the Billy and Ruth catalog in 1949 also offered the lithographed metal house for sale. The two-story, six-room house was priced for $4.95 unfurnished. It measured 18.5" high x 28" wide x 13" deep. *Courtesy of Marcie Tubbs. Photograph by Bob Tubbs.*

Right:
A similar T. Cohn house was advertised in *Playthings* magazine in March 1951. This house included an additional one-story section that was to be used as a garage. It included five rooms plus a garage. Both houses featured inside decorations. The house measured 16" high x 28.5" wide x 9.75" deep. Also pictured are two T. Cohn metal service stations.

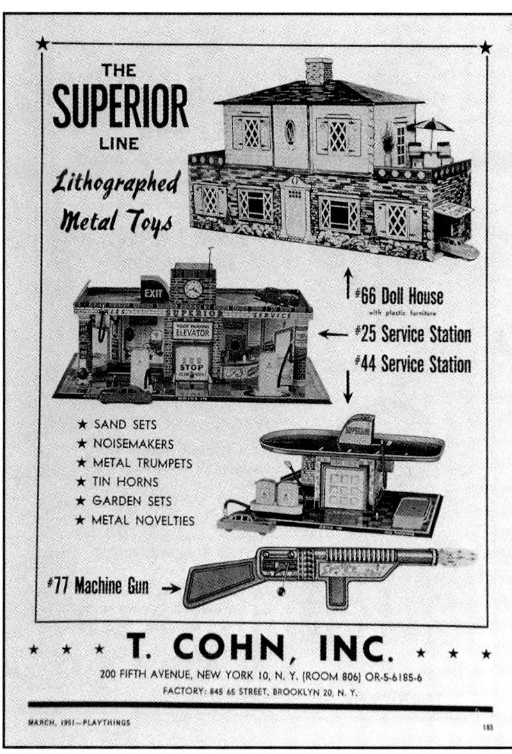

The T. Cohn metal ranch house is also pictured in the 1956 company catalog. It is a one-story, four-room house that includes a kitchen, living room, bedroom and bathroom. It was furnished with sixteen pieces of plastic furniture. It measured 10.5" high x 25" wide x 9.5" deep. *Tubbs Collection.*

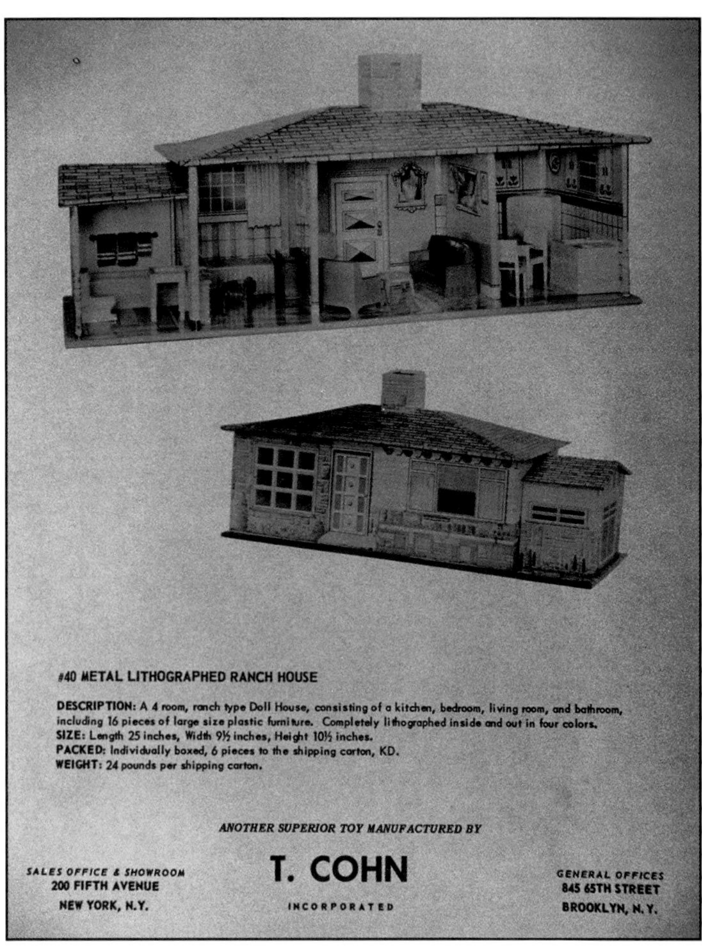

#40 METAL LITHOGRAPHED RANCH HOUSE
DESCRIPTION: A 4 room, ranch type Doll House, consisting of a kitchen, bedroom, living room, and bathroom, including 16 pieces of large size plastic furniture. Completely lithographed inside and out in four colors.
SIZE: Length 25 inches, Width 9½ inches, Height 10½ inches.
PACKED: Individually boxed, 6 pieces to the shipping carton, KD.
WEIGHT: 24 pounds per shipping carton.
ANOTHER SUPERIOR TOY MANUFACTURED BY
SALES OFFICE & SHOWROOM 200 FIFTH AVENUE NEW YORK, N.Y.
T. COHN INCORPORATED
GENERAL OFFICES 845 65TH STREET BROOKLYN, N.Y.

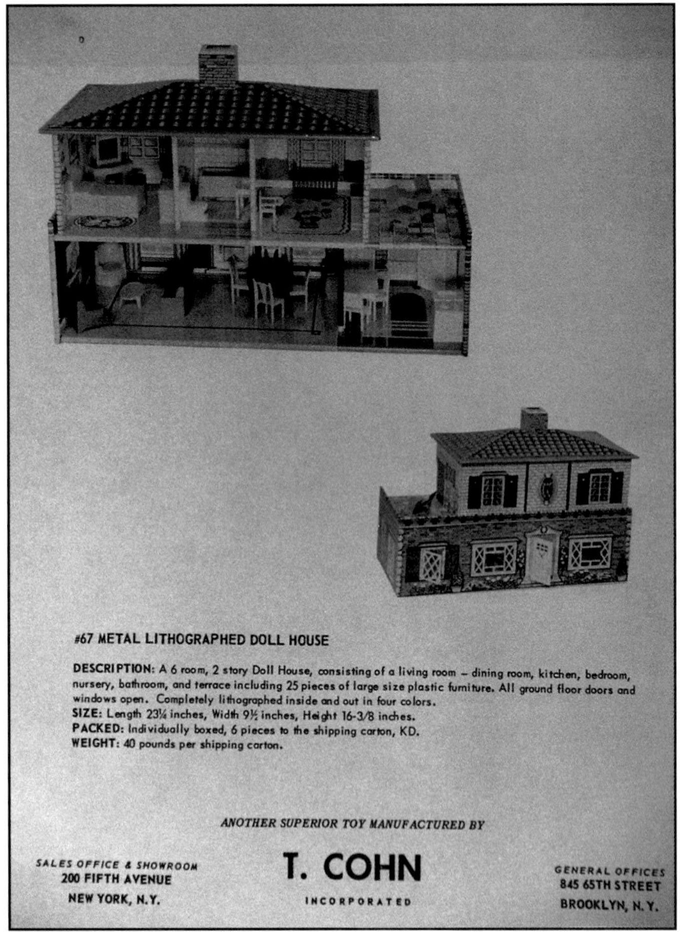

#67 METAL LITHOGRAPHED DOLL HOUSE
DESCRIPTION: A 6 room, 2 story Doll House, consisting of a living room – dining room, kitchen, bedroom, nursery, bathroom, and terrace including 25 pieces of large size plastic furniture. All ground floor doors and windows open. Completely lithographed inside and out in four colors.
SIZE: Length 23¼ inches, Width 9½ inches, Height 16-3/8 inches.
PACKED: Individually boxed, 6 pieces to the shipping carton, KD.
WEIGHT: 40 pounds per shipping carton.
ANOTHER SUPERIOR TOY MANUFACTURED BY
SALES OFFICE & SHOWROOM 200 FIFTH AVENUE NEW YORK, N.Y.
T. COHN INCORPORATED
GENERAL OFFICES 845 65TH STREET BROOKLYN, N.Y.

This page from a T. Cohn company catalog for 1956 pictures the newer version of the 1951 house. The garage has been removed to make it a five room house with one deck. The 3/4" to 1 foot scale plastic furniture is pictured inside. The description states that twenty-five pieces of furniture came with the house to furnish six rooms (living room, dining room combined). 16 .5" high x 23.25" wide x 9.5" deep. *Courtesy of Marcie Tubbs, photograph by Bob Tubbs.*

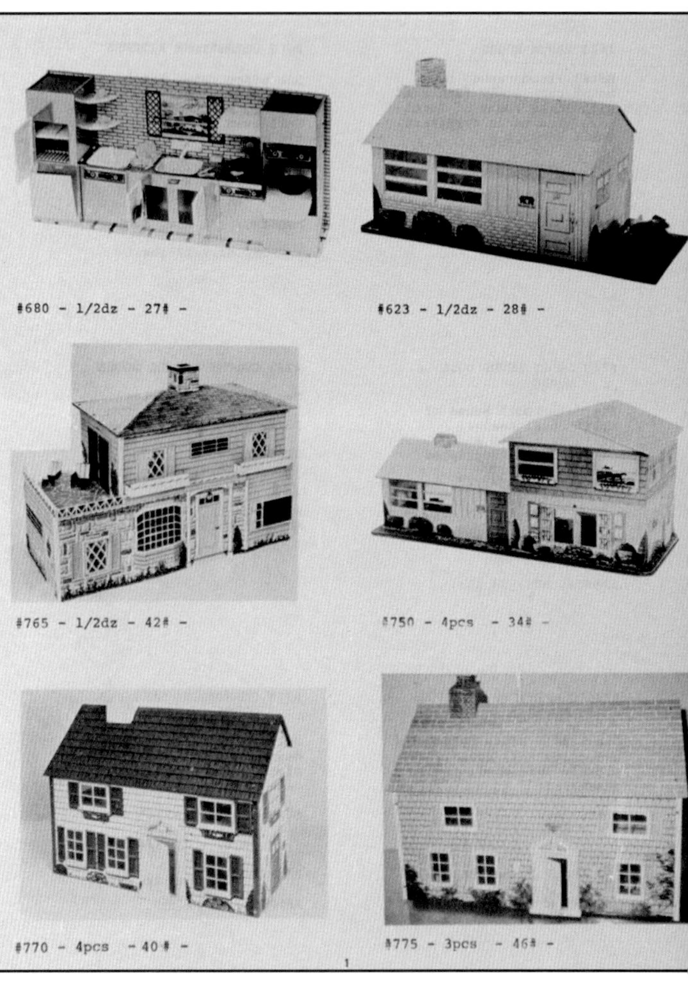

This page of the T. Cohn 1956 catalog pictures one of the houses already mentioned plus a toy kitchen room, a split level house and two houses at the bottom of the page that were probably made of hardboard. The house on the right was pictured in the Cullum & Buren wholesale catalog in 1961 with added shutters. It included five rooms and measured 30" tall x 30" wide x 12" deep. It was furnished with plastic Superior furniture. The 1961 house was identified as a T. Cohn product in the catalog. The split-level house shown in the middle right was also pictured in the 1961 Cullum & Buren catalog. The T. Cohn house at the lower left is like one offered for sale by the Brumberger Co. during the 1970s. This house contained five rooms and measured approximately 23.5" high x 30" wide x 13" deep. It was also made of hardboard and came furnished with Superior plastic furniture. *Tubbs Collection.*

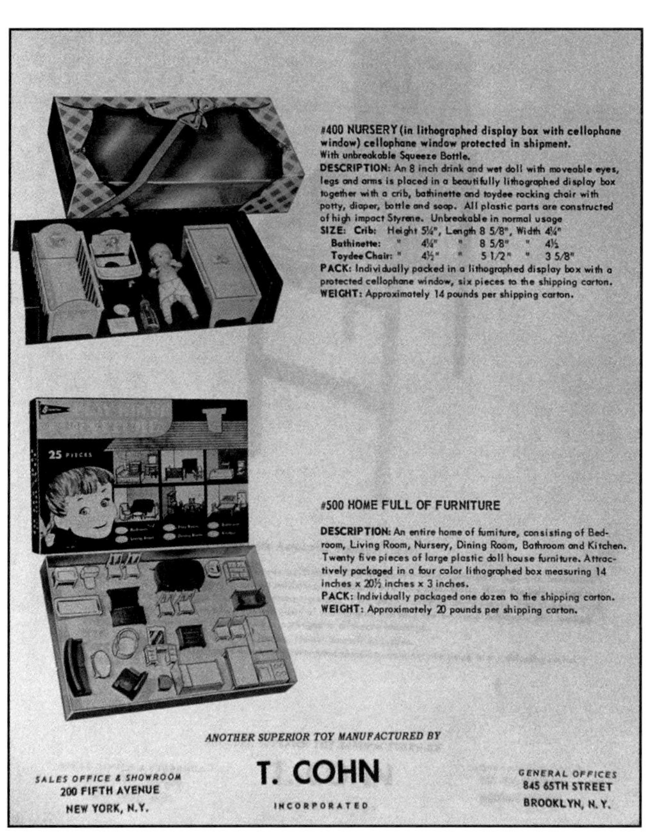

An additional page of the 1956 catalog offers a nursery set with an 8" doll and a set of the firm's 3/4" to 1 foot scaled plastic furniture. The boxed set included twenty-five pieces of furniture, enough to furnish a six-room house (includes nursery pieces). *Tubbs Collection.*

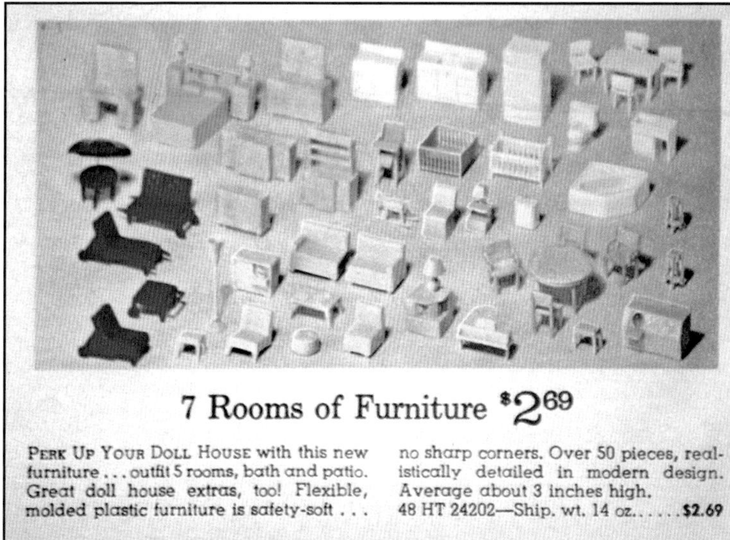

Furniture identical to this small 1/2" scaled "Superior" plastic furniture was used by T. Cohn for many years to furnish their houses. This ad appeared in the Montgomery Ward Christmas catalog for 1966. The seven rooms of furniture were priced at $2.69.

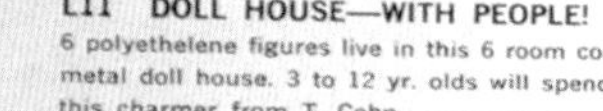

This later T. Cohn house was featured in the Hollywood Toys, Inc. catalog for 1959-60 (located in Hollywood, California). Several slightly different versions of this house were produced. Examples were also made with green or blue decoration. Some had an opening front door and window, while others did not. This one appears to have that feature. Two different doors were used on various models. This six-room house came completely furnished and sold for $5.98. It measured approximately 16.5" high x 23" wide x 9.5" deep. *Courtesy of Marge Meisinger.*

This small T. Cohn Ranch house was pictured in the 1963 Aldens Christmas catalog for the low price of $2.97 complete with furnishings. The small Superior furniture was used to furnish the house. The house was also produced in a four-room model with an extra wing. It measured 9.5" high x 23" wide x 11.25" deep. *Courtesy of Marilyn Pittman.*

1960s Advertisements

The 1960s brought an end to most of the dollhouse and furniture manufacturers of earlier years. Strombecker continued to offer wood dollhouse furniture as well as furniture for the 8" dolls until they closed their toy line circa 1962. Rich Toy Co. suffered losses when they moved South, and they ceased operation as well in 1962. The plastic furniture from Renwal, Plasco, and Ideal dating from the late 1940s was no longer popular, and although Marx continued to sell metal houses and plastic furniture, the goods were no longer much in demand.

In order to rekindle sales in the 3/4" to one foot scaled plastic furniture, both Marx and Ideal brought out new lines of more expensive "fancy" plastic furniture. Ideal's Petite Princess line appeared in 1964 and Marx's Little Hostess line soon followed. Neither line was successful.

The dollhouses that did meet with success were those made in larger sizes to be used with the Tressy, Tammy, Penny Brite, Heidi, and, of course, the Mattel Barbie dolls.

Hall's Lifetime Toys continued to produce dollhouses and wood furniture in the smaller sizes as well as in the new larger models. FAO Schwarz still stocked nicely made regular sized dollhouses throughout the decade and new firms such as Woodmaster added additional designs to the regular dollhouse supply. The T. Cohn firm was still in business, at least during the first part of the decade, and they produced some masonite or wood type houses as well as their older metal designs.

The decade offered some gimmick houses in which magnets were used to activate plastic doll figures so they could be moved from room to room. In addition, interior decoration sets were marketed to give little girls practice in decorating their houses.

Except for a few examples, most feel the 1960s ended the "Golden Years" of the production of toy dollhouses and their furnishings.

This decade also marks the beginning of adult interest in new miniatures and houses, and the hobby that developed from these new products. Perhaps manufacturers that might have been attracted to the toy dollhouse field concentrated their efforts instead in producing products for this new adult field.

The advertisements in this chapter follow the changes that took place in the industry during the decade of the 1960s.

American Character

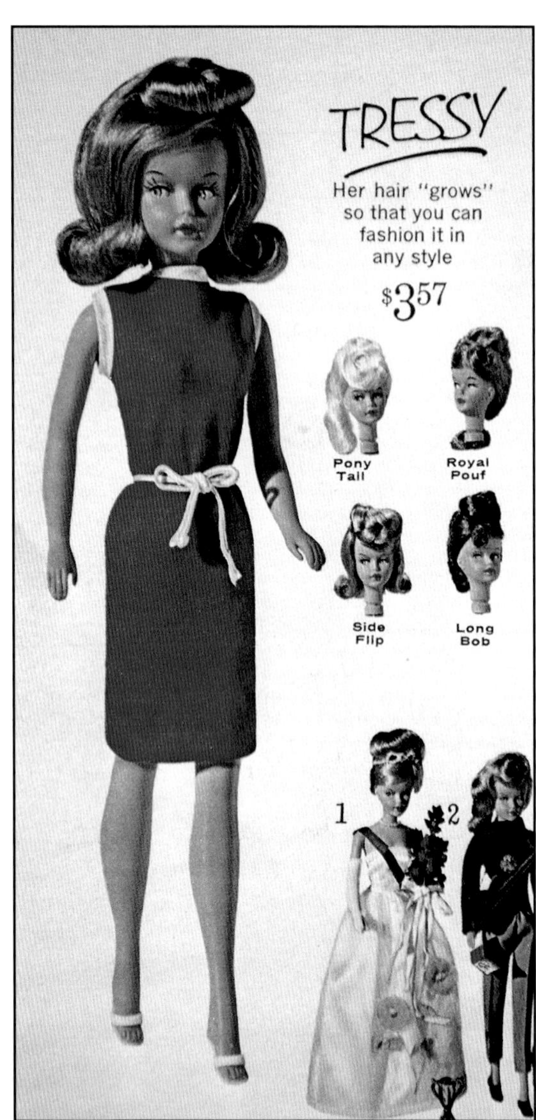

The American Character Doll Company of New York City had its beginning in 1919. After producing fine composition and later hard plastic dolls, the firm was making dolls of vinyl by the 1960s. Their vinyl Tressy doll was pictured in the 1964 Sears Christmas catalog. Her hair could change length with the turn of a magic key. She measured 11.5" tall and was made of plastic. She sold for $3.57.

Here's Tressy's modern Penthouse Apartment

$6^{99}

Floor plan in-the-round is complete with kitchen, studio-type bedroom with fold-out bed; wardrobe and dressing area, dinette, living room, terrace. All in decorator colors . . including put-together furnishings, accessories. Sturdy chipboard opens 27x39x20 in. high.
79 N 9367C—Shpg. wt. 9 lbs. . . $6.99

The same Sears 1964 Christmas catalog also offered Tressy's Penthouse Apartment. It was made of chipboard and included a kitchen, studio-type bedroom with fold-out bed, dinette, living room and terrace (on the top level). It measured 27" x 39" x 20" high and sold for $6.99.

Chestnut Hill Studio

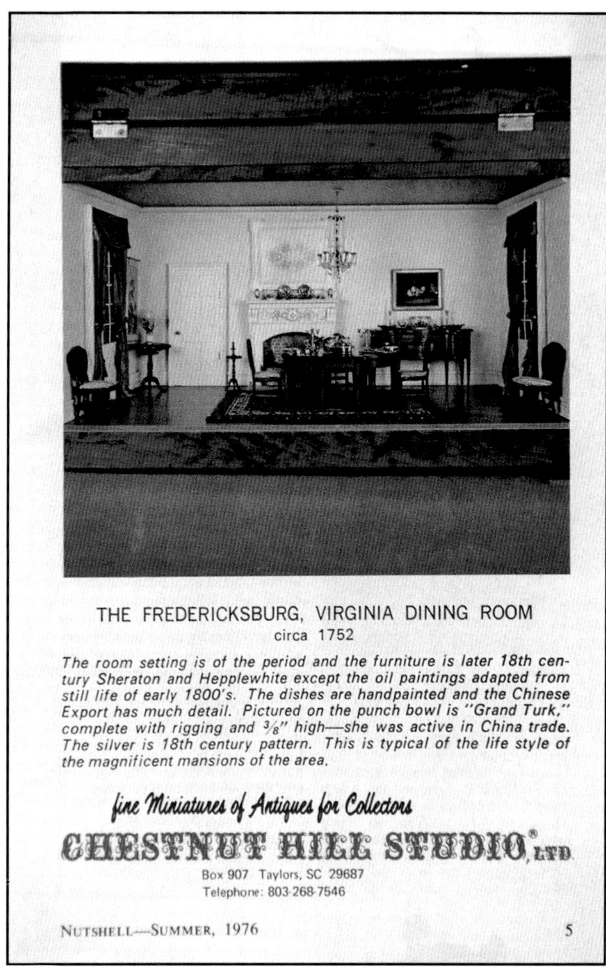

THE FREDERICKSBURG, VIRGINIA DINING ROOM
circa 1752

The room setting is of the period and the furniture is later 18th century Sheraton and Hepplewhite except the oil paintings adapted from still life of early 1800's. The dishes are handpainted and the Chinese Export has much detail. Pictured on the punch bowl is "Grand Turk," complete with rigging and 3/8" high—she was active in China trade. The silver is 18th century pattern. This is typical of the life style of the magnificent mansions of the area.

fine Miniatures of Antiques for Collectors

CHESTNUT HILL STUDIO, LTD

Box 907 Taylors, SC 29687
Telephone: 803-268-7546

NUTSHELL—SUMMER, 1976 5

This Chestnut Hill Studio advertisement is from the Summer 1976 issue of *Nutshell News*. It pictures the Fredericksburg, Virginia Dining Room circa 1752. The mail order firm was located in Churchville, New York and began marketing miniature furniture in 1947. It was founded by Reta Cowles Johnson. *Courtesy of Gail Carey.*

Blue Box

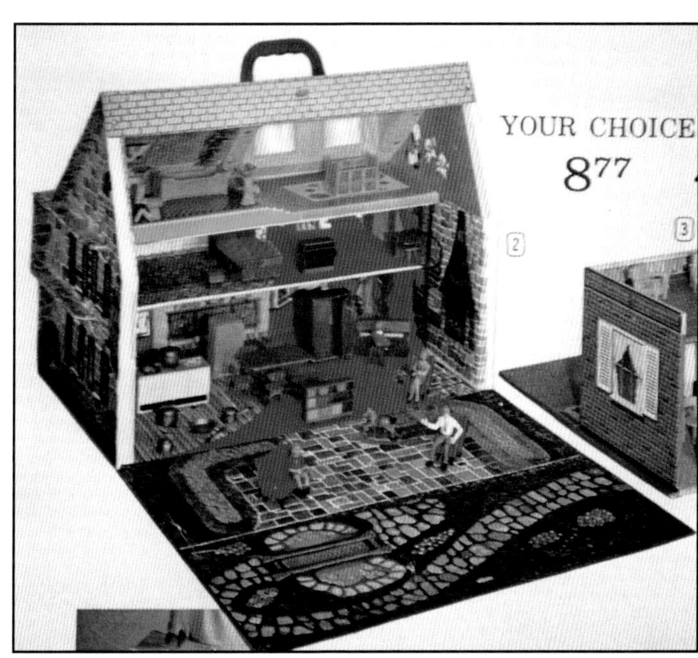

Blue Box plastic furniture was used to furnish this vinyl dollhouse pictured in the Montgomery Ward Christmas catalog for 1969. The furniture was made in Hong Kong and was mostly in the small scale of 1/2" to one foot. The house, which folded into a carrying case, was probably made by Ideal. The front folded down to provide a patio for the three-story house. It measured approximately 14.5" x 17" x 12.5" and sold for $8.77 furnished.

Pictured is Chestnut Hill's 1775 Drawing Room from their 1968 catalog. Included was a Queen Ann Wing Chair 4.25" high ($40.00), Secretary 7.25" tall ($50), Oriental Rug ($165), and a Tier Table ($22.50). *Courtesy of Linda Boltrek.*

The Chestnut Hill 1968 catalog also pictured an 1812 hallway including a Sheraton card table ($17.50), Grandfather Clock ($7.50), and a Chippendale chest of drawers ($21). All of the handmade furniture was 1" to one foot in scale. *Boltrek Collection.*

The Late Victorian bedroom from 1968 included a corner what-not ($10.50), Victorian bureau ($21.00), and a brass bed ($21.50). *Boltrek Collection.*

The Chestnut Hill traditional living room included a Duncan Phyfe sofa ($15.00) and a piano and bench with a music box ($32.00). The firm's catalog also featured Country Pine furniture, a Shaker room, and many other examples of furniture and accessories. *Boltrek Collection.*

Child Guidance

$3.33
Manage This Household Your Way With Magnetic Wand
THIS FAMILY WILL COME ALIVE WITH A TOUCH OF THE MAGIC WAND. As you move the wand under the table, it guides the family members anywhere you want them—in the patio, yard or beautiful 5-room ranch house—without touching them! It's fun to help mother with the chores while father works in the yard.
The completely furnished house even has real mirrors. The open top reveals the doll house family in action inside their house. Plastic house is mounted on 26x20-in. playboard with sturdy plastic legs. Wands have lifetime magnets.
48 T 7936 MO—Shipping weight 7 lbs. $3.33

A magnetic Child Guidance house was advertised in the Montgomery Ward Christmas catalog in 1965. The five plastic "people" who came with the house could be moved from room to room through the use of a "magic wand" (doll's wand included magnets). The five-room house came with over forty pieces of furniture and accessories. It was mounted on a 26" x 20" play board with plastic legs. It sold for $3.33. *Courtesy of Marilyn Pittman.*

Move cars up to gas pumps . . in for service . . or through car wash
Magnetic Service Station by Child Guidance Toys
$4.99
Six cars and attendants spring mysteriously into action. You control them secretly—with a touch of the Magic Mover wand underneath the gas station. You boss a 70-piece outfit, complete even to dummy gas tanks, traffic signals, and pedestrians. Business is brisk. Take off car bodies for inspection if you like; they can be interchanged at a flip of your finger. High-impact plastic station can be permanently assembled. Base 19¾x26x5 inches.
79 N 6070C—Shipping weight 7 pounds. $4.99

The Child Guidance firm also produced a Magnetic Service Station using the same type of magnetic figures and wands. It was advertised in the Sears 1964 Christmas catalog. The set came with seventy pieces which included cars, trucks, signs, gas pumps, and much more. The base for the station measured 19.75" x 26" x 5". It sold for $4.99.

Deluxe Reading Corp.

The 8" vinyl Penny Brite doll was made by the Deluxe Reading Corp., located in Elizabeth, New Jersey, and was featured in the 1965 Montgomery Ward Christmas catalog. Several different sets of furniture could also be purchased for the doll. The basic doll was priced at $1.17. Surprisingly, two of the sets of furniture were later sold as a boxed set titled "Dawn's Apartment." See page 227 of *American Dollhouses and Furniture* for photographs of this plastic furniture. The Dawn furniture from the early 1970s was issued by Amsco toys so it is likely that the firm was also responsible for the Penny Brite pieces. The Penny Brite bedroom suite sold for $4.99 and included a bed with canopy, vanity table with mirror, two lamps, a bench, and pajama set. The kitchen set was priced at $4.79 and included a cabinet-sink, table, two chairs, plastic dishes, and a dress and an apron for Penny. Other sets included a Beauty Parlor, Schoolroom, and sports car. *Courtesy of Marilyn Pittman.*

Eldon

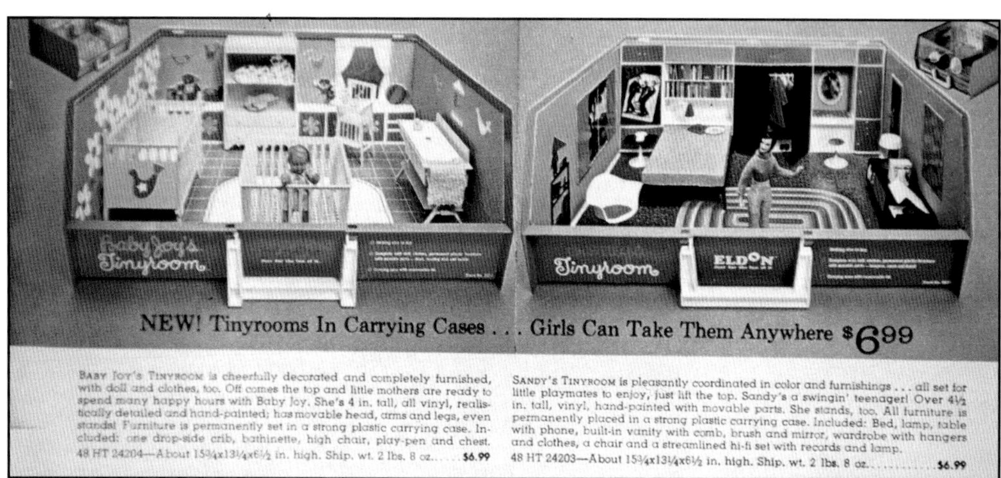

Two "Tinyroom" sets, marketed by Eldon, were advertised in the Montgomery Ward Christmas catalog in 1966. One was called "Baby Joy's Tinyroom" and the other was "Sandy's Tinyroom." Baby Joy was 4" tall, made of vinyl, and fully jointed. Her furniture was permanently mounted in the case and included a crib, playpen, highchair, bathinette, and chest. The vinyl Sandy doll was 4.5" tall with movable parts. Her furniture included a bed, chair, lamp, table, vanity, wardrobe, and hi-fi set. Both rooms measured 6.5" high x 15.25" x 13.25". Each set was priced at $6.99.

Erna Meyer

The German Erna Meyer cloth dollhouse dolls were advertised in the Franz Carl Weber 1961-62 catalog. Eighteen different models were pictured. The features on all of the dolls are painted and each is fitted with a small wig. Their shoes have cardboard soles. More recent dolls have plastic feet. *Courtesy of Linda Boltrek.*

Hall's Lifetime Toys

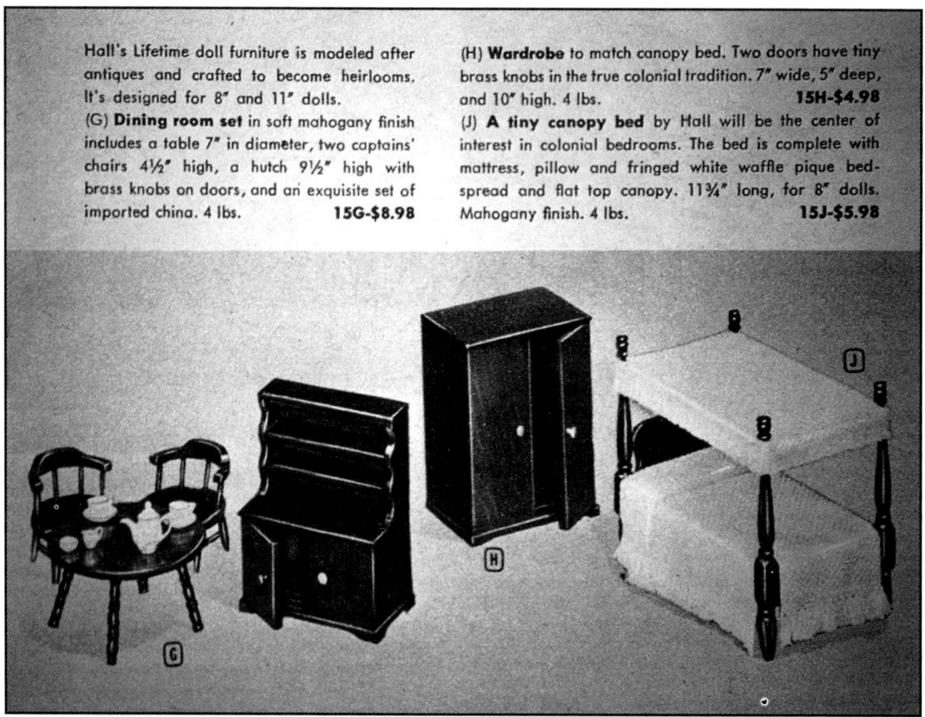

Hall's Lifetime Toys was based in Chattanooga, Tennessee and the firm produced both dollhouse and doll size furniture for many years. This advertisement appeared in the Los Angeles May Co. Toy Time catalog in 1957. These pieces of furniture were designed for the 8" to 11" dolls then popular. The pictured dining set included a table, two chairs, and a hutch priced at $8.98. The bedroom furniture featured a wardrobe for $4.98 and a canopy bed for $5.98. *Courtesy of Marge Meisinger.*

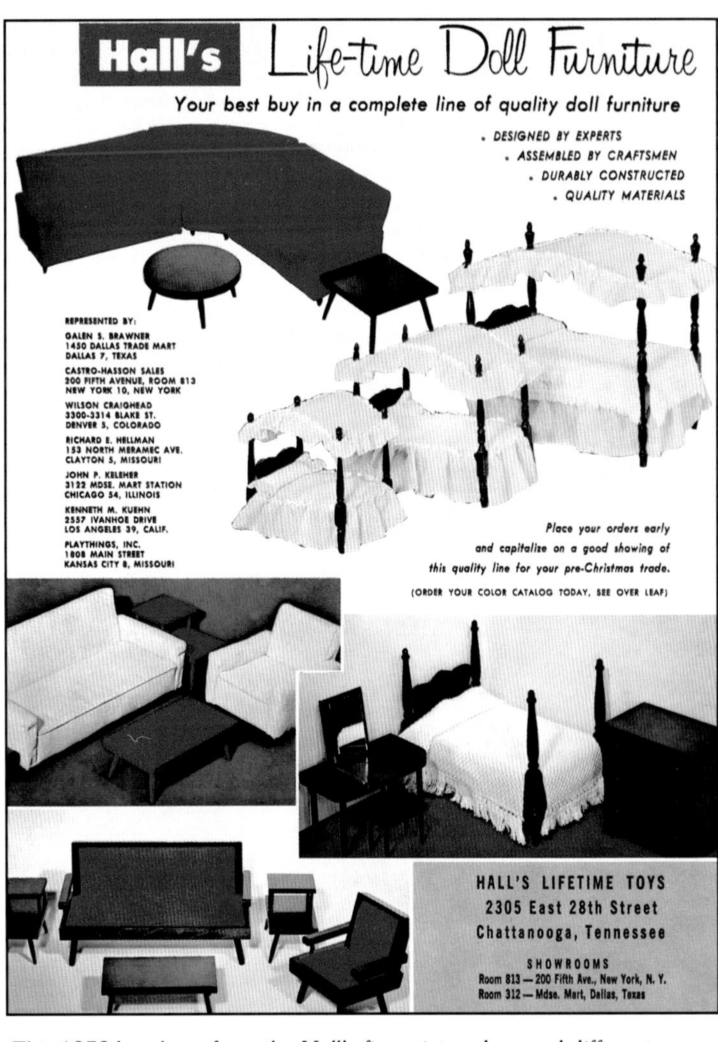

This 1959 brochure from the Hall's firm pictured several different styles of doll furniture. Most of the pieces were to be used with the 10" dolls but the canopy bed was offered in several sizes.

The F.A.O. Schwarz Christmas catalog for 1959 pictures four rooms of Hall's furniture, using the firm's folding dollhouse as backgrounds. Madame Alexander dolls were pictured in the rooms but were sold separately. The bedroom set included a four poster bed, three drawer chest, dressing table with mirror and matching stool, and a 6" rocking chair. All were finished in mahogany. The set was priced at $12.95. The two folding walls and a 20" x 20" floor of ply covered veneer-wood could be purchased for $4.00. The kitchen furniture consisted of a table, two chairs and a stool priced at $3.50. Most of the furnishings were printed on the wall. The dining room pieces included a table, two chairs, hutch, and buffet priced at $8.95. The living room was furnished with a sofa, easy chair, two end tables, and a coffee table priced at $8.95 for the set. Both the dining room and living room sets were finished in mahogany. The living room upholstery was red corduroy. Each of the Hall's backgrounds was priced at $4.00.

In the 1966 Hall's company catalog, their set of wood 1" to one foot scaled dollhouse furniture was labeled "new" but it was pretty much like the furniture pictured in the 1965 catalog. A different television, hutch, toilet, baby dresser, and the elimination of the baby's shoofly (replaced with a night stand) apparently were responsible for the term "new." Each set was priced at $5.00. A Ranch House and an A-Frame house were to be used with the furniture. The two-story Ranch House could be furnished with all six sets of furniture. It measured 17" high x 36" wide x 15" deep and was to retail for $25 unfurnished. The A-Frame was 22" high x 24" wide x 12" deep and sold for $15.00. *Courtesy of Marcie Tubbs. Photograph by Bob Tubbs.*

Right:
Hall's offered a Country Pine Line of furniture in its catalog for 1976. It was larger in scale and was to be used with the 8"-12" size dolls. The same catalog featured the Independence Row Houses Line, produced in conjunction with the Bicentennial celebration of the United States. The houses included the Molly Pitcher, Abigail Adams, Betsy Ross, and an Inn. The smaller houses were 30" high x 14" wide x 12" deep. Each contained three rooms in three stories. The Inn included five rooms and measured 29" high x 23" wide x 13" deep.

"Dolly Doll Houses" from Greenwich, Connecticut featured the Hall's houses in a 1976 catalog. Included was the Country Classic House at the top left that sold for $52.50. The basic design of this house had been used by Hall's since the late 1960s but this model had been changed somewhat from the first houses. It measured 21" high x 38" long x 25" deep.

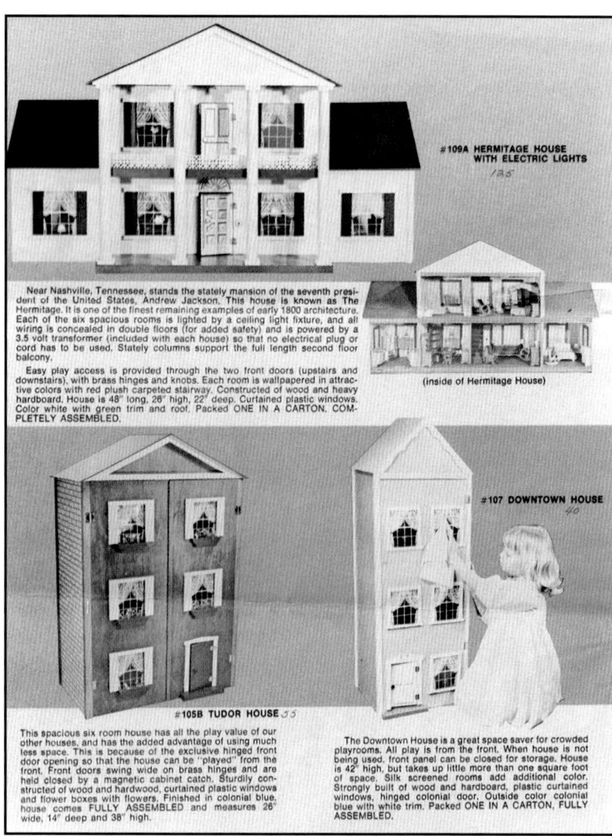

The Hermitage House, another Hall's favorite, was also pictured in the Dolly Doll Houses catalog in 1976 at the top of the page. It was based on the house of Andrew Jackson, located near Nashville, Tennessee. The two-story, six-room house was made of wood and heavy hardboard with plastic windows. It was priced at $125 with electric lights. The house measured 48" long x 26" high x 22" deep.

Honor House Prod. Corp

The Electric split-level dollhouse from Honor House Prod. Corp. of Lynbrook, New York was advertised in the "Linda Carter, Student Nurse" comic book in September 1961. The six-room house came with thirty pieces of plastic furniture made from Renwal molds. The lighting system was battery operated. A dollhouse family and a car were also part of the $2.98 package. No mention is made of what material was used to make the house. It measured 12" high x 24" wide x 12" deep. *Courtesy of Judy Mosholder.*

Another Honor House was advertised in 1969. This house was large enough that a child could get inside and play with the small plastic furniture arranged beside the two end walls. The two-story house had eight rooms and the package included a five-piece doll family, a thirty-three piece furniture set, and a battery powered electric system. The advertisement does not mention the material used in producing the house. The outfit sold for $5.98 and measured 30" x 34" x 36".

Ideal

(See also 1940s section)

Ideal's Tammy family dolls were featured in the Aldens 1963 Christmas catalog. Pictured are the dolls dressed in special outfits which were priced separately. The basic dolls could be purchased dressed in simple clothing. They included Tammy priced at $1.92; mother and father for $2.87 each; Ted, priced at $2.47 and Pepper for $1.88. The vinyl dolls ranged in size from 8" to 14" tall. *Courtesy of Marilyn Pittman.*

Special furniture was provided for Ideal's Pepper and Patti in the Montgomery Ward Christmas catalog for 1965, The two rooms of furniture included a living room sofa, two armchairs of vinyl coated fiberboard, vinyl coffee table, twin beds, vanity, and bench. The two 9" dolls and the furniture were priced at $6.99. *Pittman Collection.*

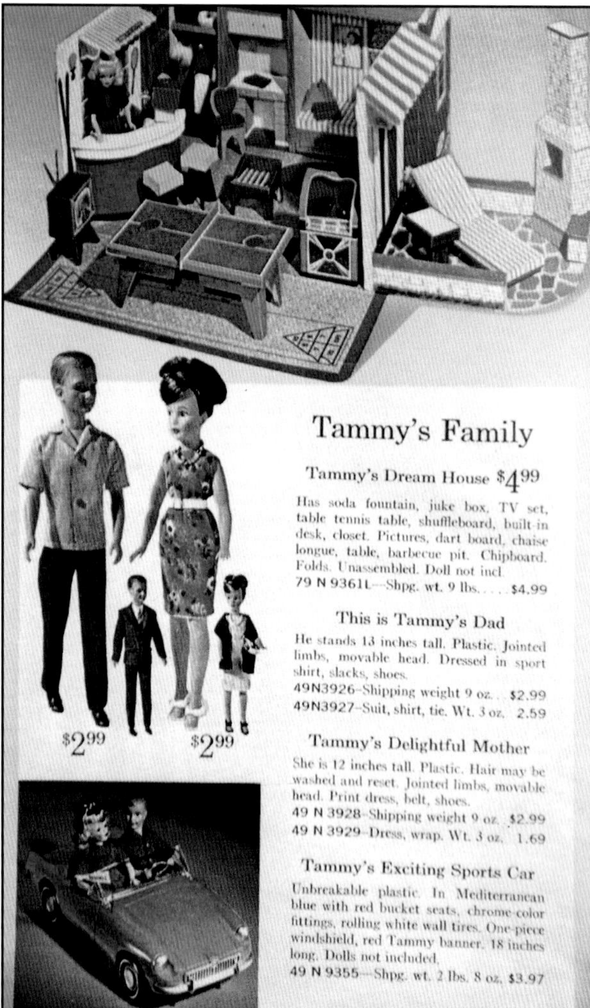

The Sears Christmas catalog for 1964 advertised Tammy's Dream House, priced at $4.99. The house was made of chipboard and included a soda fountain, juke box, TV. set, table tennis table, shuffle board, built-in desk, closet, chaise lounge, table and barbecue pit. A sports car was also available for $3.97. See page 131 of *American Dollhouses and Furniture* for a photograph of the house.

This "Cavehouse" was advertised in the Montgomery Ward Christmas catalog in 1965 to accompany Ideal's Pebbles and Bam-Bam dolls then popular. The dolls were based on characters from the Flintstones. The house was made of corrugated fiber board and also included several pieces of furniture. The ad copy stated the house could be used with either the 8" or 12" sets of dolls. The house sold for $1.99, not including the dolls. The 8" vinyl dolls sold for a little less than $3.00 each. *Pittman Collection*.

Irwin Corp.

The New York based Irwin Corp. produced an Interior Decoration set in the mid 1960s. The complete set included 236 pieces which provided enough furniture for five rooms. These included a dining room, kitchen, bedroom, bathroom, and living room. The furniture came with wall panels and floor coverings so the young decorator could design her own room. It was made to be mixed and matched, with chair bottoms and cushions that could be used in several different ways. The Irwin Studio Apartment set was advertised in the Montgomery Ward Christmas catalog in 1965. The doll family to be used with the furniture was also pictured. The studio apartment sold for $4.99. The plastic furniture was approximately 3/4" to one foot in scale. The magazine *House and Gardens* was credited for the coordinated colors. Rooms-in-Miniature are pictured at the bottom of the advertisement. These products were produced by Miner Industries, Inc. *Courtesy of Marilyn Pittman.*

Miner Industries, Inc.

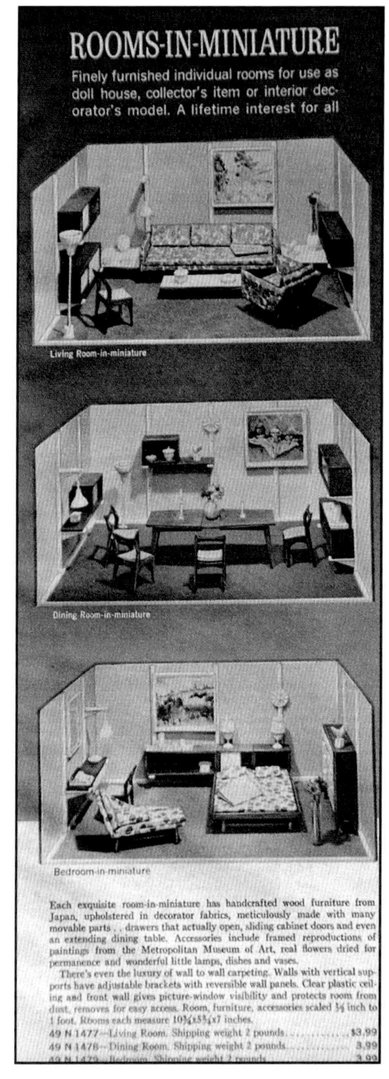

The Rooms-in-Miniature were also featured in the Sears 1964 Christmas catalog. They were marketed by New York based Miner Industries, Inc. Each of the three rooms sold for $3.99 and measured 10.75" x 5.75" x 7". The hand crafted wood furniture for all three rooms was from Japan and was approximately 1/2" to one foot in scale. The rooms included a living room, dining room, and bedroom.

Mattel, Inc.

Dozens of homes for the popular Mattel, Inc. Barbie dolls have been marketed over the years. During the 1960s and early 1970s, a variety of vinyl suitcases were produced for Barbie dolls as well as for members of Barbie's family. Pictured is "Barbie and Skipper's Deluxe Dream House" from the Sears Christmas catalog of 1965. The front dropped down to allow access to the built-in furniture provided for a bedroom, living room, and kitchen. The house sold for $9.99 and measured 27" x 7" x 18" when folded into the case.

Miniature Mart

The Miniature Mart, located in San Francisco, offered a full line of miniatures for many years. John M. Blauer was the owner of the company, which catered to adult collectors. The pictured catalog is circa 1967. *Courtesy of Roy Specht.*

In 1966, Sears offered a smaller Mattel, Inc. model home for the approximately 6.5" tall Mattel Inc. Tutti and Todd dolls. It included two beds, hangers and a space for clothes, and an outside play area. The two dolls and house sold for $7.99.

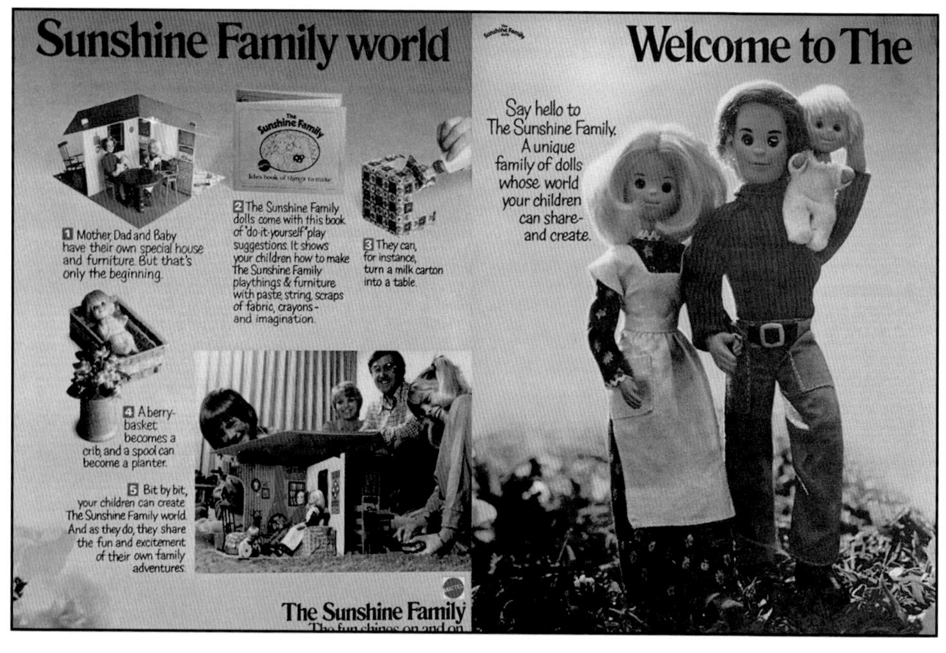

In the mid-1970s, the Sunshine Family was introduced by Mattel, Inc. This vinyl doll family consisted of a 9.5" male doll called Steve, a 9" female doll named Hattie, and a 3" baby doll called Sweets. There was also a black family called Happy Family. This two-page ad is dated 1975. It pictures the dolls and the four-room vinyl "Sunshine Family Home." The plastic furniture that came with the house was to be supplemented with items made by the consumer, following suggestions included with the house. See page 228 of *American Dollhouses and Furniture* for photographs of the dolls and house.

This page of lamps is from the Miniature Mart catalog circa 1967. They ranged in price from 65 cents each (232-234) to $16.00 each (222-223). *Specht Collection.*

Remco Industries

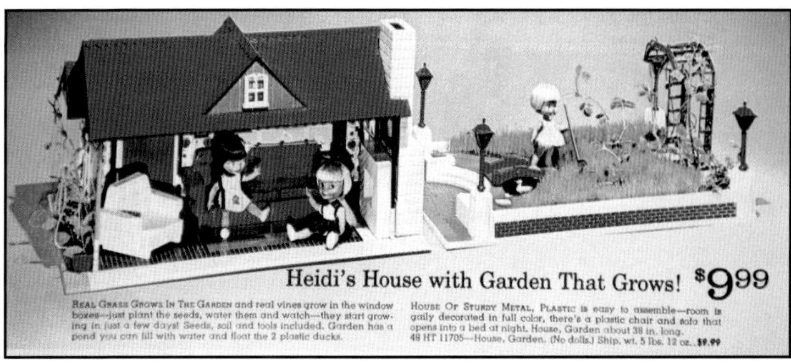

"Heidi's House with Garden that Grows" was advertised in the Montgomery Ward catalog for 1966. The 5.5" tall vinyl Heidi doll (the Pocket Doll) was produced by Remco Industries in the mid 1960s. The house was made of metal and plastic and came complete with a growing garden. The house contained one room. The roof of the house was plastic and the walls and floor were metal. The house was furnished with a plastic sofa and chair. The garden was attached to the side and included seeds, a pond, and tools. The house and garden measured 10.5" high x 38" long x 13" deep and sold for $9.99 with no dolls. Other plastic furniture that could be purchased for Heidi included a table, chairs, buffet, modern bathroom with corner tub and vanity, bunk beds, dresser, chair, table and lamp. See page 226 of *American Dollhouses and Furniture* for a photograph of this house.

Schwarz, F.A.O.

F.A.O. Schwarz sold this house through their stores and catalogs from the late 1950s until the early 1970s. The two-story house included seven rooms and a two-story porch. In this 1961 F.A.O. Schwarz Christmas catalog, the house was priced at $125.00 unfurnished. It was made of white pine plywood and included electric ceiling lights in each room. This particular model had an open back but some models came with removable fronts and backs. It measured 26" high x 36" wide x 20" deep. The furniture available to furnish the house included fifty-four pieces of period pieces in 1" to 1 foot scale plus curtains, rug, mattresses, and bedspreads. The furniture was probably the later Lynnfield design sold by Henry Messerschmidt or Block House. The furniture set sold for $108.00. Two sets of German Caco dolls were also available. The Peasant Family dolls measured from 2.25" to 4" tall and sold for $4.50. The larger Caco family set of dolls were from 3.5" to 5.5" tall. This set of dolls included a maid and sold for $5.95. See page 140 of *Antique & Collectible Dollhouses* for a photograph of this house.

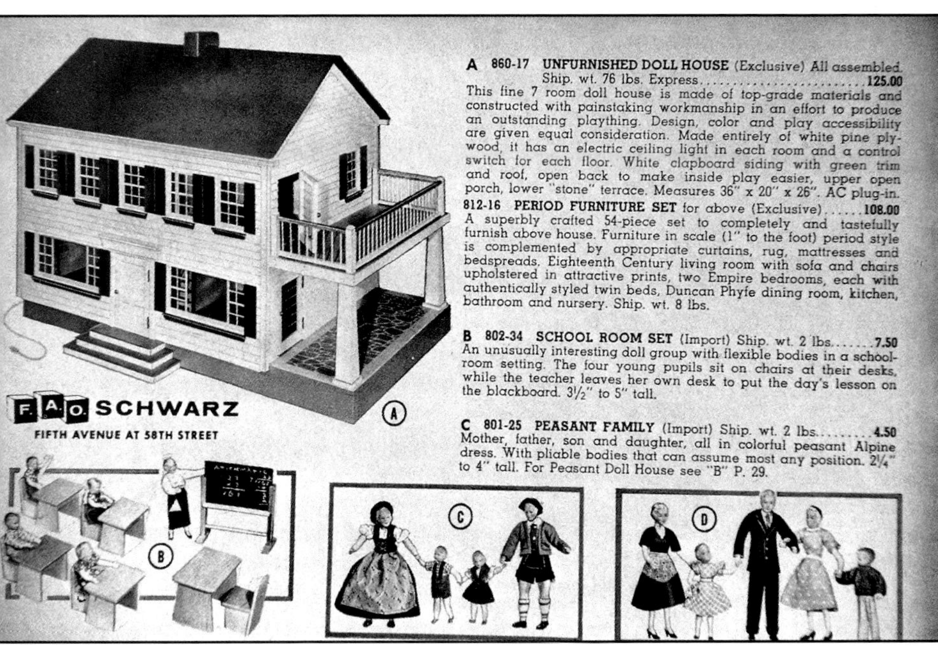

A 860-17 UNFURNISHED DOLL HOUSE (Exclusive) All assembled. Ship. wt. 76 lbs. Express........................125.00
This fine 7 room doll house is made of top-grade materials and constructed with painstaking workmanship in an effort to produce an outstanding plaything. Design, color and play accessibility are given equal consideration. Made entirely of white pine plywood, it has an electric ceiling light in each room and a control switch for each floor. White clapboard siding with green trim and roof, open back to make inside play easier, upper open porch, lower "stone" terrace. Measures 36" x 20" x 26". AC plug-in.

812-16 PERIOD FURNITURE SET for above (Exclusive)......108.00
A superbly crafted 54-piece set to completely and tastefully furnish above house. Furniture in scale (1" to the foot) period style is complemented by appropriate curtains, rug, mattresses and bedspreads. Eighteenth Century living room with sofa and chairs upholstered in attractive prints, two Empire bedrooms, each with authentically styled twin beds, Duncan Phyfe dining room, kitchen, bathroom and nursery. Ship. wt. 8 lbs.

B 802-34 SCHOOL ROOM SET (Import) Ship. wt. 2 lbs.......7.50
An unusually interesting doll group with flexible bodies in a schoolroom setting. The four young pupils sit on chairs at their desks, while the teacher leaves her own desk to put the day's lesson on the blackboard. 3½" to 5" tall.

C 801-25 PEASANT FAMILY (Import) Ship. wt. 2 lbs.........4.50
Mother, father, son and daughter, all in colorful peasant Alpine dress. With pliable bodies that can assume most any position. 2¼" to 4" tall. For Peasant Doll House see "B" P. 29.

A
A 819-80 WEEKEND HOUSE 26.95
A delightful spot for a country weekend is this tastefully furnished, attractively finished two-section Weekend House, complete with family—mother and father, son, daughter, and 2 guests. One section, 18"x8½", comprises an informal living room with curtains, rug, table, chairs — even plants — and bedroom with bunk beds and closet. The other section, 18" x 5½", has a second bedroom with bunk beds for the children, a modern kitchen, and the W.C. For outdoor relaxation there is an airy patio with furniture. Carefully constructed of wood, with red roof, colorful flower boxes, and "stone" patio. 9½" high. Ship. wt. 10 lbs.

The F.A.O. Schwarz Christmas catalog also featured a weekend house priced at $26.95 completely furnished. The house came in two sections. One section included the living room and bedroom and the other section contained a kitchen and a bedroom for the children. It included bunk beds and a tiny bathroom. An outside furnished patio was also provided for the family of dolls. The house measured 9.5" high x 18" wide x 24" deep.

This two-story house was also sold by the F.A.O. Schwarz firm for several years. The house was probably made by Keystone (see 1940s chapter under Keystone). Pictured is the fanciest model of the house from the Schwarz 1961 Christmas catalog. A platform could be purchased for the basic house, which offered a patio and yard. It sold for $6.95. The basic two-story house contained six rooms when movable partitions were in place. The house had clear plastic windows, a television antenna, two chimneys, and a cupola. It was made of wood and hard board. The house measured 23" high x 37" wide x 16.5" deep. It sold for $28.95 unfurnished. Wood furniture in a 1" to 1 foot scale could be ordered for $28.95 to furnish the house. It was not pictured, but the set was probably a variation of the German pieces pictured with the house on page 110 of the *International Dollhouses* book. The German Peasant House is also shown in that book, on page 113.

This German Peasant dollhouse was also carried by the Schwarz firm for a number of years. This one dates from 1961. It was labeled "Exclusive" in the ad copy. The chalet type house included three large furnished rooms and sold for $59.50 in 1961. Twenty-five decorated pieces of wood furniture came with the house. The open-backed house measured 17" high x 29" wide x 16" deep. The Peasant doll family recommended for the house was too small for the larger 1" to one foot scaled home.

Toymaster

This corrugated fiberboard three story Toymaster dollhouse was advertised in the Cullum and Boren Co. Fall and Winter catalog in 1961. The house also included fiberboard furniture for a kitchen, living room, and bedroom. The house sold in the Sears 1960 Christmas catalog for $4.33. It measured 52.75" high x 28.5" wide x 13" deep, and was to be used with the larger dolls then popular.

Weber, Franz Carl

1 Zweiteilige Puppenstube, mit Türe vom einen zum anderen Zimmer, je einem Fenster und mit Wandspiegel. Zu den modernen Farben passen die modernen Möbeli! Puppenstube wie oben, leer . . . . . Fr. 24.80

Neu: Schlafzimmer-Möbeli wie Bild . . . . . . Fr. 13.50

Neu: Wohnzimmer-Möbeli wie Bild . . . . . . Fr. 7.80

2 Einteilige Puppenstube mit verschiedenfarbigen Wänden und einem Fenster. 47,5x28 cm gross, ohne Möbeli . . . . Fr. 13.90

Neu: Wohnzimmer-Möbeli wie abgebildet, Holz-Kombination hell/dunkel . . . . Fr. 15.80

3 Neu: Zweiteilige Puppenstube, schöne Holzausführung mit halber Trennwand und zwei Fenstern mit Vorhängen. 35x60 cm gross mit 11 cm breitem «Dachgarten» und garniert mit schönen, modernen Wohn- und Schlafzimmer-Möbeln. Komplett wie Bild,

Alleinverkauf Franz Carl Weber! Fr. 49.80

4 «Decor»-Puppen-Sommerhaus, für das Weekend, zweistöckig
Treppe und Dachgarten. 3 Zimmer, ausgestattet mit soliden M
als Schlafzimmer, Wohnküche und Wohnstube. Die linke Hausseit
der Wohnstube kann nach rechts zugeklappt werden, wodurch
fertiges hübsches Einfamilienhaus entsteht. Komplett Fr.
Einfachere Ausführung . . . . Fr.

5 Moderner, grosser Kaufstand, in dem ein Kind bequem Platz
Total-Tiefe 70 cm, Höhe der Rückwand 83 cm. Solide Holzausführ
10 Plastik-Schubladen, richtiggehende Uhr! . . . . Fr.
Verkaufsstand mit 10 kleinen Schubladen und Tablaren, ohne
62½ cm lang, 66½ cm breit und 79½ cm hoch . . . . . . Fr.

6 Modernes schwedisches Puppenhaus, mit Küche, Bad, Wohn
und 2 Dachzimmern, Treppe, durchbrochenen Fenstern und 2 T
Verschieden tapeziert und bemalt. In allen Räumen elektrische Bel
tung und verschiedene Anschlüsse. Stromquelle normale Taschenlam
Batterie. Alle Räume mit reizenden Puppenmöbeli reichhaltig ausge
tet (wie Abbildung). Puppenhaus 71 cm breit, 26 cm tief und 45 cm h
Alleinverkauf bei Franz Carl Weber! Komplett Fr.

28

This Franz Carl Weber catalog page from 1961-62 features both dollhouses and furniture made in Germany. Rooms are pictured in both one and two room sizes and the two houses shown range from the simple (note TV antenna) to the more complicated. The house at the top appears to open from the middle to allow access to its rooms. The descriptions are in German. *Courtesy of Linda Boltrek.*

Winthrop-Atkins Co., Inc.

Several different designs of the Instant Doll Houses were made by the Winthrop-Atkins Co. in the 1960s. The firm, based in Middleboro, Massachusetts, advertised their Instant Doll House in *Chain Store Age* in December 1967. The houses were made of heavy "Plasticized" fiberboard that flipped open easily to form a ranch-style house with three rooms and a patio. Seven pieces of furniture were included as pictured. The house was made in two sizes to fit the 4" and 6" size dolls. The house, which was designed to be used with 6" dolls, measured 9" high x 17.5" wide x 12.5" deep.

Woodmaster – Metal Master Corp.

Woodmaster dollhouse featured in the Sperry and Hutchinson Green Stamp catalog circa 1967. The five-room house was made of hardboard and came with Plastic Multiple Products furniture. It measured 18.5" high x 24" wide x 13.5" deep. Woodmaster, of Newark, New Jersey, also produced a smaller size of the house measuring 14" high x 20" wide x 10" deep. See page 210 of *American Dollhouses and Furniture* for a photograph of the house. The inside walls are nicely decorated. Woodmaster was a division of Metal Master Corp. of Newark, New Jersey. *Courtesy of Linda Boltrek.*

Deluxe 6-Room Furnished Doll House 11.87
A HOME OF HER OWN ... she'll be delighted Christmas morning. Full color doll house durably constructed of fine quality wood hardboard. 6 Rooms, 2 floors completely furnished in the latest decorator styles. She will have fun playing decorator and re-arranging furniture. 24-inches wide, 18½-inches high, 13½-inches deep: ideal for todays most popular sized dolls. Easy to assemble. Place your Christmas order early. Mailable.
34 Y 5976E—Doll House. Shipping weight 13 lbs.......... 11.87

The Aldens Christmas catalog in 1967 offered a six-room Woodmaster house for sale at a cost of $11.87. This house was the larger model. *Courtesy of Marilyn Pittman.*

Uneeda Doll Co.

Several different companies produced Troll dolls during the 1960s. The most popular were the Wishnik models made by the Uneeda Doll Co. of Brooklyn, New York. A Wishnik house and clothing was offered for the trolls in the Sears Christmas catalog for 1967. The two-room house included built-in furniture. When the suitcase-type house was opened, a patio folded down from the main house. The vinyl carrying case measured 9" high x 10" wide x 8 " deep. It sold for $2.49. A separate 3" vinyl Uneeda troll could be purchased for only 69 cents.

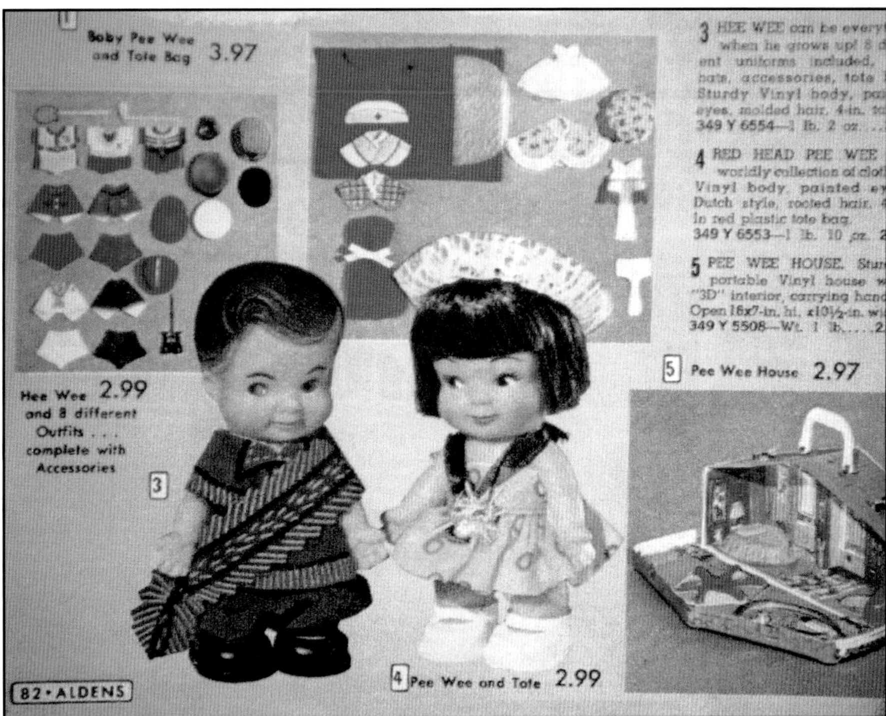

In addition to trolls, the Uneeda firm was also responsible for production of the small "Pee-Wee" dolls in the mid to late 1960s. Aldens Christmas catalog for 1967 featured a page of the dolls, clothing, and a small vinyl suitcase house similar to the one made for the Wishnik troll dolls. It contained molded furniture and sold for $2.97. The house measured 7" high x 18" wide x 10.5" deep when it was opened. The vinyl Pee-Wee dolls were 4" tall. *Pittman Collection.*

Unidentified

This unidentified dollhouse family was offered for sale in the Montgomery Ward catalog in 1965. The five plastic flexible dolls had very large hands. The father was 4.5" tall. All of the dolls had molded hair. The family sold for $1.59. *Pittman Collection.*

1970s Advertisements

As toys for little girls, dollhouses in the 3/4" to one foot or the 1" to one foot scale continued to decline in popularity as playthings for little girls in the 1970s. Larger houses for the Mattel Barbie dolls continued to dominate the market. Even the Marx firm experimented with this new concept in dollhouses and furniture when they became involved with the larger 11" tall Sindy doll and her houses and furniture. The venture was not successful and by 1980, the once powerful toy company filed for bankruptcy. Most of the other dollhouses and furniture was produced for adult collectors. Catalogs and brochures were issued by B. Shackman, Mark Farmer, Sonia Messer Imports, Spielwaren (Germany), Woodesigns, and many others featuring furniture and accessories geared to the adult collector.

There were a few toy companies producing items for the dollhouse field. Hall's Lifetime Toys was still active in the business until the late 1970s, producing both dollhouses and furniture. The new Brumberger Co. apparently bought out the T. Cohn firm, as they sold several of the old T. Cohn designed dollhouses under their own name in the late 1960s and 1970s. Newly designed houses were also part of the Brumberger line. They furnished many of these houses with the T. Cohn "Superior" plastic furniture.

One new company did make an impact on the dollhouse market during the 1970s and into the 1980s. It was the Lundby firm from Sweden. Even the Montgomery Ward and Sears catalogs featured their houses, furniture, dollhouse dolls, and accessories. Many collectors are now adding Lundby products to their dollhouse collections. The firm produced so many different styles of furniture, a collector will have trouble choosing the best. Examples from the firm's various brochures are pictured in this chapter.

A new character from the American Greeting Corp. called Holly Hobbie did inspire at least three different designs of dollhouses. Two of the houses are pictured in ads in this chapter and the third house is shown in the *American Dollhouses and Furniture* book on page 230.

As the decade of the 1970s ended, the dollhouse market was booming in the adult miniature field but remained slow in the toy industry.

American Greeting Corp.

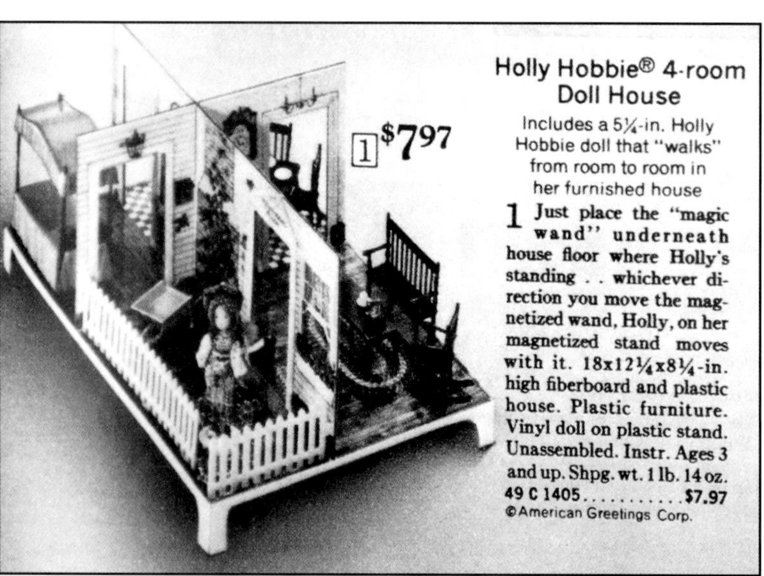

Holly Hobbie® 4-room Doll House
1 $7.97
Includes a 5¼-in. Holly Hobbie doll that "walks" from room to room in her furnished house
1 Just place the "magic wand" underneath house floor where Holly's standing . . whichever direction you move the magnetized wand, Holly, on her magnetized stand moves with it. 18x12¼x8¼-in. high fiberboard and plastic house. Plastic furniture. Vinyl doll on plastic stand. Unassembled. Instr. Ages 3 and up. Shpg. wt. 1 lb. 14 oz.
49 C 1405..........$7.97
©American Greetings Corp.

A Holly Hobbie four-room dollhouse was advertised in the 1975 Sears Christmas catalog. Holly Hobbie products were copyrighted by the American Greeting Corp. The house was made of fiberboard and plastic. A 5.25" vinyl Holly Hobbie doll came with the house. She could be mounted on the magnetized stand and moved from room to room with the help of a magnetized wand. The house was furnished with plastic furniture. It was priced at $5.33 and measured 8.25" high x 18" wide x 12.15" deep.

1 Holly Hobbie© doll house . . . a 2-story charmer, completely furnished and ready for 6-in. Amy and Carrie to move right in. Dolls sold separately, below.
FEATURES: Front porch and rear staircase make it a delightful place to live. Prettily decorated inside and out. Made of plastic/fiberboard. About 18x17x18 in. high overall. Put together without tools.
INCLUDES: Old-time "brass" bed, patchwork quilt, kitchen table and chairs, rocking chair, sofa, "cast iron" stove, hope chest, plates, teakettle. Made of plastic.
48 T 11602—Ship. wt. 7 lbs. **15.96**

2-3 Carrie and Amy, only 6 in. tall, just the right size to play in doll house sold above.
DETAILING: Vinyl dolls have rooted hair, painted features. Movable arms, legs. Hands that hold things. Old-fashioned clothing.
INCLUDES: Each doll comes with tiny baby doll and plastic accessories shown. Ages over 3.
Ship. wt. each 6 oz.
(2) 48 T 10469—Carrie **4.44**
(3) 48 T 10470—Amy **4.44**

4-6 Dream-Along™ dolls. Holly, Carrie and Amy, dressed for bed and sweet dreams.
DETAILING: 12 in. tall. Soft, cuddly rag bodies and heads. Yarn hair. Painted features.
COSTUMES: Pastel print nightgowns and night caps. Each doll has her own tiny plush pet tucked in the pocket of her nightie. Ship. wt. each 5 oz.
(4) 48 T 10327—Holly **4.33**
(5) 48 T 10329—Carrie **4.33**
(6) 48 T 10330—Amy **4.33**

A different Holly Hobbie dollhouse was featured in the Montgomery Ward 1979 Christmas catalog. The American Greeting Corp. Holly Hobbie dolls could be purchased separately. The two-story house featured a front porch and stairway, and came completely furnished with plastic furniture. Included were a bed, quilt, table and chairs, rocking chair, sofa, kitchen stove, hope chest, plates, and tea kettle. The house measured 18" high x 17" wide x 18" deep and sold for $15.96. It was scaled for 6" dolls. The dolls sold for $4.44 each. *Courtesy of Marilyn Pittman.*

Brumberger Co.

#757 Colonial Wooden Doll House

A beautifully designed Doll House with authentic Dutch Colonial styling complete to its GAMBREL type roof.
Sturdily constructed of top grade composition wood, laminated in realistic full color for beauty and long life.
Complete with plastic windows, hinged door which opens and closes, chimney and staircase plus a full assortment of unbreakable plastic furniture including kitchen, dining room, living room, bedroom and bathroom pieces.
Doll house is easy to assemble with all nut and bolt construction and is complete with heavy duty brackets to withstand rough child's play.
Assembled size is approximately 14" wide, 11" deep and 12" high.

Packed 6 to master carton. Shipping Weight—30 pounds.

760 CONTEMPORARY DOLL HOUSE
With handsome deck, canopy and patio furniture this Contemporary Doll House will make a beautiful playtime possession for any young miss. Ruggedly constructed of top grade composition wood, laminated in realistic full color for long life and easy to assemble with all nut and bolt construction. Complete with plastic windows, hinged door which opens and closes, chimney and a full assortment of unbreakable plastic furniture. Assembled size is approximately 21" wide, 11" deep and 12" high.
Packed 6 To Master Carton. Shipping Wt. 35 lbs.

The new Brumberger Co., located in Brooklyn, New York, apparently bought out the T. Cohn firm as they sold several of the old T. Cohn designed dollhouses under their own name in the late 1960s and 1970s. Newly designed houses were also part of the Brumberger line. They furnished many of these houses with the T. Cohn "Superior" plastic furniture. The 1977 Brumberger Co. catalog featured five different dollhouses as well as toy structures for boys. It included this #757 "Colonial Wooden Doll House." It was made of composition wood laminated in color. The windows and door were plastic. The house included two rooms and plastic furniture to furnish a living room, kitchen, bedroom, and bathroom. It measured 12" high x 14" wide x 11" deep.

The #760 "Contemporary Doll House" was also made of composition wood and contained six rooms. The open-backed house included a front deck and was furnished with plastic furniture for all its rooms. It measured 12" high x 21" wide x 11" deep.

The Chalet Dollhouse #754 is most often found by dollhouse collectors. This open-backed model also included a "flip-top roof" to make access easier. The composition wood house came with plastic furniture for a kitchen, dining room, living room, bedroom, and bathroom. A carport is part of the design. The base is 20" wide x 11" deep and the house is 11" high.

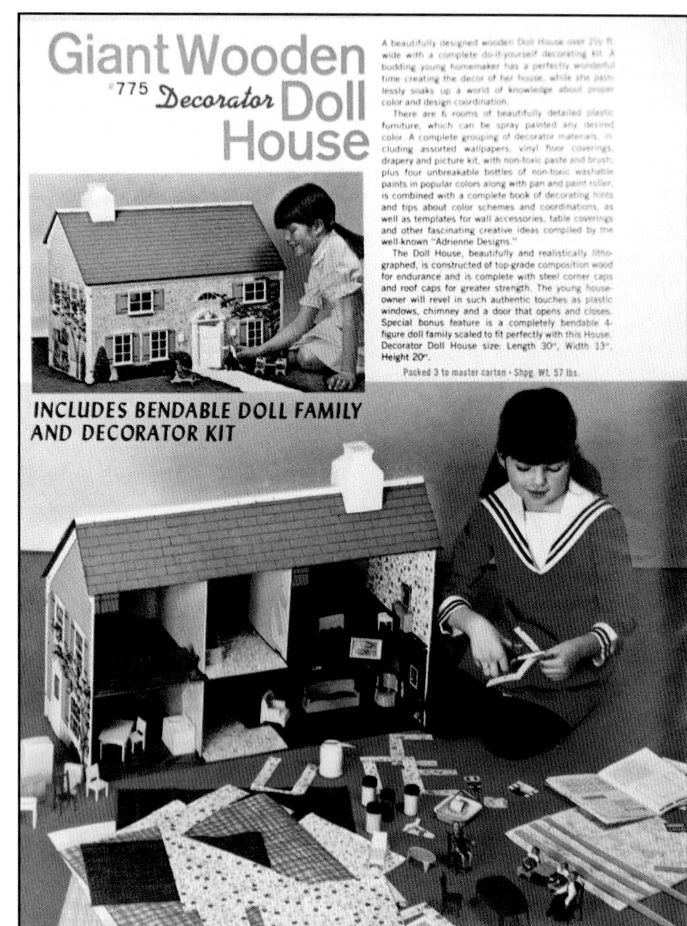

The Brumberger "#775 Decorator Doll House" came with six rooms of plastic furniture (appears to be very early Superior mold). Washable paint was included to paint the furniture. Wallpapers, vinyl floor coverings, drapery, and picture kits were also included as part of the decorating kits. A booklet offering hints for decorating and a bendable doll family were part of the package as well. The composition wood house measures 20" high x 30" wide x 13" deep.

Left:
"Colonial Two Story #770 Wooden Doll House" also from the Brumberger 1977 catalog. The products were all manufactured in their factory in Brooklyn, New York. This unusual house includes composition wood construction along with tin lithographed floors, plus plastic chimney, windows, and door. The five-room house came with six rooms of plastic furniture. It measured 20" high x 24" wide x 10" deep.

The same Colonial house was featured in the True Value Christmas catalog in 1968. It sold for $8.88.

#789 — Wooden FIRE HOUSE

ire fighting holds an ever-esh excitement, and the fire ouse is the center of the ction — where the colorful rama starts and ends. This ing-size station is constructed f finest-grade composition vood for strength and endur-nce, beautifully lithographed n realistic colors and complete vith steel corner caps and roof rackets for added rugged-ess. Plastic doors open and lose.

The taut reality of the setting s emphasized by some half-ozen warning and road signs n bold colors and 3 sets of road lockades.

The Fire House is designed or use with most plastic or teel fire trucks. Size: Length 7½", Width 26½", Height 15".

acked 4 to a master carton. hipping wt. 39 lbs. (Trucks ot included).

In addition to dollhouses, Brumberger's also produced several toy buildings for boys. These boy toys included a "Wooden Fire House" #789. It was produced of composition wood lithographed in bright colors. Although signs and roadblocks were part of the package, no fire trucks were included. 15" high x 26.5" wide x 17.5" deep.

Irene Miniatures Co. Ltd.

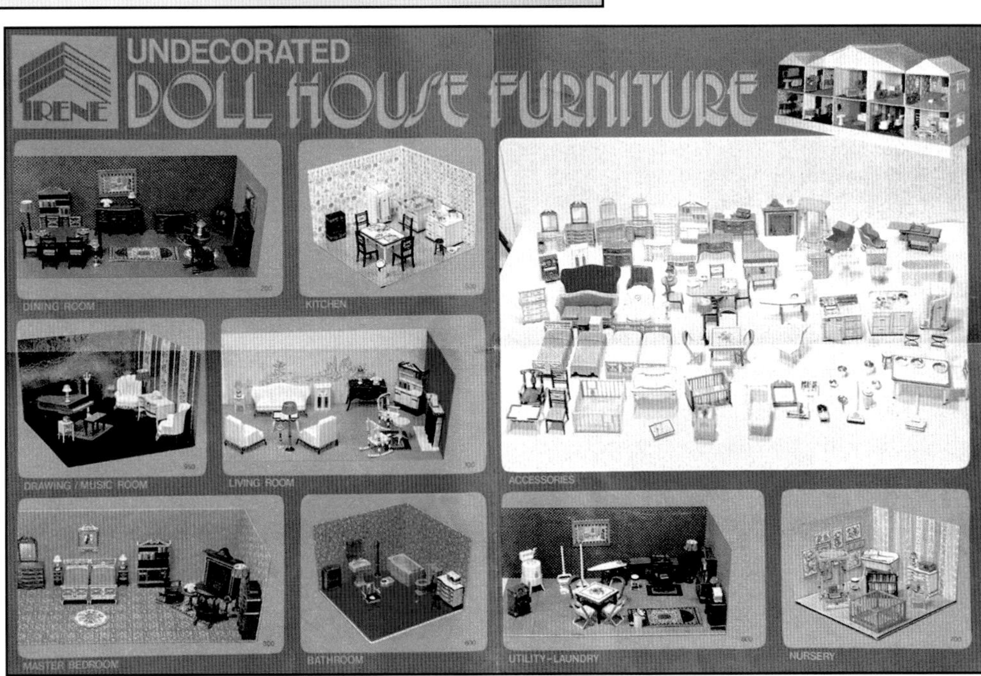

Pictured here is a circa 1977 brochure from the Chicago based Irene Miniatures. The plastic furniture was 3/4" to one foot in scale and produced in Hong Kong using many of the earlier Renwal designs. The brochure shows pieces for a dining room, kitchen, music room, living room, master bed-room, utility-laundry room, and nursery. Even the Renwal card table and chairs were reproduced. See page 228 of *Antique & Collectible Dollhouses* for photo-graphs of the actual furniture. *Courtesy of Judy Mosholder*.

Lundby of Sweden

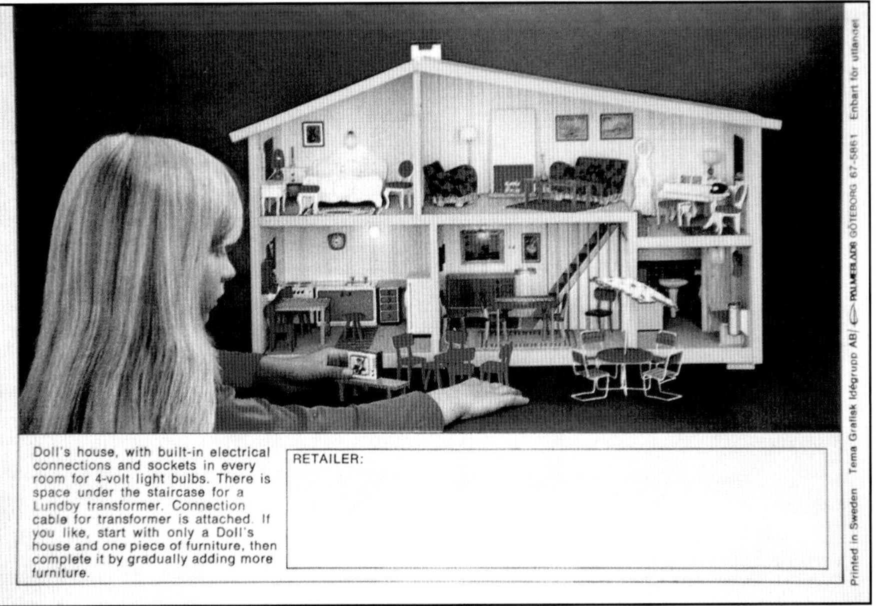

Doll's house, with built-in electrical connections and sockets in every room for 4-volt light bulbs. There is space under the staircase for a Lundby transformer. Connection cable for transformer is attached. If you like, start with only a Doll's house and one piece of furniture, then complete it by gradually adding more furniture.
RETAILER:
Printed in Sweden

The Lundby of Sweden firm was located in Lerum, Sweden and was very successful in marketing their 3/4" to one foot scale furniture and dollhouses during the 1970s and 1980s. The firm began producing furniture shortly after the end of World War II and the line grew until it consisted of over two hundred items by the late 1980s. The basic Lundby house is pictured here in one of the company catalogs. This two-story example included built-in electrical connections. Six rooms of furniture could be used in the house. *Courtesy of Judy Mosholder.*

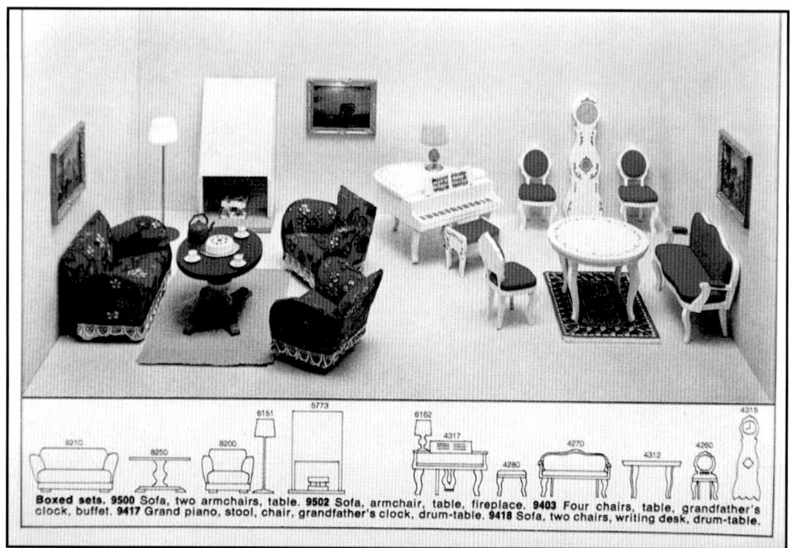

Another page of the Lundby brochure pictured pieces that could be used in a living room and music room. Accessories and dollhouse dolls were also supplied by the Lundby firm. *Mosholder collection.*

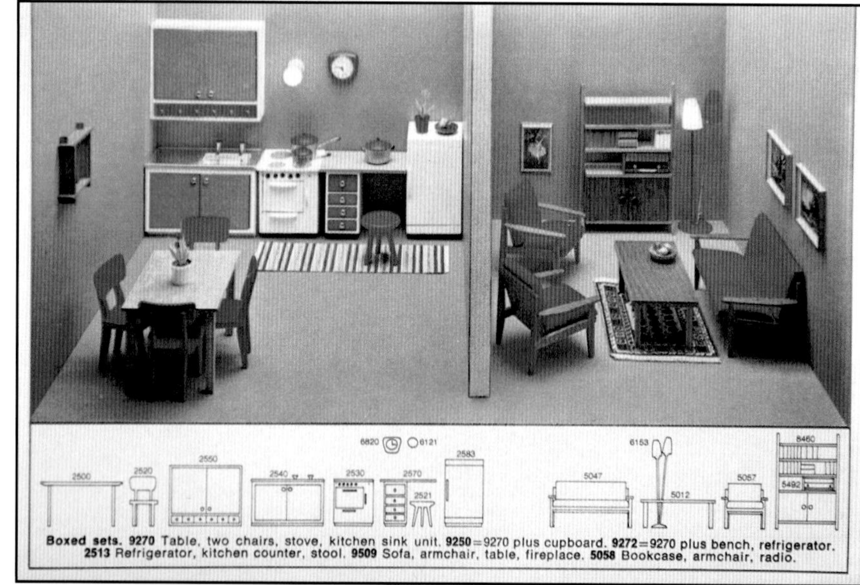

These two rooms of very modern Lundby pieces were shown in the same brochure. Many of the drawers and doors were operational in the Lundby furniture. *Mosholder collection.*

The basic Lundby house was offered in the 1979 Montgomery Ward Christmas catalog. It measured 15.5" tall x 30" wide x 10" deep and sold for $34.95 unfurnished.. The sets of furniture to furnish the house included a kitchen ($21.99), bathroom ($14.99), bedroom ($12.99), music room ($12.99), dining room ($18.99), and living room ($18.99). The family of bendable dolls came as a set for $14.99. *Courtesy of Marilyn Pittman.*

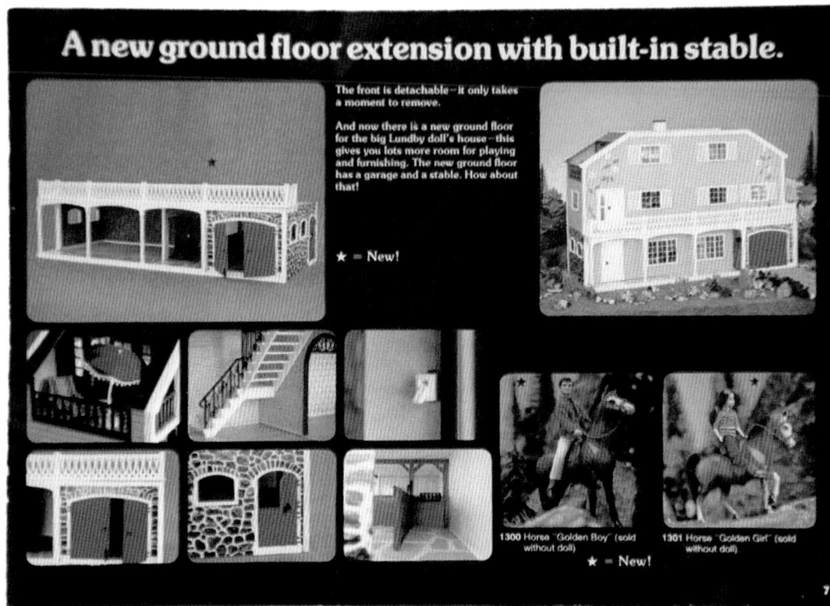

A more recent brochure pictured several different sizes of the Lundby houses. Pictured is the outside of the house with an additional story added on the bottom. The front of the house was detachable. *Courtesy of Carol Stevenson.*

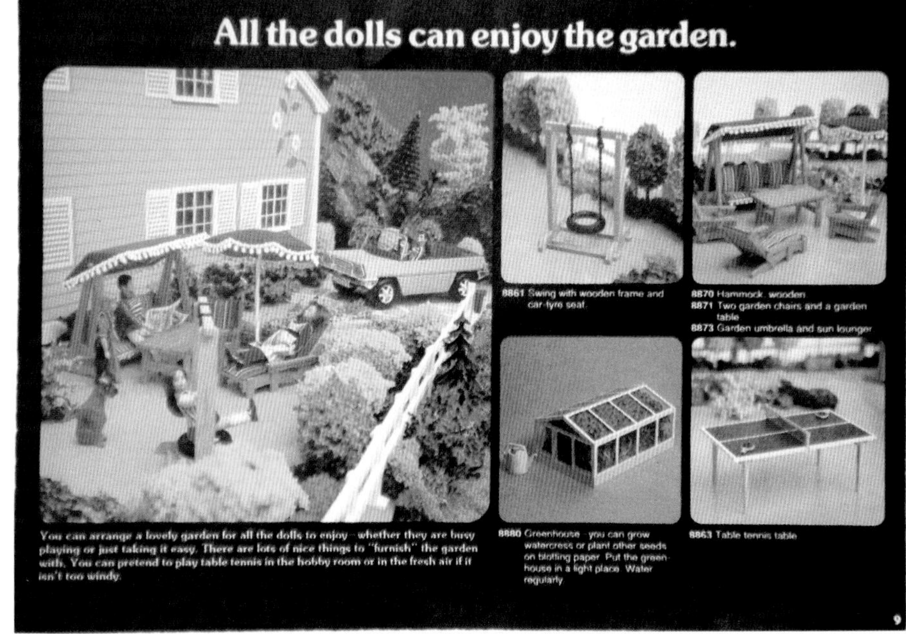

In addition to furniture for inside the house, outdoor accessories were also provided by Lundby. Included were a tire swing, ping pong table, and outside chairs, table, swing and umbrella. *Stevenson Collection.*

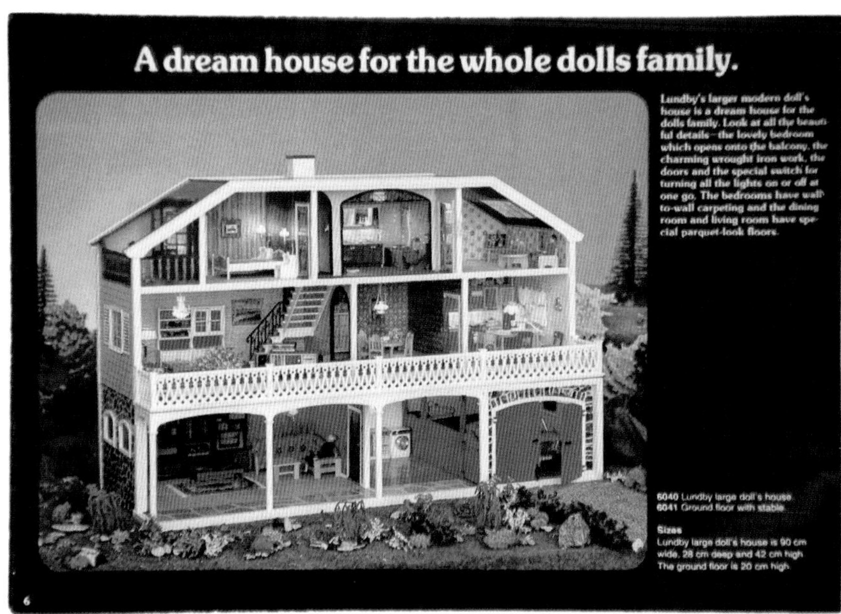

The later Lundby brochure pictured their largest house consisting of three stories. It was sold unfurnished in the 1981 Sears catalog for $119.98. *Stevenson Collection.*

Several rooms of furniture are pictured from the later Lundby brochure. The same dining room as the one pictured on the lower left was offered by Sears in 1981 with a light finish for $19.99. The same kitchen was priced at $23.99. *Stevenson Collection.*

This Lundby brochure pictured a total of twenty-one dolls that could be purchased to live in the dollhouses. The Sears 1981 catalog offered a four-piece deluxe doll family priced at $17.99. The dolls had soft vinyl bodies with flexible joints. The children were 3.24" tall and the parents measured 4.75" in height. *Stevenson Collection.*

B. Shackman & Co.

B. Shackman & Co. was a wholesale importing firm located in New York City. The company was founded in Wilkes Barre, Pennsylvania in the 1890s by Bertha Shackman. Eventually the business moved to New York City. In the 1970s, the company was managed by Shackman descendents when their catalogs featured many pieces of 1" to one foot scaled furniture as well as dolls and accessories. This upholstered living room furniture was featured in the Shackman 1973 catalog and included a high back chair, club chair, sofa, and Queen Anne settee.

um piece. Features a slide that fits into notched staff. 4" tall.
3849 . . . Sold ½ dz. $25.20 dz.

3927 $10.40 dz. sets

3375 . $14.00 dz.

Candle & Plate Hol
Replica of antique original. Plate h er is adjustable. With hook for h ing on wall; also suitable on table. 1 high. Plate & Candle incl. Sold 2
3746 . $18.90 d

4786

Cape Cod Candleholder
A beauty! Of pewter-type metal ¾" dia. Has hole for party size candle Sold 2 dz.
4786 . . . $6.05 dz.

6501

Chandelier —
Beautifully proportioned metal classic. 2¼" dia., 2" deep. With hanger.
6501 . . . $12.15 dz.
Sold 1 dz.

CANDLESTAND with CANDLEHOLDER — Cherrywood
A magnificent and authen replica of the actual m seum original. For d houses, collectors, etc. F hard smooth wood, natu stain finish, hand rubb Table 2½", candlest 1½". Sold 1 dz.
3386 . $14.60 dz

4787

Candelabra
A tiny gem! Pewter-type metal with 3 red tipped candles. 1⅛" tall. Sold 2 dz.
4787 . . . . $6.05 dz.

6509

2-Candle Wall Sconce
Embossed design. 1¾" high. Sold 2 dz.
6509 $8.15 dz.

3188

Metal Candelabra
Very graceful. Unusual. Early-American model. 2-pronged, 1" x 1¾".
3188 $10.50 dz.
Sold 2 dz.

6523

1-Candle wall Sconce
Embossed design with mirrored reflector. 2¼" high. Sold 2 dz.
6523. $8.15 dz.

Leaf Candle Holder
Art nouveau! 1½" dia. Sol 2
6522 . . $8.15

"COME IN AND VISIT US"

This page from the 1973 Shackman catalog included a metal chandelier, a candelabra, and wall sconces. Sometimes these pieces are thought to be much older than the 1970s because of their period look.

3918

Floor Lamp
Silk rick-rack trimmed shade is removable. Cherry-wood base with table, stands 5" high. Lovely and graceful. Sold ½ dz.
3918 . . . $21.95 dz.

5028

Sold 1 dz.

Lamp and Battery Box Set
Charming Cape Cod lantern with brass shade and base, glass chimney. Lamp is 2" tall, complete with bulb and its own battery box. In 2½" x 3" gift box.
5028 . $26.00 dz. sets
Battery not incl.

Oil Lamp
1908
1908
For desk or table top. 1⅜" high. Plastic. Sold 3 dz.
1908 $5.20 dz.

5647E

Glass Oil Lamp
Copy of antique original. 2 pc. in hand blown glass with shade decorated in contrasting color. 2". Sold 1 dz.
5647E . . . $8.15 dz.

5644E

Glass Candelabra
Hand blown with lovely spiral striped effect. Glass candles with red tip. 2" tall.
5644E. $6.60 dz.
Sold 2 dz.

These glass oil lamps from the same Shackman catalog may also be advertised as "antique" by unknowing sellers. Most of the Shackman miniatures were imported from Japan, Germany, or Taiwan.

Sonia Messer Imports

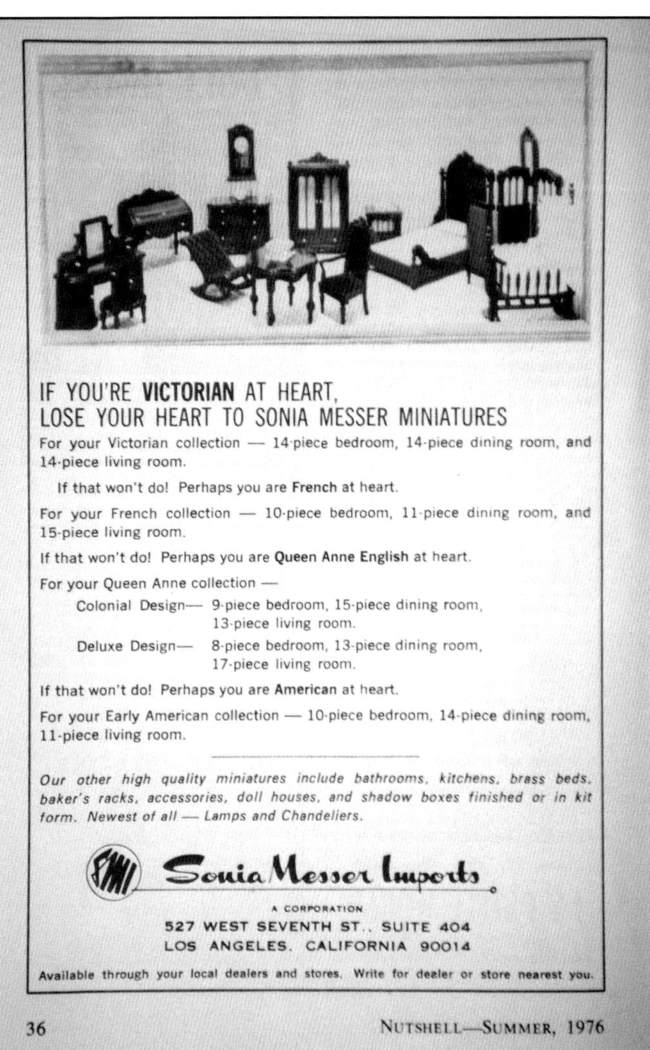

This Sonia Messer Imports ad appeared in the 1976 Summer issue of *Nutshell News* magazine. The firm marketed furniture especially made in Columbia for Sonia Messer Imports from the late 1960s until the early 1980s. Pictured are Victorian pieces. The company sold bedroom, dining room, and living room furniture in this style. They also carried Early American pieces for the same three rooms. *Courtesy of Gail Carey.*

A Sonja Messer brochure from the 1970s pictured the French 18th Century Collection furniture. The dining room set shown here included eleven pieces. This furniture was quite expensive. The table was priced at $34.95, a chair for $21.95, and the buffet for $45.95.

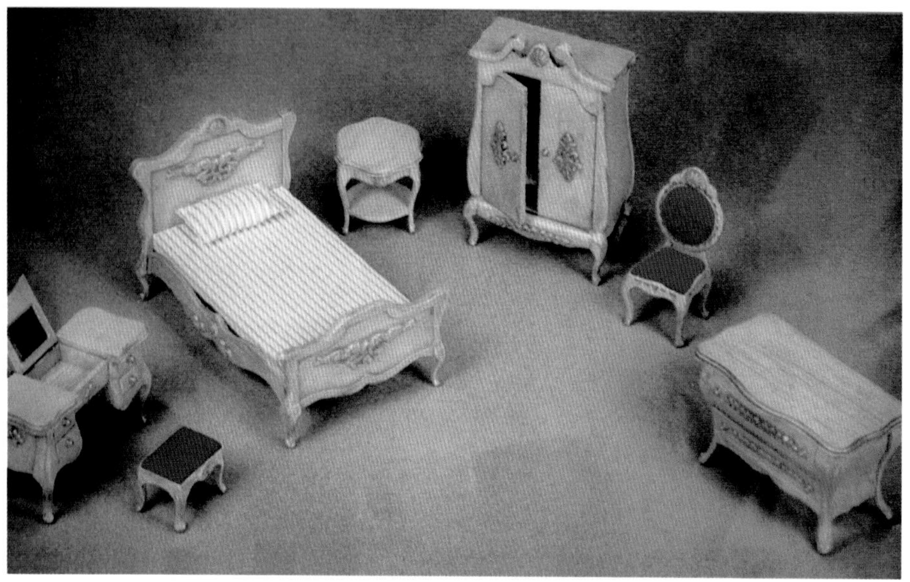

Matching sets to be used in a bedroom and living room were also available. Shown here is the bedroom set. The doors and drawers were functional on this furniture. See page 134 of *Antique & Collectible Dollhouses* for a picture of the 18th Century French living room pieces. Also available was the Queen Anne English Deluxe design in bedroom, dining room, and living room sets.

Spielwaren (Germany)

The German Spielwaren firm was responsible for producing a very unusual "fairy land" type of furniture during this time period. The basic furniture was 1" to one foot in scale and was made of wood with plaster type material used to provide the extra fancy decorations that adorned each piece. The result was miniature furniture "fit for a queen." Fancy room settings were also made to be used with the furniture. Pieces could be purchased individually or in room sets. Sets included those made for bedrooms, living rooms, music rooms, and dining rooms. Accessories featuring pictures, candle sticks, vases, and clocks were also available. Some of the firm's ads included "Seit 1952," perhaps a founding date for these products.

Woodesigns Co.

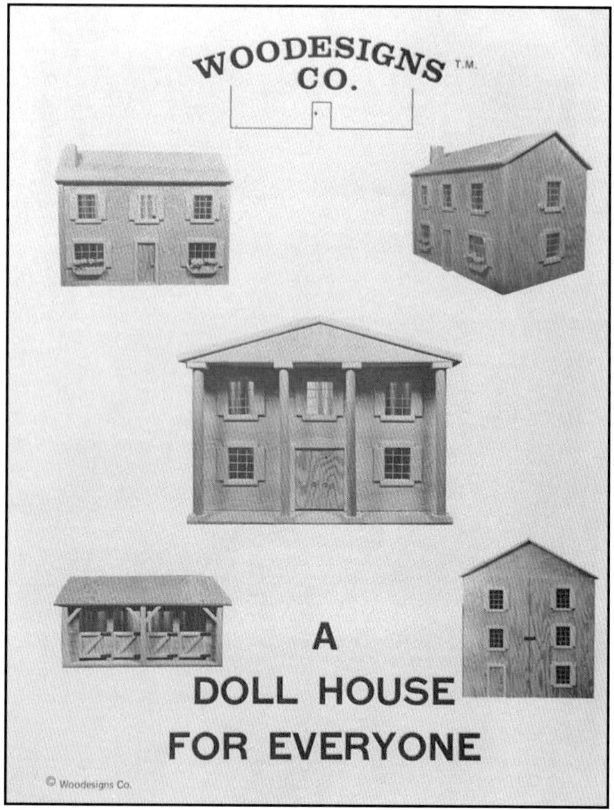

The Woodesigns Co. of Hawthorne, New Jersey offered catalogs in the 1970s and 1980s picturing dollhouses that could be purchased either assembled or unassembled. Houses, as well as a stable, are pictured on the front of the firm's catalog. Adult collectors were just beginning to show interest in the miniature hobby during this period and Donald Giannella, the owner, began his business at a good time to take advantage of this new market. *Courtesy of Linda Boltrek.*

1980s Advertisements

Although the 1970s marked the end of many of the earlier firms involved in the dollhouse industry, the 1980s offered some fine dollhouses from new as well as older firms.

By this decade, most American dollhouses and furniture were being produced in foreign countries for companies in the United States.

Several different lines of houses were marketed for younger children in the 1980s. These included houses offered by Fisher Price, Kenner (Strawberry Shortcake), and Mattel, Inc. (Littles). All of these houses were made of plastic and each package included special furniture and dolls designed especially for that particular house.

Two special houses were also offered during the decade for older girls. The plastic Tomy Smaller Homes was first marketed in 1980. Perhaps borrowing a concept used by Lundby, special rooms of furniture, accessories, and dollhouse dolls were marketed for the house. A more unique house from the era was the Craftmaster-Fundimensions house from 1982. This plastic house was special because electronic accessories could be purchased so the house would make the sounds of a grandfather clock, shower, piano, and more. Both of these houses and their furnishings are now considered very collectible.

The older Wolverine Toy Co. (Today's Kids) became very active in the dollhouse field in the 1970s and 1980s. The firm was still selling the old-styled metal dollhouses as late as 1984. The newer houses and furniture produced by the company are more collectible today. The Rite Scale line of houses were made of masonite, plastic and metal. The finely crafted plastic furniture was in a 1" to one foot scale.

Lesser known firms offered inexpensive plastic furniture labeled "Merry Toys" or "Blue Box," which had been produced in foreign countries.

Although the decade of the 1980s did not have the quality or variety of dollhouses from the 1930s, some very fine houses were produced that will remain as collector items for years to come. The advertisements and brochures in this chapter picture the products from the era. Maybe they will inspire a collector to add a more recent dollhouse to a collection. After all, some of these house are already twenty-five years old.

Arco Merry Toys

Box cover from set of Arco Merry Toys, circa early 1980s. The plastic 1/2" to one foot scaled furniture was marked "Arco Inc. Ltd. Made in Hong Kong." Pieces were made for a bedroom, bathroom, living room, dining room, family room, and kitchen as well as for a patio. This boxed set also included a 40" "Play Stage." *Courtesy of Judy Mosholder.*

Craftmaster-Fundimensions

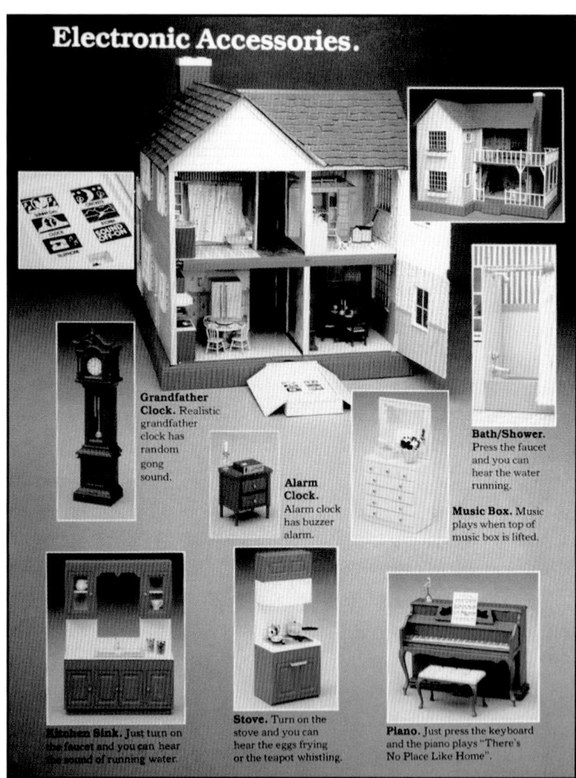

This page is from part of a booklet advertising the "Sounds Like Home" dollhouse marketed in 1982 by Craftmaster-Fundimensions, a division of General Mills Toy Group. The plastic dollhouse contained six rooms and could be furnished using fourteen special sets produced to accompany the house. Pictured are the electronic accessories. For a photograph of the actual house, see page 235 of the *Furnished Dollhouses* book. *Courtesy of Kathy Garner.*

Fisher-Price

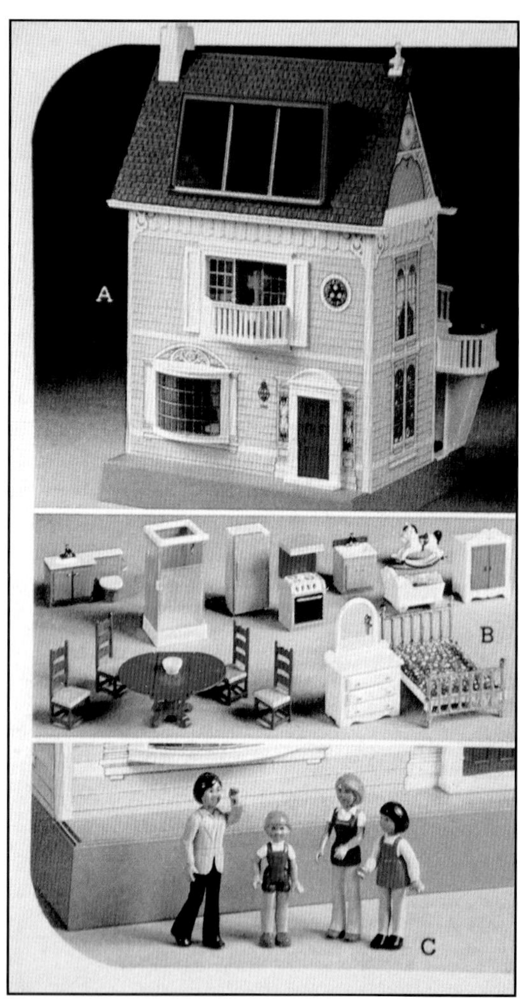

This Fisher-Price yellow plastic dollhouse was advertised in the Montgomery Ward Christmas catalog in 1984. The first floor included a kitchen-dining room-living room. The second floor featured a bedroom and bathroom and the third floor was an attic room. The house was priced at $39.99 unfurnished and measured 23.5" high x 15.5" wide x 13.5" deep. A set of plastic furniture was available to furnish the house at a cost of $29.99. A set of four family dolls was also available for $7.99. The dolls had movable heads, arms, and bendable legs. The entire Fisher-Price set of house, furniture and dolls was listed as 1" to one foot in scale.

Goebel Miniatures & Co.

The Butterfly Collection, by Goebel Miniatures & Co., was advertised in the August 1980 *Nutshell News*. Beginning in 1979, the firm offered several rooms of historically accurate furniture made of resin castings in the 1" to one foot scale. Each piece was marked with the year of production and a butterfly. The Stuart Library pieces were priced from $18 to $48 each. The pictured secretary is from that room. *Courtesy of Gail Carey.*

Kenner Products Co.

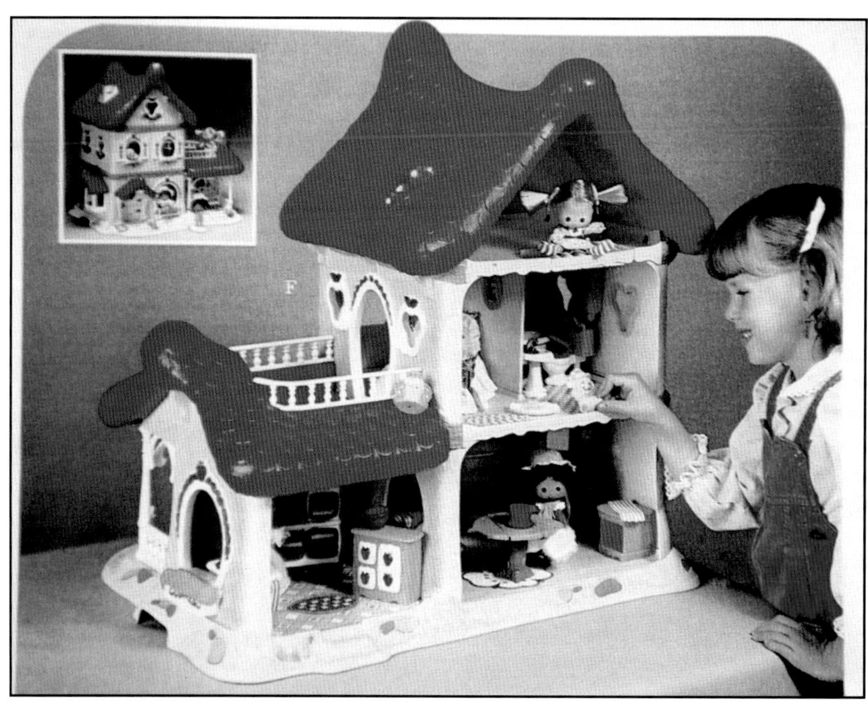

The "Strawberry Shortcake Berry Happy Home" was pictured in the Montgomery Ward Christmas catalog for 1984. It was marketed by Kenner Products Co. of Cincinnati, Ohio and made of molded plastic. The two-story house included a kitchen, combination dining room-living room, bedroom, and bathroom. A stairway which led to an attic was also included. The front porch was decorated with a swing. The house came completely furnished and measured 27" high x 27" wide x 20" deep. The 5.5" dolls were not included. It was priced at $149.99.

Mattel, Inc.

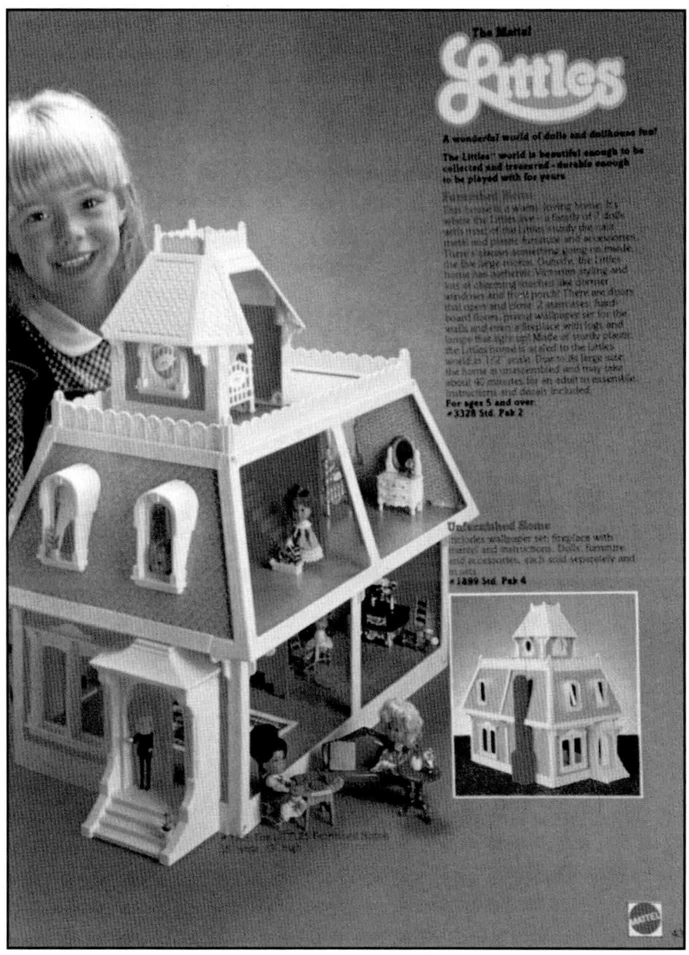

The Littles house was made by Mattel, Inc., in 1981 and 1982. Pictured is an advertisement from Mattel, Inc. showing the four-room plastic Victorian house. An attic room was also part of the house. The house and furniture were 1/2" to one foot in scale. *Courtesy of Marcie Tubbs. Photo by Bob Tubbs.*

A smaller and cheaper plastic "Carrying Case" house was also available to use with the Littles furniture and dolls and was pictured in the Mattel, Inc. brochure. It included three floors. *Tubbs Collection.*

Mattel, Inc. brochure picturing all of the furniture pieces and dolls produced in the Littles line. Most of the furniture was made of metal. Included were pieces for a family room, living room, bathroom, kitchen, and bedroom. Smaller sets and individual pieces were also available. The dolls were 2.5" to 3" tall. *Tubbs Collection.*

Tomy

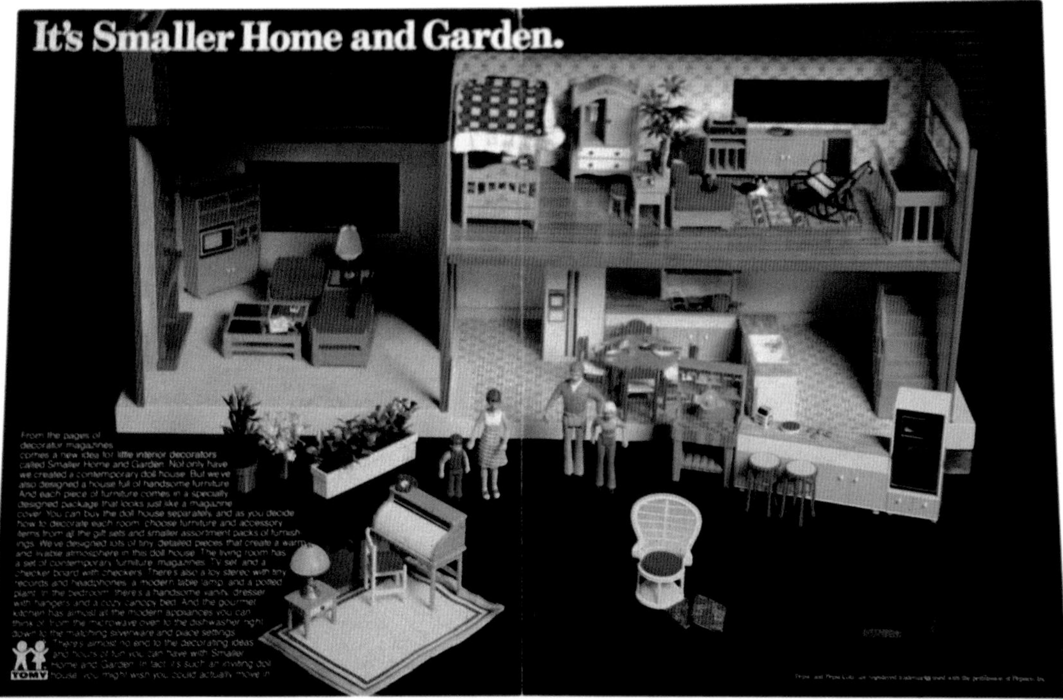

Brochure for Tomy Smaller Homes from 1982. The contemporary plastic houses were first marketed in 1980. Although the products were manufactured in Japan, the company was headquartered in Carson, California. The inside of the house included four rooms and a stairway. The windows were plastic. The house measured 14" high x 31" wide x 13" deep. The furniture was made of plastic in the 3/4" to one foot scale. *Courtesy of Marcie Tubbs. Photograph by Bob Tubbs.*

Many different sets of furniture as well as individual pieces could be purchased for the house. A living room and bedroom set were pictured in the 1982 company brochure. *Tubbs Collection.*

From the same brochure, the "new" nursery set as well as bathroom pieces are pictured. *Tubbs Collection.*

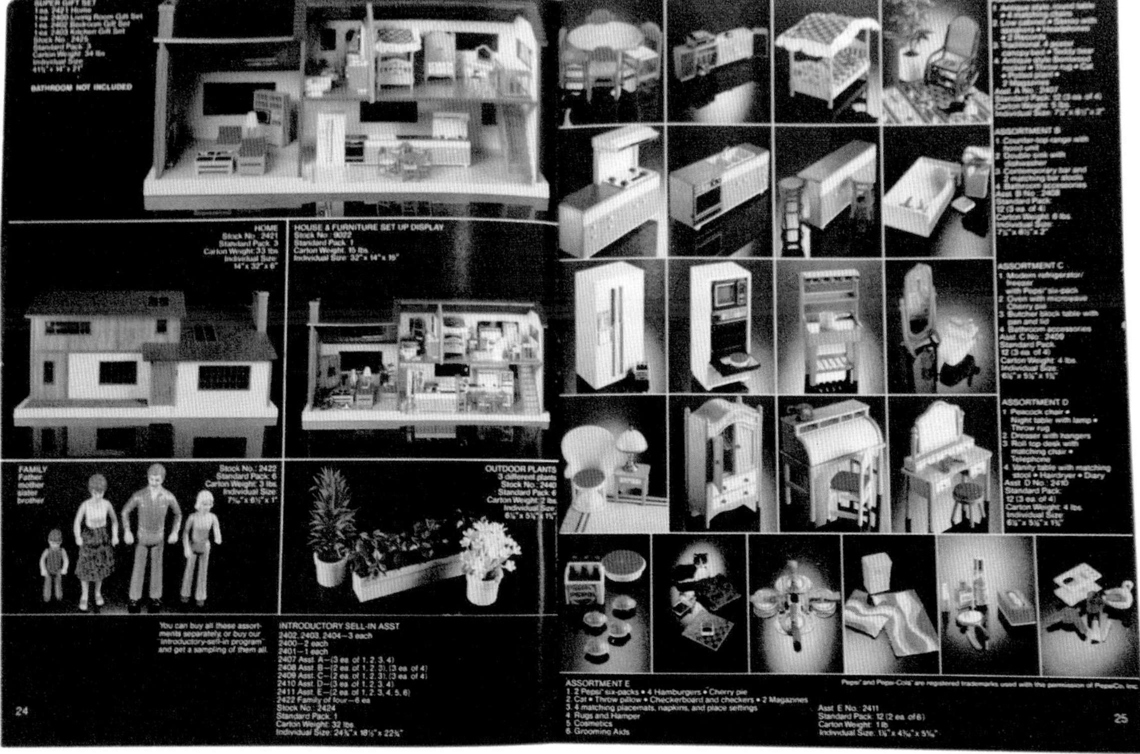

This 1982 Tomy brochure pictures the house, dolls to live in the house, plants, furniture and a variety of accessory packages. See page 236 of *Furnished Dollhouses* for photographs of the house and furniture. *Tubbs Collection.*

Wolverine Toy Co. (Today's Kids)

The 1984 catalog from the Wolverine Toy Co. (then located in Booneville, Arkansas) offered a variety of interesting dollhouses. Pictured are two different styles of metal dollhouses. The two-story "Town and Country " house was of steel construction and came with plastic furniture to furnish the living room/dining room, kitchen, master bedroom, children's bedroom, and bathroom. Male and female figures also were included in the package. The house measured 17.5" high x 22.25" wide x 12" deep. The metal Augusta dollhouse was also pictured. The exterior was decorated differently and a front porch had been added, but the plastic furniture (approximately 3/4" to one foot in scale) and the inside décor were the same as that of the Town and Country house. With the addition of a base, the house measured 25" wide x 15" deep and 17.5" high. *Courtesy of Marcie Tubbs.*

Unidentified

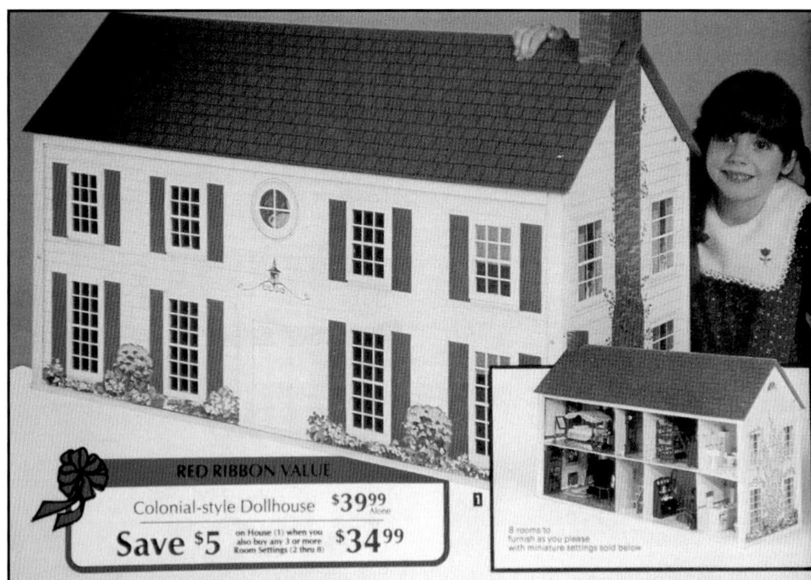

The Sears Christmas catalog in 1981 featured this unidentified Colonial-style dollhouse for $39.99. The two-story house included eight rooms. This was a do-it-yourself house which was sold unassembled. The furniture offered to furnish the house was similar to other pieces being marketed to the adult miniature collectors of the era. This house was produced for little girls, however.

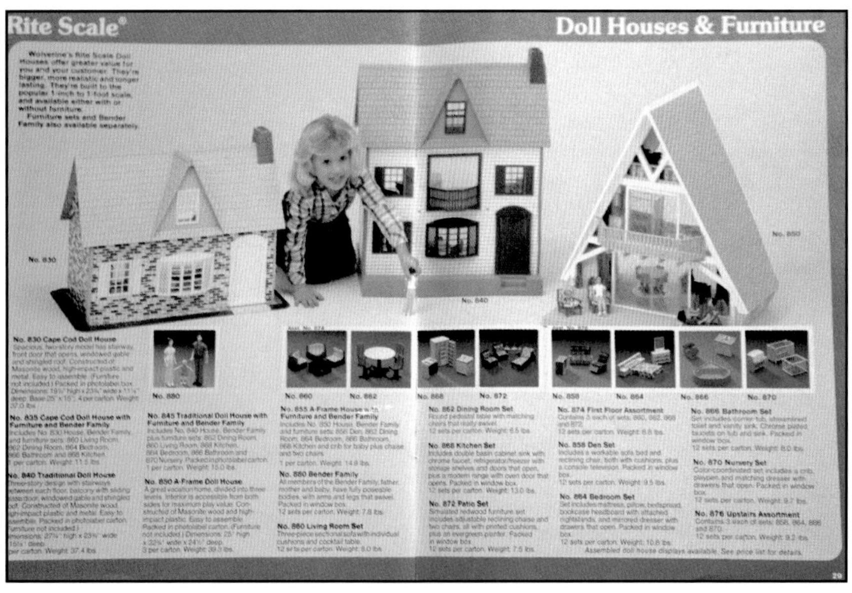

In addition to the traditional metal houses, the Wolverine firm (first founded in 1903 in Pittsburgh, Pennsylvania) also produced a line of Rite Scale houses in the 1" to one foot scale. Included was the Cape Cod house on the left made with masonite walls, metal flooring, and a plastic roof. It had four rooms and measured 19.5" tall x 23.75" wide x 11.25" deep. The house was sold either unfurnished or with five furniture sets plus the dollhouse family. The "Traditional" dollhouse pictured in the middle was also made of masonite, metal, and plastic. It included five rooms in three stories, a stairway, and a sliding door on the balcony. It could also be purchased with or without the furniture and dolls. It measured 27.75" high x 23.75" wide x 15.25" deep. The third house pictured was an A-Frame house. It was constructed of masonite, wood, and plastic. It was made on three levels and included a living room, dining room, and kitchen on the first floor, a sleeping area on the second floor, and a bathroom on the top level. Plastic furniture in a 1" to one foot scale was made to be used in all of the firm's Rite Scale houses. Included were sets for the living room, dining room, kitchen, patio, den, bedroom, bathroom, and nursery, plus a first floor assortment and second floor assortment. A boxed family set which featured posable dolls to represent a mother, father, and baby was also available. See page 187 of the *International Dollhouses* book for pictures showing several of these houses. *Tubbs Collection.*

Dollhouse and Furniture Magazine and Newspaper Plans

Plans for making dollhouses and their furnishings have been printed in a variety of magazines for nearly a century. Women's magazines often featured these types of articles in their November or December publications. Early issues of *Ladies Home Journal, Woman's Home Companion, Woman's World*, and *McCalls* often provided articles of this type. Children's magazines, especially *Child Life*, also printed similar articles. Usually the entire directions for making the houses or furniture were printed in the magazines but sometimes patterns needed to be ordered for a small fee to complete the project.

By the 1930s, men's magazines like *The Home Craftsman, Popular Mechanics*, and other similar publications offered patterns or printed articles on how to build a variety of different dollhouses. Beginning in the 1940s, *Woman's Day* magazine also contributed many different designs for making dollhouses.

Patterns sold through newspapers were usually to be used for sewing family clothing but infrequently, dollhouse patterns were also advertised. These patterns could be purchased for $1.00 or less from the address printed in the newspaper.

All dollhouse collectors have a dollhouse or two that they know were not commercial products. The question is, did a father or other relative design the house or was it made from a pattern from another source? It is hoped that this chapter may answer that question for some collectors when they are able to identify one of their houses by comparing it to a pictured pattern in this chapter.

A comfortable bedroom and library for the doll tenants. Note their grandfather's clock

Real meals can be cooked in this doll kitchen and eaten in the dining-room

A DOLLS' FOUR-ROOM BUNGALOW

With a Complete Outfit of Dolls' Furniture

DESIGNED BY JOHN D. ADAMS

DOES some father or big brother want to make the little daughter or sister of the household very happy this coming Christmas? If he is somewhat of a carpenter he can do so by following the plans and directions shown on this page.

"Oh, what a wonderful little house!" Mrs. Doll is sure to exclaim (if she is a talking doll) when she first sees it, on Christmas morning. "The kitchen is so convenient, the living-room is so ...

... stage in the diagram showing the method of erecting. (Fig. 1.) When the two ends already prepared are set up and nailed to the bottom, the second stage is reached. (Fig. 2.) The partition running from back to front comes next, and when the two doorways are cut, this should be set up and secured with nails driven up through the flooring. (Fig. 3.) The partitions between the dining- and living-rooms and between the bedroom and kitchen are next in order. (Fig. 4.) Note that these are connected with the other walls by means of corner strips, which may well be nailed to their respective walls before the latter are set up.

This *Women's Home Companion* article dates from November 1914. It is called "A Doll's Four-Room Bungalow," designed by John D. Adams. The house was to be made of 1/2" wood and wallboard. It included four rooms: a kitchen, bedroom, dining room, and living room. It measured 34" high x 52" wide x 42" deep. In addition to the house, complete directions to make fifteen pieces of furniture could be ordered from the magazine for ten cents.

Dollhouse and Furniture Magazine Plans

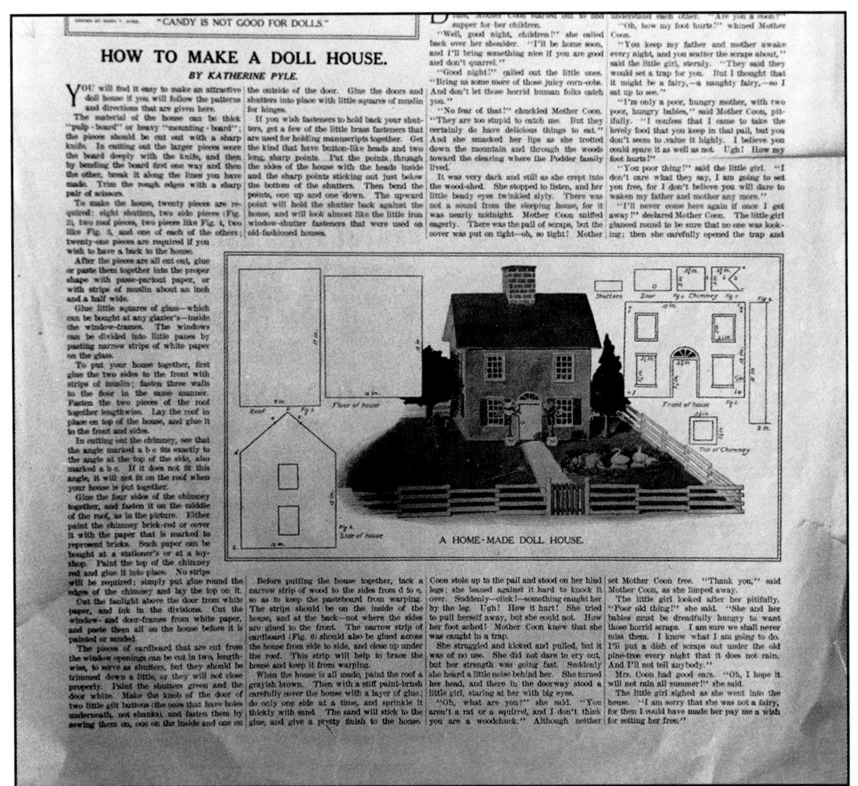

"CANDY IS NOT GOOD FOR DOLLS."

HOW TO MAKE A DOLL HOUSE.

BY KATHERINE PYLE.

A HOME-MADE DOLL HOUSE.

This early dollhouse plan appeared on the "Children's Page" in *The Companion* magazine for January 23, 1913. The article was titled "How To Make a Dollhouse" by Katherine Pyle. The house was to be made of a heavy cardboard material and glued together using strips of muslin material. The outside walls were to be sprinkled with sand after glue had been applied to give a stucco look. The finished house was 15" wide x 12" deep and apparently had only one room.

The Dining-Room Furniture

The Sideboard for the Dining Room

The Dining-Room Table

The Pretty China Closet

Paper Furniture for Your Betty Bonnet Doll

Which Can be Made Without Either Mucilage or Glue

By John V. Horr

The Armchair for the Head of the Table

There are Five Side Chairs Like This One

The Furniture for the Bedroom

THIS doll's furniture is lovely, and I know you will like it. The flower designs on the bedroom pieces are outlined in black, so that you can color them pink, blue or violet, whichever you like best. While the diagrams are on white paper, still you can color the furniture for the dining room with the paints in your paint box, but the bedroom furniture will be prettier in white, with only the design colored.

NOTE—In the December number we shall give pictures of the furniture for the hall, the living room and the kitchen. Diagrams will be offered.

"Paper Furniture For Your Betty Bonnet Doll," by John V. Horr, was published in the *Ladies Home Journal* magazine circa 1915. That firm printed Letty Lane paper dolls in each issue beginning in 1908, and in 1915 the feature was changed to monthly Betty Bonnet paper dolls. Both series of paper dolls were drawn by Sheila Young. Diagrams of this paper furniture could be obtained from the magazine. Included were furniture pieces for a dining room and bedroom. Furniture for a hall, living room, and kitchen were to be pictured in the December issue of the magazine, which also planned to offer diagrams for those rooms of furniture. *Courtesy of Carol Stevenson.*

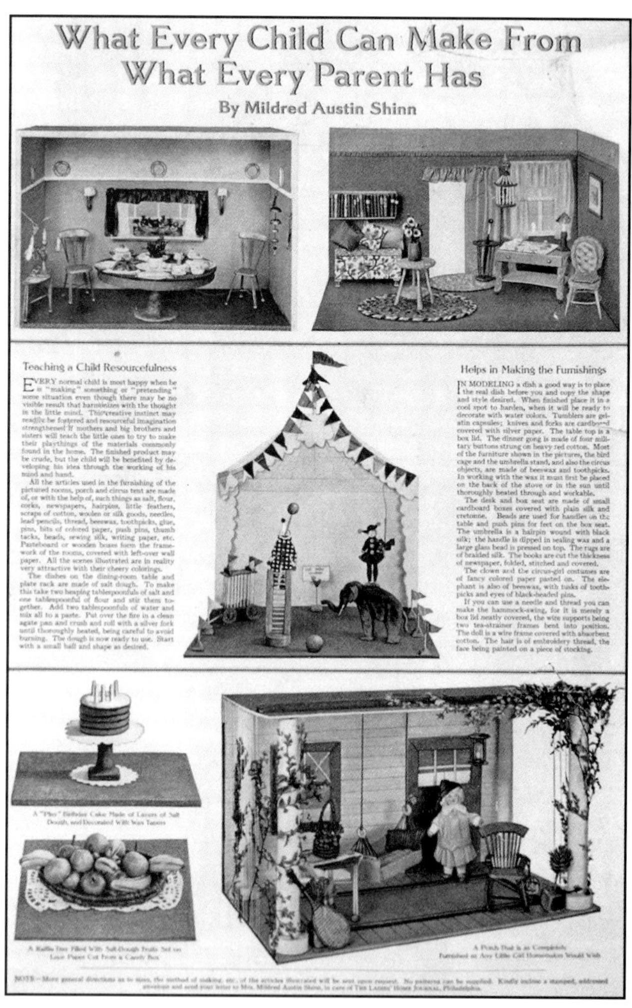

What Every Child Can Make From What Every Parent Has

By Mildred Austin Shinn

Teaching a Child Resourcefulness

EVERY normal child is most happy when he is "making" something or "pretending" some situation even though there may be no visible result that harmonizes with the thought in the little mind. This creative instinct may readily be fostered and resourceful imagination strengthened if mothers and big brothers and sisters will teach the little ones to try to make their playthings of the materials commonly found in the home. The finished product may be crude, but the child will be benefited by developing his idea through the working of his mind and hand.

All the articles used in the furnishing of the pictured rooms, porch and circus tent are made of, or with the help of, such things as salt, flour, corks, newspapers, hairpins, little feathers, scraps of cotton, woolen or silk goods, needles, lead pencils, thread, beeswax, toothpicks, glue, pins, bits of colored paper, push pins, thumb tacks, beads, sewing silk, writing paper, etc. Pasteboard or wooden boxes form the framework of the rooms, covered with left-over wall paper. All the scenes illustrated are in reality very attractive with their cheery colorings.

The dishes on the dining-room table and plate rack are made of salt dough. To make this take two heaping tablespoonfuls of salt and one tablespoonful of flour and stir them together. Add two tablespoonfuls of water and mix all to a paste. Put over the fire in a clean agate pan and crush and roll with a silver fork until thoroughly heated, being careful to avoid burning. The dough is now ready to use. Start with a small ball and shape as desired.

Helps in Making the Furnishings

IN MODELING a dish a good way is to place the real dish before you and copy the shape and style desired. When finished place it in a cool spot to harden, when it will be ready to decorate with water colors. Tumblers are gelatin capsules; knives and forks are cardboard covered with silver paper. The table top is a box lid. The dinner gong is made of four military buttons strung on heavy red cotton. Most of the furniture shown in the pictures, the bird cage and the umbrella stand, and also the circus objects, are made of beeswax and toothpicks. In working with the wax it must first be placed on the back of the stove or in the sun until thoroughly heated through and workable.

The desk and box seat are made of small cardboard boxes covered with plain silk and cretonne. Beads are used for handles on the table and push pins for feet on the box seat. The umbrella is a hairpin wound with black silk; the handle is dipped in sealing wax and a large glass bead is pressed on top. The rugs are of braided silk. The books are cut the thickness of newspaper, folded, stitched and covered.

The clown and the circus-girl costumes are of fancy colored paper pasted on. The elephant is also of beeswax, with tusks of toothpicks and eyes of black-headed pins.

If you can use a needle and thread you can make the hammock-swing, for it is merely a box lid neatly covered, the wire supports being two tea-strainer frames bent into position. The doll is a wire frame covered with absorbent cotton. The hair is of embroidery thread, the face being painted on a piece of stocking.

"What Every Child Can Make From What Every Parent Has" by Mildred Austin Shinn appeared in the *Ladies Home Journal* for July 1916. The article explains how to make the dollhouse and porch furnishings from boxes, beads, pins, buttons, beeswax, toothpicks, silk, cretonne, hairpins, salt, flour, corks, newspaper, glue, and colored paper.

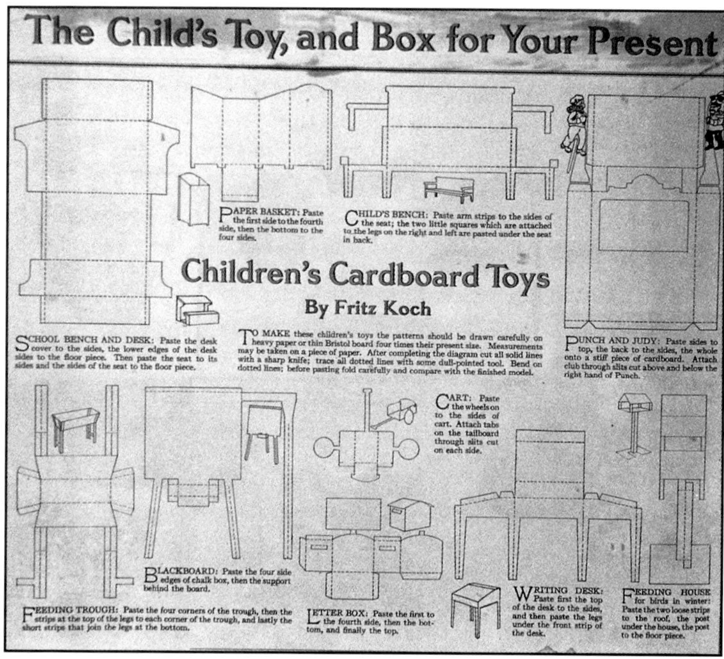

The Child's Toy, and Box for Your Present

PAPER BASKET: Paste the first side to the fourth side, then the bottom to the four sides.

CHILD'S BENCH: Paste arm strips to the sides of the seat; the two little squares which are attached to the legs on the right and left are pasted under the seat in back.

Children's Cardboard Toys

By Fritz Koch

SCHOOL BENCH AND DESK: Paste the desk cover to the sides, the lower edges of the desk sides to the floor piece. Then paste the seat to its sides and the sides of the seat to the floor piece.

TO MAKE these children's toys the patterns should be drawn carefully on heavy paper or thin Bristol board four times their present size. Measurements may be taken on a piece of paper. After completing the diagram cut all solid lines with a sharp knife; trace all dotted lines with some dull-pointed tool. Bend on dotted lines; before pasting fold carefully and compare with the finished model.

PUNCH AND JUDY: Paste sides to top, the back to the sides, the whole onto a stiff piece of cardboard. Attach club through slits cut above and below the right hand of Punch.

CART: Paste the wheels on to the sides of cart. Attach tabs on the tailboard through slits cut on each side.

BLACKBOARD: Paste the four side edges of chalk box, then the support behind the board.

FEEDING TROUGH: Paste the four corners of the trough, then the strips at the top of the legs to each corner of the trough, and lastly the short strips that join the legs at the bottom.

LETTER BOX: Paste the first to the fourth side, then the bottom, and finally the top.

WRITING DESK: Paste first the top of the desk to the sides, and then paste the legs under the front strip of the desk.

FEEDING HOUSE for birds in winter: Paste the two loose strips to the roof, the post under the house, the post to the floor piece.

The *Ladies Home Journal* for October 1916 offered several diagrams that could be used to make cardboard dollhouse furniture. It was suggested that the diagrams be enlarged before the furniture was cut-out. Included were a bench, desk, waste basket, writing desk, and blackboard, as well as other items.

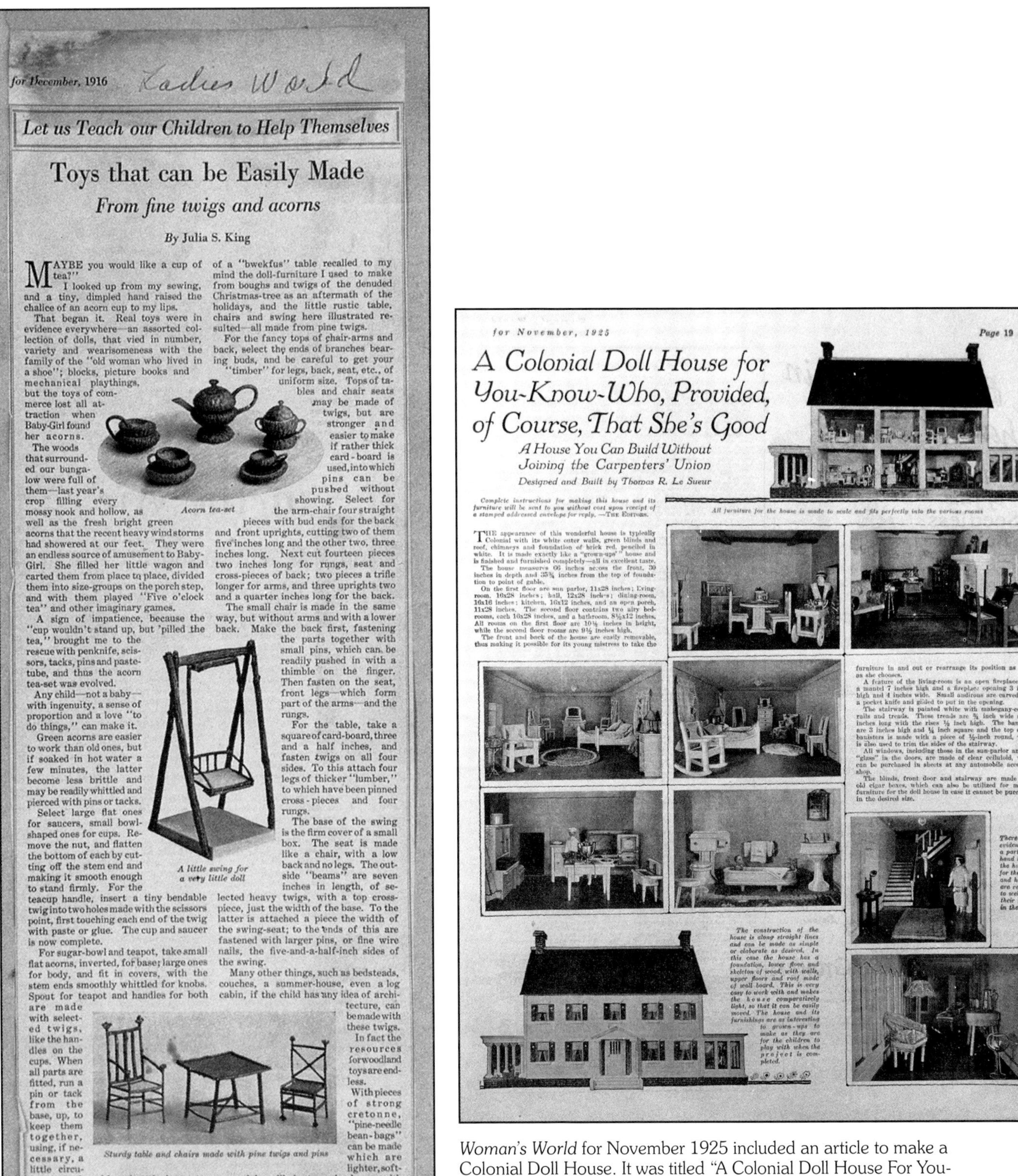

for December, 1916 Ladies World

Let us Teach our Children to Help Themselves

Toys that can be Easily Made

From fine twigs and acorns

By Julia S. King

MAYBE you would like a cup of tea?"

I looked up from my sewing, and a tiny, dimpled hand raised the chalice of an acorn cup to my lips.

That began it. Real toys were in evidence everywhere—an assorted collection of dolls, that vied in number, variety and wearisomeness with the family of the "old woman who lived in a shoe"; blocks, picture books and mechanical playthings, but the toys of commerce lost all attraction when Baby-Girl found her acorns.

The woods that surrounded our bungalow were full of them—last year's crop filling every mossy nook and hollow, as well as the fresh bright green acorns that the recent heavy windstorms had showered at our feet. They were an endless source of amusement to Baby-Girl. She filled her little wagon and carted them from place to place, divided them into size-groups on the porch step, and with them played "Five o'clock tea" and other imaginary games.

Acorn tea-set

A sign of impatience, because the "cup wouldn't stand up, but 'pilled the tea," brought me to the rescue with penknife, scissors, tacks, pins and paste-tube, and thus the acorn tea-set was evolved.

Any child—not a baby—with ingenuity, a sense of proportion and a love "to do things," can make it.

Green acorns are easier to work than old ones, but if soaked in hot water a few minutes, the latter become less brittle and may be readily whittled and pierced with pins or tacks.

Select large flat ones for saucers, small bowl-shaped ones for cups. Remove the nut, and flatten the bottom of each by cutting off the stem end and making it smooth enough to stand firmly. For the teacup handle, insert a tiny bendable twig into two holes made with the scissors point, first touching each end of the twig with paste or glue. The cup and saucer is now complete.

For sugar-bowl and teapot, take small flat acorns, inverted, for base; large ones for body, and fit in covers, with the stem ends smoothly whittled for knobs. Spout for teapot and handles for both are made with selected twigs, like the handles on the cups. When all parts are fitted, run a pin or tack from the base, up, to keep them together, using, if necessary, a little circular piece of card-board at the bottom to keep the pinhead from pushing through.

The pitcher is the most difficult, acorns not lending themselves to a pitcher's outline. But, with a large stock of acorns to select from and some whittling to shape the "nose," a fairly good cream-jug can be made.

The sugar-bowl and teapot, having removable covers, were especially alluring to Baby-Girl.

Many other things, suggested by Baby-Girl's gift of imagination, were manufactured from the acorns. The need of a "bwekfus" table recalled to my mind the doll-furniture I used to make from boughs and twigs of the denuded Christmas-tree as an aftermath of the holidays, and the little rustic table, chairs and swing here illustrated resulted—all made from pine twigs.

For the fancy tops of chair-arms and back, select the ends of branches bearing buds, and be careful to get your "timber" for legs, back, seat, etc., of uniform size. Tops of tables and chair seats may be made of twigs, but are stronger and easier to make if rather thick card-board is used, into which pins can be pushed without showing. Select for the arm-chair four straight pieces with bud ends for the back and front uprights, cutting two of them five inches long and the other two, three inches long. Next cut fourteen pieces two inches long for rungs, seat and cross-pieces of back; two pieces a trifle longer for arms, and three uprights two and a quarter inches long for the back.

The small chair is made in the same way, but without arms and with a lower back. Make the back first, fastening the parts together with small pins, which can be readily pushed in with a thimble on the finger. Then fasten on the seat, front legs—which form part of the arms—and the rungs.

A little swing for a very little doll

For the table, take a square of card-board, three and a half inches, and fasten twigs on all four sides. To this attach four legs of thicker "lumber," to which have been pinned cross-pieces and four rungs.

The base of the swing is the firm cover of a small box. The seat is made like a chair, with a low back and no legs. The outside "beams" are seven inches in length, of selected heavy twigs, with a top cross-piece, just the width of the base. To the latter is attached a piece the width of the swing-seat; to the ends of this are fastened with larger pins, or fine wire nails, the five-and-a-half-inch sides of the swing.

Many other things, such as bedsteads, couches, a summer-house, even a log cabin, if the child has any idea of architecture, can be made with these twigs. In fact the resources for woodland toys are endless.

Sturdy table and chairs made with pine twigs and pins

With pieces of strong cretonne, "pine-needle bean-bags" can be made which are lighter, softer and less likely to make havoc with mirrors and bric-a-brac than those made with hard beans—to say nothing of their delicate fragrance.

Even a realistic tiny, topographical landscape, such as the Japanese make so daintily, can be made from the spoils of our woods—bits of lichen, velvety moss, miniature rocks and trees, with sandy paths, toy houses and glass lakes.

Let us teach our children to help themselves to the material of our woods, allowing them to fit the things together and make their own toys.

for November, 1925 Page 19

A Colonial Doll House for You-Know-Who, Provided, of Course, That She's Good

A House You Can Build Without Joining the Carpenters' Union

Designed and Built by Thomas R. Le Sueur

Complete instructions for making this house and its furniture will be sent to you without cost upon receipt of a stamped addressed envelope for reply. —THE EDITORS.

All furniture for the house is made to scale and fits perfectly into the various rooms

THE appearance of this wonderful house is typically Colonial with its white outer walls, green blinds and roof, chimneys and foundation of brick red, penciled in white. It is made exactly like a "grown-ups'" house and is finished and furnished completely—all in excellent taste.

The house measures 66 inches across the front, 30 inches in depth and 35¾ inches from the top of foundation to point of gable.

On the first floor are sun parlor, 11x28 inches; living-room, 16x28 inches; hall, 12x28 inches; dining-room, 16x16 inches; kitchen, 16x12 inches, and an open porch, 11x28 inches. The second floor contains two airy bedrooms, each 16x28 inches, and a bathroom, 8½x12 inches. All rooms on the first floor are 10½ inches in height, while the second floor rooms are 9½ inches high.

The front and back of the house are easily removable, thus making it possible for its young mistress to take the furniture in and out or rearrange its position as often as she chooses.

A feature of the living-room is an open fireplace with a mantel 7 inches high and a fireplace opening 3 inches high and 4 inches wide. Small andirons are carved with a pocket knife and gilded to put in the opening.

The stairway is painted white with mahogany-colored rails and treads. These treads are ¾ inch wide and 4 inches long with the rises ½ inch high. The banisters are 3 inches high and ¼ inch square and the top of the banisters is made with a piece of ½-inch round, which is also used to trim the sides of the stairway.

All windows, including those in the sun-parlor and the "glass" in the doors, are made of clear celluloid, which can be purchased in sheets at any automobile accessory shop.

The blinds, front door and stairway are made from old cigar boxes, which can also be utilized for making furniture for the doll house in case it cannot be purchased in the desired size.

There is evidently a party on hand in the house, for the host and hostess are ready to welcome their guests in the hall

The construction of the house is along straight lines and can be made as simple or elaborate as desired. In this case the house has a foundation, lower floor and skeleton of wood, with walls, upper floors and roof made of wall board. This is very easy to work with and makes the house comparatively light, so that it can be easily moved. The house and its furnishings are as interesting to grown-ups to make as they are for the children to play with when the project is completed.

Woman's World for November 1925 included an article to make a Colonial Doll House. It was titled "A Colonial Doll House For You-Know-Who, Provided, Of Course, That She's Good." It included a kitchen, bathroom, living room, dining room, two bedrooms, and two halls. *Courtesy of Carol Stevenson.*

This article was featured in *Ladies World* in December 1916. It gives instructions on how to make miniature furniture using evergreen twigs from used Christmas trees. Pictured are chairs, a table, and a swing made in this manner.

A Doll House for Small Folks that Any Grown-Up Can Make

By Mary Grace Ramey

The upper hall is 13 inches across and has a real closet with hooks for the doll dresses and a shelf for bonnets. In this cozy hall grandfather's old-fashioned mahogany-stained chair is kept, cut with the jig saw from a cigar box. It is 5 inches high with a seat 2 inches square, the sides and legs cut in one piece and firmly glued to the back and seat. Knit a small rug from bright bits of wool.

The bedroom, with its set of painted white furniture decorated in rose and blue to match the wall paper, is a dainty nook, 16 inches across. Baby's bassinet, draped in white, stands conveniently by the bed. The curtains are of dotted Swiss tacked on small strips of wood before they are hung, while a bit of fringe makes a very pretty valance over the curtains and conceals the tacks.

The telephone table in the entrance hall has a circular top, two inches in diameter, cut through the center and one half glued upright to give it a fashionable tilt. A sharp knife or jig saw—with lathe attachment if possible—cut the legs.

The kitchen lifts completely off to facilitate moving. It is 12 inches in depth and 8½ inches in width. The sides—to allow for the sloping roof—are 9½x12½ inches, the window is 5½x3½ inches. Both kitchen and bathroom (page 117) are papered in the thinnest grade of waterproof paper, and their plumbing fixtures—purchasable in toy stores—glued to the walls. The wooden range is painted black, and curtains are blue-and-white checked gingham.

THE dearest dream of a little girl's heart, especially at Christmas, is to own a doll house. The one pictured here and on page 117 is complete in every detail.

Fifty feet of a good quality bass lumber, at ten cents a square foot, was used for its construction, and this forms the largest item of expense in making. Cigar boxes furnished wood for the furniture, which is all substantially made. Many of the articles required in building it are left-overs found in almost every household. But if one had to purchase all materials the following list would be sufficient:

50 Feet of bass or poplar lumber, a quarter of an inch thick.
6 Cigar boxes.
1 Packet of ⅝-inch brads.
1 Packet of 1-inch brads.
5 Small pairs of brass hinges.
1 Half-pint can of paint, any desired color for outside of house.
1 Small can (less than half pint) of paint for roof.
1 Small can (less than half pint) of mahogany stain for doors, stairs, etc.
1 Small can (less than half pint) of light oak stain for floors.
1 Small can (less than half pint) of mission stain for dining-room furniture.
Glass for windows.
Glue.
Scraps of silk, cretonne, lace, etc., for furnishings.
Odds and ends of worsted and embroidery floss for crocheting rugs.
Small favors, such as a bird cage, telephone, sewing machine, and talking machine; many of which may be purchased in confectioner's shops and five and ten cent stores.

The base of the house was made first; this is forty-three inches long by thirteen inches deep, and these measurements provide for a ledge of one inch across the front and each end of the house. The sides of house are cut twenty-four inches high; the back is cut and made after the rest of the house is all assembled.

Two pieces of lumber forty and a half inches long and twelve inches wide are next cut for the second-story and the attic floors. In the center of the second-story floor, at the back, a space eight inches long by four inches wide is cut, which allows for the stairs in the hall. A keyhole saw is very useful for cutting all the openings, doors and windows. Of course all the windows and doors should be cut in the partitions before the actual work of building the house is begun.

When the lumber is all cut the assembling of the house is the next step. It is well to glue all the edges of the lumber together, as well as to nail them. Put on the end pieces of the house, then fasten the second-story and attic floors into position, placing the second-story floor twelve inches from the base, the attic floor ten and a half inches from the second story. Do not put the roof or back on house until inside carpenter work in the main portion is complete.

In the partitions between the living room and hall, and the hall and dining room, arches are cut instead of the conventional doorways, as they give a more spacious air to the house. These arches are eight inches high by four inches wide. In the partitions on the second floor, doorways seven inches high by three and a half inches wide are cut, and doors made of the basswood, stained with mahogany, are hung with tiny brass hinges. The door knobs are bits of wood turned on the lathe and painted.

All door frames are finished with strips half an inch wide, cut from the cigar-box wood and tacked to both sides. All the windows are finished on the outside of the house in the same way, the strips being fitted on large enough to hold the glass in place. Narrow strips tacked inside the windows also help to keep the glass secure and act as window sills as well.

For the roof two boards twenty-five inches long by twelve inches wide are cut and fastened in place with glue and nails, and a nine-and-a-half-inch support in the center of the attic floor is further used as a brace.

The fireplace is put in before back is fastened to house. The chimney measures twelve inches in height, and six inches in width at base. It is two inches deep, and the opening is three and a half by three and a half inches.

(Continued on Page 117)

The *Ladies Home Journal* featured an article called "A Doll House for Small Folks that Any Grown-Up Can Make" in their November 1923 issue. The house was to be made of bass lumber. Wood from cigar boxes was used to make some of the furniture. Other pieces were purchased in toy stores.

vember, 1923 The Ladies' HO

The living room measures 12x16 inches. It boasts a piano made from a block of wood, with white paper, heavily inked, for the keyboard. A davenport, 7 inches long by 2¼ inches high and 2½ inches deep, has a tiny molding to give a professional finish. The floor lamp—6 inches high with a 1-inch base—was a curtain pole. Strong copper wire is used for frame of silk shade. Framed pictures are cut from magazines.

A Doll House for Small Folks

(Continued from Page 114)

Before the boards for the back of the house are fitted into place all necessary windows should be cut in them. The back is then fastened to the house and chimney added. Just beneath each of the second-story end windows, strips of lumber five inches long by one inch thick and one inch wide are securely fastened and painted green. In these, small holes are bored for tiny artificial flowers.

To build the stairway, place the landing where grandfather's clock stands midway between the first and second floors. This should be three inches wide and extend the entire width of the hall. Fasten it in place with glue and one-inch brads. The stairs from first floor to landing are made of pieces of lumber seven and a half inches long by two and a half inches wide. The steps, which are two and a half inches long by one inch wide, are one inch apart, glued, and fastened on with small brads. A similar set extends to second floor.

All of the inside trimming is painted white, the floors are stained, and the walls papered with light, small-figured wall paper. The chimney and fireplace are covered with red and white brick paper, and the outside of the house is given two coats of paint, with the roof in a contrasting color.

The bathroom, 12x11 inches, has tiles of painted blue cardboard and a towel rack of heavy wire. The towels are scraps of linen, embroidered in blue to match the rugs, which are made of strands of blue and white embroidery cotton, effectively crocheted in round and oval shapes.

Complete in all details is this little house. The dining room measures 12x16 inches, with high windows, 8x3 inches, giving space for sideboard—once a cigar box. The sideboard opens easily, as hinges are brads driven through the top and bottom and the knobs are brass tacks. It measures 7 inches in length.

The open front "Doll House For Small Folks…" included five rooms, two halls, and an attic. The base of the house was 43" wide x 13" deep. The kitchen wing was removable.

A Colonial House for the Children's Christmas

By EDWARD THATCHER

"A Colonial House For the Children's Christmas" by Edward Thatcher was featured in the *Ladies Home Journal* magazine for November 1926. The elaborate house included a living room, dining room, two bedrooms, nursery, bathroom, and kitchen. The house opened both in the front and the back and measured 32.75" high x 38.75" wide x 36" deep. Complete instructions on how to build the house were included in the several page article.

Easily-Made Doll Furniture

By Three Contributors

A TINY set of dolls' furniture, similar to the one illustrated at the top of this page, may be made at a cost of fifteen cents. The materials required are five small corks, two large ones, two rows of pins, and less than half a skein of two-ply Saxony wool, brown in color.

Cut the tops of the corks the depth desired for the small chairs, and twice the depth for the easy-chair. Crochet the covers. Put the pins in slanting for the legs, and form the backs of the small chairs, easy-chair and sofa of pins. When the pins are in position wind the Saxony wool in and out to form the backs of the furniture, and around the legs as shown in the illustrations.

An oblong piece cut from one of the large corks, with a crocheted cover, forms the body of the sofa. The tidies on the easy-chair and small chair are crocheted, and the sofa-pillow is made from two small squares of red silk. The table is made in the same way as the chair, using a large cork. The mat, is made from net, run with zephyr.

LEILA T. COLLINS.

THIS pretty set of dolls' furniture, which is made of broom sedge in its green stage, can be made for ninety-eight cents. It is painted with white enamel paint and held together with pins. The sedge must be accurately measured. The materials required for it are: pins, five cents; enamel, ten cents; toilet set, five cents; gilding, ten cents; mirror, five cents; broom sedge, five cents; a quarter of a yard of silk, thirteen cents; one yard of number two ribbon, five cents; two yards of baby ribbon, two cents; one ounce of single zephyr, five cents; three yards of lace, fifteen cents; cambric, three cents; organdy, five cents; Swiss muslin, five cents; lining, five cents.

DAISY BROOKE.

TO MAKE the paper farmhouse illustrated below take a square of wall paper nineteen inches by nineteen and lay it down with the colored side uppermost. Fold the two front corners to the back corners, and the front edge to the crease in the centre; do the same with the back edge, making four oblongs. Fold the right corners over to the left corners; turn the right edge to meet the middle crease; fold the left edge to meet this crease, making a large square, with sixteen small squares as in diagram. The four squares on the front should be slit to meet the second row of squares, and the four squares on the back to meet the third row of squares. Fold the two centre squares on the front edge and place one over the other to form a gable. The first and fourth squares on the front edge must then be folded in front of this gable. Fold the back edge in the same way to form a gable, and fold the first and fourth squares in front of the gable thus made. Paste the pieces forming the gables together; paste the front and rear pieces to the gables. Slip the roof of the front porch into place, before the front gable and the front of the cottage are pasted; then paste the porch roof and the fronts of the cottage together to the gable. The floor of the porch is pasted in position by folding down one edge in the same way. The railing and stairs are pasted in position by folding down a tiny edge on each, and pasting the edges down. The double doors and the windows are made by cutting a slit in the centre of the front and two slits on the top and bottom at each side of the centre slit, and folding the others back in place. The chimney is an oblong strip folded into four oblongs. One edge of this is turned down and pasted to the opposite edge, making a hollow oblong.

The fence and the animals in the farmyard were also made from paper.

All the pieces of dolls' furniture may be made by folding a square of paper seven inches by seven into sixteen squares, and then folding it into the square box, or, by cutting off one strip, into the oblong box.

FLORA E. JACKLIN.

Another page from the vintage dollhouse scrapbook included this unidentified magazine article, which gave directions on making three different types of dollhouse furniture. The furniture in the top picture was made using corks, pins, and crocheted covers. The middle photograph shows a more attractive set of furniture made of broom sedge in its green stage. It was painted with white enamel and held together with pins. The furniture in the bottom photograph was made "by folding a square of paper seven inches by seven into sixteen squares, and then folding it into the square box, or, by cutting off one strip, into the oblong box."

A CHILD'S CHRISTMAS DOLL SET FOR $1.50

By Emily Ross Bell

ANY little maiden's heart would rejoice over a Christmas present of a set of doll's furniture such as the one shown here, which is made from wooden boxes, and draped with an inexpensive silkoline.

A LITTLE BED WITH CANOPY

The bed is made of one of the shallow boxes in which condensed milk is packed. Nail on strips to form a frame for the top of the canopy; cover these sticks and the box with silkoline, adding ruffles of the same.

THE COMFORTABLE SOFA

The sofa is made of a prune box. Remove the lid and one side. Use the side for the seat, sawing off enough to let the seat slip in easily. Pad the inside of the box.

DRESSING-TABLE

PADDED ARMCHAIR

The chair is made of the same sized box as the sofa; one end is taken off for the seat. Remove the lid and end, cut the sides slightly curved, and make like the sofa.

The dressing-table is made of a cube-shaped box. Remove the lid and it will serve for shelves for the dolly's clothes if little cleats are tacked inside.

THE DOLL'S TABLE

Put a heavy piece of wood in the lower part of the box to prevent top-heaviness.

The table is made from a box similar to the bed. Nail an inch stick on each corner, and cover box and sticks with the silkoline.

These interesting pieces of doll furniture are from an unidentified magazine, perhaps from the 1920s. The item comes from a dollhouse scrapbook which included magazine features from several decades. The pieces were constructed by Emily Ross Bell. Prune and condensed milk boxes were used for several of the pieces. A silkoline material provided the "upholstery."

Right:
Child Life magazine for December 1926 featured plans for a doll bungalow in its "Our Workshop" feature by Neely Hall. The house was made of wallboard. The Spanish Bungalow included four rooms and was 32" wide x 32" deep.

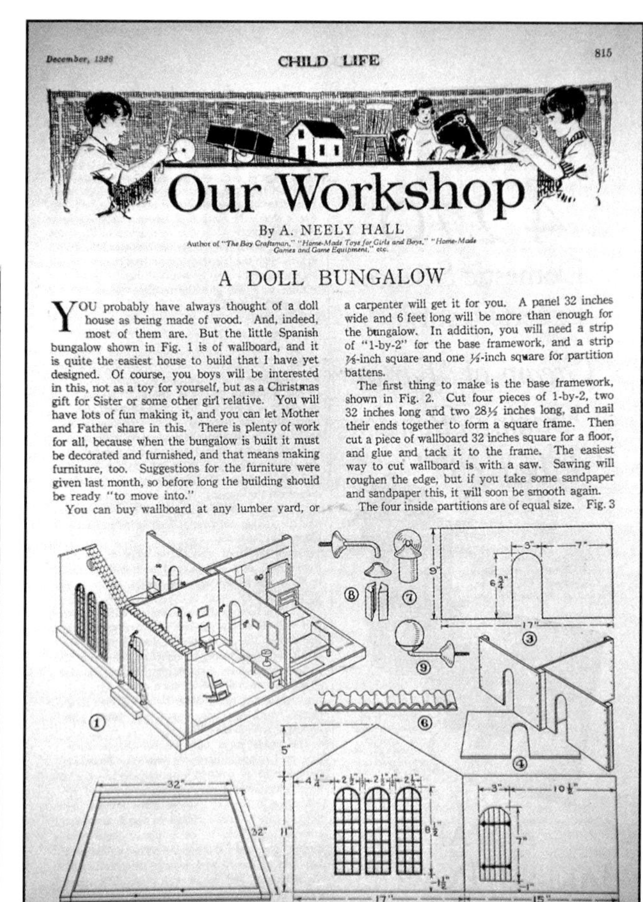

December, 1926 CHILD LIFE 815

Our Workshop

By A. NEELY HALL

Author of "The Boy Craftsman," "Home-Made Toys for Girls and Boys," "Home-Made Games and Game Equipment," etc.

A DOLL BUNGALOW

YOU probably have always thought of a doll house as being made of wood. And, indeed, most of them are. But the little Spanish bungalow shown in Fig. 1 is of wallboard, and it is quite the easiest house to build that I have yet designed. Of course, you boys will be interested in this, not as a toy for yourself, but as a Christmas gift for Sister or some other girl relative. You will have lots of fun making it, and you can let Mother and Father share in this. There is plenty of work for all, because when the bungalow is built it must be decorated and furnished, and that means making furniture, too. Suggestions for the furniture were given last month, so before long the building should be ready "to move into."

You can buy wallboard at any lumber yard, or a carpenter will get it for you. A panel 32 inches wide and 6 feet long will be more than enough for the bungalow. In addition, you will need a strip of "1-by-2" for the base framework, and a strip ⅞-inch square and one ½-inch square for partition battens.

The first thing to make is the base framework, shown in Fig. 2. Cut four pieces of 1-by-2, two 32 inches long and two 28½ inches long, and nail their ends together to form a square frame. Then cut a piece of wallboard 32 inches square for a floor, and glue and tack it to the frame. The easiest way to cut wallboard is with a saw. Sawing will roughen the edge, but if you take some sandpaper and sandpaper this, it will soon be smooth again.

The four inside partitions are of equal size. Fig. 3

654 CHILD LIFE December, 1930

OUR WORKSHOP

Doll House Furniture

By A. Neely Hall

Author of "Making Things with Tools," "Big Book of Boys' Hobbies," "Home Made Toys for Girls and Boys," etc.

AFTER you have built the bungalow doll house shown upon last month's page, make the furniture. Making furniture is a big job in itself, and you must start work early so there will be time to complete it and have the bungalow in readiness to place beside the tree on Christmas Eve.

On this page are designs for some easily built doll furniture. It has been designed to a scale of 1 inch to 1 foot. A table that measures 2½ feet high will be 2½ inches high for the doll house, and a chair's seat that measures 1½ feet high will be 1½ inches high. By using this system of measurement, you can get all of the dimensions needed for the doll furniture by measuring furniture in your home, then using inches instead of feet. For this reason, I haven't crowded our page with dimensions.

There is nothing better for doll furniture than the thin wood from cigar boxes. You can procure boxes at a drug store or a cigar store. Some of the wood used in cigar boxes has a grain similar to that of mahogany. You can finish it with a mahogany stain, fill the grain with wood filler, and then apply varnish. Or you can give it a coat of boiled linseed oil, and then wax the surfaces. Other wood used in cigar boxes has a close grain. The best way to finish it is with lacquer or enamel. The bright red, orange, yellow, green and blue colors, which you can buy in small-sized cans, make pretty doll furniture.

After obtaining a supply of cigar boxes, remove the paper linings and labels. Place the boxes in a tub of hot water, weight them down, and allow them to soak until the paste has softened. Then peel off the paper. Place the covers flat against the bottoms, and bind with string, to prevent them from warping, and place the boxes near a radiator or stove. When the boxes are dry, knock them apart.

[Continued on page 668]

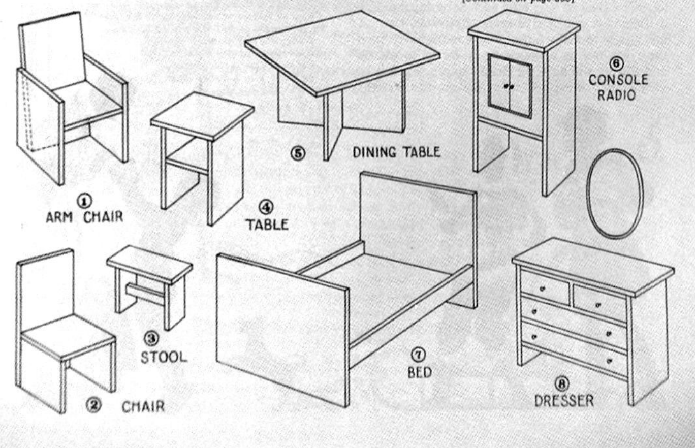

The "Our Workshop" feature from the December 1930 issue of *Child Life* magazine included plans for dollhouse furniture. The 1" to 1 foot scaled furniture included a bed, dresser, radio, table, chair, armchair, end table, and stool. The furniture was to be constructed from wood cigar boxes.

Right:
The *Ladies Home Journal* continued its tradition of printing dollhouse articles with this one that appeared in the December 1930 issue. It was called "Building Little Sister's Doll House" and was written by Bernice Carter Davis. The Colonial house had the look of one of the Tynietoy houses being produced at the same time. Plans for this house could be obtained from the magazine for $1.00. The front and rear sides of the house were detachable. It included a kitchen, dining room, living room, children's room, two bedrooms, bathroom, and halls. Many of the furniture pieces appeared to be made by Tynietoy.

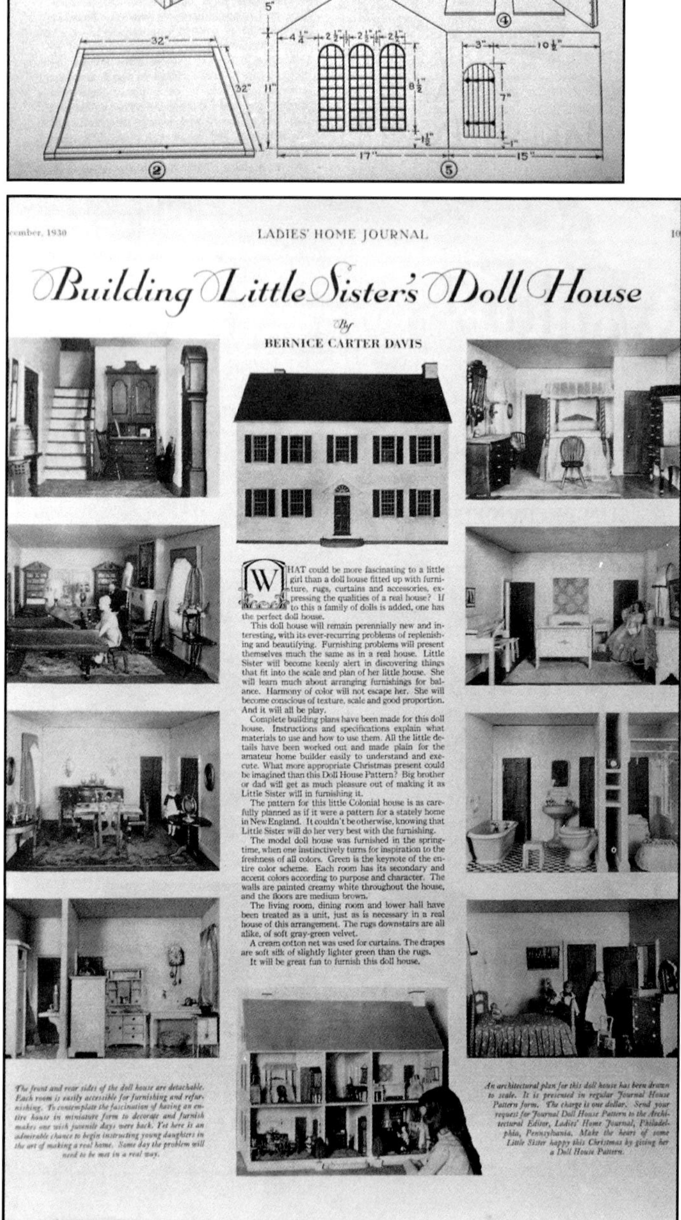

LADIES' HOME JOURNAL

Building Little Sister's Doll House

By BERNICE CARTER DAVIS

WHAT could be more fascinating to a little girl than a doll house fitted up with furniture, rugs, curtains and accessories, expressing the qualities of a real house? If to this a family of dolls is added, one has the perfect doll house.

This doll house will remain perennially new and interesting, with its ever-recurring problems of replenishing and beautifying. Furnishing problems will present themselves much the same as in a real house. Little Sister will become keenly alert in discovering things that fit into the scale and plan of her little house. She will learn much about arranging furnishings for balance. Harmony of color will not escape her. She will become conscious of texture, scale and good proportion. And it will all be play.

Complete building plans have been made for this doll house. Instructions and specifications explain what materials to use and how to use them. All the little details have been worked out and made plain for the amateur home builder easily to understand and execute. What more appropriate Christmas present could be imagined than this Doll House Pattern? Big brother or dad will get as much pleasure out of making it as Little Sister will in furnishing it.

The pattern for this little Colonial house is as carefully planned as if it were a pattern for a stately home in New England. It couldn't be otherwise, knowing that Little Sister will do her very best with the furnishing.

The model doll house was furnished in the springtime, when one instinctively turns for inspiration to the freshness of all colors. Green is the keynote of the entire color scheme. Each room has its secondary and accent colors according to purpose and character. The walls are painted creamy white throughout the house, and the floors are medium brown.

The living room, dining room and lower hall have been treated as a unit, just as is necessary in a real house of this arrangement. The rugs downstairs are all alike, of soft gray-green velvet.

A cream cotton net was used for curtains. The drapes are soft silk of slightly lighter green than the rugs.

It will be great fun to furnish this doll house.

The front and rear sides of the doll house are detachable. Each room is easily accessible for furnishing and refurnishing. To contemplate the fascination of having an entire house in miniature form to decorate and furnish makes one wish juvenile days were back. Yet here is an admirable chance to begin instructing young daughters in the art of making a real home. Some day the problem will need to be met in a real way.

An architectural plan for this doll house has been drawn to scale. It is presented in regular Journal House Pattern form. The charge is one dollar. Send your request for Journal Doll House Pattern to the Architectural Editor, Ladies' Home Journal, Philadelphia, Pennsylvania. Make the heart of some Little Sister happy this Christmas by giving her a Doll House Pattern.

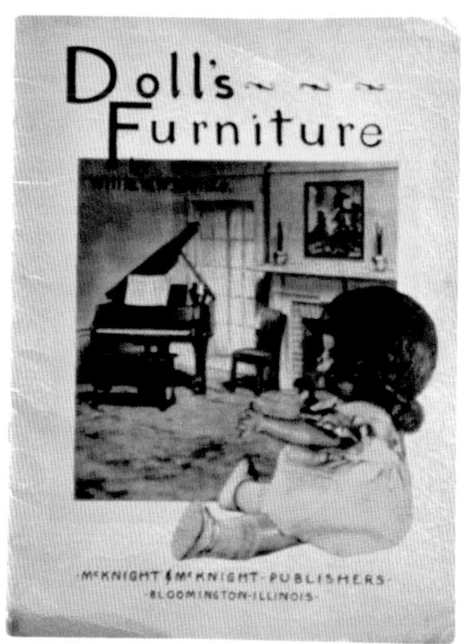

This booklet called "Doll's Furniture" was published by McKnight and McKnight in Bloomington, Illinois in 1935. It included instructions for making twenty-five pieces of miniature furniture. A side chair measures 3.75" tall by 1.75" deep. Included were pieces for a living room, dining room, and bedroom, plus a table and chairs and kitchen cabinet. A secretary, overstuffed sofa and chair, various tables, chairs, bed, and dresser were also featured in the booklet. *Booklet and photo courtesy of Becky Norris.*

Another *Popular Homecraft* magazine, dated November-December 1938, featured an interesting wood Colonial dollhouse on its front cover. Plans for the back-opening house, which had nine rooms, were included inside the magazine. Four rooms were upstairs and five rooms were downstairs, including a kitchen wing. A porch was also part of the structure. The basic house was 20" deep and the platform was 72" wide. *Norris Collection.*

A Doll Bungalow was featured on the cover of *Popular Homecraft* magazine in December 1937. Plans to make the house were printed in an article inside the publication. The Bungalow included six rooms plus a porch and was approximately 36" wide x 49" deep. The roof could be removed for easy access to the rooms inside. *Norris Collection.*

Home Craftsman magazine for November-December 1940 featured a "Doll House in Monterey Style" on its cover, with the plans printed inside in an article called "Plywood Makes a Monterey Type Take-Apart Doll House." The large two-story house included a living room, dining room, kitchen, two bedrooms (or could be a bathroom), and hall. A covered patio and garage were also part of the plan. It measured 54" wide but the patio could fit in the garage, which could then be placed in the house for storage. Access to the inside of the house was gained by unhooking the back panel.

Art Deco dollhouse plans from a booklet called "Little Library of Useful Information, Doll Houses Number 60." The plans were first published in *Popular Mechanics* magazine in 1937. This booklet is dated 1942. The Popular Mechanics Co. was based in Chicago, Illinois. The house base measured 26.5" high x 4' wide x 27" deep. See a house made from this pattern in *Furnished Dollhouses* on page 154. *Norris Collection*.

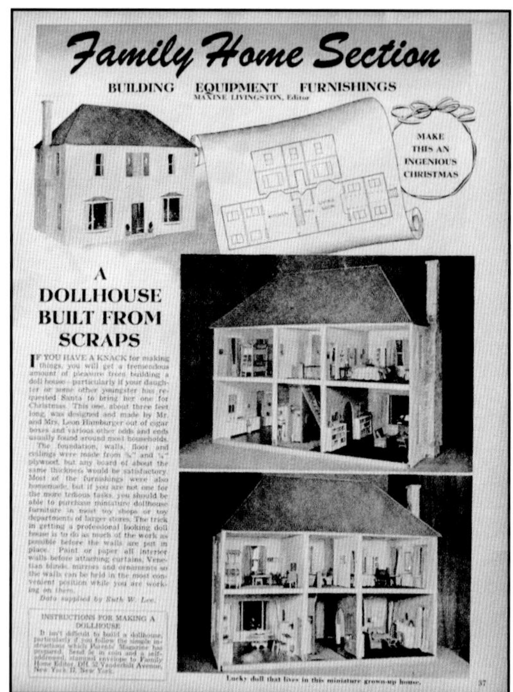

Family Home Section

BUILDING EQUIPMENT FURNISHINGS

MAKE THIS AN INGENIOUS CHRISTMAS

A DOLLHOUSE BUILT FROM SCRAPS

IF YOU HAVE A KNACK for making things, you will get a tremendous amount of pleasure from building a doll house—particularly if your daughter or some other youngster has requested Santa to bring her one for Christmas. This one, about three feet long, was designed and made by Mr. and Mrs. Leon Hamburger out of cigar boxes and various other odds and ends usually found around most households.

The foundation, walls, floor and ceilings were made from ... plywood, but any board of about the same thickness would be satisfactory. Most of the furnishings were also homemade, ...

Data supplied by Ruth W. Lee.

This open-backed dollhouse was featured in *Parents* magazine circa 1943. The house was made of plywood and the plans could be obtained from the Family Home Editor. The open-backed house included six rooms. *Courtesy of Judy Mosholder.*

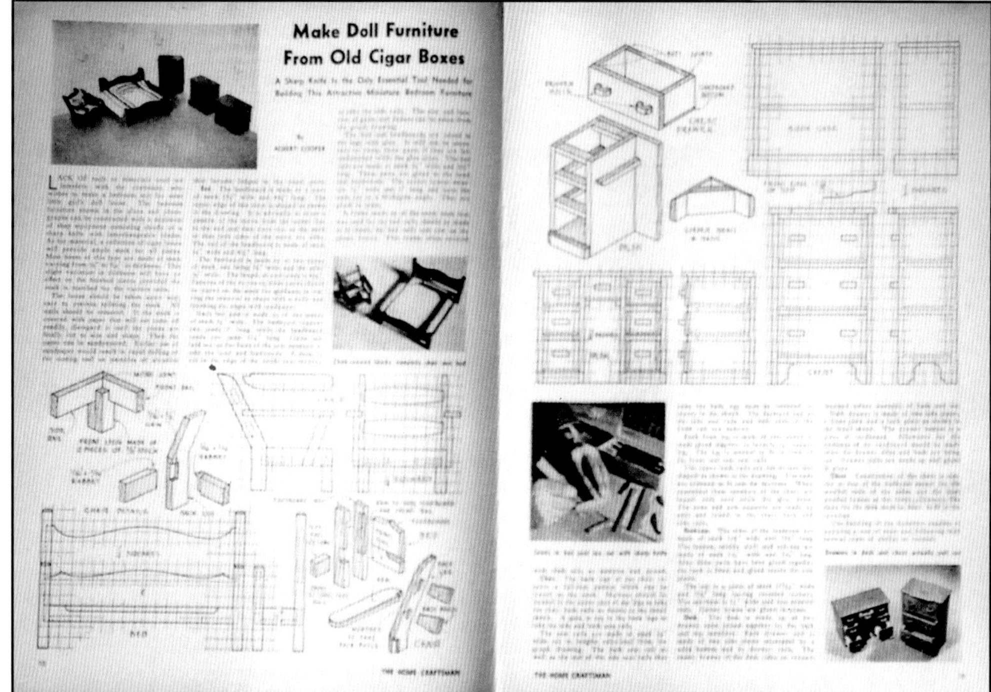

Make Doll Furniture From Old Cigar Boxes

A Sharp Knife Is the Only Essential Tool Needed for Building This Attractive Miniature Bedroom Furniture

By ROBERT COOPER

"Make Doll Furniture From Old Cigar Boxes" was an article featured in *The Home Craftsman* magazine for March-April 1944. Instructions were given on how to construct a bed, side chair, dresser, desk, and book case. Working drawers were part of the dresser plans. *Article and photograph courtesy of Becky Norris.*

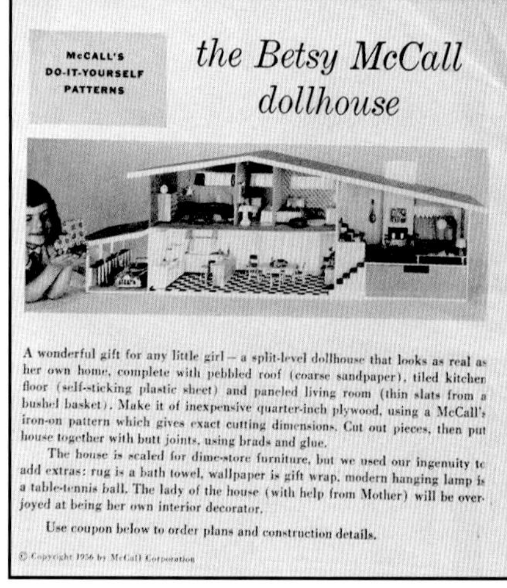

McCALL'S DO-IT-YOURSELF PATTERNS

the Betsy McCall dollhouse

A wonderful gift for any little girl—a split-level dollhouse that looks as real as her own home, complete with pebbled roof (coarse sandpaper), tiled kitchen floor (self-sticking plastic sheet) and paneled living room (thin slats from a bushel basket). Make it of inexpensive quarter-inch plywood, using a McCall's iron-on pattern which gives exact cutting dimensions. Cut out pieces, then put house together with butt joints, using brads and glue.

The house is scaled for dime-store furniture, but we used our ingenuity to add extras: rug is a bath towel, wallpaper is gift wrap, modern hanging lamp is a table-tennis ball. The lady of the house (with help from Mother) will be overjoyed at being her own interior decorator.

Use coupon below to order plans and construction details.

Plans for a Betsy McCall dollhouse were advertised in *McCall* magazine in May 1956. The house was a split-level model to be made of plywood. It included a kitchen, living room, two bedrooms, bathroom, and carport.

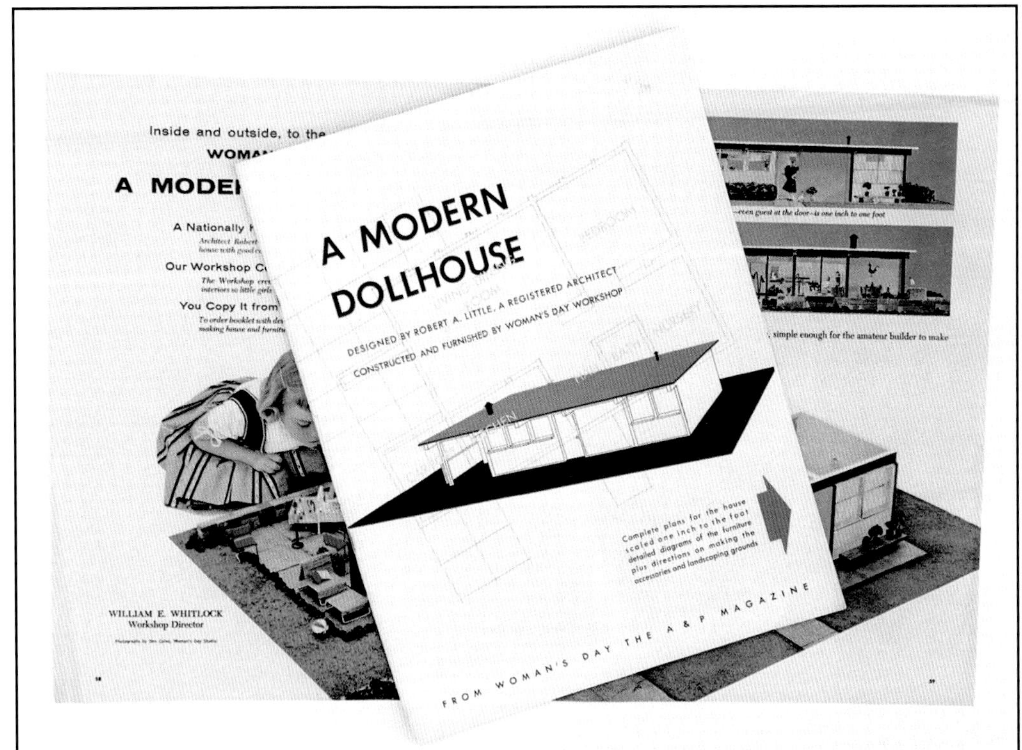

This Modern Doll House was featured in *Woman's Day* magazine in September 1956. It was designed by Robert A. Little and constructed and finished by Woman's Day Workshop. The plans could be ordered through the magazine. The house was built in two sections for easier storage. The 1" to one foot scaled house included a living room-dining room, bedroom, kitchen, hall, bathroom, nursery, and carport. It measured 40.5" wide by 25.5" deep.

Woman's Day magazine offered another pattern for a dollhouse in their July 1961 issue. The pattern could be purchased for 35 cents. The house was made of four heavy cartons and included a kitchen, child's room, bedroom, and living room.

Enchant A Little Girl

By STEVE ELLINGSON

An enchanted little girl completely absorbed in a miniature world is a rich reward for the time spent in building this beautiful doll house. If you decide to build it, we think it's only fair to warn you that working on it is sort of hypnotic, and playing with it is even more so. It's quite likely that the youngsters will have to send you adults to the movies in order to get at it at all. Even so, here's another project that will help you to ease the expenses for the Christmas gift season that lies ahead.

For centuries doll houses have been one of the best loved playthings a youngster could receive. Its popularity goes undiminished year after year. It will give your daughter hours of quiet indoor pleasure, a treat enjoyed by mothers as much as children. A few scraps of wood are all you need. The furnishings are of the inexpensive plastic variety found in all dime stores.

The base of this doll house is on casters—making it easy to maneuver during play, and when it comes time to put it away. The pattern is full-size. You need only trace the pattern parts on plywood, then saw them out, and finally put them together. It is that easy. A list of required materials along with lots of illustrations are included with each pattern. It's something that any amateur can undertake with success.

To obtain the full-size doll house pattern number 411, send $1.00 (add 25 cents per pattern if airmail is desired) by currency, check or money order to:

Steve Ellingson
Nashville Tennessean Pattern Dept.
P. O. Box 2383
Van Nuys, California 91409

Other patterns you will enjoy:

No. 56 Rocking horse 50c
No. 113 Giraffe clothes tree 50c
No. 248 Toy chest $1.00
No. 383 Delivery truck $1.00
Booklet picturing over 480 projects 75c
No. 419 Jeep $1.00
No. 361 Teenage doll furniture $1.00

This dollhouse pattern was featured in a newspaper circa early 1960s. The open-backed house included six rooms. It was furnished with plastic dollhouse furniture. The pattern could be ordered for $1.00 from Steve Ellingson at the Nashville Tennessean Pattern Dept. in Van Nuys. California.

Bibliography

Aldens Christmas Catalogs. Chicago: Aldens, Inc. Various issues, 1950-1967.

Barlow, Ronald S. *The Great American Antique Toy Bazaar 1879-1945*. El Cajon, California: Windmill Publishing Co., 1998.

Block House, Inc. Catalogs 1940, 1950, 1977. New York: Block House, Inc.

Brett, Mary. *Tomart's Price Guide to Tin Litho Doll Houses and Plastic Doll House Furniture*. Dayton, OH: Tomart Publications, 1977.

Butler Brothers Catalogs. Chicago: Various issues, 1920-1940s.

Cooper, Patty, and Dian Zillner. *Toy Buildings 1880-1980*. Atglen, PA: Schiffer Publishing Ltd., 2000.

Children's Activities Magazine. Chicago: Child Training Association, Inc. Various issues, 1930s-1950s.

Cieslik, Marianne and Jurgen, eds. *Moritz Gottschalk 1892-1931*. Reprints of Catalog Illustrations. Theirault's Gold Horse Publishing, 2000.

Dolly Dear Accessories. Rives, Tennessee: Dolly Dear, 1958.

Firestone Catalog. Fall and Winter 1948. Chicago.

Grandmother Stover's Doll House Accessories. Columbus, OH: Grandmother Stover, 1977.

Hall's Lifetime Toys Catalog. Chattanooga, Tennessee. Various issues.

Jacobs, Flora Gill. *Dolls' Houses in America*. New York: Charles Scribner's Sons, 1974.

Keystone Toy Catalog. Boston, Mass: Keystone Mfg. Co., 1942-43 & 1955.

Lundby of Sweden Catalogs. Lerum, Sweden: 1970s-1980s catalog.

Mark Farmer, Inc. Catalog. El Cerrito, California: Mark Farmer, Inc. 1968.

Marshall Field & Company Catalogs. Chicago, IL. Various issues.

Mason & Parker Mfg. Co. Catalog 1914. Winchendon, Mass.: Mason & Parker.

Miniature Mart Doll House Catalog. San Francisco: John M. Blauer, 1967.

Montgomery Ward. Catalogs. Chicago: Montgomery Ward. Various issues, 1923-1980.

Morton E. Converse and Son Company. Catalogs 1915, 1919. Winchendon, Mass.: Morton E. Converse and Son.

Schmuhl, Marian. "Pliant Playthings of the Past." *Dolls: The Collectors Magazine*, December 1993, pp. 50-56.

Sears, Roebuck and Company Catalogs. Chicago: Sears, Roebuck and Company. Various issues, 1900-1982.

Shackman, B. and Co. Catalog. New York City: B. Shackman & Co. 1973.

Snyder, Dee. "The Collectables." *Nutshell News*, "Dolly Dear Accessories," July-August, 1979.

Sonia Messer Imports Catalogs. Los Angeles, California: 1970s.

Stirn, Carl P. *Turn-of-the-Century Dolls, Toys and Games*. The Complete Illustrated Carl P. Stirn Catalog from 1893. New York: Dover Publications, Inc., 1990.

The Toy Yearbook 1955-1956. Norberry's Toy Headquarters. West Seattle, Washington.

Tynietoy Catalog. Toy Furniture Shop. Providence, Rhode Island: 1920s.

Whitton, Blair, ed. *Bliss Toys and Dollhouses*. New York: Dover Publications, Inc., 1979.

Whitton, Margaret, ed. *Dollhouses and Furniture Manufactured by A. Schoenhut Company, 1917-1934* (reprinted).

Wisconsin Toy Company. Catalog circa mid-1930s. Milwaukee, WI: Wisconsin Toy Co.

Zillner, Dian. *American Dollhouses and Furniture From the 20th Century*. Atglen, PA: Schiffer Publishing Ltd., 1995.

Zillner, Dian. *Furnished Dollhouses 1880s-1980s*. Atglen, PA: Schiffer Publishing Ltd., 2001.

Zillner, Dian. *International Dollhouses & Accessories 1880s-1980s*. Atglen, PA: Schiffer Publishing, Ltd., 2003.

Zillner, Dian, and Patty Cooper. *Antique & Collectible Dollhouses and Their Furnishings*. Atglen, PA: Schiffer Publishing Ltd., 1998.

Index

A

Althof, Bergmann & Co., 6
American Character, 102, 103
American Greeting Corp., 118, 119
American Toy & Furniture Co., 72, 73
Andrews, O.B., 59
Arcade Manufacturing Co., 12-15
Arco Merry Toys, 127

B

Banner Plastics Corp., 60
Barbie and Family, 102, 111, 112
Biedermeier, 11
Bliss, R. Mfg. Co., 5
Blue Box, 102, 103
Brinkman Engineering Co., 26
Brumberger Co., 118-121
Built-Rite, 26-30, 59
Butterfly Collection, 128

C

Caco Dolls, 85
Cannon, Florence V. Co., 16
Carrom Co., 15
Cass, N.D., 6
Chestnut Hill Studio, 103, 104
Child Guidance, 105
Child Life, 138
Child Life Toys, 86
The Companion, 133
Concord House, 90
Converse, Morton E., 5, 7, 26, 30
Cooke, Adrian, 5, 7
Cozytown Houses, 12, 16
Craftmaster-Fundimensions, 127, 128
Craftsman's Model Co., 31
Cranford Doll House Co., 8

D

De Luxe Game Corp., 59-61
Deluxe Reading, 105
Dinky Toys, 26, 31, 32
Dollyhome, 86
Dolly Dear, 59-62
Dollyzown, 18
Donna Lee, 59, 62, 63
Dorothy's Doll House, 9
Dowst Brothers – Dowst Manufacturing, 12, 20-22
Durrel Co., 12, 23

E

ECA Toys, 63
Elastic Tip Co., 12, 15
Eldon, 106
Electric Game Co. Inc., 63
Embossing Co., 32
Erna Meyer Dolls, 106

F

Faber, David H., 64
Fibre-Bilt, 85, 86
Fisher Price, 127, 128
Flagg Doll Co., 85-88
Forslund, Carl Inc., 88
French Penny Toys, 16
Frier Steel Co., 12, 16

G

Gerber Plastic Co., 84
Goebel Miniatures & Co., 128
Gottschalk, Moritz, 5, 9, 12
Grandmother Stover's Inc., 85, 89, 90
Grimm & Leeds, 5

H

Hall's Lifetime Toys, 85, 102, 106-108, 118
Heidi's House, 113
Holly Hobbie, 118, 119
The Home Craftsman, 139, 140
Honor House Prod. Corp., 109
Hubley Mfg. Co., 17
Hugh Specialty Co. (Miniaform), 36

I

Ideal Novelty & Toy Co., 64-66, 102, 109, 110
Irene Miniatures Co. Ltd., 121
Irwin Corp, 111

J

Jacobs, Flora Gill, 5
Jayline Toys, Inc., 90, 91
Jenny Wren House, 12, 15

K

Katz Co., 17
Keith, Max L., 9
Kenner Products Co., 127, 129
Keystone Mfg. Co., 66-70, 85, 114
Kiddie Brush & Toy Co., 26, 36
Kiddies Treasure Line, 91, 92
Kilgore, 5, 12, 17, 18

L

Ladies Home Journal, 134, 136-138

Ladies World, 135
Letty Lane, 10
Lincoln, 26, 32
Lines-Tri-ang, 12, 26, 53
Littles House, 127, 129, 130
Lundby, 118, 121-124
Lynnfield, 59

M

Macris Co., 26, 32, 33
Mark Farmer, 118
Marshall Fields, 33, 34
Marx, Louis & Co., 26, 34, 35, 59, 85, 92-98, 102, 118
Mason & Parker, 5, 10
Mattel, Inc., 102, 111, 112, 127, 129, 130
McCall, 140
Meccano Ltd., 26, 31, 32
Melco Toys, 71
Menasha Woodenware Corp., 35
Meritoy, 71
Miniaform, 36
Miniature Mart, 112, 113
Miner Industries, Inc., 111
Moss, Marion (Doll House), 61

N

Nancy Forbes, 59, 72, 73, 90
National Can Corp., 59, 77, 78
Nels Doll House, 64
Nit-Sal Co., 18

P

Parents, 140
Pebbles & Bamm Bamm, 110
Pee-wee Dolls, 117
Penny Brite, 102, 105
Plasco, 73-77
Plastic Art Toy Corp., 59, 73-77
Playroom Equipment Co., 19
Playskool Institute, 26, 36
Playsteel Dollhouse, 59, 77, 78
Popular Homecraft, 139

R

Rapaport Bros., 72, 73
Remco, 113
Renwal Manf. Co., 59, 78-81
Rich Toy Co., 26, 36-41, 59, 90, 102
Richwood Toys, Inc., 99

S

Sam'l Gabriel Sons & Co., 19
Sandra Sue Doll (Richwood Toys), 99
Santa Claus Supply House, 19
Schmidt Lithograph Co., 19
Schoenhut, A. Co., 26, 42-45
Schwarz, F.A.O., 113, 114
Shackman, B., 118, 124, 125
Sindy Doll (Marx), 98
Sonia Messer Imports, 118, 125, 126
Sounds Like Home, 128
Spielwaren, 118, 126
Star Novelty Works, 9
Stirn, Carl P., 5
Strawberry Shortcake Berry Happy Home, 129
Strombeck-Becker Mfg. Co., 26, 45-52, 59, 85
Strombecker, 26, 45-52, 59, 85
Strong, Ethel R., 85, 89
Sunshine Family, 112
Sutherland Paper Co., 26, 52

T

Tammy and Family Dolls, 102, 109, 110
T. Cohn, Inc., 59, 85, 99-101
Terry Lynn Doll House, 91, 92
Today's Kids, 127, 132
Tomy Smaller Homes, 127, 130, 131
Tootsietoy, 5, 12, 20-22
Toy Gro Educational Toys, 22
The Toymakers, Inc., 23
Toymaster, 115
Toy Tinkers, Inc., 53
Tressy Doll (American Character), 103
Tri-ang, 12, 26, 53
Trixytoy, 12, 23
Twinky Dolls, 85, 89
Tynietoy, 12, 23, 24, 59

U

Uneeda Doll Co., 116, 117

V

Vista Toy Co., 26, 54

W

Warren Paper Products (Built-Rite), 26-30
Wayne Paper Goods Co., 12, 24
Weber, Franz Carl, 115
Whitney-Reed, 5
Whitton, Blair, 5, 26
Winthrop-Atkins Co., Inc., 115
Wisconsin Toy, 26, 54-57
Wishnik Trolls, 116
Wolverine Toy Co., 57, 127, 132
Woman's Day, 141
Women's Home Companion, 133
Woman's World, 11, 135
Woodburn Manufacturing Co., 59, 62, 63
Woodesigns Co., 118, 126
Woodmaster-Metal Master Corp., 116
Wright, J.L., 26, 32

Y

Youth's Companion, 11